Symbol Glossary

Symbol	Stands for	Symbol	Stands for
$\hat{s}_{\overline{X}_D}$	estimated standard error of the differences	RT	row total
$\hat{s}_D$	estimated standard deviation of the differences	CT	column total
		R	number of rows
D	difference between a pair of scores	C	number of columns
$\overline{X}_{\text{tot}}$	total mean	U or M–WU or U'	statistic computed for the Mann–Whitney (M–W) test of significance
X_g	score within a group		
$\overline{X}_g$	mean of a group	N_1, N_2	number of subjects in the first and second groups, respectively
SS_{tot}	total sum of squares	R_1, R_2	rank of the scores in the first and second groups, respectively
SS_w	sum of squares within a group		
SS_b	sum of squares between groups	d	differences between pairs of scores in the Wilcoxon test
N_g	number of subjects within a group	T	sum of the ranks of the scores with the less frequent sign (Wilcoxon test)
N	total number of subjects		
$\sum_g$	sum over or across groups	H or K–WH	statistic computed for the Kruskal–Wallis (K–W) test
MS_b	mean square between groups	N_i	number of observations in a particular sample
MS_w	mean square within groups		
df_b	degrees of freedom between groups	R_i	sum of the ranks for a particular sample
K	number of groups	K	number of samples
df_w	degrees of freedom within groups	r	Pearson r, Pearson product-moment correlation coefficient
df_{tot}	total degrees of freedom		
F	F ratio, ANOVA test	z_X, z_Y	z scores for the X and Y variables, respectively
HSD	honestly significant differences	ρ	rho, the population correlation coefficient
LSD	least significant differences		
q	studentized range statistic	$\hat{Y}$ or $\hat{X}$	Y-carat or X-carat: predicted values for Y or X based on the regression equation
HSD$_{.05}$, HSD$_{.01}$	honestly significant difference at the 5% or 1% level, respectively	s_Y, s_X	standard deviation of the Y variable and the X variable, respectively
χ^2	chi-square	r^2	coefficient of determination
O	observed frequency	r_s	Spearman rank order correlation coefficient
E	expected frequency		
K	number of categories	b	regression coefficient

STATISTICS FOR THE BEHAVIORAL SCIENCES

SECOND EDITION

B. Michael Thorne
Mississippi State University

Steve Slane
Cleveland State University

Mayfield Publishing Company

Mountain View, California

London • Toronto

Library of Congress Cataloging-in-Publication Data
Thorne, B. Michael (Billy Michael)
    Statistics for the behavioral sciences / B. Michael Thorne, Steve Slane.—2nd ed.
        p.   cm.
    ISBN 1-55934-637-X
    1. Social sciences—Statistical methods. 2. Psychometrics.
I. Slane, Steve. II. Title.
HA29.T54   1997
300'.1'5195—dc20   96-32313
                                                                                    CIP

Manufactured in the United States of America
10 9 8 7 6 5 4 3 2 1

Mayfield Publishing Company
1280 Villa Street
Mountain View, California 94041

Sponsoring editor, Franklin C. Graham; developmental editors, Brooks Donnelly and Kathleen Engelberg; production editor, Carla L. White; manuscript editor, Janet Greenblatt; text designer, Richard Kharibian; cover designer, Steve Naegele; art manager, Susan Breitbard; artist, Joan Carol; manufacturing manager, Randy Hurst. The text was set in 10/12 Palatino by Dovetail Publishing Services and printed on 45# Penntech Penn Plus by R. R. Donnelley & Sons, Company.
Cover photo: © M. Yamashita/Westlight
Back cover: "A good world" by Kobayashi Issa (1763–1827) from *The Dumpling Field: Haiku of Issa* by Lucien Stryk. Copyright © 1991 by Lucien Stryk. Reprinted with permission of Ohio University Press/Swallow Press, Athens, Ohio.

To Wanda, my wife and friend,
and to my children, Dean and Erin
B.M.T.

To my family—Michelle, Stephenie, Drew, and Narda,
and all those students in my classes over the years who
taught me statistics.
S.S.

Brief Contents

Contents

Preface

This textbook uses the metaphor of learning a second language to introduce students to statistics. Just like learning French or Italian, learning statistics involves acquiring a new vocabulary and discovering how to combine terms and phrases into longer and more useful "sentences." Like language students, students of statistics often find that they are already familiar with many of the basic concepts and simply have to learn new "words" for them. Also like language students, statistics students find they benefit from immersion in the new subject and from regular practice.

Another similarity is that students often enter their first statistics course with trepidation, worrying that they may not have the necessary background or talent. Many students are traumatized by textbooks that introduce too many statistical concepts and formulas too quickly. In this book, we show that statistics can be approached and appreciated on different levels. We aim for comprehension on two levels: (1) the practical level, involving the ability to use statistical tests and methods in applied settings, and (2) the intuitive level, involving a feel for the principles underlying statistical procedures. Our goal has been to write a simplified text without sacrificing essential content. At all times we have kept the less well prepared student in mind. All students, well prepared in math or not, can succeed on the levels at which this book is aimed. Just as students *can* learn a second language with good instruction and regular practice, students *can* learn stastistics.

Our emphasis has been on teaching the student to use statistical tests and procedures. At least two completely solved examples illustrate each new technique. Sections labeled "Checking Your Progress" follow the solved examples to give students feedback about their ability to use the technique. Additional exercises at the end of each chapter strengthen the student's computational skills.

Many chapters begin with a brief vignette designed to illustrate the material to be encountered in the chapter, engage the student, and alleviate anxieties. Beginning with Chapter 5, most chapters also have a section called "Troubleshooting Your Computations." Each of these sections identifies the common errors that can result if the chapter techniques are misapplied and shows the student what to do about them. Thus, the student doesn't have to give up if he or she arrives at an incorrect answer; the troubleshooting sections provide hints about likely problem spots.

The text is divided into two parts, following a short introductory chapter. In Part I, Descriptive Statistics, Chapters 2–8 cover basic concepts of measurement, the frequency distribution, graphing, measures of central tendency, measures of dispersion and standard scores, the normal curve, and correlation and regression. In Part II, Inferential Statistics, Chapters 9–14 cover probability, confidence intervals and hypothesis testing, significance of the difference between two sample means, one-way analysis of variance, post hoc comparisons, and two-way analysis of variance. Chapters 15 and 16 cover popular nonparametric inferential tests.

Important resources for students are provided in five appendixes at the end of the book. Appendix 1 is a math-algebra review for students who need to brush up on their math skills. Appendix 2 is a glossary of statistical terms. Appendix 3 contains the most important definitional and computational formulas in the book, organized by chapter. (Formulas are also listed inside the front and back covers of the book.) Appendix 4 contains the tables needed for the inferential tests, simplified for this text. And Appendix 5 provides answers to the odd-numbered exercises at the end of each chapter.

Available with the text are an Instructor's Manual, a Computerized Test Bank, a Study Guide, and a Solutions Manual. The Instructor's Manual contains answers to all the even-numbered exercises in the text, a sample syllabus with formulas, and a test bank of problems the instructor can use either for in-class exercises or for constructing tests. (This test bank is also available in computerized format for either IBM-compatible or Macintosh computers.) Each chapter of the Study Guide contains additional exercises for the student, a comprehensive chapter review, a listing of all chapter formulas, terms to identify, fill-in-the-blank exercises, and a self-test to enable students to check their mastery of concepts and techniques. Many chapters also include exercises using the SPSS data set found in Appendix 6 of the Study Guide. The answers to all Study Guide problems and step-by-step solutions to the odd-numbered problems are provided. The Solutions Manual contains complete step-by-step calculations from formula to final answer for every problem in the text, including the Checking Your Progress exercises, and for the even-numbered problems from the Study Guide.

We would like to thank the reviewers of this book who have added immeasurably to the final product: Dennis Berg, California State University-Fullerton; Bernardo J. Carducci, Indiana University Southeast; William A. Frederickson, University of Central Oklahoma; Richard T. Grow, Weber State University; Jan Kottke, California State University-San Bernadino; and John F. Walsh, Fordham University.

We are grateful to the literary executor of the late Sir Ronald A. Fisher, F.R.S., to Dr. Frank Yates, F.R.S., and to Longman Group Ltd., London, for permission to reprint portions of Tables IV and VII from their book *Statistical Tables for Biological, Agricultural and Medical Research* (6th edition, 1974).

1

The Language of Statistics

Statistics are all around us. We use them every day, perhaps without realizing we are doing so. Statistics help us make sense of the information we receive about events in our community, nation, and world. Consider the following typical day in the life of a young American woman:

After waking up, Maria makes herself a cup of coffee and turns on a morning news show. One of the stories is about recent college admissions. The reporter says that 8 out of 10 students who score in the 90th percentile or above on the SAT are admitted to the college of their choice. Because Maria is working to save enough money to go to college, she is particularly interested in this report. She wonders if her scores will be good enough to get her into the school she wants to attend or if, despite the fact that she scored in the 90th percentile, she will be one of the 20% who are not accepted by their first-choice school.

On her way out the door, Maria grabs the morning newspaper. While riding to work on the bus, she reads that car thefts have risen 67% nationally in the last 25 years. The article states that in New York and Miami, 1 out of every 29 cars is reported stolen. In addition, the dollar losses from car thefts have jumped 134% in the same 25-year period. She figures that part of the greater increase in dollars lost is due to the rapid rise in car prices. She then wonders how much insurance costs have escalated. Maybe she won't be able to get a car anytime soon.

That night, Maria relaxes with the sports section of the paper. An avid baseball fan, she wants to know the results of last night's game. She is thrilled to read that the pitcher on her home team gave up only two runs in eight innings, lowering his earned run average to 1.80. The first baseman went 4 for 4 with two home runs, raising his batting average from .287 to .301. The team won and went over the .500 mark for the first time this season, moving into third place in the division.

You may not be a baseball fan, and you may have read different stories in today's paper, but, like Maria, you are surrounded by statistics. Most people who use statistics are average citizens, not professional statisticians. But whether their purpose is personal or professional, most people need and benefit from a basic understanding of statistics. That is what this book is designed to provide.

WHAT IS STATISTICS?

Before we look more closely at Maria's day, let's consider the term **statistics.** What does it really mean? Actually, the term is used in two different ways. We use it to refer to the summary numbers, or **indices,** that result from an analysis of **data** (numbers). An example is the summary number, or statistic, that expresses a grade point average or baseball batting average.

We also use the word *statistics* to refer to all the procedures and tools used to organize and interpret facts, events, and observations that can be expressed numerically. Throughout this book, we demonstrate how to make sense of facts, events, and observations by converting them into numbers and organizing and analyzing them by using the tools of statistics.

We use the term *statistics* in both these senses in this book. You will know from the context which use is intended.

WHY STUDY STATISTICS?

Personal Reasons

Maria's day illustrates two important points about statistics. The first has already been stated: We are surrounded by statistics. We encounter statistics in the newspaper, on television, in magazines, and in conversation. We are a statistical society. In fact, all civilizations, ancient and modern, have been statistical societies.

As a student, you are no doubt interested in your average grade in a course. Your average grade is a statistic. What's the weather going to be like tomorrow? If the TV weather reporter says that there is a 70% chance of rain, you'll probably take your umbrella with you. The likelihood of showers, expressed as a 70% chance, is a statistic.

What is the latest news in scientific studies? What food additives have been found to increase the probability of cancer, and by how much? What is the effectiveness rate of various contraceptives? What does it mean to say that heart disease is the leading cause of death in the United States, but injuries, homicide, and suicide are responsible for more potential years of life lost? How successful is the latest AIDS drug? Statistical techniques are used to organize and analyze the results of the studies conducted to answer these questions.

Furthermore, to evaluate such studies critically, you need to understand the statistical methods and procedures that were used to arrive at the stated conclusions. A working knowledge of statistics is essential in sorting out the diverse claims and counterclaims that you encounter in daily life. Although this text and a first course in statistics are not going to make you a professional statistician, they will help you become an informed consumer of statistics.

The second point illustrated by Maria's story is that we are all amateur statisticians. Because of our continual exposure to statistics, we have developed a practical and working knowledge of rudimentary statistical concepts. For example, most of us understand the probabilities associated with coin tosses and card games. As with other practical knowledge, it tends to be incomplete and is often misused or misunderstood, but it is knowledge nonetheless. In this book, we hope to build on your current understanding of statistics, filling in the gaps in your knowledge and enhancing your ability to use statistics to describe and understand the world around you.

Professional Reasons

Statistics has more than everyday uses, of course. It is also an essential tool for people who study and do research in the social and behavioral sciences. To understand why this is so, consider this typical definition of psychology: Psychology is the scientific study of behavior and cognition. The term *scientific* refers to the fact that psychologists perform experiments, manipulate variables, make objective observations, and quantify their results. Just as important, however, is the word *behavior*. Examples of behavior studied by psychologists are the disk-pecking behavior of pigeons, language production in humans, food intake by rats in a free-feeding situation, and heart rate as a response to a threatening stimulation.

What is there about behavior that requires the use of statistical procedures? Behavior is ordinarily quite variable. Consider, for example, an experiment designed by a colleague of ours to evaluate the flexibility and adaptability of visual perception. Our colleague asks his students to wear special goggles that reverse what a person sees. Everything is upside down and backward: Right appears left, left appears right, up is down, and down is up. Each student is then asked to play catch with the professor using a small rubber ball. As you can imagine, the results are often hilarious. But after a time most students' visual systems accommodate, and they begin to see normally. Despite the goggles, they are able to throw and catch the ball.

Our colleague measures the length of time it takes each student to begin to throw and catch normally after putting on the goggles. This measure is an index of the adaptability of each student's visual system. Some students adapt quickly; others experience vertigo and don't adapt at all. The majority fall somewhere in between.

What accounts for this variability—the differences in the amount of time it takes students to adapt? It may be that some students have more coordination than others. Or maybe some students are affected by performing in front of the class, whereas others aren't. Or perhaps the professor gets better at throwing and catching with the students as the demonstration goes on, so that students coming toward the end appear to do better. No doubt you can think of some other factors that might influence the outcome of this experiment.

In short, there is variability not only among the subjects of a study but in the characteristics of the study and in the procedures used to measure the subjects' behavior. The variability that characterizes all living things is one of the main reasons we need statistics.

When we measure some stable object or phenomenon with great precision and under rigidly controlled conditions, we have little need for statistics beyond certain basic descriptive measures. We can report our results in one or a few numbers that anyone can appreciate. In chemistry, for example, instruments are often so precise and the processes underlying an observation so well known that variability is practically nonexistent. Unfortunately, as the goggles experiment illustrates, things are not so precise in psychology. Instruments of measurement are often very crude; psychologists frequently do not have control over all extraneous conditions; and psychologists are rarely aware of all the factors that could affect the subjects' performance. Psychologists and other behavioral scientists need ways to describe their data and methods that will help them relate their results to the "real world." Statistics was created to deal with uncertainty and variability. Thus, behavioral scientists especially need to study statistics.

Our Goals

As you can see, we consider the study of statistics to be important for a number of reasons. We have written this text with several goals in mind. First, we want to help you learn the basic vocabulary, procedures, and logic of statistics. Second, we want to assist you in becoming a better everyday consumer of statistical information. Third, we want to show you how to improve your ability to read and understand the professional literature—journal articles, for example—in the behavioral sciences. And finally, we want to give you the tools with which to calculate and interpret statistics on data you or others collect, whether as part of a lab class or as part of your job.

STATISTICS AS A SECOND LANGUAGE

At the level that most of us understand it, mathematics involves memorizing "proven" rules for the manipulation of numbers. The fact that there are mathematical laws governing these manipulations is comforting. By contrast, statistics is composed of indices and procedures that have evolved over time, often by trial and error, because they have "worked" to convey certain information. Much of our choice is influenced by culture and convention—that is, what is commonly done by other people in our field. So even though statistics uses numbers, it isn't truly mathematical; it is more like a language. In statistics, there are conventions that must be learned, and the best way to learn them is by practice.

Our first step will be to present a vocabulary of statistics, including the concepts of central tendency, variation, probability, and other descriptive statistics introduced in the first several chapters of the text. Later, basic statistical "grammar" and "syntax" will be introduced. This is where you will learn to combine the indices of central tendency and variation to draw inferences about hypotheses.

Approaching the study of statistics as a second language should help you learn the basic concepts. In the course of this book, we will try to help you acquire an intuitive feel for the rationale behind the various statistics. However, a more sophisticated understanding will have to await more advanced course work. This parallels the way we master a second language. After one course in Spanish we are probably not going to be comfortable conversing in Spanish. Moreover, so long as Spanish is a second language, we will never be as fluent as a native speaker, and no matter how many courses we take, we will probably always experience some anxiety and uncertainty.

In statistics, don't let that anxiety and uncertainty inhibit your progress. As with a second language, the most important way to learn statistics is to do it. Practice, repetition, and daily use are essential. Our best advice in mastering statistics is to immerse yourself in the material. Do the homework, use the study guide, and practice, practice, practice.

WHAT YOU NEED TO USE THIS BOOK SUCCESSFULLY

This is not a mathematics text. However, it does require some mathematical skill. The statistical calculations in this book will involve computations of squares and square roots as well as the use of summation and simple algebra. Because this level of skill is required to enter most colleges, you probably already have all the math skills you will need to understand this text. Nevertheless, if you haven't had a math class in a number of years or if you substituted business math for high school algebra, you may want to read Appendix 1 to review your math skills.

An indispensable tool for the beginning statistics student is a good, relatively simple and inexpensive pocket calculator. There are many different brands on the market, and features vary almost as widely as the different model types. We recommend a calculator with at least an eight-digit display, four basic functions (add, subtract, multiply, divide), square root function, percentage function, at least one memory function, and a clear current entry key separate from a clear total key. Most calculators have all these functions except possibly the separate clear current entry key.

One other recommendation is that you purchase a light-powered calculator rather than a battery-operated one. Over the years, we have observed the inevitable operation of Murphy's law: If something *can* go wrong, it will. Battery-powered calculators seem especially prone to fail during exams or at midnight (when all the battery stores are closed) the day before the homework assignment is due.

Many calculators are considerably more sophisticated than the one recommended here. Some of these are quite useful for statisticians because they compute a number of important statistics directly. However, for our purposes, a simple calculator is preferable because it will be easily mastered.

Perhaps most important to your success in statistics is your orientation to the material. For most students, statistics is easily mastered so long as they are willing to confront the material and to practice. More than most disciplines, statistics requires regular use. Don't assume that studying statistics once a week while watching television will suffice. Follow a regular study schedule—and practice!

SUMMARY

Statistics refers either to summary numbers resulting from data analysis or to the procedures used to organize and analyze facts numerically. We are all amateur statisticians, but we need to extend and sharpen our understanding, because we are increasingly surrounded by statistics in our everyday lives.

This text has four goals: to teach you the basic vocabulary, procedures, and logic of statistics; to help you become a better consumer of statistical information; to teach you how to read and understand the professional literature in the behavioral sciences; and to enable you to calculate and interpret statistics on data that you or others collect.

It is helpful for us to approach statistics as we would a second language. This orientation places more emphasis on practice than on proof and does not demand immediate fluency, focusing instead on a progressive understanding.

To use this text successfully, you will need a basic understanding of mathematical operations and algebra, a good inexpensive calculator, and a willingness to practice.

EXERCISES

1. How was statistics defined for this course? Why should you take a statistics course?
2. What are the three things you will need for this course?
3. Read the instructions that accompanied your pocket calculator and work through the examples provided. Learn to use the memory function.

DESCRIPTIVE
STATISTICS

Our most common experience with statistics is descriptive. It is so common, in fact, that we usually don't think about the information we receive as "statistical." Descriptive statistics involves using indices, usually numerical, to summarize larger amounts of data so that they become easier to understand and digest. News reports are full of statistics. The weather forecaster on television may say that today's temperature is 67 °F, 10° lower than normal for this time of year. The sports pages of a newspaper are loaded with box scores, batting averages, strokes under par, and yards per rushing attempt. The business section gives us stock prices, the Dow Jones average, and the interest rates of T-bills.

A working knowledge of descriptive statistics is useful for two reasons. First, given the huge amount of statistical information we are exposed to each day, it is important that we be good consumers of statistics. It will help us properly interpret the wealth of statistical information around us. Second, at some point we are likely to be in the position of presenting statistical information, and we need to know which statistics are appropriate to use and how to determine them.

In this part of the book, we discuss several different kinds of descriptive statistics. In Chapter 3, we discuss how to organize data in a frequency distribution. A frequency distribution is a simple way to summarize a lot of numerical information in an orderly way; it also allows for the computation of other statistics, such as the median. One common use of frequency distributions is to summarize scores on class exams. Scores are listed from highest to lowest, with the numbers of people scoring at each level indicated.

Chapter 4 deals with the graphing of data. Graphs give a pictorial representation of data. They are useful as a kind of snapshot of information. There are many different types of graphs, and there are rules for graphing as well. We discuss all these issues in the chapter.

Chapter 5 presents measures of central tendency—indices of the "center" or "most typical" score in a set of scores. If we were required to select one score that would be most representative of a set of scores, what would it be? Most people think of the average, or mean. But there are others, such as the median and the mode. We discuss these statistics as well as the situations most appropriate for their use.

When we are describing our data, it is important to know not only the most typical score but also the "width," "spread," or dispersion of a set of scores. Distributions with the same measures of central tendency might differ greatly in the dispersion of the scores. In Chapter 6, we present several indices used to describe dispersion.

In Chapter 7, we discuss the normal distribution. Using the normal distribution, we can find the probability of obtaining a score of a particular value, given certain knowledge of the population from which the score was drawn. Conversely, we may wish to find a score that corresponds to a particular probability, such as the 90th percentile. The ability to attach a score to a probability or a probability to a score is a very useful descriptive technique.

Another powerful statistical tool is correlation. It allows us to describe the strength of relationship between two sets of scores, such as IQ scores and test scores. Based on the strength of this relationship, we can use scores on one variable to predict scores on the other. Chapter 8 describes the procedures for calculating and using correlation.

In Chapter 1, we introduced the metaphor of statistics as a second language. In terms of that metaphor, descriptive statistics are the vocabulary. They are the words and phrases of the language called statistics. Learning the vocabulary of statistics is a necessary first step before learning the inferential uses of statistics, just as learning the vocabulary of any language precedes learning the grammar and syntax. After completing Part One, you will be a more sophisticated consumer of statistical information. You will also be better able to communicate with others using the language of statistics.

CHAPTER 2

Definitions and Scaling

Do you prefer the routine and predictable? Do you value a life of security, comfort, and peacefulness? Or do you like excitement, change, and risk? Would you rather experience "life on the edge"? According to work initiated by Marvin Zuckerman in the 1970s, if you prefer excitement and change, you are considered a sensation seeker (SS). If you prefer predictability and security, you are considered a non–sensation seeker (non-SS).

A great deal of research has been performed on the concept of sensation seeking, including the development of a scale, known as the SS Scale, to measure it. Among other attributes, sensation seekers are hypothesized to have a low threshold for boredom; we expect them to be more easily bored than non–sensation seekers. If we wanted to investigate this hypothesis, we could have the students in our classes respond to the SS Scale and use the scores to divide the students into SS and non-SS groups. Based on our experience with the students in class, we could then categorize them into people who are "easily bored" and people who are "not easily bored." If our hypothesis is correct, we would expect more "easily bored" than "not easily bored" students to fall into the SS group and more "not easily bored" than "easily bored" students to fall into the non-SS group.

This is just one of several ways we might work with data and hypotheses about sensation seekers and non–sensation seekers. In this chapter, we introduce some of the terms that scientists and statisticians use when they are designing research, deciding what kind of data they want to collect, and planning how they will organize the data that result from their studies. Although many terms will be introduced and defined throughout this book, some terms are so basic and pervasive that they need to be identified at the outset. After defining these basic terms, we will discuss the measurement scales that statisticians use to make sense of their data.

STATISTICS: SOME BASIC VOCABULARY

The terms that will be formally defined in this section are *variable (dependent* and *independent), population, parameter, sample, statistic,* and *sampling.*

Variable

A current edition of *Webster's Dictionary* says that a **variable** is anything that is likely to change, and synonyms include *changeable, inconstant,* and *fluctuating.* Thus, a variable is anything that can take on different values or amounts over a period of time. As scientists, we are interested in variables because it is through observing the ways things vary together that we can, for example, better describe personality traits, make sense of interactions between people, and build models of the world.

What are some things that vary? We could begin with the size of textbooks, the heights of students in a class, or the dosage of a given drug prescribed by a doctor to different patients. Blood pressure varies from person to person and within a person from time to time. The same is true for IQ scores. In psychology, there are many different types of variables—personality traits, reaction times, test scores, degree of extraversion versus introversion, and galvanic skin response (a measure of the skin's electrical conductivity), to name just a few.

In research, there are two important classes of variables. The **independent variable** is the variable that is controlled, or manipulated, by the researcher. The **dependent variable** is the variable that the researchers observe to see if it changes as a result of changes in the independent variable. The dependent variable's scores or values *depend* on—or may vary because of—changes in the independent variable. In the behavioral sciences, the dependent variable is the measurement of an organism's behavior. In our colleague's experiment with the goggles (see Chapter 1), the goggles were the independent variable that was used to manipulate the students' visual systems. The time it took the students to adjust to the goggles was the dependent variable.

In a typical experiment, we might be interested in the effect of various drugs on driving ability. To study this, we might administer different drugs (the independent variable) to separate groups of people. Then we would measure driving ability (the dependent variable) by recording reaction time (the time it takes a person to react to a suddenly occurring stimulus) or the number of steering wheel adjustments in a simulated driving test.

Sometimes the independent variable isn't something that can be manipulated directly. In psychology, this is encountered most often when the independent variable of interest is an existing attribute of a person, such as gender, height, IQ, sensation seeking, or self-esteem. In these cases, people are typically assigned to groups representing different levels of the independent variable based on an assessment. The experimenter is thus manipulating the independent variable through group assignment. We could compare males with females, short with tall, high IQ with low IQ, and so on. At the beginning of this chapter, we proposed selecting people high or low on a scale of sensation seeking (our independent variable) and comparing their tolerance for boredom (our dependent variable).

Population and Parameters

As psychologists studying sensation seeking, we are interested in more than just the level of boredom among SS and non-SS students in our classes. We would like our results to generalize to a broader group of individuals of whom our students are representative. We may want our findings to be applicable to all college students, to all adults in the United States and Canada, or to all students at a particular university. This group, which our subjects represent and to which we want to generalize, is called a population.

If pressed for a definition from everyday life, most of us would probably say that a population is a very large group of things, living or nonliving. Actually, this is not a bad definition except that we shouldn't put a size restriction on the term. Populations can be any size at all, from very large to very small. Thus, a **population** is a complete collection of anything, no matter what the size of the collection.

Even though populations may be small, most researchers are primarily interested in large populations. Specifically, they are often interested in **parameters**, numerical summary characteristics of populations. Consider the population consisting of all the students at your school. The average ACT or SAT score is an example of a population **parameter**. Unfortunately, it is usually too difficult, time-consuming, and/or costly to measure large populations. If you want to know, for example, how many households in America watched a particular TV show last week, can you really afford to call or write them all to get the answer? Or if you want to know how much support a political candidate has nationwide, is it feasible to ask every voter? No, and for this reason most research relies on sample data.

Sample, Statistic, and Sampling

A **sample** is a portion or subset of the population, and a measurable characteristic of a sample is called a **statistic.** Again, think of the population of all the students at your school. Your statistics class is a sample, and the average ACT or SAT score in your class is a statistic. A major application of statistical procedures, such as those described in this text, is to use sample statistics to make inferences about populations and population parameters. From your sample of American households, you could make inferences about the popularity of a TV program, and from your sample of voters, you could make inferences about your candidate's chances of winning. (Making inferences is discussed in more detail later in this chapter.)

Sampling is the process of selecting a sample from the population. Entire books have been written on the topic of sampling, but here, let's just briefly consider the most common sampling procedures.

If we intend to generalize the results from our sample to the population from which it came, we need to select a sample in such a way that it is **unbiased.** That is, the sample should accurately reflect the population from which it came. A **biased** sample is one that is not representative of the population of interest.

A famous example of biased sampling occurred during the 1936 U.S. presidential election. The *Literary Digest* sent postcards to people selected from telephone directories and automobile registration lists, asking whether people would vote for Alf Landon or Franklin Delano Roosevelt. They received over 2.5 million responses, with the overwhelming majority preferring Landon. The *Literary Digest* went to press predicting Landon the winner. FDR won handily. The sample of voters was unrepresentative because it contained too many affluent people—voters who could afford telephones and automobiles during the Great Depression—relative to the U.S. population at the time.

One way to get a representative sample is with random sampling. **Random sampling** is a sampling method in which each member of the population theoretically has an equal chance of being selected into the sample. Random sampling is sometimes called **random and independent sampling** or just **independent sampling,** where *independent* means that picking one person or object for a sample has no effect on the probability of selecting another person or object. Random sampling is also **sampling with replacement,** which simply means that each individual selected from the population is returned to the population before the next selection. In **sampling without replacement,** each chosen individual is not returned to the population before the next selection.

Why is replacement necessary? Think about the definition of a random sample. If individuals are not replaced as they are drawn from the population, the probability of each later selection is increased because the population is decreased by 1 each time. For example, suppose we have a population of 1,000 individuals. The probability of selecting any one person for our sample is $\frac{1}{1000}$ before we make our selection, and if we replace that person, the probability continues to be $\frac{1}{1000}$. However, if the person is not replaced, the population no longer has 1,000 individuals and the probability of selecting a particular individual on the second selection is $\frac{1}{999}$. Obviously, if the population is large, replacement or nonreplacement will have little effect.

To illustrate random sampling, suppose we are interested in the population consisting of all full-time students at a university. Because of the size of the population, we decide to select a random sample of 100 students. For our sample to be truly random, each student must have an equal chance of being included. That is, we can't just go to the student union and select the first 100 students who walk through the door. It may be that some students never go to the student union, and the probability of their selection would be zero.

One way to obtain a random sample would be to put each student's name on a slip of paper, put all the slips into a big drum, and mix the slips thoroughly. Then we would select 100 names, one at a time, with replacement and remixing after each selection. An easier procedure would be to enter all the student ID numbers into a computer and then program the computer to select 100 numbers randomly with replacement.

Of course, even with completely random sampling, it is still possible to obtain a nonrepresentative sample. Suppose the computer has randomly selected 100 students from the university. We convert the ID numbers to names and discover that 90 of the subjects are females even though we know that only 40% of the student body are women. If gender is not a factor in what we're studying, then the unrepresentative nature of our sample may be unimportant. But if we're interested in height, or experience playing football, or any of the myriad things on which we might reasonably expect males and females to differ, the unrepresentative sample may give us spurious results.

If we know in advance that different groups in the population differ in the characteristic we're interested in measuring, then **stratified random sampling** may be preferable to random sampling. Suppose we are interested in individuals under 5 feet 5 inches in height, and we suspect that women are more likely to fit this description than men. If we want our sample results to truly reflect the population, and we know that 40% of the student body are women, then we should specify in advance of sampling that our sample will contain 40 females. The 40 females are then randomly selected from the population of females. Thus, the population has been stratified into males and females, and within the strata random samples are taken.

But what if you don't have access to all members of the population of interest? For example, what if you're studying rats and would like to generalize your sample results to the population of all laboratory rats? How can you use random sampling? The answer is that you can't. In most experiments, researchers use **randomized sampling,** in which all *available* subjects are assigned at random to the different experimental conditions. For example, if you have 50 rats and two experimental conditions, you could assign the animals to the conditions in such a way that each animal has an equal chance of being assigned to either condition. That is, you have randomized the process of assigning subjects to groups.

SCALES OF MEASUREMENT

Statistics involves using tools to make sense of numbers (data). **Scaling** is the assignment of numbers or labels to objects or events. The rules that we use to assign numbers to objects or events are called **scales** or **scales of measurement.** The particular scale used often suggests the statistical tool we should employ.

There are four measurement scales we need to consider. In order of complexity from least to most, they are the nominal scale, the ordinal scale, the interval scale, and the ratio scale.

The Nominal Scale

The word *nominal* comes from the Latin word for "name," and a **nominal scale** does just that. It provides a name, or label, for different objects or events. If numbers are assigned in a nominal scale, they serve only to identify, and it would make little sense to manipulate them mathematically. For example, the numbers assigned to horses before a race serve only to identify particular animals and tell us nothing about the order of finish in the race, the size of the horses, the amount of money each has won, or any other measurable characteristic.

There is nothing inherent in nominal scales that requires that numbers be assigned. Examples of nominal scales that we are all familiar with are plentiful. Shirt manufacturers spend vast sums of money on advertising to ensure product differentiation, and we could probably assign our shirt wardrobe to categories such as Izod, Polo, Arrow, Sears, Guess, Salvation Army, and so on. Rat researchers in psychology may be interested in comparing rat strains, and the different strain names constitute another type of nominal scale. Again, nominal scales are used for identification purposes only.

We must be alert to the fact that numbers are commonly used in a nominal fashion. When they are, common arithmetic and statistical operations, such as computing an average (mean), are not appropriate. For example, the assignment of room numbers in a building is a use of a nominal scale. Suppose you have classes in rooms 103, 235, and 300. Is there any reason to compute your average room number? No, the only function of the numbers is a qualitative one: to identify a spatial location.

In the example at the beginning of the chapter, students were categorized into "easily bored" or "not easily bored." This is an example of a nominal scale. Other frequently encountered nominal data include gender, Social Security numbers, license plate numbers, and street addresses.

In trying to convey information using nominal scales, the best that can be accomplished is to count the frequency (number) of members or observations in each category. For example, we might count the number of girls and the number of boys in an elementary school class or the number of people voting yes or voting no on a piece of legislation. The numbers assigned by a nominal scale differentiate the objects or events that they categorize. Thus, room 103 is different from room 235, and horse 1 in a race is not the same as horse 5.

The Ordinal Scale

The numbers assigned by an **ordinal scale** not only serve to identify objects or events—that is, have a nominal function—they also tell us the **ranking,** or **rank ordering,** of each object or event. In other words, ordinal scale values tell us which object or event is greater than another.

Instead of classifying our students into "easily bored" and "not easily bored" categories (nominal scale), we could produce an ordinal scale by ranking our students from most to least easily bored. Ben, who shuffles into class, finds a seat in the back of the room, and immediately falls asleep, would receive the lowest rank. Steph, who has laserlike intensity, sits in the front row, and even understands our jokes, would rank highest. The rest of our students would be ranked in between.

As another example, consider a race with 10 entrants. Their order of finish is an example of an ordinal scale in which the number 1 is assigned to the winner, 2 is given to the second-place finisher, and so on. Here the numbers tell us about the relative performance of the runners, with 1 performing better than 2, 2 better than 3, and so on; however, we don't know how much better or worse the performance of each was relative to the others. That is, although the numbers assigned are directly related to the time taken to complete the race and provide a rank ordering of the finishers, the ranks alone don't tell us how much better 1 was than 2. The ordinal scale doesn't give us this information.

The Interval Scale

The third type of scale is the **interval scale.** On an interval scale, each unit is assumed to be equal to each other unit on the scale. In psychology, scores on standardized tests, such as IQ, are examples of interval scales. The interval scale has the categorizing and ranking properties of the nominal and ordinal scales, respectively, and also has the property of having equal intervals between the scores. Celsius and Fahrenheit temperature scales are examples of interval scales. Water at 50° Celsius is different from water at 25 °C (nominal): It has more of the characteristic (heat) being measured (ordinal) and is the same number of units from 25 °C as 25 °C is from 0 °C (interval). Unfortunately, we cannot say that 50 °C is twice as hot as 25 °C because the Celsius scale has an arbitrarily determined zero point, as does the Fahrenheit scale. That is, 0° on either scale does not mean an absence of temperature. Zero on the Kelvin scale, however, does mean an absence of temperature. Figure 2-1 (on page 16) illustrates this point.

The Ratio Scale

The **ratio scale** has all the properties of the preceding scales in addition to having a true zero. The Kelvin scale is a ratio scale. Other ratio scales specify time, length, height, and weight. Thus, it is meaningful to say that 2 hours is twice as long as 1 hour and that a person weighing 130 pounds is half as heavy as someone weighing 260 pounds. We are using the ratio scale in psychology when we measure the running speed of rats in a maze or the incidence of head banging in autistic children. In our example of sensation seeking and boredom, if we had measured the minutes and seconds it took for each of our students to become bored, we would have been using a ratio scale. Even though it is the most useful scale from a mathematical standpoint, examples of the ratio scale are hard to find outside the physical sciences. In fact, variables studied in the behavioral sciences often cannot be proved to have all the characteristics of interval scales.

FIGURE 2-1   Although 50 °C is 25° warmer than 25 °C, 50 °C is not twice as warm as 25 °C, as you can see from the Kelvin scale, which has a true zero.

The statistical tools introduced in this text are neutral with regard to the origin of the numbers to which they are applied. That is, it makes no difference to a statistic such as *t* whether the numbers to which it is applied come from an interval scale, a ratio scale, or even a nominal scale. The statistic can be used to manipulate the numbers, and an arithmetically correct answer will be obtained. The problem is one of interpretation; if we feed nonsense into an equation, we will get nonsense as the result. So it is essential that we be aware of the type of data we have before we begin to compute statistics.

Remember, the type of data limits the kind of arithmetic and statistical operations that may be performed on the numbers. For example, summing and averaging are meaningless when performed on nominal and ordinal data, whereas most arithmetic operations are appropriate for interval data. Throughout the book, as we discuss each statistic, we will point out what type of data is necessary for proper computation and interpretation.

TWO BASIC USES OF STATISTICS

Statistics texts are often divided according to the two basic uses of statistics. You are certainly familiar with using statistics to describe data. This division of statistics is called, appropriately enough, **descriptive statistics.** When you compute your average test score in a course, you have computed a descriptive statistic. Most of the statistics we encounter daily—in the newspaper, for example—are descriptive statistics. Graphs also describe data and are another way to use descriptive statistics. Descriptive statistics can be used to describe numerically the variability in data.

It's often not enough just to describe data, however. A very important use of statistics for the scientific researcher involves making inferences from data. This branch of statistics is called **inferential statistics.** As an example of inferential statistics, imagine that you are interested in seeing if the color of a toothpaste tube affects toothpaste preference. To test the effect of tube color, you ask 100 people to brush their teeth with a new toothpaste. Half receive the product packaged in a white tube; the other half brush with the same product from an orange tube. Afterward, the subjects are asked to rate their experience on a scale from 1 to 10.

Suppose that the average rating assigned to toothpaste in the white tube is 8 and the average rating for toothpaste in the orange tube is 5. What does this difference mean? If you have collected good data by running this study correctly, you might infer that people prefer white tubes of toothpaste. When statistics are used to draw conclusions about hypotheses, they are inferential statistics.

The purpose of inferential statistics is to allow us to draw conclusions, or inferences, about a larger group based on the results from some portion of it. A number of inferential techniques are discussed in Part Two of this book.

SUMMARY

A variable is anything that may take on different values or amounts. The independent variable in an experiment is the variable manipulated and controlled by the experimenter to determine its effect on the dependent variable. In the behavioral sciences, the dependent variable is the measurement of behavior.

A population is a complete collection of anything, and a parameter is a numerical characteristic of the population. A sample is a subset of the population; a measurable characteristic of a sample is called a statistic. Sampling is the process of selecting a sample from the population. Random sampling is a method in which each member of the population has an equal chance of being selected. In stratified random sampling, the population is divided into relevant groups (strata), and then random samples are taken from each group. A randomized sample is constructed by assigning all available subjects at random to the different experimental conditions.

Scaling is the assignment of numbers or labels to objects or events. A nominal scale assigns a name or label to different objects or events; that is, it provides identification. Numbers assigned with an ordinal scale both identify and rank-order each object or event. Interval and ratio scales have all the properties of the ordinal scale in addition to providing equal intervals between scores. Finally, a ratio scale has a true zero point.

Descriptive statistics consists of tools used to describe or to illustrate data. Examples of descriptive statistics are averages and graphs. Inferential statistics permit us to draw conclusions about a large group based on results from some subset of the group.

EXERCISES

1. Differentiate between each of the following pairs:
   a. independent and dependent variables
   b. population and sample
   c. parameter and statistic
   d. sampling with and without replacement
   e. descriptive and inferential statistics

2. Name the type of measurement scale that each of the following represents:
   a. Fahrenheit scale
   b. Kelvin scale
   c. college course numbers
   d. the order of finish of contestants in a decathlon
   e. ratings of teaching effectiveness
   f. scores on a math test
   g. reaction time
   h. gender

3. As part of a study examining growth patterns, your task is to determine the average height and weight of all children in the fifth grade in your county. In planning your study, try to use as many of the terms (e.g., *sample, population, parameter*) and methods (e.g., *random sampling*) covered in this chapter as possible.

4. Briefly define the following:
    a. data
    b. stratified random sampling
    c. variable
    d. sampling
    e. biased sample

5. Three groups of schoolchildren receive three different types of reading instruction for a school year. At the end of the year, student reading performance is measured. Identify the independent variable and the dependent variable in this study.

CHAPTER 3

The Frequency Distribution

 Not long ago, a colleague posted the results of a class quiz on the bulletin board outside his office. The posting consisted simply of the students' codes (known only to them and the professor) and the points earned on the quiz. The posting looked like this:

Code	Score	Code	Score
BU	4	PU	8
JB	8	EZ	10
LC	10	JY	9
KS	9	TO	5
MD	2	AJ	9
BE	0	KO	8
IF	6	MM	3
OH	8	SS	4
IP	9	MT	2
XL	7	JR	1
PQ	7	TS	9
IS	6	JN	8
IT	6		

If you were a student in the class, what would you make of these data? What information, other than your own score, would you try to find out?

You would probably look for the low and high scores and try to determine how your own score fell relative to your classmates'. In other words, you would construct a crude distribution in your mind. Frequency distributions, the main topic of this chapter, are a more formal means of accomplishing this same task.

Frequency distributions are a simple way to organize and describe data. If we took the quiz scores and tried to organize them, we might first arrange them in descending order. In other words, it would be helpful to arrange them in order of value, listing them from the highest to the lowest. It would make just as much sense to list them from lowest to highest (ascending order), but by convention it is done the other way around. At any rate, after listing the scores from highest to lowest, we have the following:

X	X
10	7
10	6
9	6
9	6
9	5
9	4
9	4
8	3
8	2
8	2
8	1
8	0
7	

Note that at the top of each column of numbers is the capital letter X. The reason for this is that X is used in statistics to stand for (symbolize) a **score**. In this particular example, we have 25 Xs or scores, the highest being 10 and the lowest 0. This arrangement of scores is more informative than the previous one because we have now identified the highest and lowest values. We can also see the distance between the highest and the lowest scores, often referred to as the *range*.

However, we still have a problem with this arrangement of the 25 scores: It is too bulky and takes up too much space. How might we condense the data?

DEFINING THE FREQUENCY DISTRIBUTION

Looking at the scores, we see that two students received a perfect score of 10 on the quiz, five students earned a 9, five earned an 8, and so on. Instead of listing

Number of Daily Threats (Each mark is one threat)

Subject #	Mon.	Tues.	Wed.	Thurs.	Fri.	Sat.	Sun.	Total
1	|||	||||	||	卌	|||	|||	||	22
2	—	—	—	—	—	—	—	0
3	—			—				—	—	—	3
4								—	—			—	5
5	卌|	卌||	卌	||||	卌卌	卌||	卌|	45
6																					卌			21
7	卌					—															18
8																		10
9	卌	—	—	—	|||	||	—	10
10																				12
11	—	—	—	|||	—	—	—	3
12			—			—						—	5
13	—														—	8
14					卌																		20
15											卌										18
16																							15
17	卌	||	||||	||	||||	||||	||||	25
18	—			—	—			—	—	2
19	—																			12
20																							15
21																	—	10
22						—						—					—	10
23																	9

FIGURE 3-1   Summary sheet showing threat behavior of 23 monkeys for 1 week.

each score of 10 and each score of 9 and each score of 8, we can save space without losing any information if we list each different score only once and make a note beside it of how many times it occurred. This new arrangement, in which the scores are listed in order from highest to lowest and the number of times each score occurs is placed beside it, is known as a **frequency distribution.** A score's **frequency,** symbolized by f, is defined as the number of times the score occurs.

X (Score)	f (Frequency)
10	2
9	5
8	5
7	2
6	3
5	1
4	2
3	1
2	2
1	1
0	1

Using quiz data, we get the above frequency distribution. It is more informative than our original listing of scores because it allows us to tell at a glance the highest and lowest scores. In addition, we can readily see which scores occurred most frequently by referring to the numbers in the frequency column.

At this point, another example may help to clarify the construction of the frequency distribution. In a laboratory experiment, 23 monkeys have been observed over a 1-week period, and the number of times each engaged in threatening behavior toward another monkey has been recorded. Thus, the scores indicate the number of incidents of threat for each monkey in the colony. The monkeys were observed for 30 minutes each day. A summary sheet for this experiment is shown in Figure 3-1.

From the definition of the frequency distribution, we first arrange the scores in order numerically and then put beside them the number of times each score occurred. The result is as follows:

X	f	X	f	X	f	X	f
45	1	33	0	21	1	9	1
44	0	32	0	20	1	8	1
43	0	31	0	19	0	7	0
42	0	30	0	18	2	6	0
41	0	29	0	17	0	5	2
40	0	28	0	16	0	4	0
39	0	27	0	15	2	3	2
38	0	26	0	14	0	2	1
37	0	25	1	13	0	1	0
36	0	24	0	12	2	0	1
35	0	23	0	11	0		
34	0	22	1	10	4		

The highest incidence of aggression among the monkeys was a score of 45, and the lowest was a score of 0. Notice that in constructing the frequency distribution, we included the scores occurring with a frequency of 0. Although we could save even more space by omitting scores that have a frequency of 0, doing so can change the "look" of the distribution and convey a false impression to the casual observer. For example, all the categories between 45 and 25 have a frequency of 0, and we certainly could save space by leaving them out. However, to do so would result in a distribution that might appear to have less dispersion than it actually has. Furthermore, categories with a frequency of 0 often enter into calculations, as when we calculate percentiles, which are based on the frequency distribution. For these reasons, scores should be omitted from a frequency distribution only under very special circumstances.

⑤ CHECKING YOUR PROGRESS

For an additional exercise in constructing a frequency distribution, assume that the following numbers represent the number of trials required by each of 50 graduate students to learn a list of nonsense syllables:

22, 27, 9, 18, 9, 10, 21, 10, 19, 20, 7, 15, 8, 19, 25, 26, 20, 26, 18, 18, 12, 11, 26, 19, 23, 25, 19, 24, 17, 16, 24, 8, 23, 14, 14, 24, 18, 20, 17, 17, 20, 17, 21, 13, 16, 24, 13, 16,   21,   19

Construct a frequency distribution for these numbers.

THE GROUPED FREQUENCY DISTRIBUTION

One of the main purposes of constructing a frequency distribution is to get a clearer idea of what form the distribution actually assumes. For example, we can look at the frequency column and tell which scores occur with the highest frequency and where the scores tail off—that is, have low frequencies. If we have a fairly large range of scores, however, it may be hard to discern any trend in the frequencies. That is, we may have difficulty seeing any bunching of the scores or any tailing off. In addition, listing each individual score may require an inordinately long column. The answer to these problems is to condense the data still further into a grouped frequency distribution.

In a **grouped frequency distribution**, the total range of scores is divided into a number of mutually exclusive (nonoverlapping) and collectively exhaustive (contiguous, or "touching") intervals. Each interval will contain the same number of score units (i.e., be the same width). To illustrate, let's consider a frequency distribution of the test scores made by a large number of students in an introductory psychology class. The frequency distribution follows on the next page.

X	f	X	f	X	f	X	f	X	f
99	1	84	4	69	2	54	0	39	1
98	1	83	3	68	2	53	0	38	0
97	2	82	3	67	3	52	0	37	0
96	3	81	5	66	4	51	0	36	0
95	2	80	2	65	3	50	1	35	0
94	2	79	7	64	2	49	2	34	0
93	3	78	5	63	0	48	0	33	0
92	2	77	4	62	0	47	0	32	0
91	4	76	6	61	0	46	0	31	0
90	3	75	8	60	1	45	0	30	1
89	2	74	5	59	0	44	0	29	0
88	3	73	7	58	1	43	1	28	0
87	4	72	7	57	0	42	0	27	0
86	5	71	7	56	0	41	0	26	0
85	4	70	6	55	1	40	1	25	1

Suppose we wanted to condense this frequency distribution into approximately 10 mutually exclusive intervals. How would we go about it? The first step is to determine how wide each interval would have to be for us to have about 10 of them. We can determine the interval width, defined as the number of score units in the interval, by dividing the range of the distribution by the number of intervals wanted.

In this particular case, the desired number of intervals is 10. Because the range of the distribution is 74 (highest score minus lowest score, or $99 - 25 = 74$), the width of each interval should be $\frac{74}{10} = 7.4$ or, rounding to the nearest odd integer, 7 units.

We can put what we have just done into an equation as follows: The width (i) of the **class interval** (**ci**) is equal to the range of scores (R) divided by the number of class intervals desired:

FORMULA 3-1   *Width of class intervals*

$$i = \frac{R}{\text{number of ci's}}$$

Once we have determined i, we are almost ready to construct our grouped frequency distribution. A convention that is often used is to make the lower limit of each class interval a multiple of i to make it easier for someone to understand how the distribution was constructed. Because the lowest score in our data is 25, and $i = 7$, we need to use the closest multiple of 7 less than 25; that is, we will start construction with 21.

To begin, we take 21 and add to it $i - 1$. Adding $i - 1$ to the lower limit results in an interval with the desired number of units; adding i alone would result in an interval containing one too many units. In this case, the result is $21 + (7 - 1) = 21 + 6 = 27$, and the interval contains 7 units: 21, 22, 23, 24, 25, 26, and 27. The scores 21 and 27 are the limits of the lowest ci. To find the limits of the second lowest ci, we add $i - 1$ to 28, which gives us 34. This procedure is continued until we have determined the limits of the interval containing the highest score in our original frequency distribution, or 99. Here is the resulting grouped distribution:

ci	f
98–104	2
91–97	18
84–90	25
77–83	29
70–76	46
63–69	16
56–62	2
49–55	4
42–48	1
35–41	2
28–34	1
21–27	1

Once the class intervals have been determined, we refer back to the frequency distribution to find the frequency for each interval. Thus, the class interval from 21 to 27 contains only a single score, 25, representing a frequency of 1 for that class interval. The same process is applied to all intervals, as shown in the f column.

Compared with the original frequency distribution, from which the grouped distribution was constructed, the trends are easier to see. We can see, for example, that over half the students scored between 70 and 83 and that there are fewer scores toward the low end of the distribution than toward the high end.

However, despite the clearer picture of the distribution and despite the compactness of the grouped distribution, we have lost something by constructing it. We no longer know the exact location of each score. For this reason, in future problems involving the grouped frequency distribution, we will make the assumption that all the scores in an interval are evenly distributed across it. This assumption may or may not be true. Consider the interval from 63 to 69. There are seven score values in the interval, with a frequency of 16; for the scores to be evenly distributed, there would have to be about two of each score. Instead we see that the scores in the middle of the interval have larger frequencies than 2 (65, 3; 66, 4; 67, 3), and 63 has a frequency of 0.

You have probably noticed that, although we said we would condense the frequency distribution into 10 class intervals, we wound up with 12. What happened? Well, when the width (i) of the interval was determined, the result was the number 7.4, which was rounded to the nearest odd integer, or 7. If the grouped distribution had been constructed using $i = 7.4$ and if we had started with 25, the lowest score in our data, the result would have been 10 class intervals. However, 7.4 would have been an awkward width for any further manipulations, and it is useful to have the lowest value in each interval a multiple of i.

You may also have noted that we specified that the fractional width that was calculated should be rounded to the nearest *odd* integer. Thus, if our computed i for a particular distribution were 4.4, we would round it to the nearest odd integer, or 5, even though this seems to violate the rules of rounding. The reason we round to the nearest odd integer is to make the midpoints of the resulting class intervals whole numbers. In our example, the midpoint of the first interval (21 – 27) is 24. If we had used 8 as the width of the interval (24 – 31), the midpoint would have been 27.5, which is not nearly as handy a number as 24.

Finally, you might wonder why we chose to divide the distribution into 10 class intervals and not 5 or 20 or some other number. Well, we would not want an extremely large number of class intervals in a grouped frequency distribution because condensation was one of our original goals. For this reason, a large number of class intervals, such as 20, usually defeats one of the main reasons for the grouped frequency distribution. But if we use a very small number of class intervals, such as 5 or fewer, the resulting grouped frequency distribution may be so compact that trends in the data are obscured.

To illustrate, let's take another look at the frequency distribution we have been considering and this time divide it into 5 class intervals instead of 10. The width of each interval will be

$$i = \frac{R}{\text{number of ci's}} = \frac{74}{5} = 14.8.$$

Rounding 14.8 to the nearest odd integer gives us 15.

The limits of the intervals are determined as before. We start with a multiple of i lower than the lowest actual score—that multiple is 15—and add $i - 1$ to it. In this case, $i - 1 = 15 - 1 = 14$, and $15 + 14 = 29$; 29 is the upper limit of the lowest interval. Continuing, we arrive at the new grouped frequency distribution shown here:

ci	f
90–104	23
75–89	65
60–74	49
45–59	5
30–44	4
15–29	1

Although the new distribution is certainly more compact, it is also less informative. The assumption of equal distribution of scores across an interval is even less tenable than before. Consider the interval from 75 to 89. With 15 score values and a frequency of 65, there should be about 5 of each score. This is not the case here; in fact, such even distribution is rarely the case.

The crucial question facing the designer of a grouped frequency distribution is whether to use a small i to get more detail or a large i to get greater compression of data. In general, a useful rule of thumb is that a grouped frequency distribution should consist of between 10 and 15 class intervals. However, there may be times when fewer intervals are appropriate, depending on the information the designer wishes to convey.

Let's look at another example. At the end of the course, students in a large general psychology class are asked to define 50 commonly encountered terms in psychology. Each student receives a score indicating the number of correctly defined items. Here is the resulting frequency distribution:

X	f	X	f	X	f	X	f
45	2	37	5	29	11	21	2
44	3	36	6	28	13	20	3
43	2	35	4	27	8	19	0
42	4	34	7	26	7	18	1
41	3	33	7	25	3	17	1
40	5	32	8	24	6	16	0
39	6	31	10	23	1	15	2
38	3	30	9	22	0	14	1

Let's construct a grouped frequency distribution. To begin, we need to find i, the width of each class interval. Again, suppose we want to have approximately 10 intervals:

$$i = \frac{R}{\text{number of ci's}}$$

$$= \frac{45 - 14}{10} = \frac{31}{10}$$

$$= 3.1 \text{ or } 3 \text{ score units.}$$

Starting with the nearest multiple of i less than the lowest score in the data set (that multiple is 12), we add $i - 1$ to it, which gives us $12 + (i - 1) = 12 + (3 - 1) = 12 + 2 = 14$. Thus, the limits of the lowest interval are from 12 to 14.

Continuing, we have 15 as the lower limit of the second lowest interval. Adding $i - 1$, or 2, to 15 gives the upper limit of the second interval, which is 17. The limits and frequencies for the complete grouped frequency distribution are as follows at the top of the next page.

ci	f
45–47	2
42–44	9
39–41	14
36–38	14
33–35	18
30–32	27
27–29	32
24–26	16
21–23	3
18–20	4
15–17	3
12–14	1

Continuous Variables and Discrete Variables

You may have noticed that there are actually gaps between the class intervals. In the example we have just considered, student scores were given in whole numbers. But what if partial credit had been allowed? What if a student could get a score such as 29.5 or 17.7? Where would these scores fit into our grouped frequency distribution? The answer lies in the discussion of continuous variables and real limits.

A **continuous variable** is a variable whose measurement can take an infinite number of values. For example, time is a continuous variable; the passage of time may be broken into an infinite number of units. Between one minute and the next, we could subdivide the seconds into milliseconds (thousandths of a second) or even microseconds (millionths of a second). Weight is also a continuous variable. Suppose a student named Andrew weighs 122 pounds according to his scale. But scales are very crude; his weight might really be 122.15 pounds or 122.1497 pounds or anything near that. The number of final decimal places is limited only by the accuracy of the machine. Gaps in the measurement of a continuous variable are caused by the crudeness of our measurement and are *apparent* rather than *real*. The use of real limits rather than apparent limits will be considered further in the next two chapters.

In addition to continuous variables, there are **discrete variables,** variables capable of assuming only a finite number of values. Number of children in a family is a discrete variable, because only whole numbers are possible. Can you imagine a family with 2.16 kids? Answers on a true-or-false test are another example of discrete variables. You either miss a question or you don't, and fractional credit is impossible.

Real Limits and Apparent Limits

A grouped frequency distribution constructed from a frequency distribution in which the scores are whole numbers results in gaps between the limits of each class interval. Class interval limits with gaps between them are called **apparent limits.** Thus, our preceding examples had apparent limits rather than "real" ones.

What is a grouped frequency distribution with **real limits?** It is a distribution in which there are *no* gaps between the class intervals. In practice, real limits are constructed by subtracting a half unit from the lower apparent limit of a class interval and adding a half unit to the upper apparent limit of the same interval. The unit refers to the accuracy of our measurement, how we have rounded. In the frequency distribution we've just considered, each score is given in whole numbers; each unit difference between scores is exactly 1 point. The interval with apparent limits of 12 and 14 would have real limits of 11.5 and 14.5 (12 − 0.5, 14 + 0.5). If this procedure were continued, we would have the following distribution:

ci (Real Limits)	f
44.5–47.5	2
41.5–44.5	9
38.5–41.5	14
35.5–38.5	14
32.5–35.5	18
29.5–32.5	27
26.5–29.5	32
23.5–26.5	16
20.5–23.5	3
17.5–20.5	4
14.5–17.5	3
11.5–14.5	1

Real limits may be given for single scores as well as for class intervals. Consider again the case of Andrew's weight. Expressed as a whole number, it is 122 pounds. But because weight is a continuous variable, the real limits of his weight are from 121.5 to 122.5.

So far, all examples illustrating the construction of real limits have dealt with whole numbers. What happens if our initial number is a fraction? The rule is that a half unit is subtracted and a half unit is added. Suppose Andrew reports his weight as 122.5. What are the real limits here? The unit in this case is a tenth $\left(\frac{1}{10}, \text{ or } 0.1\right)$ and a half of the unit is (0.1)(0.5) = 0.05, also written $\left[\left(\frac{1}{10}\right)\left(\frac{1}{2}\right) = \frac{1}{20} = 0.05\right]$. Thus, the real limits of Andrew's 122.5 pounds are 122.45 and 122.55 (122.5 − 0.05, 122.5 + 0.05).

✪ CHECKING YOUR PROGRESS

As part of an experiment on the brain's control of learning, a researcher trains a large number of rats on a maze. Each animal's score is the length of time it takes the animal (in seconds) to complete an errorless traversal of the maze. The frequency distribution is as follows (scores with zero frequency have been omitted for simplicity):

X	f	X	f	X	f
55	1	33	1	21	10
50	1	32	4	20	8
45	3	31	6	19	7
42	2	30	5	18	5
41	1	29	1	17	2
40	2	28	9	16	3
39	3	27	8	15	1
38	2	26	10	14	1
37	5	25	10	12	2
36	6	24	9	10	1
35	3	23	8	9	1
34	2	22	11	8	1

(handwritten margin notes)

Apparent limits	f	Real limits	f
54-56	1	53.5-56.5	
51-53	0	50.5-53.5	
48-50	1	47.5-50.5	
45-47	3	44.5-47.5	
42-44	2	41.5-44.5	
39-41	6	38.5-41.5	
36-38	13	35.5-38.5	
33-35	6	32.5-35.5	
30-32	15	29.5-32.5	
27-29	18	26.5-29.5	
24-26	29	23.5-26.5	29
21-23	29	20.5-23.5	29
18-20	20	17.5-20.5	20
15-17	6	14.5-17.5	6
12-14	3	11.5-14.5	3
9-11	2	8.5-11.5	2
6-8	1	5.5-8.5	1

Construct a grouped frequency distribution with approximately 15 class intervals, giving both the apparent and the real limits.

To help you check your work: $i = 3$, the *apparent* limits of the lowest interval are 6 and 8, and the interval has a frequency of 1. The *real* limits are from 5.5 to 8.5.

PERCENTAGE OR RELATIVE FREQUENCY AND CUMULATIVE FREQUENCY DISTRIBUTIONS

So far, we have considered only the most basic of frequency distributions—dis-tributions consisting of scores (or intervals of scores) and their frequencies. However, it is often practical to have frequencies presented as percentages of the total sample and in cumulative fashion. **Percentage frequencies** are useful for comparing distributions that have unequal sample sizes. Let's look now at how a percentage frequency distribution (often called a relative frequency distribution) is obtained using the data from the general psychology students' quiz on definitions.

The grouped frequency distribution is repeated here for convenience:

c_i	f	%age
45–47	2	1.40
42–44	9	6.29
39–41	14	9.79
36–38	14	9.79
33–35	18	12.59
30–32	27	18.88
27–29	32	22.38
24–26	16	11.19
21–23	3	2.10
18–20	4	2.80
15–17	3	2.10
12–14	1	0.70
	$N = 143$	100.01

$\dfrac{2}{143}$
$\dfrac{9}{143}$
$\dfrac{14}{143}$
etc.

Note that the frequencies have been summed and the result given as $N = 143$, where N stands for the sum of the frequencies, or the total sample size. One way to convert the frequencies into percentages is to divide them by N and then multiply by 100. We can state this procedure as a formula:

FORMULA 3-2   *Percentage from frequency*

$$\%age \text{ (percentage)} = \frac{f}{N}(100).$$

For example, 32 students defined 27–29 terms correctly. Using Formula 3-2, we find that the percentage is

$$\%age = \frac{f}{N}(100) = \frac{32}{143}(100) = (.2238)100 = 22.38.$$

The other frequencies have also been converted and are listed in the distribution table.

The **cumulative frequency distribution** helps us interpret the frequency distribution and is useful in helping us find the median, a statistic discussed in Chapter 5. To construct the cumulative frequency distribution, we start with the distribution's lowest interval and accumulate frequencies as we ascend. For any interval, the cumulative frequency tells us the number of scores contained in that interval plus the sum of the frequencies in intervals below the one we are considering. It may sound more complicated than it really is. Let's examine a grouped frequency distribution that's been converted into a cumulative frequency distribution. This has been done with our general psychology quiz data, and the result is as follows:

Class Intervals

Apparent Limits	Real Limits	f	Cum f	Cum %age
45–47	44.5–47.5	2	143	100.00
42–44	41.5–44.5	9	141	98.60
39–41	38.5–41.5	14	132	92.31
36–38	35.5–38.5	14	118	82.52
33–35	32.5–35.5	18	104	72.73
30–32	29.5–32.5	27	86	60.14
27–29	26.5–29.5	32	59	41.26
24–26	23.5–26.5	16	27	18.88
21–23	20.5–23.5	3	11	7.69
18–20	17.5–20.5	4	8	5.59
15–17	14.5–17.5	3	4	2.80
12–14	11.5–14.5	1	1	0.70

$N = 143$

Handwritten annotations: "etc. 59", "27 etc.", "$11 \div 143 \times 100 = 7.69$", "$8 \div 143 \times 100 = 5.59$", "$4 \div 143 \times 100 = 2.80$", "$1 \div 143 \times 100 = 0.70$"

To construct the Cum f (cumulative frequency) column, we start with the frequency in the lowest interval, add to it the f in the next lowest interval, add to that the frequency in the third interval from the bottom, and so on, ending with 143, or the total sample size. What does Cum f tell us? Consider the interval with real limits 26.5 and 29.5. The Cum f for the interval is 59; that is, 59 students had scores of 29.5 or less on the quiz. The cumulative frequency through the interval ends at 29.5, the upper real limit of the interval.

The cumulative percentages making up the **cumulative percentage distribution** are also shown; these were obtained in the same way as the percentage frequencies. That is, each Cum f was divided by N and the result multiplied by 100:

FORMULA 3-3 *Cumulative percentage from cumulative frequency*

$$\text{Cum \%age (cumulative percentage)} = \frac{\text{Cum } f}{N}(100).$$

The Cum %age column indicates the percentage of scores that fall at or below a particular category. For example, 60.14% of the scores fall below 32.5, and 92.31% fall below 41.5.

ꙅ CHECKING YOUR PROGRESS

Using the distribution of psychology test scores, construct a percentage frequency distribution, a cumulative frequency distribution, and a cumulative percentage distribution. The grouped distribution is as follows:

ci	f
98–104	2
91–97	18
84–90	25
77–83	29
70–76	46
63–69	16
56–62	2
49–55	4
42–48	1
35–41	2
28–34	1
21–27	1

To help you check your work: For the interval 56–62, the %age frequency is 1.36, Cum f = 11, and Cum %age = 7.48.

SUMMARY

The frequency distribution is a preliminary method for describing data. In this method, the scores (symbolized by the letter X) are ranked from highest to lowest, with the number of times each score occurs listed beside it. The number of times each score occurs is called its frequency (symbolized by the letter f).

When we have a frequency distribution with a large range of scores (the range is the difference between the highest and lowest scores), a further condensation of the data may be desirable. The grouped frequency distribution is used for this purpose. To construct a grouped frequency distribution, we divide the range of scores into a number of mutually exclusive intervals containing several score units. The size of each class interval (ci) is found by dividing the range of scores by the number of intervals desired. There is no set rule for determining the number of intervals wanted, but 10 to 15 intervals is a reasonable division.

The width or size of the class interval (symbolized by the letter i) can be found from the formula

$$i = \frac{R}{\text{number of ci's}}.$$

The resulting answer is rounded to the nearest odd integer to make the midpoints of the resulting class interval easier to use. Thus, constructing the grouped frequency distribution begins by adding $i - 1$ to the multiple of i less than the smallest score in the data.

A grouped frequency distribution constructed from a frequency distribution in which the scores are whole numbers will have gaps between the intervals. In this case, the limits of the class intervals are called apparent limits rather than real limits. Real limits close the gaps between the intervals to accommodate continuous variables, in which gaps in measurement exist only because of the crudeness of our measuring instruments. In order to determine the real limits in a grouped frequency distribution, we subtract a half unit from the lower apparent limit of each class interval and add a half unit to the upper apparent limit. Discrete variables are variables that are capable of assuming only a finite number of values.

In addition to frequency distributions and grouped frequency distributions, we constructed percentage frequency and cumulative frequency as well as cumulative percentage distributions. In a percentage frequency distribution, frequencies for each interval are converted to percentages using the equation

$$\%\text{age} = \frac{f}{N}(100).$$

To construct the cumulative frequency distribution, we start with the frequency in the distribution's lowest interval, add to that the frequency in the next lowest interval, and continue to accumulate frequencies throughout the distribution. The equation

$$\text{Cum }\%\text{age} = \frac{\text{Cum }f}{N}(100)$$

is used to convert cumulative frequencies to percentages.

EXERCISES

1. Thirty-five soccer players were challenged to do as many sit-ups as possible in 2 minutes. Here are their scores:

37	48	29	50	13
34	47	29	40	16
27	45	25	38	18
28	33	20	35	14
23	15	18	33	38
50	11	16	25	40
44	12	13	20	14

Describe the data using techniques developed in this chapter. Construct a grouped frequency distribution with approximately eight class intervals. Give both real and apparent limits (the numbers were rounded to the nearest whole sit-up). Also construct percentage frequency, cumulative frequency, and cumulative percentage distributions.

2. In a study of the effects of hunger on the bar-pressing behavior of rats, one group of 20 rats was tested after 24 hours of food deprivation. Their response rates during a 20-minute session were as follows:

233	255	328	300
122	115	155	183
187	255	243	273
275	282	305	300
263	266	168	179

Make a frequency distribution of the scores. For simplicity, omit scores occurring with a frequency of 0.

3. In the study cited in Exercise 2, 20 rats were tested after 0 hours of deprivation. Their response rates during a 20-minute session were as follows:

98	100	105	97
128	155	152	107
123	135	141	145
133	125	107	103
95	148	140	127

Arrange the data into a grouped frequency distribution with approximately eight class intervals.

4. What are the real limits of each of the following:

   a. 7

   b. 15.5–20.5

   c. 116.2

   d. 5.62–5.63

5. Thirty-seven people got off a bus and were going into a diner when a car rounded a corner at a high rate of speed and smashed into the rear of the bus. As part of the accident report, each witness was asked independently to estimate the speed of the car before it struck the bus. Seven persons claimed they did not see the incident, and 30 people gave the following estimates:

35	40	28	40	60
25	45	30	40	55
55	37	45	35	50
40	50	40	38	45
70	30	40	30	48
25	30	35	32	37

Construct a grouped frequency distribution with about 10 class intervals. Give both the apparent and real limits. Also construct percentage frequency, cumulative frequency, and cumulative percentage distributions.

6. In a simple reaction-time test, a person tries to catch a ruler between thumb and forefinger after it has been released suddenly by another person. The following are scores generated with the test in a statistics class:

Females			Males		
5	13	7	5	5	9
9	9	9	6	6	6
2	5	6	8	8	6
9	7	10	4	6	6
7	11		7	3	

Construct a separate frequency distribution for the females and males. Combine the scores and construct a frequency distribution for the class. Why is it unnecessary to make a grouped frequency distribution with these data?

7. In an experiment on exercise physiology, the pulse rates of 30 male students are recorded before they jog a mile. Here are the pulse rates in beats per minute:

75	68	77	69	90	70
72	102	78	67	83	77
83	75	81	68	80	72
95	73	80	110	88	65
65	74	75	95	75	87

Construct a grouped frequency distribution with approximately 10 class intervals. Give the real limits and a cumulative percentage distribution.

8. After jogging a mile, the pulse rates of the male students in Exercise 7 are as follows:

85	97	110	85	128
85	95	135	80	135
91	93	125	93	120
110	100	110	97	117
125	105	115	97	118
130	80	107	110	110

Construct a grouped distribution as in Exercise 7, and compare the distributions between the two exercises.

9. Define the following terms:
   a. continuous variable
   b. range
   c. discrete variable

CHAPTER 4

Graphing Data

✳ Teresa, a coffee lover, picked up the student newspaper and was confronted with the headline "Coffee Prices Soar: Students Steam." The story went on to say that unseasonable temperatures in Brazil and other coffee-growing countries had resulted in a shortage of coffee beans. This produced a dramatic increase in wholesale coffee prices that was now being reflected in the price of a cup of coffee at the student union and coffee shops near the university. The newspaper had conducted a survey of per-cup coffee prices at local establishments, and the article included an impressive graph of the findings (see Figure 4-1). Shocked and depressed, Teresa decided that she would have to reduce her daily coffee consumption from seven cups to five cups.

In Chapter 3, we considered one preliminary way to describe data, the frequency distribution. In this chapter, we acknowledge the old adage that a picture is worth a thousand words and discuss graphing as a descriptive technique. We also discuss how some graphs—such as the coffee graph—are misleading and how they can be corrected.

Although there are many different types of graphs, in this text we consider only the ones most commonly used by behavioral scientists: the frequency polygon, the cumulative frequency polygon, the histogram, the bar graph, the stem-and-leaf plot, and the line graph. Let's begin with a look at some graphing conventions.

RULES FOR GRAPHING

A frequent criticism of statistics is that statistics can be used to mislead; that is, you can "lie" with statistics. Because it is certainly possible to misrepresent data

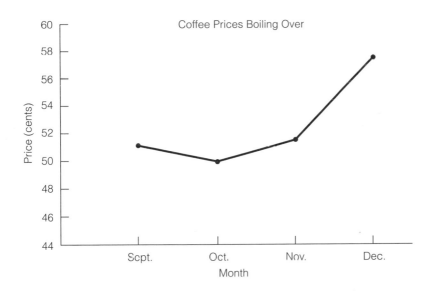

FIGURE 4-1 Coffee prices over a 4-month period.

graphically, in this section we present some graphing conventions designed to help prevent flagrant misrepresentation. The first convention concerns the relative lengths of the X axis (the horizontal axis, or the **abscissa**) and the Y axis (the vertical axis, or the **ordinate**). Specifically, the distance between the points on the axes should be chosen so that the Y axis is approximately three fourths as long as

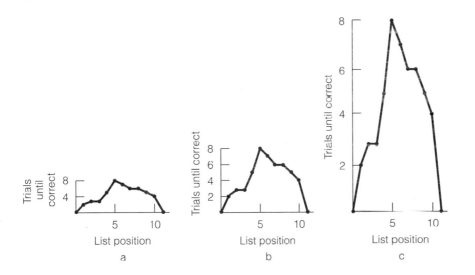

FIGURE 4-2 Three graphs illustrating distortion resulting from manipulation of the relative lengths of the X and Y axes. The middle graph conforms to the three-quarters rule. The graphs show, as a function of list position, the number of times the nonsense syllables were given incorrectly before they were given correctly.

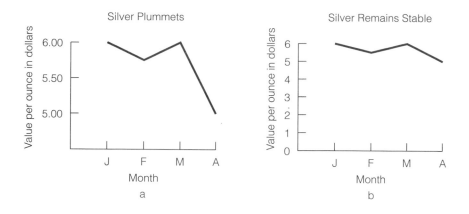

FIGURE 4-3   The price of silver, showing the effect of omitting 0 on the Y axis and using small units.

the X axis. This is sometimes called the three-quarters rule. Let's look at an example of what can happen when the three-quarters rule is violated.

A list of 10 nonsense syllables has been learned to the point where it can be repeated without error. For each nonsense syllable on the list, the number of times it was given incorrectly before it was given correctly is recorded. We will plot the list position of the nonsense syllable (1–10) on the X axis and the number of incorrect trials until it was given correctly on the Y axis. The length of the Y axis will be varied to give different impressions of the data. The graphs are shown in Figure 4-2 on page 39.

It is apparent that each graph in the figure creates a different impression. The middle portion of the curve in Figure 4-2c is greatly magnified by the expansion of the Y axis relative to the X axis, whereas just the opposite is true for Figure 4-2a. Figure 4-2b corresponds to the three-quarters rule.

Another type of misrepresentation can result when the values on the Y axis don't begin with 0 and when the units on the Y axis are very small and don't reflect reasonable variations in the data. Look at Figure 4-3a; it appears that the value of silver is plummeting. The graph in Figure 4-3b reveals a truer picture. Values on the Y axis should begin with 0. It is also apparent from the graph in Figure 4-3a that very small units on the Y axis maximize differences.

These types of misrepresentations can be seen in the graph of coffee prices in Figure 4-1. Using the three-quarters rule and starting the Y axis at 0 gives a very different picture. As can be seen in the properly constructed graph in Figure 4-4 (page 41), coffee prices are "warming up," but they are hardly "boiling over."

THE FREQUENCY POLYGON

The frequency distribution, discussed in Chapter 3, is a useful way to organize data and show overall distribution. From it, we can get an idea of where the

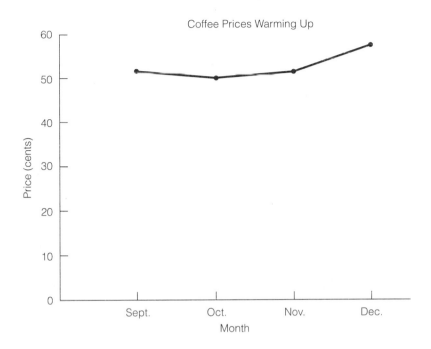

FIGURE 4-4   Coffee prices over a 4-month period.

scores are concentrated, readily see the highest and lowest scores, and tell where the scores are sparsely represented.

A graph of the frequency distribution—a **frequency polygon**—is even more useful in a descriptive sense. A frequency polygon is constructed by plotting the scores on the X axis and the frequency of each score along the Y axis. To illustrate, let's consider a frequency distribution of the number of repetitions required by 54 students to learn a list of nonsense syllables. The distribution is as follows:

X	f	X	f	X	f
33	1	24	5	15	1
32	1	23	4	14	1
31	1	22	4	13	1
30	1	21	3	12	0
29	1	20	3	11	1
28	2	19	2	10	1
27	3	18	2	9	2
26	4	17	2	8	1
25	5	16	1	7	1

The frequency polygon depicting this distribution is shown in Figure 4-5. Examining the polygon, we can see clearly the trends in the data. The majority of

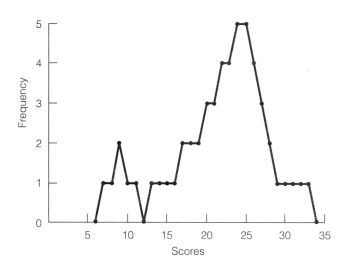

FIGURE 4-5 Frequency polygon based on the number of repetitions required to learn a list of nonsense syllables.

scores pile up in the region of scores 24 and 25, and there is a longer tail of scores to the left side of the graph than to the right. By convention, the polygon begins and ends with a zero frequency score (see Figure 4-2 for another example).

Note that the axes of the graph have been labeled, with "Scores" appearing below the X axis and "Frequency" to the left of the Y axis. It is not necessary to denote each possible score, and for this reason only selected ones have been labeled on the X axis. It is important that the axes be labeled appropriately; other-

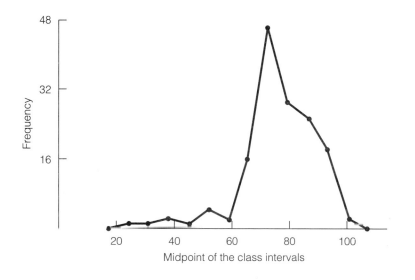

FIGURE 4-6 Frequency polygon based on a grouped frequency distribution of test scores earned by students in an introductory psychology class.

wise the graph will be meaningless. Of equal importance is the legend—in this case, "Figure 4-5 Frequency polygon. . . ." Each graph should have a legend that describes the graph and what it shows.

The Frequency Polygon from a Grouped Frequency Distribution

As you know from Chapter 3, frequency distributions are often based on grouped data. The only difference between the frequency polygon described in the last section and one based on a grouped frequency distribution is that for the latter we plot the frequencies over the *midpoints* (MPs) of the class intervals rather than over the scores themselves. For example, let's consider one of the grouped distributions from Chapter 3. The data are quiz scores made by students from a large introductory psychology class:

ci	MP	f
98–104	101	2
91–97	94	18
84–90	87	25
77–83	80	29
70–76	73	46
63–69	66	16
56–62	59	2
49–55	52	4
42–48	45	1
35–41	38	2
28–34	31	1
21–27	24	1

As you can see, the midpoint of each class interval is listed in the second column. The midpoint for any class interval can be found by adding $(i - 1)/2$ to the lower limit of the class interval. For example, consider the interval from 21 to 27. The interval width we used was $i = 7$, so $(i - 1)/2 = (7 - 1)/2 = 6/2 = 3$. Adding 3 to the lower limit of the interval gives us $21 + 3 = 24$, and this is the value shown.

The frequency polygon based on the grouped frequency distribution we have been considering is shown in Figure 4-6. As you will note, the primary difference between this figure and Figure 4-5 is that the X axis here is labeled "Midpoint of the class intervals" instead of "Scores." The graph is plotted in the same way.

A Comparison of Distributions Using the Percentage or Relative Frequency Polygon

One of the most important uses of the frequency polygon is to compare the performance of different groups (or to compare different treatments on the same group). Suppose we are interested in the difference between introverts and extraverts in the number of friends they have. We might expect (we hypothesize) that extraverts will have more friends. To investigate this, we ask 90 people, 50 extraverts and 40 introverts, how many friends they have (assume that we couldn't find equal numbers of introverts and extraverts). The frequency distributions for extraverts and introverts are as follows:

Extraverts				Introverts			
X	f	X	f	X	f	X	f
18	1	10	7	12	2	4	4
17	2	9	6	11	2	3	2
16	2	8	5	10	1	2	2
15	4	7	2	9	1	1	3
14	2	6	2	8	4	0	2
13	3	5	1	7	4		$N = 40$
12	6	4	1	6	7		
11	5	3	1	5	6		
			$N = 50$				

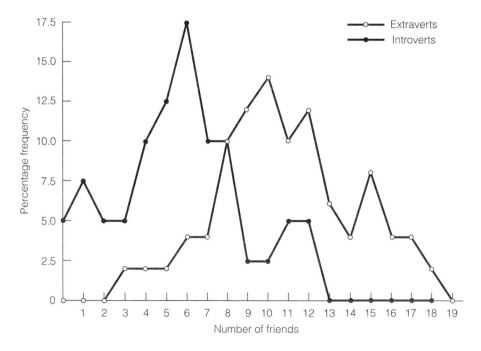

FIGURE 4-7   Percentage frequency polygon comparing introverts' and extraverts' numbers of friends.

Because there is a difference in the total N for the introverts and extraverts, we must use percentages instead of the actual frequencies. We should do this whenever we have unequal Ns in order to put groups on an equal basis. For example, what if we want to compare the number of extraverts and introverts who have eight friends? From the frequencies, it appears that more extraverts than introverts have eight friends (5 vs. 4). However, we sampled more extraverts than introverts. If we compare percentages, we see that exactly the same proportion (10%) of extraverts and introverts have eight friends.

You may recall from Chapter 3 that one way to convert each frequency into a percentage is to divide each frequency by N and then multiply by 100 (Formula 3-2). Using this procedure, we convert each of the frequencies to a percentage, with the following results:

Extraverts			Introverts		
X	f	%age	X	f	%age
18	1	2	12	2	5.0
17	2	4	11	2	5.0
16	2	4	10	1	2.5
15	4	8	9	1	2.5
14	2	4	8	4	10.0
13	3	6	7	4	10.0
12	6	12	6	7	17.5
11	5	10	5	6	15.0
10	7	14	4	4	10.0
9	6	12	3	2	5.0
8	5	10	2	2	5.0
7	2	4	1	3	7.5
6	2	4	0	2	5.0
5	1	2	$N = 40$	Total %age = 100.0	
4	1	2			
3	1	2			
$N = 50$	Total %age = 100				

Figure 4-7 gives a clear picture of the difference in the number of friends for introverts and extraverts. The percentage frequency polygon for each distribution is plotted on the same set of axes for comparison. For example, we can see that most of the distribution of scores for the introverts is shifted to the left of that for the extraverts. Therefore, our hypothesis that extraverts will have more friends than introverts would appear to have been substantiated by our findings, illustrated in Figure 4-7.

FIGURE 4-8   Examples of symmetrical curves. Curves a and b are nonnormal; curve c is normal.

Shapes of Frequency Polygons

A frequency polygon can assume many shapes, but some are more common and therefore more interesting to us than others. The normal curve is one of the most interesting curves, both because of its properties and because so much of the data in the real world approximates it. Data we often assume to be almost normally distributed include IQ scores, heights, and weights.

The **normal curve** is defined by a mathematical equation that fixes its shape while leaving certain parameters—that is, the central point and the amount of spread about the central point—free to vary. The shape of the curve is symmetrical (the left half would fold precisely over the right half), and the tails never reach the baseline. The normal curve is often called the "bell-shaped curve." Of course, many curves can be symmetrical without having the properties of the normal curve. Examples of symmetrical, nonnormal curves are shown in Figure 4-8 along with the normal curve.

Some curves that are not symmetrical are called skewed. A **skewed curve** is a curve in which a large number of scores are piled up at one end or the other, with a tail at the opposite end. If we consider the right side of the X axis to be positive and the left side to be negative, then a **positively skewed curve** is one that has its tail to the right, and a **negatively skewed curve** has its tail to the left of the X axis. Remember that the tail—not the end where the scores pile up—gives the direction of the skew. Examples of positively and negatively skewed curves are shown in Figure 4-9.

i.e. faculty teaching performance & personal income

FIGURE 4-9   Examples of positively and negatively skewed curves.

One real-life example of a negatively skewed distribution, at least from our experience, is the distribution based on the student ratings of faculty teaching performance. That is, most professors are given relatively high evaluations, and only a select few are rated as being very poor. Data based on ratio scales (e.g., time, speed, weight) are often positively skewed. This is because there is a smallest possible value (0), but there is no limit to how large the values may be. This often leads to scores clustering near the small values with a few large scores creating a long tail. Personal income in the United States is another example of a positively skewed distribution. The majority of people have incomes below $35,000, but a few individuals have eight- or nine-digit incomes. Human weights are an example of a normal distribution.

THE CUMULATIVE FREQUENCY (OR CUMULATIVE PERCENTAGE) POLYGON

The shape of the polygon created from a cumulative frequency distribution is different from the polygon shapes we considered in previous sections. The old saying "What goes up must come down" is not true for the cumulative frequency polygon.

The cumulative frequency curve, or cumulative frequency polygon, shows the relative position of individuals in a distribution. For example, suppose 23 students in an honors class are given an IQ test, and the resulting frequency distribution of their scores is as follows (possible scores that were not actually observed, such as 169, 168, and so on, have been omitted to save space):

X	f	X	f
170	1	144	1
163	1	143	1
160	1	142	1
158	2	140	2
157	1	138	1
153	3	129	1
150	3	127	1
145	2	120	1

The cumulative frequency polygon is constructed by plotting the cumulative frequencies (or percentages) over the *upper real limits* of class intervals. Therefore, the first thing we must do is convert the ungrouped frequency distribution into a grouped one. Using 10 as the desired number of class intervals, we find that the width of the class interval should be

$$i = \frac{R}{\text{number of ci's}} = \frac{170 - 120}{10} = \frac{50}{10} = 5.$$

The limits of the lowest interval are 120 and 124: $120 + (i - 1) = 120 + (5 - 1) = 120 + 4 = 124$. The rest of the grouped distribution is as follows, including the real limits of the class intervals and a cumulative frequency column:

Class Intervals			Cum f
Apparent Limits	Real Limits	f	(Cumulative Frequency)
170–174	169.5–174.5	1	23
165–169	164.5–169.5	0	22
160–164	159.5–164.5	2	22
155–159	154.5–159.5	3	20
150–154	149.5–154.5	6	17
145–149	144.5–149.5	2	11
140–144	139.5–144.5	5	9
135–139	134.5–139.5	1	4
130–134	129.5–134.5	0	3
125–129	124.5–129.5	2	3
120–124	119.5–124.5	1	1

Why is the cumulative frequency curve plotted over the upper real limits? The cumulative frequency for an interval tells us the total number of scores *through* the interval—that is, up to and including the top score. And what is the top score in any interval? The upper real limit. The cumulative frequency polygon for our data is shown in Figure 4-10.

We can also construct a cumulative frequency polygon from an ungrouped distribution. Remember that real limits are obtained by subtracting a half unit and adding a half unit. In a grouped distribution, we subtract the half unit from the lower apparent limit of a class interval and add the half unit to the upper apparent limit. We could do the same thing to score values in an ungrouped distribution. For example, suppose we have the following distribution:

X	f
13	1
12	0
11	3
10	2
9	3
8	5
7	6
6	4
5	2
4	1

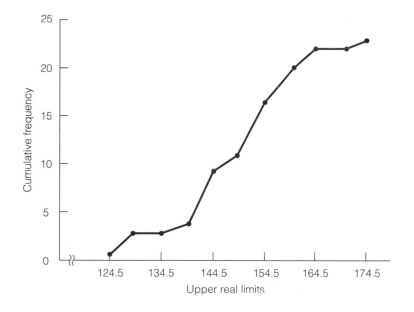

FIGURE 4-10   Cumulative frequency curve based on IQ scores of students in an honors class.

By subtracting and adding a half unit to each score value, we obtain the following distribution with real limits:

X	Real Limits	f	Cum f
13	12.5–13.5	1	27
12	11.5–12.5	0	26
11	10.5–11.5	3	26
10	9.5–10.5	2	23
9	8.5–9.5	3	21
8	7.5–8.5	5	18
7	6.5–7.5	6	13
6	5.5–6.5	4	7
5	4.5–5.5	2	3
4	3.5–4.5	1	1

Now it would be easy to plot the cumulative frequencies over the upper real limits, and we suggest that you do it for practice.

Let's return to our IQ score example. To see the relative performance of any individual on the IQ test, draw a vertical line from that person's score on the X axis up to the curve, and then draw a horizontal line from the curve across to the Y axis. The point where the horizontal line crosses the Y axis gives us an

FIGURE 4-11   Cumulative frequency curve showing the relative location in the honors class of an individual with an IQ score of 151.

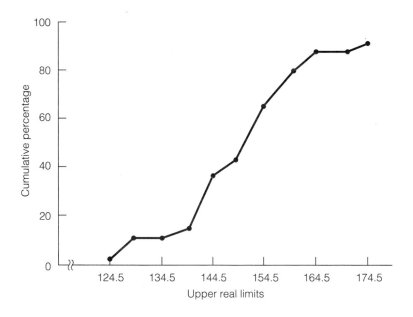

FIGURE 4-12   Cumulative percentage polygon based on the IQ scores in the honors class.

approximate idea of the number of individuals scoring at or below the score we are examining. For example, suppose we want to know the relative performance of a student who might have scored 151 on the IQ test.

First we draw a vertical line from a score of 151 on the X axis up to the point where the line intersects the curve. From this point we draw a horizontal line to the Y axis, where it intersects at a frequency of 13. We conclude that approximately 13 persons had scores of 151 or lower and 10 persons had scores this high or higher. The procedure is shown in Figure 4-11.

We may also use the cumulative polygon to plot cumulative percentages. In the following distribution, the cumulative frequencies have been converted to cumulative percentages using Formula 3-3. The **cumulative percentage polygon** is plotted in Figure 4-12.

Class Intervals

Real Limits	f	Cum f	Cum %age
169.5–174.5	1	23	100.00
164.5–169.5	0	22	95.65
159.5–164.5	2	22	95.65
154.5–159.5	3	20	86.96
149.5–154.5	6	17	73.91
144.5–149.5	2	11	47.83
139.5–144.5	5	9	39.13
134.5–139.5	1	4	17.39
129.5–134.5	0	3	13.04
124.5–129.5	2	3	13.04
119.5–124.5	1	1	4.35

The procedure for determining the relative location of a score in terms of the percentage of scores either above or below is precisely the same as that illustrated for the cumulative frequency polygon. For example, we could easily determine that someone with an IQ score of 151 is in approximately the 50th percentile of this particular distribution. That is, the person with an IQ score of 151 scored as well as, or better than, approximately half of the class.

ॶ Checking Your Progress

At a smoking clinic, each person fills out a questionnaire on smoking habits. The average number of cigarettes smoked per day for 60 people is shown in the distribution at the top of the following page.

X	f	X	f
60	1	26	3
55	2	25	5
53	2	24	2
50	3	23	5
47	1	20	10
45	2	18	3
40	3	15	2
35	4	12	1
30	5	11	1
28	3	10	2

Use the data to construct a frequency polygon, a cumulative frequency curve, and a cumulative percentage curve. If this is a representative sample, approximately what percentage of smokers smoke 20 or fewer cigarettes per day?

THE HISTOGRAM

Another way to graph a frequency distribution is with a histogram. In a **histogram, a rectangular bar is drawn over each score value** on the X axis, its height determined by the score's frequency. Each bar is centered above a particular score value and extends halfway between adjacent scores. To construct a histogram from a grouped frequency distribution, we plot each bar over the midpoint of a class interval and extend the bar the width of the class interval—that is, we extend it from lower to upper real limits. A histogram based on the frequency distribution of the number of introverts with certain numbers of friends is shown in Figure 4-13.

If you compare the histogram in Figure 4-13 with the percentage frequency polygon for the introverts in Figure 4-7, you will see that the main difference between the two is that dots are plotted over the score values in the polygon and bars are used in the histogram.

☙ CHECKING YOUR PROGRESS

Plot a histogram of the IQ scores in the honors class.

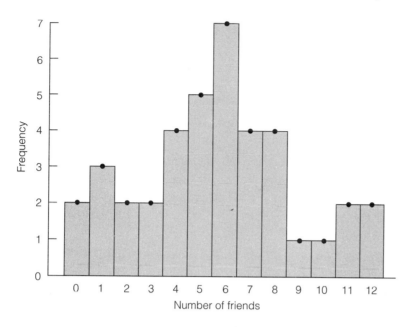

FIGURE 4-13   Histogram based on the frequency distribution of introverts' numbers of friends.

THE BAR GRAPH

The **bar graph** is a variation of the histogram used to graph nominal scale data. That is, the scale along the X axis consists of labels that are used to identify rather than labels that measure or show the amounts of something. For example, suppose we go into a parking lot and count the number of cars falling into the categories Toyota, Mazda, Chevrolet, Ford, and so on. For each of the different categories (car manufacturers), we would have a frequency of occurrence. A bar graph could be used to show this information. That is, we would draw a bar over each category or label to indicate its frequency. The bar's width would be arbitrary, and each bar would be separated from its neighbors.

Suppose a traffic planner has determined the number of vehicles passing through five different intersections at a particular time of day. Although for identification purposes the planner may label the intersections 1, 2, 3, 4, and 5, the number assigned to any particular intersection is purely arbitrary; the planner might just as well use the street names for identification or call the intersections A through E. The data generated might be as follows: Intersection 1, 25; Intersection 2, 43; Intersection 3, 10; Intersection 4, 5; Intersection 5, 26.

The bar graph of these data is plotted in Figure 4-14 on page 54. As you can see, the intersection number is shown on the X axis, and the number of vehicles (frequency) is shown on the Y axis. Instead of the bars touching and giving an

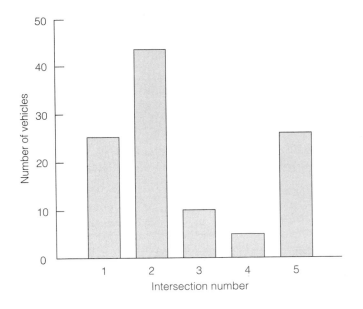

FIGURE 4-14   Bar graph showing the number of vehicles passing through particular intersections.

impression of continuity, the rectangles are slightly separated. Like their width, the spacing of the bars is arbitrary.

⟳ Checking Your Progress

In some classic research on the observational learning of aggression, psychologist Albert Bandura and his colleagues exposed children to five different models of aggression (live, film, cartoon, nonaggressive, and none). Later, the number of imitative aggressive responses made by each child was recorded. The mean number of imitative responses in each condition was as follows: live model, 22; film model, 16; cartoon model, 12; nonaggressive model, 2; no model, 4. Construct a graph of these data. Label the X axis "Type of model" and the Y axis "Mean number of imitative aggressive responses."

THE STEM-AND-LEAF PLOT

Yet another way to organize and display data that has features of both a frequency distribution and a frequency histogram is to construct a **stem-and-leaf plot.** To create the display, we split each score into two parts: a stem and a leaf. The first one or two digits constitute the stem, and the last digit is the leaf. For example, a score of 91 would have a stem of 9 and a leaf of 1. Similarly, $X = 153$ would have a stem of 15 and a leaf of 3. Let's look at some data and actually construct a stem-and-leaf plot.

In the exercises at the end of Chapter 3, the pulse rates of 30 male students were recorded before they jogged a mile. The data were as follows:

75	68	77	69	90	70
72	102	78	67	83	77
83	75	81	68	80	72
95	73	80	110	88	65
65	74	75	95	75	87

To construct a stem-and-leaf plot, the first step is to list all the different stems, from lowest to highest. In this case, the lowest pulse is in the 60s and the highest is 110. Thus, the stems are the numbers 6 through 11, and our list will be

Stems

6

7

8

9

10

11

The next step is to draw a vertical line to the right of the column of stems. Then we go through the list of scores, one at a time, and put each leaf beside its stem. Starting at the left, the first score is 75; its leaf (5) is placed beside its stem (7). We continue this procedure through all the scores. The completed stem-and-leaf display is as follows:

Stem-and-Leaf Display of Male Pulse Rates

Stems	Leaves
6	5 8 9 7 8 5
7	5 2 5 3 4 7 8 5 5 0 7 2
8	3 1 0 3 0 8 7
9	5 5 0
10	2
11	0

In actuality, the stem-and-leaf display shown is a histogram with a class interval of 10. If we rotate the display so that the stems become scores on the X axis of a graph, the result is a histogram with digits rather than bars over the scores. The beauty of the stem-and-leaf plot is that it is easily constructed; it has features of both a grouped frequency distribution and a histogram; and no information is lost (i.e., we still know the exact location of each score). Here is the rotated stem-and-leaf display based on the male pulse rates:

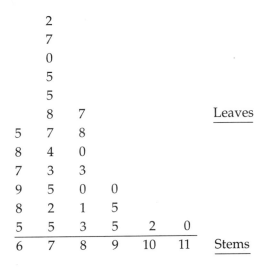

Ꙩ Checking Your Progress

Construct a stem-and-leaf plot of the male pulse rate data after exercise. The data are as follows:

85	97	110	85	128
85	95	135	80	135
91	93	125	93	120
110	100	110	97	117
125	105	115	97	118
130	80	107	110	110

THE LINE GRAPH

All of the graphs discussed to this point have been based on the frequency distribution. Although frequency polygons, cumulative frequency curves, histograms, and bar graphs are very useful in a descriptive sense, they are not the only types

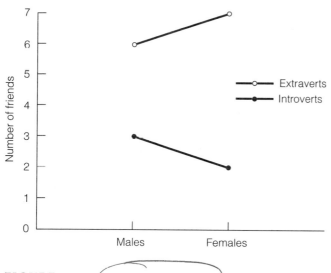

FIGURE 4-15 (A misuse of a line graph. Males and females are not a continuous dimension. Compare Figure 4-16.

of graphs employed by behavioral scientists. The line graph is another type of graph often encountered in the literature.

With the **line graph,** an independent variable is recorded on the X axis, and some measure of the dependent variable is given on the Y axis. Often the dependent variable has undergone some preliminary analysis before being graphed. That is, average scores may be used instead of individual scores or frequencies of occurrence. Also, the independent variable is assumed to be continuous, and for this reason a line is used to connect the plotted points. A common misuse of the line graph occurs when discontinuous or qualitative (nominal scale) variables, such as gender or ethnicity, are displayed on a line graph. In these cases, lines are used to connect values of a variable that cannot meaningfully be displayed on a continuous dimension.

For example, suppose we have collected data on the average number of friends of male and female introverts and extraverts. We might try presenting the data in a line graph, such as that shown in Figure 4-15. However, this is an incorrect presentation because it implies a continuous dimension connecting males and females. In this example, males and females are categories. A more appropriate presentation would be the bar graph shown in Figure 4-16.

One of the most common uses of the line graph is to show the development of some type of behavior over time. For example, the development of learning in an organism may be shown by a line graph in which a measure of the amount of practice (time, trials, etc.) is given on the X axis and a measure of performance or behavior (number correct, percentage of correct responses, number of errors, speed of performance, etc.) is shown on the Y axis.

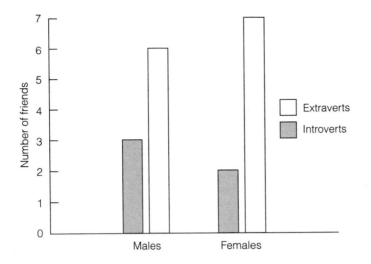

FIGURE 4-16   An appropriate way to display data on the number of friends of male and female extraverts and introverts. Compare Figure 4-15.

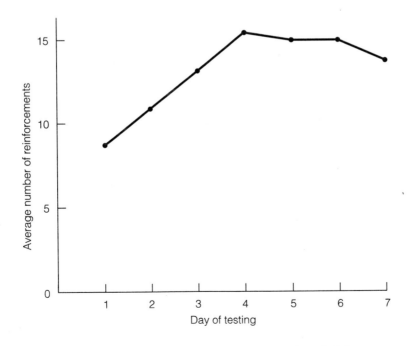

FIGURE 4-17   Line graph showing the average number of reinforcements per day of testing on a VI 30-s schedule.

Let's illustrate with a specific example. In one experiment, rats were trained to press a lever to receive a food reward. The animals were trained to bar-press on a variable interval schedule in which they received rewards on the average of every 30 seconds; that is, they followed a VI 30-s reinforcement schedule. The development of their performance is shown in Figure 4-17, where the average number of rewards is noted on the Y axis and the day of testing is shown on the X axis. Each day's training session was 20 minutes.

As you can see from the graph, the performance of the animals improved over the first 4 days of testing; that is, their average number of reinforcements increased each day. Performance on the last 3 days of testing was essentially stable.

The line graph is also useful for comparing two or more groups, as this next example illustrates. To study experimenter bias, 20 students are divided into two groups of 10 students each, and each student is given a rat. One group of students is told that their rats are very bright; the other group is informed that their animals are stupid. Each of the 20 students then trains her or his rat on a simple task and records the number of daily errors. The average number of errors per day is computed for the "smart rat" group and for the "stupid rat" group. Here are the results:

Day	"Smart Rats" Average Number of Errors	"Stupid Rats" Average Number of Errors
1	6.2	6.5
2	5.1	6.1
3	4.1	5.5
4	2.5	5.3
5	1.5	4.8
6	0	3.9
7	0	3.5
8	0	2.9
9	0	1.8
10	0	1.3
11	0	0

Figure 4-18 reveals that the "smart rats" improved much more rapidly than the "stupid rats." (Note that the lines go *down* because number of errors is recorded on the Y axis.) Incidentally, in reality there was no difference in the intelligence of the rats. The only difference was in the instructions given to the students. There are inferential techniques that will allow us to decide whether or not students who trained "smart rats" came from the same population as students who trained "stupid rats."

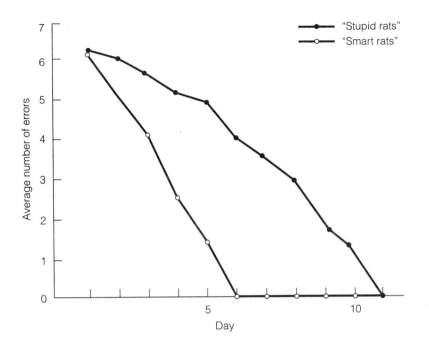

FIGURE 4-18   Line graph showing the performance of "smart rats" and "stupid rats" over days of training.

⟳ CHECKING YOUR PROGRESS

Suppose five students have learned a list of 10 nonsense syllables to the point where they can recite the list without error. The average number of errors per repetition before learning was perfected has been determined and is as follows:

Repetition	Average Errors
1	9.6
2	7.2
3	6.1
4	5.8
5	5.2
6	4.4
7	3.5
8	2.1
9	2.3 *(cont.)*

Repetition (*cont.*)	Average Errors (*cont.*)
10	1.3
11	1.1
12	0.6
13	0.0

Use the line graph to show the average number of errors per repetition.

SUMMARY

In this chapter, we have studied graphing conventions and a variety of types of graphs. One graphing convention that helps prevent misrepresentation of data is making the length of the Y axis approximately three-quarters as long as the X axis. Another graphing "rule" is to have values on the Y axis begin with 0 and reflect reasonable increments in the data.

The first type of graph introduced was the frequency polygon. To construct a frequency polygon from a frequency distribution, we list the scores across the X axis and give the frequencies on the Y axis. Each point plotted on the graph shows the frequency of a given score. The frequency polygon from a grouped frequency distribution is the same except that the midpoints of the class intervals, rather than the scores themselves, appear on the X axis.

The frequency polygon is useful for comparing frequency distributions on the same set of axes. However, if the distributions to be compared have unequal Ns, then frequencies must be converted to percentages before the graph is plotted. The resulting curve is called the percentage or relative frequency polygon.

Some commonly encountered shapes of frequency polygons were described. One very important curve is the normal, or bell-shaped, curve. Nonnormal curves with tails pulled either toward the right side or toward the left side of the X axis are called skewed curves. Positively skewed curves have a tail (relatively few scores) toward the positive, or right, side of the X axis, whereas negatively skewed curves have a tail toward the negative, or left, side of the X axis.

The cumulative frequency polygon and cumulative percentage polygon were constructed by plotting the cumulative frequencies or percentages over the upper real limits of the class intervals in a grouped or ungrouped frequency distribution. The cumulative frequency for an interval tells the total number of scores through the interval.

A frequency distribution may also be graphed with a histogram. In the histogram, a rectangular bar is drawn over each score on the X axis (or over the midpoint of a class interval in a grouped frequency distribution), with frequency of the score determined by the height of the bar. The bar graph is a variation of the histogram used to show nominal scale data. In nominal scale data, the scale along the X axis consists of labels rather than amounts of something, and the bars are separated from their neighbors.

Data can also be organized and displayed with a stem-and-leaf plot, a technique having features of both a frequency distribution and a frequency histogram. In the stem-and-leaf plot, each score is split into two parts called the stem and the leaf. The first digit(s) of the score is the stem, and the last digit(s) is the leaf; for example, for the number 85, 8 is the stem and 5 is the leaf. To construct the display, we list the stems from lowest to highest and draw a vertical line to the right of the list. Going through the scores one at a time, we then place each leaf to the right of its stem. The stem-and-leaf display results in a histogram with a class interval of 10. The advantage of a stem-and-leaf display is that no information is lost.

In a line graph, an independent variable is plotted on the X axis and some measure of the dependent variable is plotted on the Y axis. Because the independent variable is assumed to be continuous, a line is used to connect the plotted points.

EXERCISES

1. Construct a frequency polygon from the following scores:

    10, 7, 12, 8, 10, 9, 10, 10, 8, 9, 11, 10, 9, 7, 8, 6, 11, 9

2. As part of the annual study of course demands at the university, the registrar computes the average number of credit hours in the natural sciences (chemistry, biology, geology, etc.) that various majors take during the academic year. The registrar discovers that in 1996, engineering majors enrolled for an average of 15 hours of natural sciences; business majors, 3 hours; psychology majors, 6 hours; and education majors, 4 hours. Construct a bar graph to represent these data.

3. Some students in an English class have been asked to unscramble 25 sentences in 10 minutes. From the grouped frequency distribution of their scores—number of sentences correctly unscrambled—construct a frequency polygon, a cumulative frequency polygon, a cumulative percentage polygon, and a histogram. Be sure to label your axes and to add the appropriate legend.

c_i	f	c_i	f
21–23	2	9–11	9
18–20	3	6–8	5
15–17	5	3–5	4
12–14	12		

4. On a recent 50-point quiz, 30 statistics students obtained the scores presented in the following frequency distribution:

X	f	X	f	X	f
46	1	38	1	30	1
45	2	37	3	29	0
44	0	36	2	28	1
43	2	35	0	27	1
42	1	34	1	26	0
41	3	33	3	25	1
40	1	32	1	24	0
39	2	31	2	23	1

Using approximately eight class intervals, construct a grouped frequency distribution and from it plot a frequency polygon, a cumulative frequency polygon, and a histogram. Tell whether the frequency polygon is skewed in appearance, and if so, in which direction.

5. As part of a class project, students surveyed classmates about their fast-food preferences. Of 100 students surveyed, the preferences were as follows: pizza, 17; hamburgers, 39; hot dogs, 12; tacos, 22. Construct a graph from these data.

6. In a study of book-carrying style of schoolchildren, at least four different styles were noted and the percentages of each sex using a particular style recorded. The percentages were as follows:

Style	Male %	Female %
1 (side carry)	80	15
2 (front carry)	20	35
3 (both hands)	0	15
4 (balanced on hip)	0	35

Use the appropriate graph to illustrate these data.

7. Briefly define the following terms:
    a. positively skewed curve
    b. symmetrical curve
    c. negatively skewed curve

8. For each of the following graphs, define or describe the conditions under which it is used and give an example of a situation where it would be appropriate:
    a. frequency polygon   c. bar graph
    b. histogram   d. line graph

9. What two graphing conventions are often employed to help prevent misrepresentation of data?

10. Use the following data from Chapter 3, Exercise 3 (bar-pressing rats) to construct a stem-and-leaf plot:

98	100	105	97
128	155	152	107
123	135	141	145
133	125	107	103
95	148	140	127

11. Use the following data from Chapter 3, Exercise 1 (35 soccer players doing as many sit-ups as possible in 2 minutes) to construct a stem-and-leaf plot that organizes the scores:

37	48	29	50	13
34	47	29	40	16
27	45	25	38	18
28	33	20	35	14
23	15	18	33	38
50	11	16	25	40
44	12	13	20	14

12. Blood samples are drawn from a large number of young adult males and females before a study of the effects of relaxation training on blood cholesterol. Total cholesterol levels are given below. Use the appropriate graphing technique to compare females and males.

Females				Males			
X	f	X	f	X	f	X	f
265	1	235	7	283	1	218	6
262	2	230	6	255	1	215	4
260	1	225	6	243	3	214	4
255	3	220	4	240	2	210	3
253	2	219	3	239	2	208	1
250	4	215	2	235	3	206	1
248	4	210	1	233	4	200	1
245	6	208	1	230	6	195	1
242	7	185	1	225	8	173	1
240	14			220	9		

Measures of Central Tendency

✺ Incumbent Governor Jones was locked in a hard-fought and very close election race with two challengers, candidate Smith and candidate Harris. Both challengers were emphasizing the severe economic woes of the state, particularly as they affected middle- and lower-income families. Candidate Smith asserted that the median annual family income for the state was $17,500, which was insufficient to support an acceptable quality of life. Candidate Harris took an even more negative view; he pointed out that the modal annual family income was $15,000. Governor Jones, on the other hand, pointed to an unprecedented level of prosperity for families. He argued that the average family income was over $25,000, a level more than sufficient for a good quality of life.

Is one of the candidates lying? Are the candidates using different data from which to draw their conclusions? As you can see from Figure 5-1, the answer to both questions is no. All three candidates are looking at the same data, but they are selecting different indices to represent the "typical" family. Thus, they are coming to equally valid but very different conclusions.

The argument among candidates Smith, Jones, and Harris centers around a difference of opinion about which index of income best represents the typical family. (Of course, each candidate is also using the value that best supports his position!) Harris argues that the mode is best, Smith prefers the median, and Jones counters that the mean is the preferred index.

In our use of statistics, both professionally and in our everyday lives, we regularly encounter indices in the form of median income, batting averages, modal type of house or car, and so forth. Similarly, we are often asked to summarize a

FIGURE 5-1   Graph of annual family income showing three different "averages."

set of scores with a single index that represents the "center," the "most typical,"
or the "average." If we wanted a single number to convey as much information
as possible about a distribution of scores, what number should we choose? In
other words, what single score is most typical or representative of an entire distribution of scores? We would probably select a score near the middle or center of
the distribution. That is, we would locate a measure of central tendency in the
data. **Central tendency** refers to the tendency of scores in a distribution to be
concentrated near the middle of the distribution.

The measures of central tendency that will be discussed in this chapter are
the arithmetic mean, the median, and the mode. Each of these measures is a kind
of average. (The election race example illustrated all three indices.) Of the different averages, the one that is probably the most familiar is the arithmetic average,
or mean. The mean is frequently encountered in everyday life. For example, we
might hear a weather report stating that the average maximum daily temperature for the month of July was 91 °F or predicting that rainfall in August will be
below average, meaning below the arithmetic mean for previous years. Similarly,
you are probably interested in your mean test score in a class or your overall
grade point average. As you may notice from these examples, the mean is particularly useful for summarizing interval or ratio data.

Another type of average, the mode, or most frequently occurring score or category, is also encountered often. For example, we may read or hear that the sub-
field of psychology receiving the most graduate school applications is clinical
psychology. If we sell cars, it may be valuable for us to know that the most commonly requested body style is a four-door sedan. If we're politicians, it may be
important to know that the average, or modal, education level in the state is the

12th grade. That is, more voters have that level of education than any other. The mode is a particularly useful measure of central tendency for nominal scale or categorical data, although it can be found for any data.

The median, although encountered less often than the mean and mode (or perhaps more often misidentified and confused with the arithmetic mean), is nonetheless important. While watching a gymnastics meet, we might hear that a gymnast has received a median rating of 9.9 on a 10-point scale for an outstanding session on the uneven bars. That is, 9.9 is the rating in the middle of the judges' scores; half the judges' ratings are below 9.9, and half are above 9.9. On a 4-point scale, the median grade point average of a group of students might be 2.5, with 2.5 being the score in the middle (50% above and 50% below) of the distribution. The median talent rating for a group of talent show contestants might be 8.5. The median is especially useful for summarizing rank order or ordinal scale data, although it can be used with interval or ratio scale data as well.

Let's begin our discussion of the measures of central tendency with the one that is easiest to determine—the mode.

THE MODE

The mode is the simplest of the measures of central tendency to locate; unfortunately, it is the least useful for further statistical purposes. Because it is based on nominal data, it cannot be manipulated statistically. The **mode (*Mo*)** is the most frequently occurring score in a frequency distribution or the midpoint of the class interval with the largest frequency in a grouped frequency distribution. To determine its value, we have only to look down the column of frequencies to see which frequency is the largest and then look across to find the score or interval of scores that has this frequency.

The following frequency distributions, first presented in Chapter 4, give the number of friends of a group of extraverts and a group of introverts:

Extraverts				Introverts			
X	f	X	f	X	f	X	f
18	1	10	7	12	2	4	4
17	2	9	6	11	2	3	2
16	2	8	5	10	1	2	2
15	4	7	2	9	1	1	3
14	2	6	2	8	4	0	2
13	3	5	1	7	4		$N = 40$
12	6	4	1	6	7		
11	5	3	1	5	6		

$$N = 50$$

Mo = 10, score with the highest frequency

Mo = 6, score with the highest frequency

To determine the value of the mode for these distributions, we first look down the frequency column to find the highest value. Looking across from this value to the score column, we see that the mode for extraverts is 10, and the mode for introverts is 6. That is, more extraverts had 10 friends than any other number of friends, and more introverts had 6 friends.

To illustrate the location of the mode in a grouped frequency distribution, let's reconsider yet another distribution introduced in Chapter 4. The IQ test scores of 23 students in an honors class are summarized in the following grouped frequency distribution:

= MID POINT

c_i	MP	f	
170–174	172	1	
165–169	167	0	
160–164	162	2	
155–159	157	3	
150–154	152	6	$Mo = 152$, MP of c_i
145–149	147	2	with highest frequency
140–144	142	5	
135–139	137	1	
130–134	132	0	
125–129	127	2	
120–124	122	1	

In the frequency column, we see that the largest number is 6, which is the frequency for the class interval from 150 to 154. The midpoint of this interval is 152, and this value is reported as the mode.

Unfortunately, as mentioned earlier, once we have determined the mode, there is little we can do with it beyond reporting it, because we can't use it for any further statistical purposes. In addition, we may not be able to decide on just one value for it; that is, our data may contain more than one score or class interval with identical high frequencies. A distribution with two modes is said to be **bimodal**, and we report both values. The authors have occasionally obtained bimodal distributions of test scores in courses we have taught; that is, some students knew the material and did well but an equal number didn't know the material and did poorly. A bimodal, symmetrical distribution is shown in Figure 5-2. It is also possible, although rare, to obtain distributions with three or more modes. These distributions are said to be multimodal.

Yet another disadvantage of the mode is that it is determined only by the frequency of scores occurring in one category. No other scores in the distribution are included in the determination. This makes the mode vulnerable to vagaries and variations in the sample, especially if the sample is small. A measure based on all the scores would be more useful because it would have greater stability from one sample to another drawn from a population. When we say that the mode is

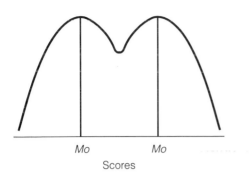

FIGURE 5-2   A bimodal, symmetrical distribution.

unstable, we mean that if we take a large number of samples from a known population and compute the mean, median, and mode for each sample, the mode will vary more than the mean or median among samples.

THE MEDIAN

The **median** (*Md*) is a point along the score scale that separates the top 50% of the scores from the bottom 50%; it is the score value at the 50th percentile. A **percentile** is the score at or below which a given percentage of the scores lie. In other words, the 50th percentile, or the median, is a point above which half the scores lie and below which half lie. The median is often easier to determine than the mean, or arithmetic average. Although not as useful for further statistical procedures as the mean, the median is at times the best descriptive measure of central tendency. We will come back to this last statement after we have looked at several ways of computing the median.

Locating the Median by the Counting Method: Even Number of Scores

In an ungrouped frequency distribution or an array of scores ranked from highest to lowest, the median is the middle score value. This means that in a frequency distribution with an even number of scores, the median will be a number halfway between the two scores in the middle of the distribution. For example, if there are 10 scores, the median will be halfway between the 5th and 6th scores; there are 4 scores above the 6th score and 4 scores below the 5th score.

Score No.	1	2	3	4	5 ↓ 6	7	8	9	10

4 scores   *Md*   4 scores

The position of the median in a frequency distribution with an even number of scores may be determined by considering that the median will be halfway between the

$$\frac{N}{2}\text{th and the }\frac{N}{2}\text{th + 1 scores.}$$

To illustrate, if you have 26 scores, the median will be between the $(N/2)$th, or $\frac{26}{2}$ = 13th score and the $(N/2)$th + 1, or 13 + 1 = 14th score. But don't forget: This procedure is designed to tell you the *location* of the median—not its value.

Let's look at some data and actually determine the median. In a study of problem solving, we have measured the number of "brainteasers" correctly solved in 10 minutes by a group of 20 students. The scores are 2, 0, 6, 5, 5, 2, 1, 7, 4, 3, 4, 6, 4, 3, 2, 0, 4, 1, 3, and 6. We want to find the median score. The first step will be to arrange the scores into a standard frequency distribution:

X	f	Cum f
7	1	20
6	3	19
5	2	16
4	4	14
3	3	10
2	3	7
1	2	4
0	2	2
	$N = 20$	

Because there are 20 scores in the distribution, the median will be halfway between the $N/2 = 20/2 = $ 10th score and the $N/2 + 1 = 10 + 1 = $ 11th score. The Cum f column tells us that the 10th score is a 3 and the 11th score is a 4. Thus, the median is the score halfway between 3 and 4, or $(3 + 4)/2 = 3.5$. This means that a median of 3.5 brainteasers were correctly solved in 10 minutes.

Let's look at another example. Suppose we have recorded the high temperature each day during the month of February in a town in Maine. We want to know the median temperature for the month. The data are as follows (each of the scores is a temperature in degrees Celsius):

X	f	Cum f	
3	1	28	
2	0	27	
1	0	27	
0	2	27	
−1	2	25	
−2	3	23	*(cont.)*

X	f	Cum f
−3	1	20
−4	3	19
−5	2	16
−6	1	14
−7	4	13
−8	2	9
−9	0	7
−10	2	7
−11	2	5
−12	2	3
−13	0	1
−14	1	1
	N = 28	

Because there are 28 scores, we know that we need to find the 14th and 15th scores: $(N/2) = 28/2 = 14$, and $(N/2) + 1 = 14 + 1 = 15$. The Cum f column tells us that the 14th score is −6 and the 15th score is −5. Thus the median is $(-6 + -5)/2 = -11/2 = 5.5$. The median temperature during February was −5.5 °C.

🌀 Checking Your Progress

A police officer monitors the speed of automobiles passing through a school zone during school hours. In a 15-minute period, the officer records the following speeds for 36 automobiles:

X	f	X	f
33	1	23	0
32	1	22	4
31	1	21	2
30	0	20	3
29	2	19	2
28	0	18	3
27	3	17	1
26	5	16	1
25	0	15	1
24	5	14	1

Handwritten: $N = 36$ $(N/2) = 18$ $18 + 1 = 19$

$(22 + 23)/2 = 45/2 = 27.5$

$(22 + 24)/2 = 46/2 = 23$

Find the median.

Answer: $Md = 23$. The median speed was 23 mph.

Locating the Median by the Counting Method: Odd Number of Scores

Now let's look at what happens when N is an odd number. Actually this is an easier situation because we need only locate the one score in the middle of the distribution. For example, if there are 9 scores, we locate the 5th score (the one with 4 below it and 4 above) and report this as the median. Or if we have 49 scores, the median will be the 25th score (24 scores below and 24 above).

The *location* of the median may be determined by computing

$$\frac{N+1}{2}.$$

That is, if we have 65 scores, the median will be the

$$\frac{65+1}{2} = \frac{66}{2} = 33\text{rd score.}$$

Consider the following example. Twenty-five students have rated a sociology professor on a 10-point scale that assesses how well prepared the professor's lectures are. The results are as follows:

X	f	Cum f
10	3	25
9	4	22
8	6	18
7	5	12
6	3	7
5	2	4
4	1	2
3	1	1
	$N = 25$	

Because there are 25 scores, the median will be the $(25 + 1)/2 = \frac{26}{2} = 13$th score. In the Cum f column, we see that there are 12 scores of 7 or less and 18 scores of 8 or less. This tells us that the 13th through the 18th scores are all 8, and so the median is 8. Thus, the sociology professor has been given a median score of 8.

It is important to note that finding the median by the counting method is an approximation. It gives the location of the median but does not always give its exact value. We know that this may seem confusing, but you only have to remember our discussion of real limits in Chapter 3 to make sense of it. Remember that each number occupies a space bounded by its real limits (a half unit above and a half unit below).

In the previous example, we know that the median is the 13th score. Twelve scores are 7 or less, so to find the 13th score, we need to go up to the next level, where the scores are 8 or less. But there are six scores of 8 and we need only one of them. A more exact method of calculating the median is to divide the category of 8 into six equal segments, beginning with the lower real limit (LRL) of 7.5. Because we need to go only one score into the interval 7.5–8.5, which is divided into six equal segments, the median $= 7.5 + \frac{1}{6} = 7.5 + 0.167 = 7.667$. This method is similar to the formula for calculating the median from a grouped frequency distribution, which we discuss in the next section.

For another example, let's look at the scores of 59 professional golfers on the last day of a tournament. The distribution is as follows:

X	f	Cum f
80	1	59
79	0	58
78	2	58
77	2	56
76	0	54
75	3	54
74	4	51
73	5	47
72	6	42
71	9	36
70	8	27
69	6	19
68	6	13
67	4	7
66	2	3
65	1	1
	N = 59	

Because there are 59 scores, the median will be the $(59 + 1)/2 = \frac{60}{2} = 30$th score. From the Cum f column, we see that there are 27 scores of 70 or less. The next 9 scores are all 71; that is, the 28th through the 36th scores are all the same. The 30th score, or median, is 71 according to the counting method. An exact computation would recognize that to obtain the 30th score requires that 3 of the 9 scores (or $\frac{1}{3}$) in category 71 be used. Thus, the exact median would be the LRL of $71 + \frac{1}{3}$ or $70.5 + 0.33 = 70.83$. The median score for the last day of the tournament was 70.83.

---

⑤ CHECKING YOUR PROGRESS

A clinical psychologist specializing in behavior therapy has used systematic desensitization to treat 23 patients for removal of phobic symptoms. In systematic desensitization, the patient is first taught how to relax. Next, a fear hierarchy is constructed in which the patient ranks fearful situations relevant to the phobia. For example, if the patient has a snake phobia, the most feared situation might be handling a live snake; the second most fearful event might be handling a dead snake; and the least feared occurrence might be to encounter a garden hose coiled in the grass. After the fear hierarchy is developed and the patient learns relaxation techniques, the two are combined. That is, the patient is asked to imagine each of the feared situations beginning with the least feared while maintaining relaxation.

The therapist has recorded the number of sessions required by each patient to achieve symptomatic relief. Unfortunately, 4 patients showed no progress after 20 sessions and were assigned an arbitrary score of 25. The data are as follows:

Number of Sessions	f
25	4
14	1
12	2
11	3
10	3
9	4
8	2
6	1
5	1
4	1
3	1

$$\frac{N+1}{2} = \frac{23+1}{2} = \frac{24}{2} = 12$$

$md = 10$

Determine the median by the counting method. Then determine the median by interpolation.

Answer: Md (counting) = 10. *Md* (interpolation) = 9.5 + 0.67 = 10.17. A median of 10 sessions—or 10.17 sessions—was required to achieve relief.

Before proceeding, let's summarize the steps involved in finding the median in an array of scores and in an ungrouped frequency distribution by the counting method:

1. Arrange the scores into a frequency distribution if they are not already so arranged.
2. Compute N and see if it is odd or even.
3. If N is even, the median will be halfway between the two scores in the middle, which we locate by looking at the Cum f column. The *location* of the median will be halfway between the $(N/2)$th score and the $(N/2)$th + 1 score.

4. If there is an odd number of scores, the median is the one in the middle, again found by looking at the Cum f column. The *location* of the median is determined by finding the $[(N + 1)/2]$th score.

Locating the Median by Interpolation: Grouped Frequency Distribution

The counting method results in a quick and useful estimate of the median. For a more precise determination, however, the interpolation method may be used.

To find the median in a grouped frequency distribution, we first locate the class interval containing the median and then interpolate to find the exact location. Let's look at a specific example to help describe the procedure.

Sixty-four very overweight people enter a weight loss program. Their weight loss after a 12-month period is represented in the grouped frequency distribution shown here:

ci		f	Cum f
63–69	62.5–69.5	5	64
56–62	55.5–62.5	6	59
49–55	48.5–55.5	8	53
42–48	41.5–48.5	7	45
35–41	34.5–41.5	8	38
28–34	27.5–34.5	10	30
21–27	20.5–27.5	9	20
14–20	13.5–20.5	5	11
7–13	6.5–13.5	4	6
0–6	–0.5–6.5	2	2
		$N = 64$	

According to the definition of the median, we need to find the case at the 50th percentile. Because there are 64 scores, we need to find the 32nd score (50% of 64 = 32). From the Cum f column, we see that the 32nd case is in the interval with apparent limits from 35 to 41 or with real limits from 34.5 to 41.5. That is, there are 30 scores of 34.5 or less (34.5 is the upper real limit of the interval from 28 to 34) and 38 scores of 41.5 or less.

If we assume that the 8 scores in the interval from 35 to 41 are evenly distributed across it, how far into the interval must we go to find the 32nd case? Because there are 30 scores up to the top of the preceding interval and we want the 32nd score, the median will be the second score from the bottom of the interval from 35 to 41 (32 − 30 = 2). That is, the median will be the second of 8 scores in the interval. Thus, it is $\frac{2}{8}$ (or $\frac{1}{4}$) of the way into an interval containing 7 score units, or $7 \times \frac{2}{8}$ths of the way into the interval. Because $7 \times \frac{2}{8} = 1.75$, we conclude that the median is 1.75 score units into the interval with a lower real limit of 34.5.

In conclusion, Md = 34.5 + 1.75, or 36.25. The median weight loss for the group was 36.25 pounds. Note that this is the same logic we used to calculate the median in the previous section. Remember that all frequency distributions can be thought of as grouped. We have only to recognize that in the previous section, we were dealing with grouped frequency distributions where the interval width was 1 unit.

The procedure for computing the median is summarized in the following formula:

FORMULA 5-1   *Median for a frequency distribution*

$$Md = \text{LRL} + i\left(\frac{N/2 - \text{Cum}\,f}{f}\right),$$

where LRL = lower real limit of the interval containing the $(N/2)$th case,

i = width of the class interval (range of scores in the interval + 1),

Cum f = cumulative frequency in the interval below the one containing the $(N/2)$th case, and

f = frequency in the interval containing the $(N/2)$th case.

Actually, Formula 5-1 may be used to find the score value at any percentile, not just the 50th. To do this, we simply substitute any proportion of N for $N/2$. For example, to find the score at the 25th percentile, we take 25% of N ($N \times .25$) or find the $(N/4)$th case.

To see how Formula 5-1 works in finding the median, let's use it to redetermine the median number of pounds lost:

$$Md = 34.5 + 7\left(\frac{32 - 30}{8}\right) = 34.5 + 7\left(\frac{2}{8}\right) = 34.5 + \frac{14}{8}$$

$$= 34.5 + 1.75 = 36.25.$$

Let's consider another example to be certain that the procedure is clear. A test is given to 83 students to assess their apathy toward current events. The test consists of 60 items taken from a weekly news magazine, and each student is asked to indicate interest in the item. The score for each student is the number of items marked "no interest." The grouped frequency distribution follows on the next page.

ci	f	Cum f
40–44	4	83
35–39	5	79
30–34	11	74
25–29	18	63
20–24	7	45
15–19	11	38
10–14	13	27
5–9	14	14
	$N = 83$	

The first step is to find the interval containing the median. Thus, the total N is divided by 2, giving $N/2 = \frac{83}{2} = 41.5$. The interval containing the 41.5th score or case is the one with limits from 20 to 24 (real limits: 19.5–24.5). There are 38 scores of 19 or less and 45 scores of 24 or less; thus, the 41.5th score must be in the interval from 20 to 24. Using Formula 5-1, we find

$$Md = \text{LRL} + i\left(\frac{N/2 - \text{Cum} f}{f}\right)$$

$$= 19.5 + 5\left(\frac{41.5 - 38}{7}\right)$$

$$= 19.5 + 5\left(\frac{3.5}{7}\right)$$

$$= 19.5 + 5(.5) = 19.5 + 2.5 = 22.$$

The median number of items marked "no interest" is 22.

Locating the Median by Interpolation: Ungrouped Frequency Distribution

Earlier, we introduced the calculation of a median when the interval width is 1. This involves an extension of the method of interpolation from grouped to ungrouped frequency distributions.

In Chapter 3, we noted that real limits could be given for single numbers in addition to class intervals. For example, a score of 9 has real limits from 8.5 to 9.5. Using this information, let's use Formula 5-1 to compute the median for the sociology professor's lecture ratings. The data appear again on the following page.

X	Real Limits	f	Cum f
10	9.5–10.5	3	25
9	8.5–9.5	4	22
8	7.5–8.5	6	18
7	6.5–7.5	5	12
6	5.5–6.5	3	7
5	4.5–5.5	2	4
4	3.5–4.5	1	2
3	2.5–3.5	1	1
		$N = \overline{25}$	

Again, the first step is to find the interval containing the median, or $N/2$th, score:

$$\frac{N}{2} = \frac{25}{2} = 12.5.$$

The interval containing the 12.5th score is the interval with real limits from 7.5 to 8.5, because the Cum f column tells us that there are 12 scores of 7.5 or less and 18 scores of 8.5 or less. Thus, the 12.5th score is just inside the interval from 7.5 to 8.5, and we can use Formula 5-1 to find it:

$$Md = \text{LRL} + i\left(\frac{N/2 - \text{Cum} f}{f}\right)$$

$$= 7.5 + 1\left(\frac{12.5 - 12}{6}\right)$$

$$= 7.5 + \frac{0.5}{6}$$

$$= 7.5 + 0.08 = 7.58.$$

The professor's median rating was 7.58.

ꙅ CHECKING YOUR PROGRESS

In Chapter 3, we presented some data based on correctly defined items on a test in general psychology. The distribution is shown here. Find the median using Formula 5-1.

ci	f
45–47	2
42–44	9
39–41	14
36–38	14
33–35	18
30–32	27
27–29	32
24–26	16
21–23	3
18–20	4
15–17	3
12–14	1

Answer: $Md = 30.89$. The median score for the psychology test was 30.89.

For additional practice with Formula 5-1, use it to compute the median for the distribution of scores for the students solving the "brainteasers" (p. 70).

Answer: $Md = 3.5$. A median of 3.5 brainteasers was correctly solved in 10 minutes.

THE MEAN, OR ARITHMETIC AVERAGE

The mean, or arithmetic average, is a value that most people have been exposed to since elementary school. The **mean** is the sum of the scores in a distribution divided by the number of scores. The symbol for the mean of a sample is $\overline{X}$ (read "ex-bar"), and the definitional formula is

FORMULA 5-2 *Mean*

$$\overline{X} = \frac{\Sigma X}{N}.$$

If you have all the values for a population, you use μ instead of $\overline{X}$:

$$\mu = \frac{\Sigma X}{N}.$$

As you know, Σ (capital Greek letter sigma) means to add or sum everything following it, in this case all the Xs, or scores. For example, if the Xs were 5, 3, and 2, then ΣX, or the sum of X, would be $5 + 3 + 2 = 10$. N is the number of scores, or Xs, that are summed. In this example, $N = 3$ and $\bar{X} = \frac{10}{3} = 3.33$.

Formula 5-2 assumes a distribution in which the frequency of each score is 1. But suppose we have the following quiz scores of 25 students: 6, 5, 5, 10, 9, 8, 0, 2, 4, 7, 7, 6, 5, 6, 6, 7, 9, 9, 8, 6, 6, 5, 2, 7, 5. We could certainly find the mean by using Formula 5-2, but this would involve adding all 25 scores to obtain $\Sigma X = 150$, from which we could then get $\bar{X} = \frac{150}{25} = 6$. With this number of scores, it would make more sense to put the data into a frequency distribution:

X	f
10	1
9	3
8	2
7	4
6	6
5	5
4	1
3	0
2	2
1	0
0	1
	$N = \overline{25}$

To find the mean for a frequency distribution, we use the following formula:

FORMULA 5-3   *Mean for a frequency distribution*

$$\bar{X} = \frac{\Sigma f X}{N}.$$

Again, if you have all the values for a population, you use μ rather than $\bar{X}$.

The first step in computing the mean should always be to write the formula and look at it for a moment to see what it tells us to compute. In this case, the numerator tells us first to multiply each score (X) by its frequency (f) and then to sum the result (ΣfX). These operations give the following results:

X	f	fX
10	1	10
9	3	27
8	2	16
7	4	28
6	6	36
5	5	25
4	1	4
3	0	0
2	2	4
1	0	0
0	1	0
	$N = 25$	$\Sigma fX = 150$

The denominator of the formula is N, which is the total number of students in the class, or the total number of scores. In the case of the frequency distribution, N is the sum of the numbers in the f column. In this case, the total is 25.

Why does the formula require us to multiply each score by its frequency? Why couldn't we just sum the Xs and divide by N? Look at the distribution again. Was there just one student with a quiz score of 9? No, there were three students with that score. To find an average, we sum *all* the scores in a distribution before dividing by N, and to sum all the scores in a frequency distribution, we must first multiply each score by its frequency.

To find ΣfX, we need a column labeled fX that we can sum. Again, the values in the column are produced by multiplying each score by its frequency. Adding the column results in the number 150.

The final step is to plug the values we have determined for N and ΣfX into Formula 5-3:

$$\overline{X} = \frac{\Sigma fX}{N} = \frac{150}{25} = 6.$$

The mean quiz score for the 25 students is 6.

The mean may also be determined from a grouped frequency distribution. In this case, we use the midpoint of each class interval for X. To illustrate, let's look at the grouped frequency distribution from the earlier example of participants in a weight loss program. The grouped frequency distribution of their weight loss after a 12-month period is repeated at the top of the following page.

ci	MP	f	fX (f times MP)
63–69	66	5	330
56–62	59	6	354
49–55	52	8	416
42–48	45	7	315
35–41	38	8	304
28–34	31	10	310
21–27	24	9	216
14–20	17	5	85
7–13	10	4	40
0–6	3	2	6
		$N = 64$	$\Sigma fX = 2{,}376$

As you can see, the sum of the f column is 64, and ΣfX, the sum of every frequency multiplied by the midpoint of its class interval, is 2,376. Thus, the mean of the distribution is

$$\overline{X} = \frac{\Sigma fX}{N} = \frac{2{,}376}{64} = 37.13.$$

The mean weight loss for the group was 37.13 pounds.

↻ Checking Your Progress

Suppose we have determined the digit span (number of digits that can be held in memory for a brief time period) in 37 4-year-olds. What is the mean digit span for our sample?

X	f
6	2
5	7
4	17
3	5
2	3
1	2
0	1

Answer: $\overline{X} = 3.73$. The mean number of digits the 4-year-olds can hold in memory is 3.73.

Rounding Conventions

In the preceding "Checking Your Progress," you should have gotten $\overline{X} = \frac{138}{37} = 3.7297297$. It would be quite tedious to list all digits after the decimal for each computation. Thus, we need to consider some rounding conventions. How should decimal fractions be rounded off? Should they be rounded to hundredths or tenths or not at all? If we do need to round, what rules should we use to make a rounding decision?

Rule 1: The convention adopted in this text is to round all final answers to hundredths. That is, we will carry out computations to at least three decimal places before deciding to increase the digit in the hundredths place or to leave it alone in our final answer.

Rule 2: If we're doing a series of operations, less inaccuracy will be introduced in our final answer if we round *only* the final answer. A corollary to this rule is: Learn to use your calculator's memory function.

Rule 3: In all preliminary calculations leading up to the final answer, maintain at least three decimal places. That is, these calculations should be rounded to the nearest thousandth.

Rule 4: In rounding the final answer, if the digit in the thousandths place is less than 5, drop it and everything that follows it. For example, if we have the number 88.764623, the number in the thousandths place (4) is less than 5, so drop it and everything that follows it. In other words, 88.764623 rounds to 88.76.

Rule 5: In rounding the final answer, if the number in the thousandths place is 5 or greater, round the preceding digit up and drop the following numbers. For example, the number 8.335221 rounds to 8.34 because the number in the thousandths place is 5.

The Mean as a Balancing Point

The mean is often called the balancing point in the distribution. In a distribution of scores, some scores have values greater than the mean and others have values below the mean. That is, scores in the distribution differ from the mean either positively or negatively—and, of course, some may be equal to it. If we sum all the positive and negative differences from the mean (the difference between each score and the mean is symbolized by $X - \overline{X}$), the result will be 0. In statistics, differences from a standard or reference value (in this case, the mean) are known as **deviations.**

The reason the sum of the deviations of the scores from the mean is 0 and the reason the mean is called the balancing point in the distribution is that the sum of the positive deviations is exactly equal to the sum of the negative deviations. Symbolically, this property of the mean is expressed as

$$\Sigma(X - \overline{X}) = 0.$$

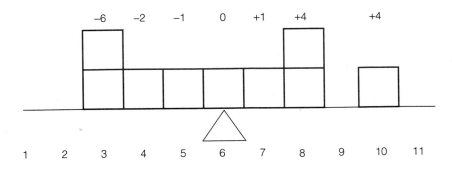

FIGURE 5-3   Seesaw with the mean as the balancing point. The weights above the mean exactly balance the weights below the mean.

To illustrate the property, let's consider the following example. Nine students have been given 10 problems to solve, each requiring some creative ability. The number of problems solved in a 20-minute period is recorded, and the frequency distribution of the scores and the computation of the mean are as follows:

X	f	fX
10	1	10
8	2	16
7	1	7
6	1	6
5	1	5
4	1	4
3	2	6
	$N = 9$	$\Sigma fX = 54$

$$\overline{X} = \frac{\Sigma fX}{N} = \frac{54}{9} = 6.$$

Imagine that the problems solved are objects placed on a seesaw. Their weights are determined by how far from the mean they are placed (Figure 5-3). As you can see, the score of 7 is 1 unit above the mean and has been given the weight of +1. There are two scores of 8, which are located 2 units above the mean and have been given the combined weight of +4. Also above the mean is the score of 10, which is 4 units from the mean and has been given the weight of +4. The four scores above the mean have a combined weight of $1 + 2 + 2 + 4 = +9$.

Because the score of 5 is 1 unit to the left of (below) the mean, it has been assigned a weight of –1; the score of 4 is 2 units below the mean and has the weight of –2; and the two scores of 3 are 3 units below the mean and together have been assigned a weight of –6. The sum of the weights below the mean is

$(-1) + (-2) + (-3) + (-3) = -9$. Adding the weights above and below the mean yields $(+9) + (-9) = 0$. Thus, we see that the weights above the mean exactly equal the weights below the mean, and the mean is the balancing point for this and any other distribution.

Earlier we said that this property of the mean could be expressed symbolically as $\Sigma(X - \bar{X}) = 0$, or, by extension, $\Sigma f(X - \bar{X}) = 0$ for a frequency distribution in which the frequencies are different from 1. Let's demonstrate this now:

X	f	$X - \bar{X}$	$f(X - \bar{X})$
10	1	+4	+4
8	2	+2	+4
7	1	+1	+1
6	1	0	0
5	1	−1	−1
4	1	−2	−2
3	2	−3	−6

$$\Sigma f(X - \bar{X}) = 0$$

The mean is still 6, and in the column labeled $X - \bar{X}$, the mean has been subtracted from each score and the appropriate sign retained. In the next column, labeled $f(X - \bar{X})$, each deviation is multiplied by its frequency. Summing this last column, we see that the sum of the deviations about the mean is indeed equal to 0. It is important to keep this property of the mean in mind when we talk in the next chapter about ways of determining the amount of variability (or deviation) in a distribution.

COMPARING MEASURES OF CENTRAL TENDENCY

As the example at the beginning of the chapter illustrates, the three measures of central tendency can have markedly different values and therefore lead to very different conclusions from the same data. Therefore, it is important to understand when the use of each index is appropriate and what advantages or limitations are associated with each.

The mode is the measure of choice in three instances: when we need the quickest possible estimate of the central tendency in the data, when we want to report the score obtained by the largest number of subjects, or when we have nominal scale or categorical data, so the computation of a median or mean is not appropriate, and yet we want to report a summarizing statistic. Thus, the mode is a good descriptive measure, but it is not used in inferential procedures. It is useful as a rough estimate of the mean and the median, and it can be used as a rough check of how accurately these latter statistics were computed.

The median is a very useful statistic and should be used when we have a fairly small distribution and a few extreme scores, when the distribution is badly skewed, or when some scores in the distribution were not actually determined (missing scores).

Because the median is based on the number of scores and not on their values, it will not be influenced by very deviant or extreme scores. To illustrate, suppose we have a distribution consisting of the scores 5, 5, 5, 5, and 35. Using our simple counting method to estimate the median, we find that it is the third score, which is a 5. The mean, on the other hand, is the sum of the scores divided by their number, or $\frac{55}{5} = 11$. As you can see, in a small distribution with extreme scores, the mean is dramatically influenced, whereas the median is not. In this case, the median is much more representative of the data.

In some studies, it may be impossible to determine an exact score for every subject. Some data that illustrate this point were obtained in a study with rats. As part of a study of the effects of diet on behavior, nine rats were trained to press a lever for a reward, and then the reward was omitted so that their lever pressing eventually ceased (extinguished). The response measure, or dependent variable, to be analyzed was the number of days it took the animals to stop responding. Because it was expected that some animals would continue to respond much longer than others, it was arbitrarily decided to terminate the participation of any animal that continued to respond beyond 15 days. That is, if an animal were still responding at 15 days, its training would be discontinued; but in actuality, it would not be known how long it would have taken the rat to extinguish its bar-pressing behavior if it had been allowed to continue. This sort of arbitrary cutoff point is often necessary in learning experiments.

The scores recorded for the nine subjects were 15, 15, 15, 15, 12, 6, 5, 4, 3. Because the first four scores were arbitrarily determined, the median is the most appropriate measure of central tendency. Remember, because the median depends on the number of scores and not on their values, the arbitrary cutoff scores do not affect the value calculated for the statistic. The mean, on the other hand, depends on the value of each score, so that an arbitrary ceiling depresses its value. In the example presented, the mean is 10. We know that this value is too low because each of the animals scoring 15 would have had a higher score if its participation hadn't been arbitrarily terminated. The value of the median would be 12 even if we had allowed each animal to continue until it achieved the criterion.

The mean is the most useful of the three measures of central tendency because many important statistical procedures are based on it. In addition, the mean has merit because it is based on *all* the data in the distribution and not on just a limited portion of it, as the median and the mode are. Also, the mean is a more reliable (more stable) measure than either the median or the mode. Specifically, if several samples are taken from a known population and each of the three measures of central tendency is computed for each sample, the mean will vary least of the three measures, followed by the median and the mode, in that order.

FIGURE 5-4   The relative locations of the three measures of central tendency in a normal distribution, a positively skewed distribution, and a negatively skewed distribution.

One of the most important uses of the mean of a sample is to estimate the population mean, symbolized by μ (Greek letter mu). (Note that Greek letters are used to symbolize population parameters; sample statistics are symbolized by letters of our own alphabet.) The sample mean is neither always above the population mean nor always below it. Instead, if we took successive samples from a population, the mean of the sample means would equal the population mean. For this reason, we say that the sample mean is an **unbiased estimate** of the population mean. This property of the sample mean as an unbiased estimator of the population mean will be especially important in Chapter 10.

As the example at the beginning of the chapter illustrates, there are times when the mean is not the best measure of central tendency to report. As we noted earlier, in small samples with extreme scores or in badly skewed distributions, the mean may be a poor representative of the distribution. The same is true when we have missing scores or arbitrarily determined cutoff scores. In all of these situations, the median is the preferred measure of central tendency.

POSITIONS OF MEASURES OF CENTRAL TENDENCY ON A FREQUENCY POLYGON

In a symmetrical, unimodal distribution, the mean, median, and mode are all the same. In a skewed distribution, however, the mean is pulled in the direction of the extreme scores (tail), and the median is between the mean and the mode. Examples of the relative locations of the three measures are shown in Figure 5-4.

To further illustrate the positions of the three measures and also review computational procedures, suppose we have the highly simplified but negatively skewed frequency distribution shown at the top of the following page.

X	f	Cum f	fX
9	5	34	45
8	5	29	40
7	7	24	49
6	6	17	36
5	5	11	25
4	3	6	12
3	1	3	3
2	1	2	2
1	1	1	1
	$N = 34$		$\Sigma fX = 213$

$Mo = 7$, because this is the score with the highest frequency.

Md = score halfway between the $(N/2)$th score and the $(N/2)$th + 1 score:

$$\frac{N}{2} = \frac{34}{2} = 17\text{th score} = 6,$$

$$\frac{N}{2} + 1 = 17 + 1 = 18\text{th score} = 7,$$

$$Md = \frac{6+7}{2} = \frac{13}{2} = 6.5.$$

$$\overline{X} = \frac{\Sigma fX}{N} = \frac{213}{34} = 6.26.$$

The frequency polygon based on this distribution is plotted in Figure 5-5. On it are shown the relative locations of the measures of central tendency.

Because the mean is pulled in the direction of the tail in a skewed distribution, if we are given any two of the measures of central tendency, we should be able to guess both the shape of the distribution and the location of the missing value. For example, if we know that the mean of a distribution is 13 and the mode is 20, we will probably guess that the distribution is negatively skewed and the median is somewhere between 13 and 20. If we are told that the mode is 10 with a median of 15, then the distribution will probably be positively skewed and the mean will be above 15.

SUMMARY

Three measures of central tendency are the mode, the median, and the mean (or arithmetic average). The mode (Mo) is the most frequently occurring score in the distribution and is determined by locating the score(s) with the highest fre-

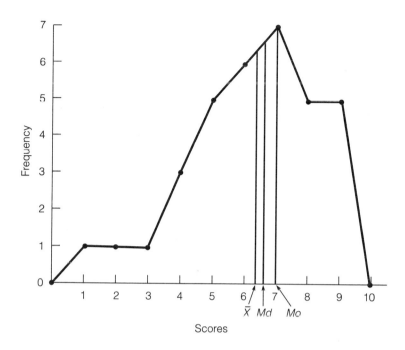

FIGURE 5-5 The relative locations of the three measures of central tendency in a negatively skewed distribution.

quency. A distribution with two modes is bimodal, and both values are reported. In a grouped frequency distribution, the mode is the midpoint of the class interval with the highest frequency. The mode is valuable in a descriptive sense but is not useful for further statistical procedures. Because it is so easily determined, it is useful as a first approximation of the central tendency in the data. It is also useful for summarizing central tendency in categorical or nominal scale data.

The median (*Md*) is a point along the score scale separating the top 50% of the scores from the bottom 50%; it is the score at the 50th percentile. The counting procedure for estimating the median from an ungrouped frequency distribution is as follows:

1. If *N* is even, the median will be halfway between the (*N*/2)th score and the (*N*/2)th + 1 score. To determine the value of the median, first locate the two scores and then take their average.

2. If *N* is odd, the median will be the [(*N* + 1)/2]th score.

To find the median from a grouped frequency distribution, the class interval containing the (*N*/2)th score is found, and interpolation is used to find the point where the score is located. The following formula is used to determine the median from a grouped frequency distribution:

$$Md = \text{LRL} + i\left(\frac{N/2 - \text{Cum } f}{f}\right),$$

where LRL = lower real limit of the interval containing the $(N/2)$th case,

i = width of the class interval (range of scores in the interval + 1),

Cum f = cumulative frequency in the interval below the one containing the $(N/2)$th case,

f = frequency in the interval containing the $(N/2)$th case.

The interpolation method can also be used to find the median in an ungrouped frequency distribution if you remember to use the real limits of each single score value. Be sure to use all possible scores, even with frequencies of 0. The median is the preferred measure when the distribution is skewed or when there are missing scores.

The mean, or arithmetic average ($\overline{X}$ for a sample, μ for a population), is defined mathematically as the sum of the scores divided by the number of scores. The formula is

$$\overline{X} = \frac{\Sigma X}{N}$$

or, in the case of a frequency distribution,

$$\overline{X} = \frac{\Sigma fX}{N}.$$

The midpoint of each class interval is used as a score in computing the mean from a grouped frequency distribution.

The mean is the balancing point in the distribution, symbolized by $\Sigma(X - \overline{X}) = 0$; that is, the sum of the deviations about the mean is 0. The mean is the least variable of the three measures of central tendency and is used in many other statistical procedures. It may not be the most representative measure in situations favoring the median—that is, where there are badly skewed distributions and/or missing scores in the distribution. The mean of a sample is an unbiased estimator of the population mean.

We also presented a set of rounding conventions:

1. Round everything to hundredths.
2. Wait until the final answer to round.
3. Maintain at least three decimal places in all preliminary calculations.
4. If the digit in the thousandths place is less than 5, drop it and everything that follows.
5. If the number in the thousandths place is 5 or more, round up the preceding digit and drop all following numbers.

In a symmetrical distribution with only one mode, the mean, median, and mode will all have the same value. In a skewed distribution, however, the mean will be pulled in the direction of the tail, and the median will be between the mean and the mode.

✳ *Troubleshooting Your Computations*

No matter how simple the statistic, computational errors are possible. How will you know (or suspect) that an error has been made?

The most basic piece of advice we can give is this: Be aware of what constitutes a reasonable answer. Try to estimate the type of answer that makes sense for the given problem. For example, if you are computing a measure of central tendency for a sample distribution, the value you obtain should be not only in the distribution of scores you have but also in the *center* (more or less) of the distribution. Thus, before starting to plug numbers into an equation, look at the distribution of scores and try to guess a value for the statistic desired. In this way, if you make a mistake and obtain an impossible answer for the distribution, at least you'll recognize it.

If you are working with a frequency distribution, be sure to take the frequencies into account; that is, be sure to use the appropriate formula (e.g., $\Sigma fX/N$ rather than $\Sigma X/N$) and to multiply each score by its frequency before summing. A common error is to add the scores (Xs) without multiplying each score by the corresponding frequency.

The mode is so easy to determine that mistakes are difficult to make. Be sure to report the *score* (or midpoint of the class interval) with the highest frequency rather than the highest frequency itself.

Finally, to help prevent computational errors, perform all computations twice, being sure you get the same answer each time.

EXERCISES

1. A sports psychologist worked with a basketball team to improve the players' free throw shooting. One technique she used was visualization. She asked each player, before taking the shot, to imagine the entire act of shooting, including the path of the ball and the sound it would make as it passed through the net. To see how good the team was before introducing the procedure, she had each of the 20 players take 25 shots, and she recorded the number each one made. The data are given on the following page.

X	f	X	f
24	1	15	0
23	0	14	0
22	2	13	0
21	3	12	1
20	2	11	0
19	4	10	2
18	1	9	2
17	0	8	1
16	1		$N = 20$

For the given data, determine each of the measures of central tendency, tell which you think is most appropriate for this situation, and say what you can about the shape of the distribution based on the three measures.

2. After a week of practicing with the visualization technique, the 20 players again shot 25 free throws, and the sports psychologist recorded the number made:

X	f	X	f
25	1	18	0
24	1	17	0
23	1	16	1
22	4	15	0
21	4	14	1
20	3	13	0
19	3	12	1
			$N = 20$

Compute the measures of central tendency, using both the counting and the interpolation methods to find the median.

3. Determine the median and the mean for each of the following:

a.   27, 33, 10, 9, 6, 7, 11, 23, 27

b.

X	f	X	f
150	5	108	3
148	5	65	5
145	8	64	5
133	7	62	5
110	4	37	3

c.

X	f	X	f
5	2	–3	3
4	3	–10	2
3	4	–15	3
2	1	–30	2

4. Which measure of central tendency is most appropriate when:

   a. you have extreme scores or missing scores?

   b. you need a quick estimate?

   c. you need the value that will be most consistent from sample to sample?

5. a. A unimodal distribution with $Mo = 30$ and $\bar{X} = 25$ is an example of a _____ skewed distribution.

   b. If $\bar{X} = 27$ with $Md = 22$, this will probably be a _____ skewed distribution.

6. A developmental psychologist is interested in the attention of infants to human faces. To study this, he shows infants either a set of geometric figures or a photograph of a human face. He then records the number of seconds the infants look at the stimuli (geometric figures or faces) without looking away for more than 5 seconds. Infants who attend for more than 100 seconds are given a score of 100. The data are as follows:

Geometric Figures		Faces	
Number of Seconds	f	Number of Seconds	f
27	1	100+	3
25	2	52	2
21	3	46	4
20	3	33	2
18	5	24	3
16	2	21	2
15	3	19	3
14	1	18	2
12	1	13	1

Determine the three measures of central tendency. Which is the most appropriate for this experiment? Suppose we discard the data for the three infants who attended for more than 100 seconds. Recalculate the measures of central tendency and tell which is most appropriate.

7. In Chapter 1, we described a classroom demonstration in which students tried to catch a ball while wearing goggles that reversed the visual field. The frequency distribution of the number of successful catches out of 10 trials for 20 students is given at the top of the following page.

X	f
10	1
9	0
8	2
7	1
6	1
5	2
4	2
3	4
2	5
1	1
0	1
	$N = 20$

Determine each of the measures of central tendency. Compute the median using both the counting and the interpolation methods.

8. In this chapter, we stated that the mean is the balancing point in the distribution. Make up a simple example to illustrate this important property of the mean.

9. Thirty rats were weighed. Find the mean, median, and modal weights from the grouped frequency distribution. The weights are given in grams.

ci	f
480–491	1
468–479	2
456–467	2
444–455	2
432–443	3
420–431	5
408–419	4
396–407	4
384–395	3
372–383	2
360–371	2

10. Using the rounding rules introduced, round the following:
    a. 43.85492
    b. 2.875
    c. 3.33333
    d. 73.66666

11. The following data represent the number of sentences correctly unscrambled by students in an English class. Determine each of the measures of central tendency.

ci	f
21–23	2
18–20	3
15–17	5
12–14	12
9–11	9
6–8	5
3–5	4

Measures of Dispersion and Standard Scores

One of our colleagues does research on the ways people solve arithmetic problems "in their heads." His approach is to ask people to solve different types of problems (such as how close together two numbers to be added are) and to measure the frequency of errors and the amount of time taken to solve the problem. In analyzing his data, he has observed that some people are highly consistent in the number of errors they make across sets of problems. If they make few (or many) errors on one set of problems, they tend to make few (or many) errors on the next set. Our colleague has also observed that there are people who are very inconsistent. They may make few errors on one set of problems but many errors on the next. The mean (or median or modal) number of errors for both types of participants is the same, but the spread of scores differs markedly. Examples of the types of distribution produced in this situation are presented in Figure 6-1. As you can see, the indices of central tendency are identical, but they do nothing to convey the differences in the shapes of these distributions. It is clear that we need an index of the spread, width, or distribution of scores if we are to adequately describe our data.

In Chapter 2, we talked about the two basic uses of statistics: to describe data and to make inferences from them. In Chapters 3, 4, and 5, we discussed different ways to describe data: by organizing them into a frequency distribution, by graphing them, and by determining a number in the central part of the distribution to summarize the data. To have a complete description of our data, we must also have a measure of the spread of the distribution, or its **dispersion.** There are three terms used frequently throughout this chapter to refer to the spread of the scores around the mean in a distribution. They are *dispersion*, *deviation*, and *variability*.

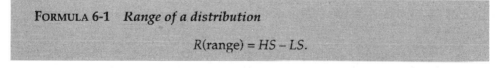

FIGURE 6-1 Graph of the spread of scores for consistent and inconsistent problem solvers.

Another example will help clarify the need for measuring the variability in the data. Suppose we look at the amount of rainfall in 1 year for two cities and find that each received a total of 150 inches, or a mean of 12.5 inches a month. Just knowing the mean will tell us nothing about how the rainfall was distributed during the year. We might find that in one city the climate was extremely dry for 10 months, with most of the 150 inches coming during a 2-month period. By contrast, a small amount of rain fell on the other city almost every day. If we simply reported our measure of central tendency, there would be no way to distinguish the two cities in terms of rainfall. What we need is a measure of dispersion, deviation, or variability. In this chapter, we discuss four such measures: the range, the average deviation, the variance, and the standard deviation.

THE RANGE

The range is similar to the mode in that it is easy to determine. Although it is useful in a descriptive sense, it is not used in statistical tests in this text. The **range** is the difference between the highest score (*HS*) in the distribution and the lowest score (*LS*).

> **FORMULA 6-1** *Range of a distribution*
>
> $$R(\text{range}) = HS - LS.$$

The range is a quick and useful way of communicating the spread of a distribution. A course instructor, for example, might announce that the average score on the midterm was 72, with a high score of 98 and a low of 40. By giving the high and low scores, the instructor is indicating the range. Or suppose we have obtained the IQ scores of most of the population in the United States and have found a low score of 0 and a high score of 200. The range is from 0 to 200 or 200 − 0 = 200. In Exercise 3c at the end of Chapter 5, a distribution was given where the high score was 5 and the low score was –30. What was the range? In this case,

$$R = HS - LS = 5 - (-30) = 5 + 30 = 35.$$

The range is a useful measure if we are interested only in a basic approximation of the variability in the data. But because the range is based on only two scores in the distribution, and these are the two extremes, it is obviously not a very sophisticated measure. It is entirely possible to have two distributions with the same range but different variabilities. Consider the following two distributions of scores in math classes:

> Class A: 13, 23, 33, 43, 53, 63, 73, 83, 93, 100
> Class B: 13, 85, 85, 86, 87, 87, 88, 88, 89, 100

In each case, the range of scores is from 100 to 13, or 87. However, the scores are much more evenly distributed across the range in Class A than in Class B. In fact, if we omitted the two extremes in Class B, its range would be only 4 (89–85).

This example illustrates a major problem with the range as a measure of dispersion. If the extreme scores are not representative of the distribution (as in Class B), the range will be unrepresentative as well. Now let's consider a statistic to measure dispersion based on the "best" measure of central tendency.

THE AVERAGE DEVIATION

One way of quantifying the dispersion of a set of scores is to use the distance between scores and the center of the distribution. Because the mean, as we discussed in Chapter 5, is the "best" measure of central tendency, we can create an index of dispersion by subtracting the mean from each score $(X - \bar{X})$. The greater the spread, or dispersion, of a set of scores, the greater these distances should be, on average. Thus, we can create an index called the **average deviation** (*AD*)—the average amount that each score in a distribution deviates from the mean. To do this, we first calculate the deviation of each score from the mean $(X - \bar{X})$, then sum these deviations $[\Sigma(X - \bar{X})]$, and finally divide by the number of scores:

$$\frac{\Sigma(X - \bar{X})}{N}$$

The problem with this procedure is that the negative deviations of the scores below the mean exactly balance the positive deviations of the scores above the mean, so their sum is 0, as we found in Chapter 5. If we used this procedure, we would find that the average deviation was always 0. Clearly, this would not be very useful, and we must try another method—one that finds the sum of the deviations without getting 0 every time.

There are actually several methods for doing this; one requires the summation of the absolute values of the deviations. The **absolute value** of a number (symbolized by parallel vertical lines on either side of the number; e.g., $|-3|$) is the value of the number itself, without regard to sign. The absolute value of -5 is just 5, and the absolute value of $+5$ is likewise 5. The absolute value of the difference between a score and the mean is simply the number of units, or distance, between them regardless of whether the score is above or below the mean. Because it is the distance and not the direction that captures the spread of the scores, it is appropriate to replace $(X - \overline{X})$ with $|X - \overline{X}|$. Therefore, the formula for computing the average deviation of a sample is

FORMULA 6-2   *Average deviation when f = 1*

$$AD = \frac{\Sigma|X - \overline{X}|}{N}.$$

The formula for computing the average deviation for a frequency distribution is

FORMULA 6-3   *Average deviation for a frequency distribution*

$$AD = \frac{\Sigma f|X - \overline{X}|}{N}.$$

Although the average deviation tells us the average amount that each score in a distribution deviates from the mean of the distribution, its application is limited because absolute values have little use in other statistical procedures. However, there is another way to avoid the problem of negative signs when finding the deviation of each score from the mean: We can simply square each of the deviations, because a minus times a minus is a plus. We discuss this in the next section.

THE VARIANCE AND THE STANDARD DEVIATION

The Variance

In the previous section, we discussed the average deviation. In the formulas for *AD*, we avoided obtaining 0 when we summed the deviations from the mean by taking the absolute value of each deviation before summing. Unfortunately, as we noted, the resulting statistic is not very useful for further procedures.

instead
use sample 6-6
$$\frac{\Sigma(X-\bar{X})^2}{N}$$

Another way to avoid getting 0 each time we sum the deviations is to square the deviations before summing. That is, we could sum the squared deviations and divide by their number. This would give us the **variance**—the average of the squared deviations. Here are the formulas for the population variance, symbolized by σ^2 and read "little sigma squared":

FORMULA 6-4   *Population variance when f = 1 (definitional formula)*

$$\sigma^2 = \frac{\Sigma(X-\mu)^2}{N},$$

FORMULA 6-5   *Population variance for a frequency distribution (definitional formula)*

$$\sigma^2 = \frac{\Sigma f(X-\mu)^2}{N}.$$

Remember from Chapter 1 that a population is a broad group of individuals to which we want to generalize our results. Most populations are very large. For example, we might be interested in all college students enrolled in statistics courses in the United States, or all graduating high school seniors, or all people with hypertension.

Usually, we know population values in one of three situations. In the first, the value is defined by probability, such as our knowledge that in the population of coin tosses, heads occur 50% of the time. In the second, we may have extensive data on a variable, such as our knowledge from census data that the mean family size in the United States is 3.1. In the third, scales may be constructed so they have defined parameters, such as IQ tests that have a mean (μ) of 100. More often, we are faced with the necessity of estimating population parameters from sample statistics. This process of estimation is the foundation of inferential statistics, which we begin discussing in Part Two of this book.

There are situations, however, where populations are quite small—that is, where we have scores for all members of the group (population) in which we are interested. A good example of this situation is when we have scores on a class examination and we are interested only in the mean and variance of this class. We are not interested in using these scores to estimate the scores of any other group. We have scores from all the people of interest (the population), even though it is a relatively small group. In this case, sample variance (s^2) and population variance (σ^2) are the same, and we use the sample variance formulas to compute population variance.

FORMULA 6-6 *Sample variance when f = 1 (definitional formula)*

$$s^2 = \frac{\Sigma(X - \overline{X})^2}{N}.$$

[handwritten: on quiz, make on index card]

FORMULA 6-7 *Sample variance for a frequency distribution (definitional formula)*

$$s^2 = \frac{\Sigma f(X - \overline{X})^2}{N}.$$

In Chapter 10, we will use sample variance to estimate population variance. In that case, we will have to modify our variance formula by using $N - 1$ instead of N in the denominator. This modification is necessary because sample variance, as calculated using Formula 6-6, underestimates population variance. But that story will have to wait until Chapter 10.

Now let's use Formula 6-6 to compute a sample variance. As a preliminary to a study of the effects of antihistamines on driving ability, researchers determined the number of movements of the steering wheel in a 1-minute simulated driving exercise for 11 normal people. The data and computations are as follows:

Steering Adjustments X	$X - \overline{X}$	$(X - \overline{X})^2$
25	−17.91 = 7.09 × 7.09	= 50.27
24	− 17.91 = 6.09	37.09
23	−17.91 = 5.09	25.91
22	− 17.91 = 4.09	16.73
20	2.09	4.37
18	0.09	0.01
17	−0.91	0.83
16	−1.91	3.65
14	−3.91	15.29
10	−7.91	62.57
8	−17.91 = −9.91	98.21
$\Sigma X = 197$		$\Sigma(X - \overline{X})^2 = 314.93$

[handwritten annotations: ① find the mean $\overline{X} = \frac{\Sigma X}{N}$ 197 − 17.91 $\frac{197}{11}$ N = 11 $\overline{X} = 17.91$ $\Sigma = 314.93$ $s^2 = 28.63$]

[handwritten: $\frac{7.09}{\sqrt{50.27}}$; 17.91 − 5.35 = 12.56 , 1 standard deviation below the mean ; 17.91 + 5.35 = 23.26 = 1 standard deviation above the mean ; 5.35 = standard deviation]

$$\overline{X} = \frac{\Sigma X}{N} = \frac{197}{11} = 17.91$$

$$s^2 = \frac{\Sigma(X - \overline{X})^2}{N} = \frac{314.93}{11} = \frac{314.93}{11} = 28.63$$

[handwritten: $5.35\ \sqrt{28.63}$]

To compute s^2, the researchers first found the mean by summing the X column (197) and dividing by N (11) to get 17.91. Next, they obtained the values in the $X - \bar{X}$ column by subtracting the mean from each score. Squaring each of the deviations and summing the resulting column, $\Sigma(X - \bar{X})^2$, gave the total 314.93. To obtain s^2, they divided 314.93 by N (11) to get the sample variance of 28.63.

If we wanted to use Formula 6-7 to compute s^2 from a frequency distribution, we would need to add one more step before summing the squared deviations. We would need to multiply each of the squared deviations by its frequency. That is, we would need an additional column headed $f(X - \bar{X})^2$.

In addition to the definitional formulas, there are *computational* or *raw score* formulas. These formulas require fewer computations than the definitional formulas and are easier to use when computing the statistics with a pocket calculator. The computational formulas are derived from and produce equivalent values to those obtained from the definitional formulas:

FORMULA 6-8   *Sample variance when $f = 1$ (computational formula)*

$$s^2 = \frac{\Sigma X^2 - \frac{(\Sigma X)^2}{N}}{N},$$

mean

FORMULA 6-9   *Sample variance for a frequency distribution (computational formula)*

$$s^2 = \frac{\Sigma f X^2 - \frac{(\Sigma f X)^2}{N}}{N}.$$

only the X is squared

Consider an example. As part of a study on Down's syndrome, the number of physical abnormalities has been determined for a group of 23 children diagnosed with this syndrome. Use Formula 6-9 to compute s^2 for the distribution:

X	f	fX	fX^2
14	1	14	196
13	2	26	338
12	3	36	432
11	3	33	363
10	5	50	500
9	3	27	243
8	2	16	128
7	1	7	49
6	2	12	72
5	1	5	25
$N = 23$		$\Sigma fX = 226$	$\Sigma fX^2 = 2{,}346$

$$s^2 = \frac{\Sigma fX^2 - \frac{(\Sigma fX)^2}{N}}{N} = \frac{2,346 - \frac{(226)^2}{23}}{23} = \frac{2,346 - \frac{51,076}{23}}{23}$$

$$= \frac{2,346 - 2,220.70}{23}$$

$$= \frac{125.30}{23} = 5.45.$$

Using Formula 6-9, we first need to determine values for three terms: N, ΣfX, and ΣfX^2. Note that in order to find ΣfX^2, we need to multiply the values in the X column by the corresponding numbers in the fX column. Equivalently, we could have squared the values in the X column and then multiplied by the frequencies.

Many students make the mistake of thinking that all they have to do is square the values in the fX column to obtain the numbers under the heading fX^2. But by squaring the values in the fX column, they really have found f^2X^2; that is, they have squared the frequencies as well as the scores. This is not what is needed. Remember the following:

$$(fX)^2 = f^2X^2 \neq fX^2$$

but

$$(fX)(X) = fX^2 \quad \text{or} \quad (X^2)(f) = fX^2.$$

The Sum of Squares

The numerator in the formulas for variance (Formulas 6-6, 6-7, 6-8, and 6-9) is sometimes called the **sum of squares,** or SS:

> **FORMULA 6-10** *Sum of squares (definitional formulas)*
>
> $$SS = \Sigma(X - \bar{X})^2 \, [\Sigma f(X - \bar{X})^2 \text{ for a frequency distribution}],$$

> **FORMULA 6-11** *Sum of squares (computational formulas)*
>
> $$SS = \Sigma X^2 - \frac{(\Sigma X)^2}{N} \left[\Sigma fX^2 - \frac{(\Sigma fX)^2}{N} \text{ for a frequency distribution} \right].$$

Any formula in this chapter for the variance or the standard deviation could be rewritten in terms of the sum of squares. For example, Formula 6-8 could become

FORMULA 6-12   *Sample variance using sum of squares (computational formula)*

$$s^2 = \frac{SS}{N},$$

where $SS = \Sigma X^2 - \dfrac{(\Sigma X)^2}{N}$.

The sum of squares is one of the most frequently used calculations in statistics. There will be occasions to use it in working with correlation (Chapter 8), computing *t* tests (Chapters 10 and 11), and doing analysis of variance (Chapters 12, 13, and 14). Because it is so frequently used, it is a good idea to memorize the formula for *SS* or at least to make careful note of it. By using *SS*, we can simplify many formulas we encounter. Where appropriate in the sections and chapters that follow, this simplified version will be included along with the longer computational formula.

The Standard Deviation

The variance is in squared units; now let's look at a statistic that has the same units as the distribution from which the variance has been computed. The **standard deviation** is the square root of the sum of the squared deviation of the scores from the mean divided by the number of scores. That is, the standard deviation is the square root of the average squared deviation, or, more simply, the square root of the variance. For a population, the definitional formulas for the standard deviation (symbolized by σ) are

whole

FORMULA 6-13   *Population standard deviation when f = 1 (definitional formula)*

$$\sigma = \sqrt{\frac{\Sigma(X - \mu)^2}{N}},$$

whole

FORMULA 6-14   *Population standard deviation for a frequency distribution (definitional formula)*

$$\sigma = \sqrt{\frac{\Sigma f(X - \mu)^2}{N}}.$$

As with the variance, when the population is small and we know all the scores, the population standard deviation (σ) and the sample standard deviation (s) are the same. Here are the formulas:

FORMULA 6-15 *Sample standard deviation when f = 1 (definitional formula)*

$$s = \sqrt{\frac{\Sigma(X - \bar{X})^2}{N}},$$

see 6.6 formula for variance

FORMULA 6-16 *Sample standard deviation for a frequency distribution (definitional formula)*

$$s = \sqrt{\frac{\Sigma f(X - \bar{X})^2}{N}}.$$

Let's use a simple distribution to illustrate the use of the definitional formula for s. Suppose we have a distribution consisting of the scores 20, 19, 14, 12, and 10. What is s for this distribution?

X	$X - \bar{X}$	$(X - \bar{X})^2$
20	+5	25
19	+4	16
14	−1	1
12	−3	9
10	−5	25
$\Sigma X = 75$		$\Sigma(X - \bar{X})^2 = 76$

$$\bar{X} = \frac{\Sigma X}{N} = \frac{75}{5} = 15$$

$$s = \sqrt{\frac{\Sigma(X - \bar{X})^2}{N}} = \sqrt{\frac{76}{5}}$$

$$= \sqrt{15.2} = 3.90$$

The first step is to find the mean (15) and then to subtract the mean from each score ($X - \bar{X}$). Next we square the deviations and sum the squared deviations (76). Then we divide the sum of the squared deviations by N (5) to get the variance (15.2). Finally, we find the square root of the variance, 3.90, which is the standard deviation.

A faster and easier approach to the standard deviation is to use the sum of squares as computed in Formula 6-10. Here is the computational formula:

FORMULA 6-17   *Sample standard deviation when f = 1 (computational formula)*

$$s = \sqrt{\dfrac{\Sigma X^2 - \dfrac{(\Sigma X)^2}{N}}{N}} \quad \text{or} \quad \sqrt{\dfrac{SS}{N}}.$$

By using Formula 6-17, we avoid the steps of computing the mean, subtracting the mean from each score, and squaring the difference. These steps are time-consuming and prone to error, especially when the numbers are computed to several decimal places. But even when the numbers are simple, Formula 6-17 is easier. To illustrate, let's use Formula 6-17 in the previous example:

X	X^2
20	400
19	361
14	196
12	144
10	100
$\Sigma X = 75$	$\Sigma X^2 = 1{,}201$

$$s = \sqrt{\dfrac{\Sigma X^2 - \dfrac{(\Sigma X)^2}{N}}{N}} = \sqrt{\dfrac{1{,}201 - \dfrac{(75)^2}{5}}{5}} = \sqrt{\dfrac{1{,}201 - 1{,}125}{5}}$$

$$= \sqrt{\dfrac{76}{5}} = \sqrt{15.2} = 3.90$$

For a frequency distribution, the computational formula is

FORMULA 6-18   *Sample standard deviation for a frequency distribution (computational formula)*

$$s = \sqrt{\dfrac{\Sigma f X^2 - \dfrac{(\Sigma f X)^2}{N}}{N}} \quad \text{or} \quad \sqrt{\dfrac{SS}{N}}.$$

For example, let's say we test 10 students to see how many scrambled sentences they can correctly rearrange. The data and the computation of the standard deviation are as follows:

X	f	fX	fX²
13	1	13	169
12	1	12	144
11	2	22	242
10	1	10	100
9	3	27	243
6	1	6	36
4	1	4	16
	N = 10	ΣfX = 94	ΣfX² = 950

$$s = \sqrt{\frac{\Sigma fX^2 - \frac{(\Sigma fX)^2}{N}}{N}} = \sqrt{\frac{950 - \frac{(94)^2}{10}}{10}} = \sqrt{\frac{950 - \frac{8,836}{10}}{10}}$$

$$= \sqrt{\frac{950 - 883.6}{10}} = \sqrt{\frac{66.4}{10}}$$

$$= \sqrt{6.64} = 2.58.$$

As before, we need to determine values for N, ΣfX, and ΣfX^2. The variance, or s^2, is 6.64. The square root of 6.64, or 2.58, is the standard deviation.

Now that we have gone through the computational steps of calculating the sample standard deviation, what do we actually have? Can we graphically depict the number we have computed? Fortunately, yes. To illustrate, let's take another example of a frequency distribution, calculate the standard deviation, and plot s on the X axis of the frequency polygon plotted from the frequency distribution. Suppose we have administered the same scrambled sentences test to a class of 56 introductory psychology students and have obtained the following distribution of scores:

X	f	X	f
19	1	10	6
18	1	9	6
17	1	8	5
16	1	7	4
15	2	6	3
14	3	5	2
13	5	4	3
12	5	3	1
11	6	2	1

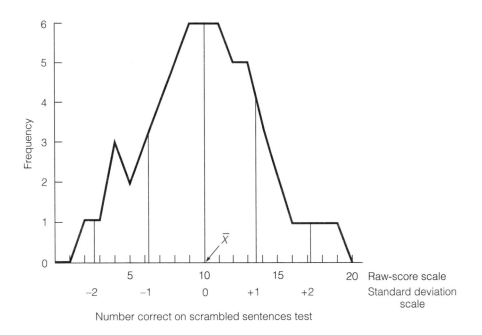

FIGURE 6-2   Visualization of the standard deviation.

Find s^2 and s. The answers are $s^2 = 13.93$ and $s = 3.73$.

Using the values from the frequency distribution, we can plot the frequency polygon shown in Figure 6-2. Then we can mark off the X axis of the polygon on either side of the mean in standard deviation units, which in this case would have a width of 3.7 raw-score units (the value we calculated for s rounded to tenths for ease in plotting).

The standard deviation can be visualized as another unit of measurement on the X axis of a frequency polygon. That is, the raw-score units we used to plot the polygon constitute one scale, the raw-score scale. But we can also plot the standard deviation scale on the X axis, and this also is shown in Figure 6-2. Later in the chapter, we will refer to the values on the standard deviation scale as either standard scores or z scores. Note that in the distribution shown, a raw score of 13.7 lies 1 standard deviation unit above the mean (mean + $1s$ = 10 + 3.7 = 13.7), whereas a score of 6.3 lies 1 standard deviation unit below the mean (mean − $1s$ = 10 − 3.7 = 6.3).

STANDARD SCORES (*z* SCORES)

We have just discussed visualizing the standard deviation as a width measure on the X axis of a frequency polygon. As mentioned, the scores plotted on the standard deviation scale are called either standard scores or z scores. Thus, a **standard score,** or **z score**, is the deviation of a raw score from the mean in standard

FIGURE 6-3 Hypothetical frequency polygon with $\bar{X} = 10$ and $s = 2$, illustrating the standard-score (z-score) scale.

deviation units. A z score tells us how far from the mean a raw score is in standard deviation units. In addition, the sign of the z score tells us the direction of the score relative to the mean: Negative z scores correspond to raw scores below the mean, and positive z scores indicate scores above the mean.

An example may help to illustrate the definition. Suppose we have a symmetrical distribution with a mean of 10 and a standard deviation of 2. How many standard deviation units away from the mean is a raw score of 14? The problem and its solution are shown in Figure 6-3. As you can see, the X axis of our frequency polygon has been divided into both raw-score units and standard-score, or z-score, units. It is apparent that 14 is 2 standard deviation units above the mean; that is, it has a z score of +2. Similarly, the z score for 8 is –1, for 6 is –2, and so forth.

Remember that the standard deviation is a kind of average amount that each score in a distribution deviates from the distribution's mean. A z score compares a score's deviation with the "average" deviation. For example, a z score of +2 means that the score is two times more deviant than all the scores are deviant, on the average. In other words, a z score of +2 (or –2, for that matter) indicates that a particular raw score is very deviant or unlikely.

There are two simple formulas for converting raw scores to z scores. On those infrequent occasions when we have population parameters of the standard deviation and the mean, we use Formula 6-19 to find z scores:

FORMULA 6-19 z score from a raw score using population parameters

$$z = \frac{X - \mu}{\sigma}.$$

More commonly, we have sample statistics, and we use Formula 6-20 to find z scores.

Box 6-1   Solving the z Score Formula for X

$$z = \frac{X - \overline{X}}{s}.$$

Multiply both sides of the equation by s to clear the fraction:

$$zs = \left(\frac{X - \overline{X}}{s}\right)s.$$

The s's cancel on the right side, leaving

$$zs = X - \overline{X}.$$

Add $\overline{X}$ to both sides of the equation:

$$zs + \overline{X} = X - \overline{X} + \overline{X},$$

which simplifies to

$$zs + \overline{X} = X.$$

Reversing terms gives us the final form of the equation:

$$X = zs + \overline{X}.$$

FORMULA 6-20   *z score from a raw score using sample statistics*

$$z = \frac{X - \overline{X}}{s}.$$

Suppose we have a sample with a mean of 7.53 and a standard deviation of 2.37, and we wish to find the z score for a raw score of 3.22. With Formula 6-20, it is quite simple:

$$z = \frac{X - \overline{X}}{s} = \frac{3.22 - 7.53}{2.37} = \frac{-4.31}{2.37} = -1.82.$$

That is, 3.22 is 1.82 standard deviation units *below* the mean.

We will also find it useful to be able to do the reverse—that is, to convert any z score to a raw score. For example, suppose we want to know what score is 2.5 standard deviation units above the mean in the distribution with a mean of 10 and a standard deviation of 2. In this case, we are told that $z = +2.5$, because the definition of z is how far a raw score is from the mean in standard deviation units. Examination of Figure 6-3 reveals that the score 2.5 standard deviation units above the mean is halfway between the scores of 14 and 16—that is, 15. Again, however, we run into problems when the mean and standard deviation are not so easy to work with. For this reason, it is handy to have a formula similar to Formula 6-20 for converting z scores to raw scores. And we do. We simply solve Formula 6-20 for X rather than for z. With the simple algebraic manipulations shown in Box 6-1, we derive Formulas 6-21 and 6-22:

SKIP

FORMULA 6-21 *Raw score from a z score using population parameters*

$$X = z\sigma + \mu,$$

FORMULA 6-22 *Raw score from a z score using sample statistics*

$$X = zs + \overline{X}.$$

For example, what is the score that lies 2.4 standard deviation units below the mean? In this case, $z = -2.4$ (negative z score, indicating that it is below the mean), $\overline{X} = 10$, and $s = 2$. Thus,

$$X = (-2.4)(2) + 10 = -4.8 + 10 = 5.2.$$

Therefore, a score of 5.2 lies 2.4 standard deviation units below the mean.

↺ CHECKING YOUR PROGRESS

Suppose we have measured the heights of all the basketball players in the National Basketball Association and have found that the average height is 77 inches, with a standard deviation of 2.2. What is the z score for a player 73 inches tall? 83 inches? What is the height of a player who is 2.6 standard deviation units below the mean?

Answer: $z = -1.82$; $z = 2.73$; $X = 71.28$. The player who is 73 inches tall is 1.82 standard deviation units below the mean; the player who is 83 inches tall is 2.73 standard deviation units above the mean; the player who is 2.6 standard deviation units below the mean is 71.28 inches tall.

One very important application of z scores is in comparing raw scores that are in different units. That is, z scores can be used as a common unit of comparison. For example, we might be confronted with the question of which is a higher score, 620 on the verbal SAT or 27 on the verbal part of the ACT. This is like asking which is more money, 9,000 lire or 50 francs. We can answer the money question by converting both lire and francs to dollars. There are about 5 francs to the dollar and 1,500 lire to the dollar, so we can convert the lire to dollars by dividing

9,000 by 1,500 and the francs to dollars by dividing 50 by 5. Our lire convert to $6 and our francs to $10. So 50 francs is more than 9,000 lire.

For our test scores, we can determine whether 620 on the verbal SAT is higher than a verbal ACT score of 27 by converting both to z scores. Suppose that the verbal ACT has a population mean of 25 and a standard deviation of 2.5; so for an ACT score of 27,

$$z = \frac{X - \mu}{\sigma} = \frac{27 - 21}{4} = \frac{6}{4} = 1.5.$$

For verbal SAT scores, $\mu = 500$ and $\sigma = 100$; so for an SAT score of 620,

$$z = \frac{X - \mu}{\sigma} = \frac{620 - 500}{100} = \frac{120}{100} = 1.2.$$

Thus, the verbal SAT score is 1.2 standard deviation units above the mean, whereas the verbal ACT score is only 1.5 standard deviation units above the mean; the ACT score is higher.

Note that both examples involved division by a constant. In the case of the money, we divided by the number of lire or francs in a dollar. For the test scores, we divided by the number of units in a standard deviation.

SUMMARY

Several measures of the spread, or dispersion, of data were discussed in this chapter. The simplest measure, but the least useful for further computations, is the range: $R = HS - LS$, where HS is the highest score and LS is the lowest score in the distribution.

The second measure presented was the average deviation, defined as the average amount that each score in a distribution deviates from the mean of the distribution. The formulas used to compute the average deviation from sample data are

$$AD = \frac{\Sigma|X - \overline{X}|}{N} \quad \text{and} \quad AD = \frac{\Sigma f|X - \overline{X}|}{N} \text{ (for a frequency distribution).}$$

Actually, a more useful pair of statistics is the variance and the standard deviation.

The variance is defined as the sum of the squared deviation of the scores from the mean divided by the number of scores—that is, the average of the squared deviations. The definitional formulas for variance are

$$\sigma^2 = \frac{\Sigma(X - \mu)^2}{N} \quad \text{and} \quad \sigma^2 = \frac{\Sigma f(X - \mu)^2}{N} \text{ (for a frequency distribution).}$$

There are two definitional formulas for variance using raw scores. They are

$$s^2 = \frac{\Sigma(X - \overline{X})^2}{N} \quad \text{and} \quad s^2 = \frac{\Sigma f(X - \overline{X})^2}{N} \text{ (for a frequency distribution).}$$

Modification of the definitional formulas results in computational formulas for s^2 that should be used when computing the statistic with a hand calculator. The formulas are

$$s^2 = \frac{\Sigma X^2 - \frac{(\Sigma X)^2}{N}}{N}$$

and

$$s^2 = \frac{\Sigma f X^2 - \frac{(\Sigma f X)^2}{N}}{N} \text{ (for a frequency distribution).}$$

The numerator of the equation for the variance is sometimes called the sum of squares (SS). The definitional formulas are

$$SS = \Sigma(X - \overline{X})^2 \quad \text{and} \quad SS = \Sigma f(X - \overline{X})^2 \text{ (for a frequency distribution).}$$

The computational formulas are

$$SS = \Sigma X^2 - \frac{(\Sigma X)^2}{N} \quad \text{and} \quad SS = \Sigma f X^2 - \frac{(\Sigma f X)^2}{N} \text{ (for a frequency distribution).}$$

The equations for the standard deviation and variance can be rewritten in terms of the sum of squares. The computational formula for s^2 is

$$s^2 = \frac{SS}{N}.$$

The standard deviation is defined as the square root of the average squared deviation or the square root of the variance, and the definitional formulas for the population standard deviation are

$$\sigma = \sqrt{\frac{\Sigma(X - \mu)^2}{N}} \quad \text{and} \quad \sigma = \sqrt{\frac{\Sigma f(X - \mu)^2}{N}} \text{ (for a frequency distribution).}$$

The definitional formulas for the sample standard deviation are

$$s = \sqrt{\frac{\Sigma(X - \overline{X})^2}{N}} \quad \text{and} \quad s = \sqrt{\frac{\Sigma f(X - \overline{X})^2}{N}} \text{ (for a frequency distribution).}$$

The computational or raw-score formulas for s are

$$s = \sqrt{\frac{\Sigma X^2 - \frac{(\Sigma X)^2}{N}}{N}} \quad \text{or} \quad s = \sqrt{\frac{SS}{N}}$$

and

$$s = \sqrt{\frac{\Sigma fX^2 - \dfrac{(\Sigma fX)^2}{N}}{N}} \text{ (for a frequency distribution).}$$

The standard deviation can be visualized as another width measure on the X axis of a frequency polygon.

A *standard score*, or *z score*, is defined as the deviation of a raw score from the mean in standard deviation units. The definitional formula for the z score using population parameters is

$$z = \frac{X - \mu}{\sigma}.$$

The formula to convert any sample raw score to a z score is

$$z = \frac{X - \overline{X}}{s}.$$

To convert a z score back to a raw score, the formulas are

$$X = z\sigma + \mu \text{ using population parameters}$$

and

$$X = zs + \overline{X} \text{ using sample statistics.}$$

✴ *Troubleshooting Your Computations*

This chapter dealt with statistics that are computationally more involved than anything encountered in Chapter 5. For this reason, we need to consider carefully some possible clues to trouble or to frequently made errors.

It is very important when computing s or any other statistic to have a "feel" for the right answer. For example, if you have a fairly large, symmetrical distribution, s will be somewhere near one sixth of the range. If you have scores that are rather tightly bunched, then s will be small relative to the case in which the scores are widely dispersed. If you obtain a value for s that is nearly the same as, or larger than, the range, you have made a gross computational error.

You must always get a positive value for s and s^2. Often, students obtain a negative number under the radical while computing s and then overlook it before reporting their final answer. In most of these cases, the value of ΣfX^2 has been improperly computed. At any rate, if you get a negative value for one of the measures of dispersion, it is incorrect.

Remember to take the frequencies into account when working with a frequency distribution. Finally, when computing s, be sure to extract the square root.

EXERCISES

1. Given that $\Sigma X = 1,000$, $N = 100$, and $\Sigma X^2 = 10,400$, what are s^2 and s?
2. Find s^2 and s for the following distribution of scores: 10, 9, 8, 7, 6, 5, 4, 3, 2, 1.
3. Find s for the following data: $\Sigma X^2 = 210$, $\Sigma X = 30$, $N = 15$.
4. Find s for the following data: $\Sigma X^2 = 416$, $\Sigma X = 48$, $N = 18$.
5. Given the following frequency distribution, find R, $\bar{X}$, s^2, and s:

X	f
9	4
8	6
7	7
6	8
5	7
4	3
3	3
2	1
1	1

In addition, plot the frequency polygon from these data and mark off the X axis in units of s.

6. On an examination in a statistics course, the scores were as follows:

   27, 36, 42, 12, 18, 15, 23, 13, 9, 26, 21, 20, 17, 14, 21, 15, 14, 2, 14, 19

   Determine R, s^2, and s.

7. Over a 3-year period, a clinical therapist recorded the number of sessions required by phobic patients to achieve relief from their symptoms. The frequency distribution of the data is shown here. Find s^2 and s.

X	f
22	1
20	2
19	2
18	3
15	4
13	4
11	2
10	1
9	2
8	1

8. Under distracting conditions, 30 people learn a list of 10 nonsense syllables. The experimenter records the number of repetitions of the list each person requires before he or she achieves an errorless trial. The results are shown here. Find s^2 and s for the distribution.

X	f	X	f
38	1	25	3
36	2	24	2
34	3	22	2
33	2	18	2
31	1	17	1
29	3	16	1
28	4	10	1
26	2		

9. In a study of mental arithmetic, each of 20 participants responded to 100 problems. The number of errors is shown here. Find R, s^2, and s.

5	7	3
4	8	2
9	0	6
3	4	8
8	6	2
2	10	6
6	7	

10. For the 20 participants in Exercise 9, the average amount of time taken to solve each problem was also recorded (in seconds). Find R, s^2, and s.

8.2	1.1	2.3
4.0	5.2	2.7
6.2	1.8	1.9
2.3	4.7	1.4
1.8	2.6	3.1
3.4	3.7	2.9
3.0	4.1	

11. Define each of the following:
    a. σ^2
    b. σ

c. μ

d. s^2

e. s

f. R

12. The average ACT score for a class of 33 students is 21.65, with $s = 2.83$. Convert each of the following to z scores: 19, 25, 33. What ACT score is 1.5 standard deviation units below the mean? What score is 2 standard deviation units above the mean?

13. For the Wechsler Adult Intelligence Scale (WAIS), $\mu = 100$ and $\sigma = 15$. Find the z score for an IQ of 92; for an IQ of 127. Find the IQ score corresponding to a z score of 1.1; to a z score of −0.5.

14. Quiz scores have been obtained for 50 students in a statistics class. The sum of scores for the class (ΣX) was 366.5, with $\Sigma X^2 = 2,836.39$. What is the z score for a raw score of 9? For a raw score of 4? What is the raw score corresponding to a z score of −1.65? Of 1.55?

15. A group of 10 college sophomores was trained on a bar-pressing task. The reward consisted of points needed to fulfill an experimental participation requirement. The schedule of reinforcement used was a fixed-interval (FI) schedule, meaning that the subject received reinforcement for the first bar press after a set period of time. The number of bar presses made by each student during a 20-minute period is shown here. Use the computational formula to find SS, s^2, and s.

Student No.	Number of Bar-presses
1	55
2	74
3	83
4	43
5	25
6	38
7	44
8	49
9	54
10	137

The Normal Distribution

Nearly all college-bound high school students take a standardized college admissions test. The two most common are the SAT and the ACT. You may recall the day you received your scores in the mail. They were accompanied by a report containing several tables with scores and percentiles and instructions about how to interpret your scores. You were probably able to figure out whether you had scored high enough to qualify for your preferred college or for certain college programs (e.g., honors programs). But you may have wondered how the tables were constructed and how your test scores were converted into percentiles.

The statistical tool used for these procedures is the *normal distribution*, which is a sort of statistical Rosetta stone. Discovered in Egypt by Napoleon's troops in 1799, the Rosetta stone contained a message written in both hieroglyphics and Greek. Scholars had been unable to decipher hieroglyphic inscriptions until the Greek translation on the Rosetta stone allowed them to break the code.

We aren't troops in a foreign country, and learning statistics isn't like deciphering hieroglyphics. But like the Rosetta stone, the normal distribution allows us to make several different translations: from scores to percentiles and probabilities, from probabilities and percentiles to scores, and from scores in one set of units to scores in other units.

In this chapter, we will learn to use the **normal distribution**—also referred to as the **normal curve**—to make translations and to answer questions such as those posed in the example about SAT and ACT scores. The normal distribution is among the handiest tools of statistics. It allows us to attach probabilities to events (or scores) and vice versa. For example, using the normal distribution, we can determine the likelihood of encountering a person with an IQ of 180 or more. Or we can calculate the score corresponding to the 25th percentile on a standardized reading test so that we can select students for a special reading program. In the example of college admissions tests, we could dispense with the tables provided and calculate the exact SAT or ACT score corresponding to the 90th percentile. The normal distribution is a useful tool indeed.

Contrary to what most people believe, including many statisticians, most data that we encounter are not normally distributed. In fact, some of our best data, numbers based on ratio scales (e.g., time and distance), are typically positively skewed. Some measurements, however, such as height, weight, and IQ, *are* normally distributed, and many empirical distributions (distributions based on actual measurement and observation) are similar enough to the normal distribution for us to treat them as if they were normal distributions. Moderate departures from "normality" usually don't disturb the statistical conclusions that we make. Thus, in answering questions about the distribution of scores, we will treat our frequency distributions as if they had the shape of the normal curve.

The normal distribution is the limiting case for a number of other distributions we will discuss. In Chapter 10, for example, we will discuss a distribution comprised of sample means. As the samples whose means comprise the sampling distribution increase in size, the distribution becomes more nearly normal. And in Chapter 15, we will discuss the distribution of chi-square, which approaches a normal distribution as N increases. Thus, even if we are working with distributions other than the normal curve, we can often assume a normal distribution with large samples. Further, through the process of sampling, all data, no matter what their original form, can be made to correspond to a normal distribution. This process is the basis of the sampling distribution of means, which we will discuss in Chapter 10.

CURVES AND PROBABILITY

All distributions of scores can be thought of as **probability distributions.** That is, a distribution represents the probabilities associated with scores in addition to the scores themselves. Think of the area under a portion of the distribution as representing the probability associated with the scores falling in that area.

For example, we can think of the curve in Figure 7-1 as representing all (100%) IQ scores. If we select a person at random and measure his or her IQ using the Stanford-Binet test of intelligence, what is the likelihood that it will be above 100? (The Stanford-Binet has been constructed to give a mean of 100, with a standard deviation of 16.) As you can see in Figure 7-1, 50% of the distribution of IQ scores fall above 100; therefore, the probability is 50%. What is the probability of selecting a person with an IQ below 100? Again, it is 50%.

What is the chance of choosing a person with an IQ above 120? The small shaded portion in Figure 7-2 represents the area of the curve corresponding to an IQ above 120. If we could determine the proportion of the curve that is shaded, we would have the answer to our question. Determining this proportion usually involves two steps using the normal distribution. The first step is to convert our

FIGURE 7-1   Normal curve illustrating the percentage area above the IQ score of 100.

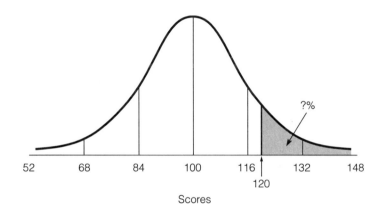

FIGURE 7-2   Normal curve illustrating the problem of finding the percentage area above an IQ score of 120.

scores to units of the standard normal distribution. This is accomplished by converting our raw scores to z scores. The second step is to use the z scores in conjunction with Table A in Appendix 4 to determine an area (proportion of the curve) that will answer our question. These steps will be discussed more fully later. But before we go any further, we must apply these ideas about probability to the normal curve.

CHARACTERISTICS OF THE NORMAL CURVE

We've alluded frequently in previous chapters to the properties of the normal curve. Actually, there are many possible normal curves, each differing in its values for the mean and standard deviation. For a given mean, the larger the standard deviation, the greater the spread of scores. That is, although each normal curve is bell shaped, as the standard deviation increases, the curve becomes flatter.

FIGURE 7-3   The standard normal curve with several areas labeled.

Normal curves all share certain characteristics. First, each normal curve is symmetrical; if you draw a line down the middle and fold the right half of the curve over the left half, the two halves will coincide. Second, each normal curve is unimodal, and its mean, median, and mode all have the same value. Third, the tails of each curve never quite reach the X axis; they stretch to minus infinity ($-\infty$) on the left side and plus infinity ($+\infty$) on the right.

The **standard normal curve** is a special example of the normal distribution in which the mean is 0 and the standard deviation is 1. If we draw the standard normal curve and mark off the X axis in standard deviation units, the result is the curve shown in Figure 7-3. Notice that some percentages have been entered on the curve. For example, between the mean and 1 standard deviation unit above the mean there is the notation 34.13%. What does this mean?

Although the standard normal curve never quite reaches the X axis, in practice we treat it as though it did. Thus, if we assume that the total area under the curve (the area between the curve and the X axis) is 100%, then 34.13% of the total area under the curve lies between the mean and 1 standard deviation unit above the mean. Because the curve is symmetrical, the same thing is true to the left of (below) the mean as well. Continuing, we find that 13.59% of the area lies between 1 and 2 standard deviation units on either side of the mean. Summing these two areas on each side of the mean, we find that 47.72% (34.13% + 13.59%) of the area lies between the mean and 2 standard deviation units on either side of it. Finally, we see that only 2.15% of the total area under the normal curve lies between 2 and 3 standard deviation units above or below the mean. Combining all the areas, we can see that almost the entire normal curve (99.74%) is contained between ±3 standard deviation units of the mean.

In other words, almost the entire normal curve is bounded by 6 standard deviation units. You may recall from the "Troubleshooting" section in Chapter 6 that if you have a fairly large, symmetrical distribution, s is going to be somewhere near one sixth of the range. Now you know why.

Because the normal curve is symmetrical, we really need to consider only one side of the distribution; the values on the other side will be identical. Fortunately for us, the areas under the normal curve have been determined for many different standard deviation units from the mean and are given in Appendix 4, Table A. However, the distances from the mean in the table are based on the *standard* normal curve, which has a mean of 0 and a standard deviation of 1. It is unlikely that we will ever encounter a sample in which the mean is exactly 0 and the standard deviation is 1. So how will we avail ourselves of the table? By converting our score values into standard scores, or z scores.

REVIEW OF *z* SCORES

We discussed standard scores, or z scores, in Chapter 6. At that time, a z score was defined as the deviation of a raw score from the mean in standard deviation units. That is, a z score tells us how far from the mean a score is in standard deviation units and in which direction. Negative z scores indicate that the score is below the mean, and positive z scores correspond to scores above the mean.

Recall the formulas for converting raw scores to z scores:

FORMULAS 6-19 AND 6-20   *z score from a raw score*

$$z = \frac{X - \mu}{\sigma} \quad \text{or} \quad z = \frac{X - \overline{X}}{s}.$$

For converting z scores back to raw scores, we introduced Formulas 6-21 and 6-22:

FORMULAS 6-21 AND 6-22   *Raw score from a z score*

$$X = z\sigma + \mu \quad \text{or} \quad X = zs + \overline{X}.$$

Let's consider an example to refresh our memories about the use of these formulas. Suppose we find for a sample of women that the average shoe size is 8.25, with a standard deviation of 1.17. What will be the z score, or standard score, corresponding to a shoe size of 10.5? Using Formula 6-20, we have

$$z = \frac{X - \overline{X}}{s} = \frac{10.5 - 8.25}{1.17} = \frac{2.25}{1.17} = 1.92.$$

In other words, based on this sample, a woman who wears a size 10.5 shoe will be 1.92 standard deviation units above the mean.

Continuing with the same example, what size shoe will be worn by a woman who is 2.25 standard deviation units below the mean? In this case, we have been given the z score, z = –2.25, and we are asked to convert it to a raw score. Using Formula 6-22, we have

$$X = zs + \overline{X} = -2.25(1.17) + 8.25 = -2.63 + 8.25 = 5.62.$$

Review what that means

That is, the shoe size corresponding to a z score of –2.25 is 5.62. This woman will probably have to try on a $5\frac{1}{2}$ and a 6 to get a pair of shoes that fits!

↻ CHECKING YOUR PROGRESS

Use the example of women's shoe sizes ($\bar{X} = 8.25$, $s = 1.17$) to determine the z score for a size 6. What shoe size lies 2.5 standard deviation units above the mean?

Answer: $z = 1.92$; $X = 11.18$. A shoe size of 6 corresponds to a z score of 1.9 and size 11 is 2.5 standard deviation units above the mean.

USING THE NORMAL CURVE TABLE

Now that we know how to convert a raw score into a z score and vice versa, what do we do with this knowledge? We can use it to give us access to the normal curve table, which can provide information about the population from which our sample was drawn.

Let's examine the portion of the normal curve table (Table A) that is shown in Table 7-1. From the normal curve table, we can find the percentage of the total area under the curve for a particular z score. Column A contains z scores to the nearest hundredth. In column B, we can find the percentage for the area between the mean and any particular z score we have. In column C, the table gives us the remaining area under the curve beyond our z score.

Let's look at a specific z score to see what information we can extract from the table. We'll use a z score of 0.52. To determine the percentage area under the curve between the mean and a z score of 0.52, we look down column A until we locate 0.52. Adjacent to this, in column B, is the number 19.85. This tells us that between the mean of a normal distribution and a z score of 0.52 lies approximately 20% of the normal curve. A glance at column C reveals that slightly over 30% (30.15, to be more precise) of the area under the curve is beyond a z score of 0.52. The z score and associated areas are shown in Figure 7-4 (on page 125).

What about negative z scores? Because the normal curve is symmetrical, there is no need to reproduce both halves. For this reason, only the right half is reproduced in the table. If we were asked to find the area under the curve between the mean and a z score of –1.06, we would look up 1.06 and report that the area was 35.54% of the area under the curve. Remember that a negative z score indicates that we are dealing with a portion of the distribution below the mean. The areas themselves are always positive.

We can also use the normal curve table to determine the z score associated with a particular area of the curve. For example, suppose we want to know the z score that has 17% of the area under the curve above it—in other words, the z

※ get explanation

TABLE 7-1

see page 365

Reproduction of a portion of Table A, the normal curve table: Areas under the normal curve (in percent). The complete table is found in Appendix 4.

(A)	(B)	(C)		(A)	(B)	(C)		(A)	(B)	(C)
z	area between mean and z	area beyond z		z	area between mean and z	area beyond z		z	area between mean and z	area beyond z
0.00	00.00	50.00		0.40	15.54	34.46		0.80	28.81	21.19
0.01	00.40	49.60		0.41	15.91	34.09		0.81	29.10	20.90
0.02	00.80	49.20		0.42	16.28	33.72		0.82	29.39	20.61
0.03	01.20	48.80		0.43	16.64	33.36		0.83	29.67	20.33
0.04	01.60	48.40		0.44	17.00	33.00		0.84	29.95	20.05
0.05	01.99	48.01		0.45	17.36	32.64		0.85	30.23	19.77
0.06	02.39	47.61		0.46	17.72	32.28		0.86	30.51	19.49
0.07	02.79	47.21		0.47	18.08	31.92		0.87	30.78	19.22
0.08	03.19	46.81		0.48	18.44	31.56		0.88	31.06	18.94
0.09	03.59	46.41		0.49	18.79	31.21		0.89	31.33	18.67
0.10	03.98	46.02		0.50	19.15	30.85		0.90	31.59	18.41
0.11	04.38	45.62		0.51	19.50	30.50		0.91	31.86	18.14
0.12	04.78	45.22		0.52	19.85	30.15		0.92	32.12	17.88
0.13	05.17	44.83		0.53	20.19	29.81		0.93	32.38	17.62
0.14	05.57	44.43		0.54	20.54	29.46		0.94	32.64	17.36
0.15	05.96	44.04		0.55	20.88	29.12		0.95	32.89	17.11
0.16	06.36	43.64		0.56	21.23	28.77		0.96	33.15	16.85
0.17	06.75	43.25		0.57	21.57	28.43		0.97	33.40	16.60
0.18	07.14	42.86		0.58	21.90	28.10		0.98	33.65	16.35
0.19	07.53	42.47		0.59	22.24	27.76		0.99	33.89	16.11
0.20	07.93	42.07		0.60	22.57	27.43		1.00	34.13	15.87
0.21	08.32	41.68		0.61	22.91	27.09		1.01	34.38	15.62
0.22	08.71	41.29		0.62	23.24	26.76		1.02	34.61	15.39
0.23	09.10	40.90		0.63	23.57	26.43		1.03	34.85	15.15
0.24	09.48	40.52		0.64	23.89	26.11		1.04	35.08	14.92
0.25	09.87	40.13		0.65	24.22	25.78		1.05	35.31	14.69
0.26	10.26	39.74		0.66	24.54	25.46		1.06	35.54	14.46
0.27	10.64	39.36		0.67	24.86	25.14		1.07	35.77	14.23
0.28	11.03	38.97		0.68	25.17	24.83		1.08	35.99	14.01
0.29	11.41	38.59		0.69	25.49	24.51		1.09	36.21	13.79
0.30	11.79	38.21		0.70	25.80	24.20				
0.31	12.17	37.83		0.71	26.11	23.89				
0.32	12.55	37.45		0.72	26.42	23.58				
0.33	12.93	37.07		0.73	26.73	23.27				
0.34	13.31	36.69		0.74	27.04	22.96				
0.35	13.68	36.32		0.75	27.34	22.66				
0.36	14.06	35.94		0.76	27.64	22.36				
0.37	14.43	35.57		0.77	27.94	22.06				
0.38	14.80	35.20		0.78	28.23	21.77				
0.39	15.17	34.83		0.79	28.52	21.48				

Source: This table is from Runyon, R. P. and Haber, A. *Fundamentals of Behavioral Statistics* (Third Edition, Addison-Wesley, 1976. pp. 377–379.) Copyright © 1976 by Addison-Wesley. Reprinted with permission of Random House, Inc.

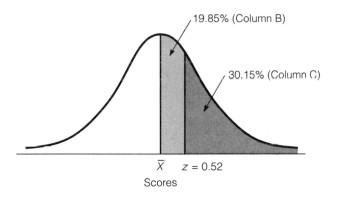

FIGURE 7-4 Normal curve showing a z score of 0.52 and associated areas from Table A, a portion of which is reproduced in Table 7-1. The number 19.85% is from column B; 30.15% is from column C.

score cutting off the upper 17% of the curve. The problem is shown graphically in Figure 7-5.

Looking at Table 7-1, we can see that for any z score, the values given in columns B and C will always add up to 50%. If we know one value, we can always find the other by subtracting from 50%. We can look in column C to find the area beyond the z score we want (17%), or we can look in column B to find the area between the mean and z (50 – 17 = 33%). Either way, we find from column A that z = 0.95. That is, we see from column C that 17.11% is closer to 17% than is 16.85% (which corresponds to a z score of 0.96), and 32.89% in column B is closer to 33% than is 33.15%. Once we've found the z score, we can use Formula 6-21 or 6-22 to convert it into a raw score.

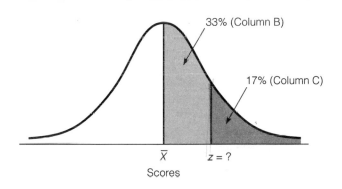

FIGURE 7-5 A normal curve illustrating the problem in which we want to find the z score cutting off the upper 17% of the curve.

Let's stop briefly at this point to see where we are and where we are going in this chapter. So far, we have had a brief introduction to the normal curve—its importance and its characteristics. Formulas have been reintroduced, two for converting raw scores to z scores and two for converting z scores to raw scores. A brief description of Table A has been presented, along with examples illustrating how to use the table to find areas under the normal curve and to find z scores cutting off specific areas. In the rest of the chapter, we will continue to encounter these two major types of problems: problems in which we need to find areas under the curve and problems in which we need to find scores cutting off particular areas. Moreover, because areas under the curve correspond to probabilities, in Chapter 9 we will also learn to convert scores to probabilities and probabilities to scores.

FINDING AREAS UNDER THE CURVE

Finding the Percentile Rank of a Score

If a person has a verbal SAT score of 700, what is his or her percentile rank? To begin with, **percentile rank** is the percentage of cases up to and including the one in which we are interested. Thus, our problem becomes one of finding the percentage of the population that scores 700 or less. Incidentally, the definition of percentile rank is the same whether we are discussing normal curve distributions or any other type of distribution. That is, even in nonnormal distributions, the percentile rank of a score is always the total percentage up to and including that score.

Before you begin working any normal curve problem, you should always first draw the normal curve and label it with the information provided in the problem; you can then go on to determine the areas or scores needed. Let's assume for this problem and for any others like it that the mean for the distribution of verbal SAT scores is 500 and the standard deviation is 100. An appropriately labeled curve is shown in Figure 7-6.

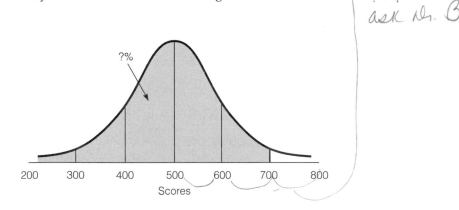

FIGURE 7-6   A normal curve illustrating the problem in which we want to find the percentile rank of a score of 700.

FIGURE 7-7 Normal curve showing an area of 47.72% (taken from Table A) between the mean and a score of 700 (z = 2.00).

Because we have been given a raw score (700), we must first convert it to a z score. The z score for a verbal SAT of 700 is

$$z_{700} = \frac{X - \mu}{\sigma} = \frac{700 - 500}{100} = \frac{200}{100} = 2.00.$$

From column B in Table A, we see that 47.72% of the curve falls between a z score of 2.00 and the mean. When we add this new information to the graph in Figure 7-6, we get Figure 7-7.

Because we are interested in the percentile rank of someone scoring 700, we need to find the total area at or *below* 700. We have just found that the area between 500 and 700 is 47.72%. And we already know that the area to the left of the mean is exactly 50% of the total curve. Therefore, the area below a score of 700 is 50 + 47.72 = 97.72% of the curve. We conclude that a person scoring 700 has a verbal SAT score equal to or higher than approximately 98% of the population.

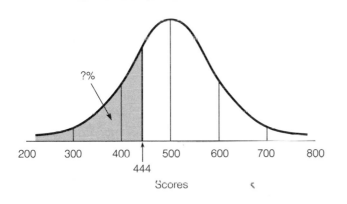

FIGURE 7-8 Normal curve illustrating the problem in which we want to find the percentile rank of a score of 444.

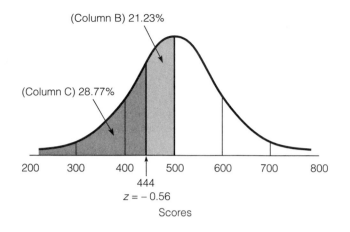

(Column B) 21.23%

(Column C) 28.77%

200   300   400   500   600   700   800

444

$z = -0.56$

Scores

FIGURE 7-9 Normal curve on which has been entered the information from Table A that 21.23% of the curve lies between the mean and the score of 444, whereas 28.77% lies below the score.

Let's try another problem. What is the percentile rank of someone with a verbal SAT score of 444? Again, the first steps are to draw the normal curve and label it appropriately. This has been done in Figure 7-8.

From the figure we can see that we need to find the area under the curve at or below the score of 444. To use the normal curve table, we must first convert the score of 444 to a z score:

$$z_{444} = \frac{X - \mu}{\sigma} = \frac{444 - 500}{100} = \frac{-56}{100} = -0.56.$$

The negative z score tells us that we are dealing with a score to the left of, or below, the mean. We find from the table that 21.23% of the curve lies between z = 0.56 (or –0.56) and the mean and that 28.77% of the curve lies beyond our z score. In Figure 7-9, this new information has been added to the previous graph, and it is evident that 28.77% is the area we want. We conclude, then, that the percentile rank of someone with a verbal SAT score of 444 is 28.77, or that the person scores as well as or better than about 29% of the population.

ꙅ CHECKING YOUR PROGRESS

As a final exercise in determining percentile rank, suppose we have trained 1,000 rats to run from one end of a 6-foot straight alley runway to the other. On the final run for each animal, we have recorded the speed of the run in feet per second. The mean running speed for the 1,000 rats was 2.4 feet per second with a standard deviation of 0.8 foot per second. What is the percentile rank of a rat that traverses the runway at a speed of 3.7 feet per second? 1.8 feet per second?

Answer: 94.84%; 22.66%. The rat that runs 3.7 feet per second is faster than 94.84% of its fellow rats; the rat that runs 1.8 feet per second equals or exceeds only 22.66% of its fellow rats.

Finding the Percentage of the Normal Curve Above a Score

To find the percentile rank of a score, we had to find the percentage of the normal curve *below* the score. A related problem is to find the percentage of the curve above a particular point. Earlier in the chapter, we asked what the likelihood was of an IQ score above 120. To answer the question, we must find the percentage of the IQ distribution falling above 120. As in the previous section, we will first draw the normal curve, this time with a standard mean of 100 and a deviation of 16, and locate the area we want to find. This problem is pictured in Figure 7-10.

As before, we have been given a raw score (120) and must first convert this score into a z score so that we can use the normal curve table:

$$z_{120} = \frac{120 - 100}{16} = \frac{20}{16} = 1.25.$$

From Appendix 4, Table A, we find that 39.44% of the curve lies between the mean and a z score of 1.25 and that 10.56% of the curve lies beyond this z score. The new information has been entered into the original diagram of the normal curve, and we can see from Figure 7-11 that the area we want is 10.56%. We conclude that approximately 11% of the population has IQ scores above 120.

Finding Percentage Frequency

Another useful piece of information about the normal curve is that the percentage area under the curve is the same thing as percentage frequency. In other

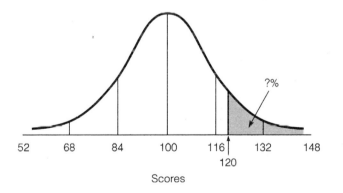

FIGURE 7-10 Normal curve illustrating the problem of finding the percentage area above an IQ score of 120.

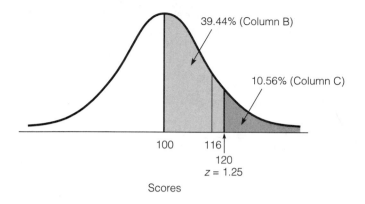

FIGURE 7-11   Normal curve illustrating the solution to the problem of finding the percentage area above the IQ score of 120.

words, when we find a percentage area under the curve, we can take that percentage of the total sample size to find how many subjects have scores in the area. For example, if we administer an IQ test to 250 randomly selected individuals, we would expect 11% of them to score 120 or above. How many would score 120 or above? The answer is 11% of 250, or 27.5 (realistically, 28) people. Let's look at another example.

How many of our randomly selected 250 would we expect to score above 80? As before, we will draw a diagram of the normal curve and enter the information we have. Then we will examine it to see if we can determine the area we want to find. The problem is shown in Figure 7-12.

To use the normal curve table, we first convert the IQ score of 80 into a z score:

$$z_{80} = \frac{80 - 100}{16} = \frac{-20}{16} = -1.25.$$

FIGURE 7-12   Normal curve illustrating the problem of finding the area above an IQ score of 80.

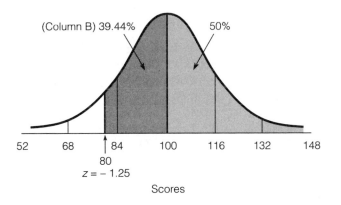

FIGURE 7-13 Normal curve showing that the area from the mean to the IQ score of 80 is 39.44%.

From Table A, we find that 39.44% of the normal curve lies between the mean and a z score of −1.25. Adding this information to Figure 7-12 results in Figure 7-13.

Because 50% of the normal curve lies above the mean, the total area above an IQ score of 80 is 50 + 39.44 = 89.44%. But this is not what the question asks us to find. We want to know how many people from the group of 250 are likely to score 80 or above. Thus, we need to find 89.44% of 250. Using a pocket calculator, we find that

$$250 \times 89.44\% = 223.6$$

or, another way,

$$250 \times 0.8944 = 223.6.$$

In other words, we would expect about 224 people to score 80 or above.

⑤ CHECKING YOUR PROGRESS

Remember our 1,000 rats trained on a straight alley runway? The mean running speed was 2.4 feet per second with a standard deviation of 0.8 foot per second. On the basis of the normal curve distribution, if we trained 300 more rats, how many could we expect to have running speeds of 3.28 feet per second or more?

Answer: 41 rats (When dealing with living organisms, such as rats and people, it makes sense to round the answer to the nearest whole number.)

Finding an Area Between Two Scores

We have learned how to find a percentage area below a score (percentile rank of the score) and how to determine an area above a score. What about determining a percentage area (or frequency) between two scores? For example, suppose we are asked to find the number of people in a random sample of 1,000 that have IQ scores between 90 and 120.

The problem, then, is to determine the area between the scores of 90 and 120 and to convert this area to a frequency based on $N = 1,000$. To use the normal curve table, we must first convert the two raw scores (90 and 120) to z scores. The z score for 90 is

$$z_{90} = \frac{90 - 100}{16} = \frac{-10}{16} = -0.625,$$

which rounds to −0.63. (Remember that when the last digit is 5 or more, we round up.) The z score for 120 is

$$z_{120} = \frac{120 - 100}{16} = \frac{20}{16} = 1.25.$$

From the normal curve table, we find that 23.57% of the curve lies between the mean and a z score of −0.63 and that 39.44% of the curve lies between the mean and a z score of 1.25. Figure 7-14 tells us that the total area from 90 to 120 is

$$23.57\% + 39.44\% = 63.01\%.$$

The last step is to find 63.01% of 1,000, which is

$$1,000 \times 63.01\% = 630.1, \text{ or } 630.$$

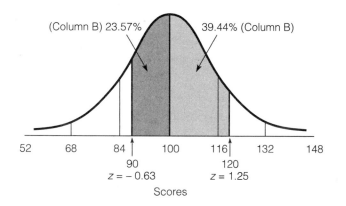

FIGURE 7-14 Normal curve on which has been entered areas obtained from Table A between 90 and the mean (23.57%) and between 120 and the mean (39.44%).

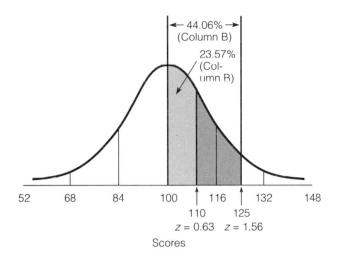

FIGURE 7-15 Normal curve on which has been entered the areas from the mean to 110 (23.57%) and from the mean to 125 (44.06%).

Thus, about 630 people would have IQ scores between 90 and 120.

A slightly more difficult problem involves finding an area between two scores when both are on the same side of the mean. To illustrate, suppose we want to know the number of people in a sample of 1,000 that have IQ scores between 110 and 125.

As before, our task is to find the area between the two scores (110 and 125) and then to convert the area into a frequency. The z scores are

$$z_{110} = \frac{110 - 100}{16} = \frac{10}{16} = 0.63,$$

$$z_{125} = \frac{125 - 100}{16} = \frac{25}{16} = 1.56.$$

Between the mean and a z score of 0.63 lies 23.57% of the curve, and between the mean and a z score of 1.56 lies 44.06% of the curve. From Figure 7-15, it is clear that the area we are seeking is

$$44.06\% - 23.57\% = 20.49\%$$

of the area under the curve. Finally, 20.49% of 1,000 is

$$1,000 \times 20.49\% = 204.9, \text{ or } 205.$$

Thus, about 205 people would have IQ scores between 110 and 125.

↻ CHECKING YOUR PROGRESS

Suppose 2,000 students have taken a test in introductory psychology, and we are told that $\bar{X} = 73.5$ and $s = 9.8$. What percentage of the students made scores between 70 and 90? How many scored between 80 and 95? Between 50 and 60? If a grade of D was given for scores of 60 to 69, how many students earned a D?

Answer: 59.41%, 481 students, 151 students, 478 students. The percentage of students scoring between 70 and 90 was 59.41%. There were 481 students scoring between 80 and 95, 151 students scoring between 50 and 60, and 478 students earning a D.

Brief Summary

We have now completed our look at problems in which we are asked to find areas under the normal curve. The specific examples considered were as follows:

1. Finding the percentile rank of a score, percentile rank defined as the total area below the score.
2. Finding the area above a score
3. Finding the area between two scores

In addition, we saw that percentage area was the same thing as percentage frequency.

In general, the procedure for finding areas under the curve consists of drawing the curve and labeling it appropriately, converting any raw scores to z scores, and then consulting the normal curve table (Table A) to find the area(s) needed. It is now time to discuss the second major type of normal curve problem: finding a score defining an area under the curve.

FINDING SCORES CUTTING OFF AREAS

So far, we have considered cases in which we have been given a particular score and asked to find some area under the curve. What if we reverse the procedure and locate a score that corresponds to some particular area of the curve? Suppose you needed to achieve a verbal SAT score at or above the 80th percentile to be considered for the honors program at your preferred university. What score would that be? Remember, when doing these problems, always begin by drawing a picture showing the information you have and what is needed.

The problem as illustrated in Figure 7-16, is to locate the score having a percentile rank of 80—that is, where 80% of the curve lies below the score. We know immediately that the score is above the mean because it has a rank higher than

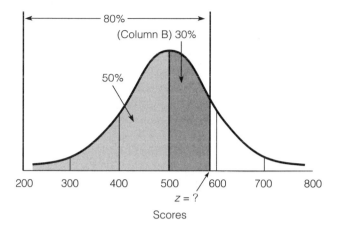

FIGURE 7-16 Normal curve illustrating the problem of finding the score at the 80th percentile.

50%. Thus, we must look in the normal curve table for a z score that has 30% of the curve between it and the mean (80% − 50% = 30%).

We will begin by looking for 30% in column B of the table, and when we find the closest number to it, we will look in column A for the z score. The closest number to 30% in column B is 29.95, which is the area between the mean and a z score of 0.84. Therefore, we will use 0.84 as the appropriate z score.

Now that we have the z score at the 80th percentile, all that remains is to convert it to a raw score using Formula 6-21.

$$X = z\sigma + \mu = (0.84)100 + 500 = 84 + 500 = 584.$$

Thus, a person at the 80th percentile on the verbal SAT has a score of approximately 584. Let's try another problem of the same general type to be sure we have the technique.

What is the verbal SAT score at the 20th percentile? Put another way, what verbal SAT score cuts off the lowest 20% of the population? The problem is shown in Figure 7-17.

To find the z score that cuts off the lowest 20% of the distribution, we can either look for 20% in column C (the area beyond the z score we need) or look for 30% in column B (the area between the mean and z). The closest number to 20% in column C is 20.05, which corresponds to a z score of −0.84. Why is z a negative value? The answer is that we are looking for a score that is below the mean; negative values of z indicate scores below the mean. Let's convert our z score into a raw score:

$$X = z\sigma + \mu = (-0.84)100 + 500 = -84 + 500 = 416.$$

In conclusion, anyone scoring below 416 on the verbal SAT would be in the bottom 20% of the population.

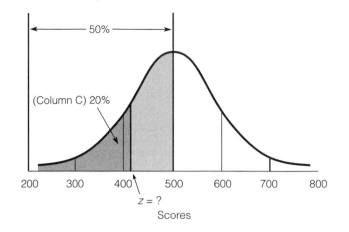

FIGURE 7-17   Normal curve showing the problem of finding the score at the 20th percentile.

---

⑤ CHECKING YOUR PROGRESS

Consider once again the 2,000 students who have taken standardized tests in introductory psychology. The average score for this group was 73.5, with a standard deviation of 9.8. What score would a student have to make to be in the upper 15% of the distribution? Lower 30%?

Answer: 83.7 or above; 68.4 or below. To be in the upper 15%, a student would have to score 84 or above; to be in the lower 30%, a student would have to score 68 or below.

Finding Deviant Scores

In another type of problem, we might be asked to determine IQ scores so deviant or unlikely that they occur 10% or less of the time. In a way, this is a trick question, because the direction of the deviance from the mean is not stated. Because the direction is unspecified, we are actually dealing with both ends of the normal curve and not just the top or bottom half. An appropriately labeled diagram of the normal curve for this type of problem is shown in Figure 7-18.

Notice in the figure that because the direction was not stated, the deviant 10% of the curve has been split into two equal parts, with 5% above the mean and 5% below it. Extremely high IQ scores are just as unlikely as extremely low ones. If we had not divided the 10% in half and had instead put 10% at the upper end and 10% at the lower end, then the z scores located would be those defining, or cutting off, the deviant 20%. Whenever we encounter a problem in which the

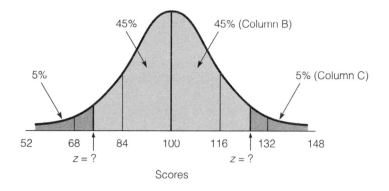

FIGURE 7-18 Normal curve illustrating the problem of finding the scores cutting off the deviant 10% of the distribution.

direction of the deviance is not given, we must halve the given area before labeling both ends of the curve.

The problem now becomes one of finding a z score when we know a percentage area under the curve and converting this z score into a raw score. As before, we can either look for 5% in column C or look for 45% in column B. Because $z = 1.64$ cuts off an area of 5.05% and $z = 1.65$ cuts off an area of 4.95%, the z score that cuts off 5% appears to be exactly halfway between 1.64 and 1.65. If it were exactly halfway, our rule of rounding would dictate the use of 1.65 (1.645 rounds to 1.65). However, the z score is actually slightly closer to 1.64 (it's 1.6449 to four decimal places). The only other situation we'll encounter that is like this is the one where the z score cuts off the deviant 1% of the distribution. In that case, the z scores to use are ± 2.58.

But for now, we have determined that the z scores that cut off the deviant 10% of the population are ± 1.64. The final step in the problem is to convert these two z scores into raw scores:

$$X = z\sigma + \mu = (\pm 1.64)(16) + 100 = \pm 26.24 + 100 = 73.76 \text{ and } 126.24.$$

Thus, the IQ scores that are so unlikely that they occur 10% or less of the time are those less than 74 and greater than 126.

Let's try another example. What IQ scores are so abnormal that they occur 5% or less of the time? This problem is shown graphically in Figure 7-19.

As before, the deviant 5% has been split, with 2.5% at either end of the curve. From column C, we find the z score cutting off 2.5% to be exactly 1.96 (± 1.96 for both tails). We now convert the z scores to raw scores:

$$X = z\sigma + \mu = (\pm 1.96)(16) + 100 = \pm 31.36 + 100 = 68.64 \text{ and } 131.36.$$

Thus, the IQ scores so unlikely that they occur 5% or less of the time are those less than 69 and greater than 131.

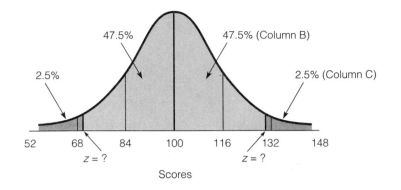

FIGURE 7-19   Normal curve illustrating the problem of finding the scores cutting off the deviant 5% of the distribution.

ᕫ CHECKING YOUR PROGRESS

In our example of 2,000 introductory psychology students, the mean score on a test was 73.5, with a standard deviation of 9.8. What scores are so deviant that they occur 1% or less of the time? Below what score would a student be in the bottom 10% of the class?

Answer: 48.22 or less, 98.78 or more; 60.96 or less. The scores occurring 1% or less of the time are 48 or less and 99 or more. (Remember to use ±2.58 rather than ±2.57.) A score of 61 or less would put a student in the bottom 10% of the class.

Brief Summary

Like all normal curve problems, the most important step in finding scores defining areas is to draw and label an appropriate normal curve. In general, the next step requires finding an area in either column B or column C of Table A to find the z score associated with it. The z score, taken from column A, is then converted to a raw score using the formula $X = zs + \bar{X}$ or $X = z\sigma + \mu$.

If the direction of the deviation of the score from the mean is not given, then we need to find scores at both ends of the distribution. To do this, we must first split the deviant area in half, putting half on each tail of the curve. In this case, the z score taken from Table A is both positive and negative (±).

SUMMARY

The normal curve is a unimodal, symmetrical curve on which the measures of central tendency are identical. Additionally, the tails of the normal curve never quite reach the X axis. For a given mean, the larger the standard deviation, the flatter the curve. The standard normal curve is a normal curve with a mean of 0 and a standard deviation of 1. Several techniques were introduced for deriving information from the standard normal curve distribution. Even if the actual distribution of scores in a sample taken from some population is not normally distributed, we can still apply the characteristics of the normal curve as long as we can assume normality in the population from which the sample was taken. For much of the data in the social sciences, this is a valid assumption.

The actual techniques for obtaining information from the normal curve table are relatively simple. You should have no difficulty as long as you remember that (1) the normal curve table gives the area under the curve from the mean to the z score you look up (column B) and the area under the curve beyond your z score (column C) and that (2) half of the area under the curve lies on one side of the mean and the other half on the other side of the mean (i.e., the normal curve is symmetrical).

Here are the steps to follow in attacking the kinds of problems discussed in this chapter:

1. Draw a small diagram of the normal curve and enter any information available.

2. Use the diagram to try to decide what area(s) or score(s) you want to find.

3. Given raw scores, first convert these into z scores so that you can use the normal curve table. The conversion formula is

$$z = \frac{X - \overline{X}}{s} \quad \text{or} \quad z = \frac{X - \mu}{\sigma}.$$

4. Given some area under the curve, look up the appropriate area in either column B or column C of the normal curve table and then find the z score from column A that is associated with it. Usually, you will want to convert this z score to a raw score using the formula

$$X = zs + \overline{X} \quad \text{or} \quad X = z\sigma + \mu.$$

5. If you are asked to find scores so deviant or so unlikely that they occur less than a certain percentage of the time, look at both ends of the distribution. Divide the percentage area in half and label your diagram accordingly.

❊ *Troubleshooting Your Computations*

Most of the errors made in solving normal curve problems come from not understanding what you are being asked to find. To avoid this problem, first draw a small curve, fill in any information you are given, and try to label it so that you can actually see what you need to find. When you have your final answer, ask yourself if it is reasonable in terms of the drawing. For example, if the area you are seeking is very small, your final answer should be correspondingly small. If you are seeking a score below the mean, your final answer should be a value less than the mean.

Failure to complete the problem is an error that is frequently made. That is, the final answer is not in the correct form. For example, if the problem requires a frequency (e.g., number of persons with a certain range of scores), then any percentage area you find must be converted to a frequency.

EXERCISES

1. What are the characteristics of the normal curve? How does the standard normal curve differ from other normal curves?

2. Using the formula for a z score, derive the formula for converting a z score into a raw score.

3. We know that a reading test has a mean ($\overline{X}$) of 10 and a standard deviation (s) of 2. Using the normal distribution, answer the following questions:

    a. What is the percentile rank corresponding to a score of 11.2?

    b. If we tested 1,000 randomly selected students, how many would be expected to score 5 or lower?

    c. What reading score corresponds to a percentile rank of 75%? 30%?

4. The verbal part of the Graduate Record Exam (GRE) has a mean (μ) of 500 and a standard deviation (σ) of 100. Use the normal distribution to answer the following questions:

    a. If we wanted to select only students at or above the 90th percentile, what verbal GRE score would we use as a cutoff?

    b. What verbal GRE score corresponds to a percentile rank of 15%? 55%?

    c. What is the percentile rank of a verbal GRE score of 628? 350?

    d. If we randomly selected 1,500 students who had taken the verbal GRE, how many would we expect to score lower than 250? Higher than 750?

5. In an introductory psychology class, 83 students have taken a sociability rating scale. The possible ratings are from 1 to 7 with a low score indicating low sociability and a high score indicating high sociability. The average rating has been 4.23, with $s = 1.02$. Using the normal curve table, answer the following:

    a. What is the percentile rank of a student with a rating of 3.11?

    b. How many of the 83 students had scores between 4.88 and 5.62?

    c. What scores are so deviant that they occurred 1% or less of the time?

    d. How many students had scores of 2.55 or less? 6.11 or more?

    e. What is the score at the 83rd percentile?

6. The police department of a major city has found that the average height of their 1,250 officers is 71 inches, with a standard deviation of 2.3 inches. Using the normal curve table, answer the following:

    a. How many officers are at least 75 inches tall?

    b. How many officers are between 65 and 72 inches tall?

    c. If an officer is at the 35th percentile in terms of height, how tall is she or he?

    d. Assuming an equal amount of service, the top 10% of the police officers in terms of height also make higher salaries than their less favored fellow officers. How tall does an officer have to be to get a better salary?

7. In an introductory English class, 100 students were given 20 words to define. The data from this test were approximately as follows: $\Sigma X = 1,000$, $\Sigma X^2 = 10,400$. Answer the following:

    a. What is the percentile rank of a person defining 9 words correctly?

    b. How many people scored above 13?

    c. What percentage of the class scored between 7 and 11?

    d. What scores are so deviant that less than 7% of the class made them?

8. Two hundred elementary school students took a 50-question math test. Their answers produced the following data: $\Sigma X = 6,000$, $\Sigma X^2 = 185,000$. Answer the following:

    a. What is the percentile rank of a score of 37? Of 22?

    b. How many students scored below 21? Above 35?

    c. How many students scored between 27 and 34?

    d. What scores are so deviant that less than 5% of the class attained them?

CHAPTER 8

Correlation and Regression

 Joe Galvan was 5 feet 2 inches tall. He was also the president of Galvan's Nuts and Bolts, a large and prosperous company. Joe picked up that day's *Wall Street Journal* and almost fell out of his chair. There, on the front page, was a story about the thing he had always suspected: "Tall Workers Earn More Money."

According to the writer, a variety of studies revealed that height is related to salary, with short individuals earning less money than their taller counterparts. The author even speculated that the salary-height relationship explained the lower salaries paid to women.

Joe considered the implications of the article. Then he decided to see if he could corroborate the article's theory by looking at his own company managers' heights and salaries. He had the human resources manager collect the information and give it to him that afternoon. The 14 managers were listed from tallest to shortest as follows:

Name	Height (in inches)	Salary (in thousands of dollars)	
Bill Robertson	77	47.1	
Sam Kline	74	45.5	
Al Krieger	73	46.2	
Sue Milanovich	72	46.1	
Mort Fein	70	42.8	
Doug Johnson	70	38.3	*(cont.)*

Name	Height (in inches)	Salary (in thousands of dollars)
Sarah Chu	69	45.4
Tom Garibaldi	68	36.5
Amelia Gonzalez	67	42.1
Ann Margulies	67	37.2
Lisa McMillen	66	34.1
Petra Dahl	64	35.1
Tashia Stone	63	33.1
Fiona Lowery	60	33.0

Joe surveyed the list in disbelief. The *Wall Street Journal* was right. There was a relationship between height and salary, and the evidence for it was right here in his own company.

In this example the relationship, spurious or not, is apparent. However, there are situations in which the relationship is less obvious, such as when we have much more data or when the scores are not strongly related. In these and many other instances, it is helpful to be able to quantify the degree of relationship. In this chapter, we will look at techniques to quantify the relationship between variables and will discover a method for prediction based on correlation.

LINEAR CORRELATION

Correlation, a term used by most of us, is defined as the degree of relationship between two or more variables. Correlation literally refers to the *co-relationship* between variables. In this chapter, we will discuss **linear correlation,** or the degree to which a straight line best describes the relationship between two variables. Of course, not all relationships are linear. Many take complex, curvilinear forms. However, the linear relationship is the simplest and most common case. The idea of a straight line, or linear relationship, between two variables will become more apparent when we look at graphs in the next section.

To illustrate what is meant by correlation, consider the variables height and weight. In general, the taller you are, the more you weigh, and we say that the two variables are highly correlated. In other words, the variables go together and are related to each other. No doubt, many of us know an exception to the rule that height and weight are related. We may know someone who is only 5 feet tall and weighs 237 pounds or someone who is 6 feet tall and weighs 135 pounds. When we said that there is a correlation between height and weight, we didn't say it is perfect! As long as the relationship between two variables is not perfect, there will be exceptions.

Classes of Correlation

The degree of relationship between two variables may assume an infinite number of values ranging from –1 to +1. It is customary to speak of three different classes of correlation: positive, negative, and zero. Correlations between 0 and +1 are called positive, and correlations between 0 and –1 are called negative.

Positive Correlation   One example of positive correlation is the relationship that Joe Galvan explored, the correlation between height and salary. A **positive correlation** between variables exists when a high score on one variable is associated with a high score on the other or when a low score on one variable is associated with a low score on the other. In other words, positive correlation implies a direct relationship between the variables.

Other examples of positive correlation include height and weight, brain size and body size, and time spent studying for an exam and the score earned on the exam. That is, we would expect taller people to weigh more, bigger animals to have larger brains, and people who spend more time studying to earn higher scores. Suppose we have actually collected some data on time spent studying and exam performance. It might resemble the following:

Student	Number of Hours Spent Studying	Exam Score
A	28	95
B	25	95
C	3	58
D	10	75
E	0	44
F	15	83
G	20	91
H	24	87
I	7	65
J	8	70

One way to study the relationship between the two variables is to look at the scatterplot of the data. The **scatterplot** is a graph that plots pairs of scores, with the scores on one of the variables plotted on the X axis and the scores on the other variable plotted on the Y axis. A scatterplot of the students' exam scores as a function of time spent studying is shown in Figure 8-1.

In general, if the pattern of points on the scatterplot of some data falls pretty closely around a straight line slanting upward to the right, we are dealing with a positive correlation. Figure 8-1 reveals a strong linear relationship between the two variables, because most of the points are close to the straight line. It is the line that best fits the data. (We will discuss how to compute such lines later in the chapter using the linear regression equation.) Because the line slants upward to the right, the correlation is positive; that is, a high score on one variable (study

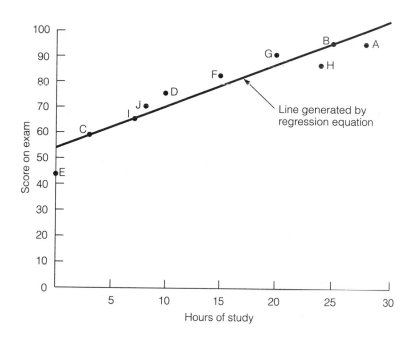

FIGURE 8-1   Scatterplot of the relationship between time spent studying and the score on an exam. The line best fitting the data is shown.

time) is related to a high score on the other variable (exam score). Later we will study how to compute statistics to represent the degree of linear relationship, but right now let's consider other types of correlation.

Negative Correlation   A **negative correlation** is one in which a high score on one variable is associated with a low score on the other. In other words, there is an inverse relationship between the two variables. One example of negative correlation is the relationship between speed over 55 miles per hour and fuel economy. That is, the faster you drive over 55, the fewer miles per gallon you get. Another example is the relationship between family size and IQ; correlational research has revealed that larger family sizes are associated with lower IQ scores. (Note that the relationship is correlational and tells us nothing about causality.) Over 100 years ago, a famous psychologist named Hermann Ebbinghaus found a negative correlation between the number of times he rehearsed a list of nonsense syllables and the amount of time it took him to relearn it 24 hours later. Specifically, frequent repetitions of a list resulted in less time to relearn.

As another example of negative correlation, suppose we have noticed that students who live off campus seem less involved in campus activities and organizations than students who live on campus. To investigate this observation, we survey students in 10 classes. We record the percentage of students in each class who live off campus and the percentage who are involved in at least one activity or group. The data are given at the top of the following page.

Class	% Off Campus	% Involved
A	100	0
B	40	95
C	95	5
D	90	20
E	92	30
F	85	40
G	55	50
H	60	70
I	98	0
J	20	100

As can be seen from the scatterplot in Figure 8-2, the points form a reasonably close approximation to a straight line that slopes downward to the right. (The line best fitting the data has been drawn.) The slope downward to the right indicates a negative correlation. Thus, our observation was correct: Living off campus is associated with less involvement in campus activities and organizations.

Zero Correlation The final category of correlation is **zero correlation.** Here there is no relationship between the variables; a high score on one variable is just as likely to be associated with a low score as it is with a high score or even with a medium score on the other variable. In other words, knowing a value for one variable provides no information that will help predict a corresponding value on the other variable. A classic example of zero correlation is the relationship

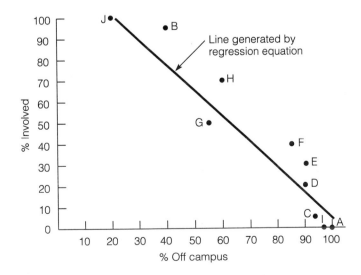

FIGURE 8-2   Scatterplot of the negative correlation between percentage of students living off campus and percentage of students involved in campus activities. The line best fitting the data is shown.

between the number and location of bumps on the skull and the intelligence or special abilities of a person. Despite the lack of such a relationship, phrenology was *the* science of the mind for a number of years and big business for many more. Another example of zero correlation is the relationship between the length of the lines in the palm of your hand and your life span.

To illustrate a scatterplot of zero correlation, suppose a professor wants to see whether there is a relationship between the order in which students turn in test papers and their scores on the exam. As the students turn in their papers, the instructor adds a number to the top of the test, indicating the order of completion. After the tests have been graded, the following data are noted:

Order of Completion	Score
1	95
2	57
3	90
4	70
5	75
6	65
7	60
8	85
9	87
10	75
11	76
12	72
13	93
14	85

The scatterplot of the data, shown in Figure 8-3, reveals essentially a random pattern of points. In other words, the scores seem to be "scattered" and don't seem to be well described by a straight line (or any other manner of line).

Before leaving the classes of correlation, we should note that negative correlation is just as meaningful as positive correlation. Knowing that a correlation is negative rather than positive just tells us that the relationship is inverse rather than direct. The strength of the relationship is given by the absolute value of the correlation. In fact, simply reversing one of the scales of measurement will convert a positive correlation to a negative one and vice versa, but the strength (absolute value) of the correlation will remain the same.

To illustrate, we earlier considered the direct relationship between amount of study time and an exam score. Suppose that instead of recording the score on the exam as the Y variable, we had noted the number of errors made by each student. Now we would find that the more time a student spent studying, the fewer mistakes he or she would make, and vice versa. In other words, we would now have an inverse relationship instead of a direct one. Thus, a negative correlation is just as meaningful as a positive one.

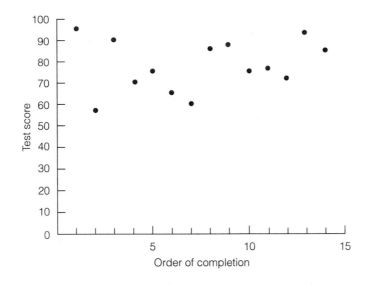

FIGURE 8-3   Scatterplot showing the lack of relationship between the order of completion of a test paper and the test score.

Correlation and Causation

A final point about correlation that is often ignored or overlooked is that correlation does not necessarily mean that one variable *causes* the other. For example, there is a positive correlation between the amount of television that children watch and their aggressiveness. Many people conclude from this that TV watching causes aggressiveness, although it is possible that highly aggressive children prefer to watch television over other activities, such as reading books. It is also possible that some other factor is responsible for both TV watching *and* aggressiveness. For example, it may be that children whose parents are more aggressive tend to watch more TV and are more aggressive. Clearly, it is not as simple as "TV causes aggression."

Similarly, many studies have reported a significant positive correlation between the level of cholesterol (a fatty substance) in the blood and heart disease. Does this mean that high cholesterol *causes* coronary artery disease? Again, the answer is not necessarily. It is possible that some other factor, such as low blood levels of vitamin B6, is responsible for atherosclerosis (clogged arteries). That is, foods high in cholesterol may be deficient in vitamin B6, with the result that a diet high in cholesterol leads to heart disease. But as you can see, coronary artery disease may result from the vitamin deficiency rather than from an excess of cholesterol.

Correlation is a necessary but not sufficient condition for causality. If two variables are causally linked, there must be some degree of correlation between them; it is *necessary*. However, the existence of correlation is not *sufficient* to determine causality.

It is possible that one variable causes the other, but the correlation between them doesn't prove it. Remember: Correlation—either high or low—doesn't prove causation.

THE PEARSON PRODUCT-MOMENT CORRELATION COEFFICIENT

Now that we have talked about what is meant by correlation and about its three classes, it is time to consider methods for determining the degree of relationship between the variables. The first method that we will discuss is the **Pearson product-moment correlation coefficient,** or the **Pearson r.** The Pearson r is the mean of the z-score products for X and Y pairs, where X stands for one variable and Y stands for the other. The term *product-moment* is used because the value of r is a function of the *moment*, or potency, of the z-score products. The formula for r based on the definition is

FORMULA 8-1 *Pearson r (definitional formula)*

$$\text{Pearson } r = \frac{\Sigma z_X z_Y}{N},$$

where z_X and z_Y are the z scores for the X and Y variables, respectively, and N is the number of pairs of scores.

To compute r with the definitional formula, we must first compute the z score for each X and for each Y. Then we multiply the z scores for each X-Y pair, sum the products, and divide by N. As you can imagine, computing r with the definitional formula is quite tedious, particularly if N is large. For this reason, we will introduce a computational, or raw-score, formula to compute r. But before we leave the definitional formula, let's use it to get an intuitive feel for why a direct relationship between variables results in a positive value for r and why an inverse relationship results in a negative value.

Suppose we have a sample of X-Y pairs in which there is a direct relationship between the variables; that is, high scores are associated with high scores and low scores with low scores. What does a z score tell us? It tells us the location of a particular score in a distribution relative to the distribution's mean. If a score is above the mean, the sign of the corresponding z score is positive; if a score is below the mean, it converts to a negative z score. Thus, with a direct relationship, a z score on the X variable is likely to be paired with a z score on the Y variable having the same sign, either positive or negative. When the products are found before summing, the majority will be positive, resulting in a positive value for r.

Similarly, for an inverse relationship, high scores on one variable will tend to be paired with low scores on the other variable, with the result that paired z scores will have opposite signs. The products will tend to be negative, resulting in a negative value for r.

In the case of no relationship, or zero correlation, there won't be any pattern to the signs of paired z scores. That is, a positive z score is just as likely to be paired with a negative z score as it is to be paired with a positive z score. The result is that the cross products will be a mixture of positive and negative values that tend to cancel each other out, resulting in a low value for r.

One final note before the computational formula is introduced: *The range of the Pearson r is from +1 to –1.* A positive value for r indicates a direct relationship between the variables; a negative value indicates an inverse relationship. The closer the value of r is to 1, the greater is the correlation. If the value of r is close to 0, in either a positive or a negative direction, we are probably dealing with an example of zero correlation.

Now we can consider the computational formula that is derived from the definitional formula:

FORMULA 8-2 *Pearson r (computational formula)*

$$r = \frac{N\Sigma XY - \Sigma X \Sigma Y}{\sqrt{\left[N\Sigma X^2 - (\Sigma X)^2\right]\left[N\Sigma Y^2 - (\Sigma Y)^2\right]}}.$$

When confronted with a formula as complex as Formula 8-2, the first thing we need to do is look at it to see exactly what we are asked to compute. Taking the components individually, we see that there is almost nothing here that we have not seen before. Specifically, we need to determine the values of the following terms: N, ΣXY, ΣX, ΣY, ΣX^2, and ΣY^2. The only new term is ΣXY, which is found by multiplying each X by each Y and summing the result. Let's use Formula 8-2 to compute the correlation between height and salary in Joe Galvan's company. Here are the data:

Employee	Height (X)	X²	Salary (Y)	Y²	XY
A	77	5,929	47.1	2,218.41	3,626.7
B	74	5,476	45.5	2,070.25	3,367.0
C	73	5,329	46.2	2,134.44	3,372.6
D	72	5,184	46.1	2,125.21	3,319.2
E	70	4,900	42.8	1,831.84	2,996.0
F	70	4,900	38.3	1,466.89	2,681.0
G	69	4,761	45.4	2,061.16	3,132.6
H	68	4,624	36.5	1,332.25	2,482.0
I	67	4,489	42.1	1,772.41	2,820.7
J	67	4,489	37.2	1,383.84	2,492.4
K	66	4,356	34.1	1,162.81	2,250.6

(cont.)

Employee	Height (X)	X^2	Salary (Y)	Y^2	XY
L	64	4,096	35.1	1,232.01	2,246.4
M	63	3,969	33.1	1,095.61	2,085.3
N	60	3,600	33.0	1,089.00	1,980.0
	$\Sigma X = 960$	$\Sigma X^2 = 66,102$	$\Sigma Y = 562.5$	$\Sigma Y^2 = 22,976.13$	$\Sigma XY = 38,852.5$

Computing for r, we get

$$r = \frac{N\Sigma XY - \Sigma X \Sigma Y}{\sqrt{\left[N\Sigma X^2 - (\Sigma X)^2\right]\left[N\Sigma Y^2 - (\Sigma Y)^2\right]}}$$

$$= \frac{(14)(38,852.5) - (960)(562.5)}{\sqrt{[(14)(66,102) - 960^2][(14)(22,976.13) - 562.5^2]}}$$

$$= \frac{543,935 - 540,000}{\sqrt{(3,828)(5,259.57)}} = \frac{3,935}{4,487.05} = .88.$$

The computations are straightforward, and the Pearson r, indicating the relationship in Joe's company between managers' height and salary is +.88. In other words, there is a high positive relationship between the variables.

Because the computational formula for the Pearson r looks so complex, we offer a more concise version that may help you remember the procedure better. Look first at the denominator of the formula (Formula 8-2):

$$\sqrt{[N\Sigma X^2 - (\Sigma X)^2][N\Sigma Y^2 - (\Sigma Y)^2]}$$

Notice that algebraically $N\Sigma X^2 - (\Sigma X)^2$ is the same as the sum of squares for $X(SS_X)$, as shown in Formula 6-11, multiplied by N:

$$SS_X = \Sigma X^2 - \frac{(\Sigma X)^2}{N}$$

That is, if we multiply each of these terms in Formula 6-11 by N:

$$\Sigma X^2 - \frac{(\Sigma X)^2}{N} = \left(\frac{N}{1}\right)\Sigma X^2 - \left(\frac{N}{1}\right)\frac{(\Sigma X)^2}{N}$$

$$= N \Sigma X^2 - (\Sigma X)^2$$

Similarly, $N\Sigma Y^2 - (\Sigma Y)^2$ is the same as the sum of squares for $Y(SS_Y)$.

Now look at the numerator of Formula 8-2:

$$N\Sigma XY - \Sigma X \Sigma Y$$

This expression is **cross products (CP)** multiplied by N; it represents the variability the two sets of scores have in common. Just as with SS_X and SS_Y, the formula for cross product can be expressed as in Formula 8-3.

> **FORMULA 8-3   *Cross products (computational formula)***
>
> $$CP = \Sigma XY - \frac{\Sigma X \Sigma Y}{N}.$$

As for SS_X and SS_Y above, multiplying each term in Formula 8-3 by N results in $CP = N\Sigma XY - \Sigma X \Sigma Y$.

Substituting CP, SS_X, and SS_Y into Formula 8-2, we obtain an alternative computational formula for r. We still have to go through all the steps to calculate SS_X, SS_Y, and CP, but it is an easier formula to remember. It is also helpful to recognize that the calculation of r involves only one term (CP) not already used in previous chapters. Here, then, is the alternative formula for r:

> **FORMULA 8-4   *Pearson r (alternative computational formula)***
>
> $$r = \frac{CP}{\sqrt{(SS_X)(SS_Y)}}.$$

Let's use Formula 8-4 to calculate r for another problem, this one with a negative correlation. Let's compute the correlation coefficient for the data on off-campus living and student involvement. The data are as follows:

Class	% Off Campus (X)	X^2	% Involved (Y)	Y^2	XY
A	100	10,000	0	0	0
B	40	1,600	95	9,025	3,800
C	95	9,025	5	25	475
D	90	8,100	20	400	1,800
E	92	8,464	30	900	2,760
F	85	7,225	40	1,600	3,400
G	55	3,025	50	2,500	2,750
H	60	3,600	70	4,900	4,200
I	98	9,604	0	0	0
J	20	400	100	10,000	2,000
	$\Sigma X = 735$	$\Sigma X^2 = 61{,}043$	$\Sigma Y = 410$	$\Sigma Y^2 = 29{,}350$	$\Sigma XY = 21{,}185$

We need to compute CP, SS_X, and SS_Y separately and then substitute the results into Formula 8-4:

$$CP = N\Sigma XY - \Sigma X \Sigma Y = (10)(21{,}185) - (735)(410)$$
$$= 211{,}850 - 301{,}350 = -89{,}500,$$
$$SS_X = N\Sigma X^2 - (\Sigma X)^2 = (10)(61{,}043) - (735)^2 = 70{,}205,$$
$$SS_Y = N\Sigma Y^2 - (\Sigma Y)^2 = (10)(29{,}350) - (410)^2 = 125{,}400,$$

and finally

$$r = \frac{CP}{\sqrt{(SS_X)(SS_Y)}} = \frac{-89,500}{\sqrt{(70,205)(125,400)}} = \frac{-89,500}{93,828.07} = -.95.$$

To evaluate a correlation coefficient of −.95, recall that the range of r is from +1 to −1. Thus, the value of r that expresses a perfect direct relationship between two variables is +1, whereas −1 expresses a perfect inverse relationship. Anything close to $r = 0$ indicates no relationship between the variables. Clearly, $r = -.95$ indicates a strong inverse relationship. In Chapter 10, we will consider whether or not r expresses a relationship different from 0; that is, we will show how to test the hypothesis that our sample came from a population in which the relationship between the variables is not 0.

The Effect of Range on Correlation

To properly determine the relationship between two variables, we must use a full range of scores on both variables. Restricting the range of either the X or the Y variable lowers the correlation. To illustrate, suppose there is a high positive correlation between SAT scores and freshman academic performance measured by grade point average. A scatterplot of data based on a large number of students is shown in Figure 8-4.

As you can see, the scatterplot of *all* the points indicates a high correlation that would be well summarized by a line sloping upward to the right. But what if we look at the restricted portion of the plot shown between the vertical lines on the graph? Within this restricted range on the X variable, the correlation may be quite low. Thus, low correlation may reflect a restricted range on either variable rather than a lack of relationship in the population.

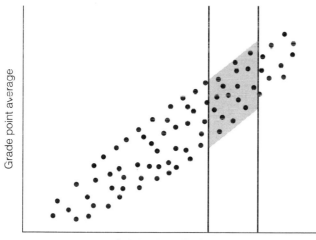

FIGURE 8-4 Scatterplot showing the effect of restricting the range on correlation.

↺ CHECKING YOUR PROGRESS

A psychologist has developed a new intelligence test based on brain wave activity, and she wants to determine its reliability. That is, she wants to see the degree to which the test yields the same score each time it is administered to a person. To measure its reliability, she gives the test to 12 selected persons on two separate occasions with an intertest interval of 3 weeks. Scores on the test range from 1 to 25, and the data from the 12 individuals are shown here. Compute the correlation coefficient.

Subject #	Score 1	Score 2	Subject #	Score 1	Score 2
1	3	5	7	11	12
2	22	17	8	13	15
3	19	21	9	7	9
4	18	16	10	6	4
5	15	17	11	20	22
6	10	8	12	18	10

Answer: $r = .85$. The correlation coefficient is .85, indicating a highly positive correlation between the two testings.

The Linear Regression Equation

So far, we've looked at r as a descriptive statistic (e.g., $r = -.95$ tells us that there is a high inverse relationship between two variables). However, as one of its most useful functions, the correlation coefficient helps us predict the value of one variable if we know the value of the other. In other words, there is a formula that allows us to predict how someone will score on variable Y if we know how he or she did on variable X. For example, we found a high correlation between height and salary in Joe Galvan's company. Given this information and an equation for prediction, we could predict a new employee's salary if we knew his or her height.

The development of an instrument for prediction, called a *regression equation*, is based on the definition given earlier of linear correlation. Correlation was defined as the degree of *linear* relationship between the variables—that is, the degree to which the relationship can be described by a straight line. The general equation for a straight line is

$$Y = a + bX \text{ or } Y = bX + a,$$

where b is the slope of the line and a is the point at which the line intercepts the Y axis.

The **regression equation** is the equation for the straight line that best describes the relationship between the variables. The question is, How do we decide which of many possible straight lines best fits the data? And in what sense do we mean best fit?

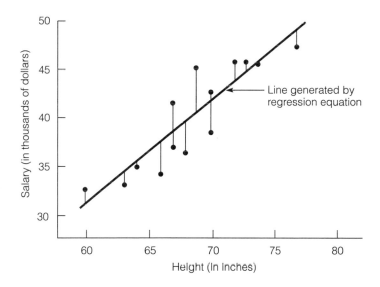

FIGURE 8-5 Scatterplot showing the relationship between height and salary in Joe Galvan's company. The line generated by the regression equation is shown.

Figure 8-5 is the scatterplot of Joe Galvan's data, and the best-fitting line has been added to it. Look at the vertical distance (the deviation) between each data point and the line. The regression line is the line that makes the squared deviations around it as small as possible. This is the sense in which the regression line is the best fit: It minimizes the squared deviations. Because it minimizes the squared deviations, the regression line is also called the **least squares line.** The word *regression* refers to regression toward the mean. That is, the regression line for Y given X yields an approximation of the mean value of Y for any given value of X.

We may think of the regression line as a "moving average." That is, the regression line gives us the average Y value that we can expect from any value of X. As X changes, so does our predicted (or average) Y. The term *moving average* also helps us understand the concept of least squares. Think of the Y value on the regression line as the mean of the Y values in a scatterplot corresponding to a particular X value. Remember from Chapter 5 that the sum of the squared deviations about the mean of a distribution is a minimum. Because the regression line can be considered a series of means (moving average), it also constitutes a line that gives us the least (minimum) squared deviations.

The equation for the regression line is

FORMULA 8-5 Y *predicted from* X

$$\hat{Y} = \left(\frac{rs_Y}{s_X}\right)X - \left(\frac{rs_Y}{s_X}\right)(\overline{X}) + \overline{Y}.$$

$\hat{Y}$ ("Y-caret") is the symbol for our estimated or predicted value of Y. All the terms in the regression equation are familiar ones. To solve the equation, we will need to know r, s_X, s_Y, $\overline{X}$, and $\overline{Y}$.

Let's determine the regression equation for the height-salary example. Earlier, we found that $r = .88$, $\Sigma X = 960$, $\Sigma X^2 = 66,102$, $\Sigma Y = 562.5$, $\Sigma Y^2 = 22,976.13$, and $N = 14$. From these values we can calculate all the other information needed to compute the regression equation:

$$\overline{X} = \frac{\Sigma X}{N} = \frac{960}{14} = 68.57,$$

$$SS_X = \Sigma X^2 - \frac{(\Sigma X)^2}{N} = 66,102 - \frac{(960)^2}{14} = 273.43,$$

$$s_X = \sqrt{\frac{SS_X}{N}} = \sqrt{\frac{273.43}{14}} = 4.42,$$

$$\overline{Y} = \frac{562.5}{14} = 40.18,$$

$$SS_Y = \Sigma Y^2 - \frac{(\Sigma Y)^2}{N} = 22,976.13 - \frac{(562.5)^2}{14} = 375.68,$$

$$s_Y = \sqrt{\frac{SS}{N}} = \sqrt{\frac{375.68}{14}} = \sqrt{28.9} = 5.18,$$

$$\hat{Y} = \left(\frac{rs_Y}{s_X}\right)X - \left(\frac{rs_Y}{s_X}\right)(\overline{X}) + \overline{Y}$$

$$= \left[\frac{(.88)(5.18)}{4.42}\right]X - \left[\frac{(.88)(5.18)}{4.42}\right](68.57) + 40.18$$

$$= 1.03X - (1.03)(68.57) + 40.18 = 1.03X - 70.63 + 40.18$$

$$= 1.03X - 30.45$$

As you can see, our regression equation is the equation for a straight line whose slope is 1.03 and whose Y intercept is –30.45.

Although the computations are fairly straightforward, there is one particular point at which many students go awry. In the step immediately before the final answer, the last two terms are –70.63 and +40.18. Written in this fashion, it should be obvious that the algebraic sum of the two is –30.45. However, there is a tendency to treat the last two terms as though they had parentheses around them— that is, –(70.63 + 40.18). If this were true, the answer would be –110.81; but because it is not true, –110.81 is not correct. Be careful on this step.

Based on Joe's data, the equation relating height (the X variable) to salary (the Y variable) is

$$\hat{Y} = 1.03X - 30.45 \quad \text{or} \quad \hat{Y} = -30.45 + 1.03X.$$

We can use this equation to predict the salary of a new employee in Joe's company, assuming Joe doesn't change the rules. For example, if a 65-inch female is hired, what would we predict for her salary? Substituting 65 for X would give us

$$\hat{Y} = 1.03(65) - 30.45 = 66.95 - 30.45 = 36.5.$$

Thus, we would predict that a person 65 inches tall would make $36,500 in Joe's company. Notice that this equation is similar to the general equation for a straight line ($\hat{Y} = a + bX$) given earlier. The equation above is in the form, $\hat{Y} = bX + a$, but remember that order makes no difference in addition. Thus, the above equation is equivalent to $\hat{Y} = -30.45 + 1.03X$ ($\hat{Y} = a + bX$).

Let's take another look at Figure 8-5. To find the points for the regression line, all we have to do is solve the regression equation for a few X values (any two will do). We've already calculated one: For $X = 65$, $\hat{Y} = 36.5$. Another is $\hat{Y} = 41.7$ for $X = 70$. Why is there some discrepancy between the regression line and the actual data points? The answer is that the correlation, high though it is, is not perfect.

As with r, there is an alternative computational formula for $\hat{Y}$ that may make it easier for you to perform the calculations. It is based on the equation for the regression line (see p. 154): $\hat{Y} = a + bX$, where a is the value of Y where the regression line crosses the Y axis, and b, called the **regression coefficient,** is the slope of the regression line. If we know a and b, we can easily find $\hat{Y}$ for any value of X. The formula for each is quite simple and uses values already calculated in the process of computing r. Here is the formula for computing b:

FORMULA 8-6 *Regression coefficient (computational formula)*

$$b = \frac{CP}{SS_X}.$$

The formula for finding a uses b:

FORMULA 8-7 *Y intercept of the regression line (computational formula)*

$$a = \bar{Y} - b\bar{X}.$$

As you can see, these formulas require fewer steps and don't involve the computation of s_Y and s_X.

Let's look at an example that will illustrate the usefulness of the regression equation and also demonstrate the use of Formulas 8-6 and 8-7. Suppose we have given a 10-point quiz in statistics class during the fourth week of the term and another during the eighth week. Twelve students have taken the quizzes. The scores are as follows at the top of the next page.

Quiz 1 X	X^2	Quiz 2 Y	Y^2	XY
8	64	7	49	56
6	36	7	49	42
7	49	8	64	56
0	0	0	0	0
9	81	9	81	81
4	16	2	4	8
2	4	2	4	4
0	0	1	1	0
4	16	5	25	20
3	9	3	9	9
7	49	5	25	35
10	100	9	81	90
$\Sigma X = 60$	$\Sigma X^2 = 424$	$\Sigma Y = 56$	$\Sigma Y^2 = 392$	$\Sigma XY = 401$

We can use the calculated relationship between the quizzes to predict Quiz 2 scores from Quiz 1 scores. For example, if a student's score on the first quiz was 8, what score would we predict for this student on the second quiz? The first step is to find r:

$$CP = \Sigma XY - \frac{\Sigma X \Sigma Y}{N} = 401 - \frac{(60)(56)}{12} = 401 - 280 = 121,$$

$$SS_X = \Sigma X^2 - \frac{(\Sigma X)^2}{N} = 424 - \frac{(60)^2}{12} = 424 - 300 = 124,$$

$$SS_Y = \Sigma Y^2 - \frac{(\Sigma Y)^2}{N} = 392 - \frac{(56)^2}{12} = 392 - 261.33 = 130.67,$$

$$r = \frac{CP}{\sqrt{(SS_X)(SS_Y)}} = \frac{121}{\sqrt{(124)(130.67)}} = \frac{121}{\sqrt{16,203.08}} = \frac{121}{127.29} = .95.$$

As you can see, there is a strong correlation between the scores obtained on Quiz 1 and the scores obtained on Quiz 2.

The next step is to compute b and a:

$$b = \frac{CP}{SS_X} = \frac{121}{124} = 0.98,$$

$$a = \overline{Y} - b\overline{X} = 4.67 - .98(5) = 4.67 - 4.90 = -0.23.$$

Finally, we can use the equation for our regression line to find the Quiz 2 score we would predict from a Quiz 1 score of 8:

$$\hat{Y} = a + bX = -0.23 + 0.98(8) = -0.23 + 7.84 = 7.61.$$

In other words, given a Quiz 1 score of 8, we would predict that the student would obtain a Quiz 2 score of 7.61. We could also use the regression equation to predict other Quiz 2 scores from the scores on Quiz 1. We need only to substitute the Quiz 1 score (X) into our regression equation $\hat{Y} = -0.23 + 0.98X$.

What if we wanted to predict X scores from Y? In other words, can we use the equation we've computed to predict Y from X to predict X from Y? Unfortunately, the answer is no. Instead, we have to interchange the Xs and Ys in the equation for r in Formula 8-5 (the regression equation). The equations for predicting X and Y are equivalent only when $r = 1.00$.

ᕦ Checking Your Progress

In a study of alcoholics, a significant correlation between blood alcohol concentration (BAC) and the score on a 50-item test of recent memory has been found. The average BAC in the persons studied was 0.01% with $s = 0.004$, and the average number of items correctly answered on the recent memory test was 35, $s = 6$. Assuming a correlation of –.83, find the regression equation and predict the score of a person with a BAC of 0.015%.

Answer: $\hat{Y} = 47.45 - 1,245X$ for the regression equation, and $\hat{Y} = 28.78$ or about 29 for the number of correct responses on the recent memory test.

The Coefficient of Determination

If we examine scatterplots such as the one in Figure 8-4, we notice that the higher the correlation between two variables, the narrower the range of Y values for any value of X. In a sense, knowing X restricts the possible values that Y might take to a certain range, and that range becomes smaller as r increases. We refer to this phenomenon of restricting the range of possible scores on one variable by knowing values on another variable as "explaining variance." The higher the correlation between X and Y, the more our knowledge of X restricts the range of Y and the more variance in Y we can "explain."

An index called the **coefficient of determination** has been developed to express the amount of explained variability. The coefficient of determination is equal to the square of r:

FORMULA 8-8 *Coefficient of determination*

$$\text{coefficient of determination} = \frac{\text{explained variation}}{\text{total variation}} = r^2.$$

To illustrate, if $r = .9$, the coefficient of determination, r^2, is .81; if $r = .8$, $r^2 = .64$; and so forth. Note that if $r = \pm 1.0$, 100% ($r^2 = 1.00$) of the variance is explained, and if $r = 0.0$ none ($r^2 = 0.00$) of the variance is explained. The coefficient of determination is important because we are often interested in knowing the percent variance in a variable that is explained by another variable.

THE SPEARMAN RANK ORDER CORRELATION COEFFICIENT

The **Spearman rank order correlation coefficient**, r_s, was originally derived as an easy-to-compute alternative to the Pearson r. In addition to being computationally simpler, it is useful when the level of measurement for one or both of the two variables does not meet the requirements for the Pearson r.

The Pearson r requires at least interval scale measurement, whereas the Spearman coefficient requires only ordinal scale measurement. Remember that with interval or ratio scale measurement, we can precisely identify the length of the interval between measurements. Sometimes, however, the crudeness of our measurement prevents us from being able to specify precisely the length of the interval between measurements.

For example, suppose one student in the class is designated a "judge" and is given the assignment of rating the tastes of five different types of coffee. On a scale from 1 to 10, the "judge" gives one cup a score of 8, another a score of 6, and a third a score of 4. Again, we cannot assume that the intervals between the scores are equal or that the coffee with a score of 8 tastes twice as good as the coffee with the 4. In other words, there's no reason for assuming either interval or ratio scaling. All we can say with any certainty is that the coffee with the score of 8 ranks higher than the coffee with the score of 6, which ranks higher than the coffee with the score of 4.

Even though numbers may be used, rating psychological variables, such as authoritativeness, confidence, or compulsiveness, is a relatively crude measure of the variable in question. This method should be used only to determine a ranking of the individual relative to other individuals; that is, the level of measurement is at best ordinal scale.

When we have either interval or ratio scale measurement, we can use either the Pearson r or the Spearman r_s to compute a correlation coefficient. The Pearson r is preferable because it takes into account more of the data. However, when we have ordinal scale measurement, we should use the Spearman r_s and not the Pearson r.

Let's consider a problem in which the Spearman r_s would be appropriate. An experimenter wants to see if anxiety level is related to perception of noise level. Ten people are first given a rating scale instrument to determine their levels of anxiety. Based on their responses to the items on the scale, each person is given a number from 0 to 10 as a summary rating of anxiety level. Later, each person is exposed to a noise at a particular level and asked to rate its loudness on a scale from 0 to 10. The paired scores are as follows on the next page.

Subject	Anxiety Rating (X)	Noise Rating (Y)
1	10	8
2	5	5
3	9	10
4	4	3
5	6	7
6	9	9
7	8	6
8	3	5
9	5	2
10	1	0

The formula for r_s is

FORMULA 8-9 *Spearman rank order correlation coefficient*

$$r_s = 1 - \frac{6\Sigma d^2}{N(N^2 - 1)},$$

where d is the difference between the ranks of individuals on the two variables and N is the number of *pairs* of observations, as it was for r.

Looking at the formula, we can see that the only thing we have to determine before calculating r_s is the value of Σd^2. To do this, we *rank* the scores on each of the variables from highest to lowest, take the difference between the ranks, square it, and then sum the squared differences. Let's compute r_s for the preceding example. Here are our data:

Number	X	Rank of X	Y	Rank of Y	d	d^2
1	10	1	8	3	−2	4
2	5	6.5	5	6.5	0	0
3	9	2.5	10	1	1.5	2.25
4	4	8	3	8	0	0
5	6	5	7	4	1	1
6	9	2.5	9	2	0.5	0.25
7	8	4	6	5	−1	1
8	3	9	5	6.5	2.5	6.25
9	5	6.5	2	9	−2.5	6.25
10	1	10	0	10	0	0
					$\Sigma d^2 =$	$\overline{21.00}$

As you can see, each subject was assigned a rank on each of the two variables; for each pair of ranks, the rank on the Y variable was subtracted from the rank on the X variable; each of the differences was squared; and the squared differences were summed to give Σd^2. Let's take a closer look at the assigning of the ranks.

We start with the highest score (10 on the X variable) and give that score the rank of 1. Two subjects had the next highest score of 9, so we give each subject the average of the tied ranks (the average of 2 and 3 is 2.5). The procedure is continued until all the scores on the X variable have been ranked; then the scores on the Y variable are similarly ranked.

Now we can compute r_s:

$$r_s = 1 - \frac{6\Sigma d^2}{N(N^2 - 1)} = 1 - \frac{6(21)}{10(10^2 - 1)}$$

$$= 1 - 0.13 = .87.$$

The value of r_s that we obtained (.87) indicates a sizable relationship between a person's rating on an anxiety scale and the same person's perception of noise level.

Let's look at another example. Suppose we rate a group of 12 students on the extent of their class participation. We assign a value of 0 to a person who never talks in class and a value of 7 to a student who frequently participates in class discussions. In addition, the same people have been rated on an introvert-extravert (I-E) scale, with a score of 0 for a person who is quiet and shy (introvert) and a score of 5 for a person who is very outgoing (extravert). We would like to determine by means of a correlation coefficient if there is any relationship between extraversion and class participation. Including rankings, the data are as follows:

Student	Participation Rating (X)	Rank on X	I-E Rating (Y)	Rank on Y	d	d^2
A	6	4	4	4.5	−0.5	0.25
B	7	1.5	4	4.5	−3	9
C	6	4	4	4.5	−0.5	0.25
D	1	12	1	11.5	0.5	0.25
E	3	7.5	5	1.5	6	36
F	3	7.5	3	7.5	0	0
G	2	10	2	9.5	0.5	0.25
H	5	6	4	4.5	1.5	2.25
I	2	10	3	7.5	2.5	6.25
J	2	10	2	9.5	0.5	0.25
K	6	4	1	11.5	−7.5	56.25
L	7	1.5	5	1.5	0	0
						$\Sigma d^2 = 111.00$

The highest scores on the X variable were earned by Students B and L; each received the rank of 1.5, the average of ranks 1 and 2. Ranking on the participation ratings continued until Student D, with a rating of 1, received the rank of 12. Similarly, the scores on the Y variable were ranked, the difference between ranks found and squared, and the resulting squared differences summed to give $\Sigma d^2 = 111$. The computation of r_s is as follows:

$$r_s = 1 - \frac{6\Sigma d^2}{N(N^2 - 1)}$$

$$= 1 - \frac{6(111)}{12(12^2 - 1)}$$

$$= 1 - \frac{666}{1,716} = 1 - 0.39 = .61.$$

The correlation between the ranks is +.61, indicating a moderately high correlation between class participation and ranking on the introvert-extravert scale. The more extraverted a person is, the more he or she talks in class.

⟲ CHECKING YOUR PROGRESS

Two "judges" have been asked to rate independently the pictures of eight individuals in terms of attractiveness on a scale of 1 to 10. Here are the ratings:

Picture	Judge A	Judge B
1	4	4
2	2	2
3	4	2
4	1	2
5	7	5
6	5	6
7	6	7
8	8	8

Find the correlation between the ratings and test it for significance.

Answer: $r_s = .89$, which indicates a high positive relationship between the ratings.

SUMMARY

Linear correlation is the degree of linear relationship between two variables; the classes of correlation are positive, negative, and zero. Two different techniques for determining the degree of relationship were discussed. The first was the Pearson product-moment correlation coefficient, or the Pearson r. The Pearson r is defined as the mean of the z score products for the X and Y variables. The computational, or raw-score, formula for the Pearson r is

$$r = \frac{N\Sigma XY - \Sigma X \Sigma Y}{\sqrt{[N\Sigma X^2 - (\Sigma X)^2][N\Sigma Y^2 - (\Sigma Y)^2]}} \quad \text{or} \quad \frac{CP}{\sqrt{(SS_X)(SS_Y)}}.$$

After r is obtained, it can be used to compute the linear regression equation, which is the equation for the straight line that best fits the data from the sample. This equation is used to make predictions about a score on one variable if we know a score on the other. The formula for predicting Y from X is

$$\hat{Y} = \left(\frac{rs_Y}{s_X}\right)X - \left(\frac{rs_Y}{s_X}\right)(\overline{X}) + \overline{Y} \quad \text{or} \quad \hat{Y} = a + bX \quad \text{or} \quad \hat{Y} = bX + a.$$

The coefficient of determination, r^2, tells the amount of variability in one variable accounted for by the variability in the other variable.

The second type of correlation coefficient introduced in this chapter was the Spearman rank order correlation coefficient, or r_S. The Spearman coefficient is based on the difference in the ranks of the two variables and is useful when the level of measurement of one or both variables is ordinal or when ease of computation is desired. The formula for r_S is

$$r_S = 1 - \frac{6\Sigma d^2}{N(N^2 - 1)}.$$

⚝ *Troubleshooting Your Computations*

When computing either correlation coefficient discussed, there is a built-in check on the accuracy of your computations. That is, always remember that the range of r and r_S is from +1 to −1. An answer outside this range is incorrect, and you need to reexamine both your formula and *all* calculations. Arithmetical errors are usually made in the *initial* calculations.

A frequently made error in computing r_S is forgetting to rank the scores on the X and Y variables. Remember the name of the statistic: the Spearman *rank order* correlation coefficient. In other words, it is the coefficient based on the relationship between the ranks, and you must obtain the ranks before any computations can be made.

Another mistake in computing r_S involves the application of the equation. You must remember that the first term in the equation, 1, is separate from the fraction

$$\frac{6\Sigma d^2}{N(N^2 - 1)}$$

and that the fraction is subtracted from it. If you're not careful, the 1 may inadvertently become part of the fraction's numerator. Also, don't become so involved in computing the fraction that you report *it* as r_s.

One major problem area in computing the regression equation is in the handling of the last two terms in the equation,

$$-\left(\frac{rs_Y}{s_X}\right)(\overline{X}) + \overline{Y}.$$

If your r is positive, simplifying the terms will result in something in the form $-A + B$. These two numbers must be added algebraically.

Remember that r_s should be used when you have ordinal scale data; that is, the precise intervals between the scores cannot be specified, and ranking, or ordering, of the scores is appropriate. When the data have been collected using either an interval or ratio scale, then the use of r is preferable.

EXERCISES

1. Consider the following data: $\Sigma X^2 = 285$, $\Sigma Y^2 = 253$, $\Sigma XY = 259$, $\Sigma X = 45$, $\Sigma Y = 43$, $N = 9$.
   a. Calculate r.
   b. Calculate the regression equation for $\hat{Y}$.
   c. Calculate b.
   d. Calculate a.
   e. Find $\hat{Y}$ when $X = 6$.

2. Consider the following data: $\Sigma XY = 1,555.2$, $\Sigma X^2 = 1,308$, $\Sigma Y^2 = 1,920$, $\Sigma X = 120$, $\Sigma Y = 144$, $N = 12$.
   a. Calculate r.
   b. Calculate the regression equation for $\hat{Y}$.
   c. Calculate b.
   d. Calculate a.
   e. Find $\hat{Y}$ when $X = 13$.

3. We are interested in the relationship between test scores on two quizzes given 2 weeks apart. Here are the scores:

Student	Quiz 1	Quiz 2	Student	Quiz 1	Quiz 2
1	10	9	6	6	2
2	9	7	7	3	1
3	7	6	8	4	1
4	8	4	9	7	5
5	8	7	10	2	6

   a. Calculate r.

   b. Calculate b.

   c. Calculate a.

   d. What Quiz 2 score would you predict from a Quiz 1 score of 5?

4. For what purpose is the regression equation used? Why is the prediction usually not perfect? What is the coefficient of determination?

5. Rank the following correlation coefficients in terms of degree of linear relationship: +.08, +.95, +.57, −.98, −.37, +.85.

6. A professor has devised a new personality test and wants to test its reliability. To do this she divides the test items in half and administers one half to 12 people. A week later she administers the other half to the same people. Determine the correlation between the two halves of the test.

Person	First Half	Second Half
1	34	37
2	25	22
3	15	15
4	17	16
5	20	19
6	23	25
7	24	22
8	31	30
9	18	14
10	10	8
11	7	10
12	16	20

7. IQ scores are determined for eight pairs of identical twins. From the following data, what is the correlation between the scores?

Pair	Twin A	Twin B
1	106	115
2	127	117
3	85	89
4	73	61
5	102	98
6	85	100
7	97	98
8	110	108

8. IQ scores are determined for eight pairs of fraternal twins. From the following data, what is the correlation between the scores?

Pair	Twin A	Twin B
1	101	110
2	153	110
3	115	107
4	97	105
5	75	68
6	120	126
7	110	112
8	105	100

9. Compute a coefficient to show the relationship between order of completion and exam score.

Order of Completion	Score	Order of Completion	Score
1	95	8	85
2	57	9	87
3	90	10	75
4	70	11	76
5	75	12	72
6	65	13	93
7	60	14	85

10. Two friends attend a wine tasting party, where they taste and rate 9 wines. Each wine is rated on a scale of 1 (undrinkable) to 20 (wine of the century). At the end of the tasting the two friends compare their ratings to see how much they agreed. Their ratings are below. Calculate the appropriate correlation coefficient.

Wine	Friend A	Friend B
1	14	12
2	7	6
3	3	4
4	12	12
5	18	18
6	10	12
7	14	19
8	9	10
9	7	8

11. In the process of selecting students for a graduate program, two faculty members read the letters of recommendation in each student's file. Each faculty member rates the letters on a scale of 1 (poor) to 10 (outstanding). The ratings for 12 applicants are below. What is the correlation between the judges' ratings?

Applicant	Judge A	Judge B
1	6	8
2	9	8
3	4	2
4	2	4
5	4	5
6	7	6
7	10	9
8	8	10
9	6	4
10	9	9
11	9	8
12	1	2

INFERENTIAL
STATISTICS

We have now spent several chapters examining the descriptive uses of statistics. Although descriptive statistics may be more common, social scientists are often much more interested in the inferential use of statistics. Inferential statistics help us make inferences about a larger population from a sample. In doing so, we are usually testing hypotheses. Thus, inferential statistics help us decide if there is support (or lack of support) for a scientific hypothesis. They allow us to make scientific judgments and to ascertain their degree of certainty. They also tell us how likely we are to be in error when we draw conclusions from our data. As a set of powerful scientific tools, inferential statistics have played a part in much of the scientific development of the 20th century.

As you will see, many of these inferential statistics involve combinations of the descriptive statistics we have already discussed. So in most cases, we will be using "old friends" in new ways to make decisions about hypotheses. In this part of the book, we discuss several inferential statistics, but we begin with a discussion of probability in Chapter 9. Probability is the foundation of statistics. Our statistical judgments are couched in probabilistic terms; that is, we draw conclusions from data based on the likelihood, or probability, of certain kinds of error. A basic understanding of probability is at the core of statistics.

In Chapter 10, we introduce confidence intervals and simple hypothesis testing. We show how to compare sample values to expected values of populations, given a very simple experimental design. This procedure involves using z scores, with which you are already familiar, as well as a related index called the t score.

Chapter 11 extends the one-sample case to two samples—situations in which population values are not available or are unknown. In the simplest case, we compare an experimental group to a control group or we compare scores on a pretest to scores on a posttest to determine the effectiveness of a manipulation or treatment. This procedure involves using different forms of the *t* test.

Chapter 12 carries the logic of *t* tests to more than two groups or testing times. For example, we might want to examine the effect of several levels of a treatment or the impact of a treatment at several points in time. The appropriate statistic in these situations is called one-way analysis of variance.

Chapter 13 explains post hoc comparisons, which apply to our one-way analyses of variance. Once we have completed our overall analysis of variance and have found at least one meaningful difference, post hoc comparisons allow us to determine more completely the exact pattern of relationships involved. If the one-way ANOVA is not significant, post hoc comparisons are not performed.

Chapter 14 introduces two-way analysis of variance, which extends the one-way analysis of variance to situations that simultaneously incorporate two independent variables instead of one. Two-way analysis of variance is a very powerful and widely used statistical technique, which we will address in an intuitive way.

Unfortunately, we often do not have the type of data we need to use *t* tests or analysis of variance. Other techniques have been developed that can be used in these situations. One is chi-square, which uses data in categories for which we have only frequencies of occurrence. In Chapter 15, we learn how to calculate chi-square.

Chapter 16 presents other alternatives to *t* tests and analysis of variance that are not as well known as chi-square. These alternatives include the Mann–Whitney *U* test, the Wilcoxen signed-ranks test, and the Kruskal–Wallis one-way analysis of variance for ranked data.

When you complete this part, you will be well equipped to perform many of the most common statistical analyses. In addition, you should be able to read and understand much of the research literature in the behavioral sciences.

CHAPTER 9

Probability

Many years ago, a wily statistics professor taught his class a valuable and expensive lesson about probability. On the first day of the semester, he offered the class a challenge. He bet that at least two people in the class had the same birthday. If he was wrong, he would pay $5 to each student who accepted the challenge. However, if he was correct and two or more people in the room did have the same birthday, each student who took the bet would owe him $5.

Students looked around the room at their 25 or so classmates. It seemed highly unlikely that two people in the room would have the same birthday. After all, there were so few students in the room (25) and so many possible birthdays (365). It seemed to many that the odds were heavily in their favor.

A number of high rollers put $5 out on their desks. Then the students began giving the month and day of their birth. After only a few birthdays had been given, a young woman exclaimed, "That's my birthday!" Ouch! Students who bet were $5 poorer, and the professor was $75 richer. "If you're hoping that I'll cancel the bet, you're mistaken," he said. "You must all learn to understand and respect the probabilities of events. Misunderstanding can be expensive!"

In this example, what forces of probability were operating? How could the students be so wrong? Had they stopped to think more carefully, they would have seen their error in judgment.

Here is how it works. The first person in the class (of 25) has 24 others with whom to match, out of 365 possible birthdays. So the chances of a "hit" on the first person is 24/365. For the second person, one birthday is expended, so he or she might match one of 23 others out of 364 remaining possibilities for a 23/364 chance. For the third person, the chances are 22/363. And so on. Across all 25 people in the class, the chances are actually very good (better than 55%) that at least two people will have the same birthday. The professor knew this and profited.

In the preceding chapters, we have discussed a number of ways to describe data, including arranging a frequency distribution, graphing, computing measures of central tendency, and determining measures of the spread, or dispersion, in the data. We are now almost ready to develop methods for testing statistical hypotheses.

Statistical hypotheses are predictions about populations based on sample results. Although we work with samples, we are often not interested in a sample itself, but rather in what the sample tells us about the population from which it came. Unfortunately, a sample is not the same as a population; it is a subset of the population and may or may not be an accurate reflection of it. Thus, when we hypothesize about a population based on a sample, we can never be certain that we are correct. However, with the help of probability, we can determine the degree of certainty we can have in our conclusions.

As mentioned earlier, this chapter marks the beginning of our study of inferential statistics. The techniques introduced here and in the next several chapters will enable you to apply decisions made from sample data to the population presumably reflected in the sample. The essence of inferential statistics is in attaching a probability to the predictions and estimates of population parameters based on sample statistics. It is for this reason that we need to begin by briefly exploring what is meant by the term *probability*.

RULES OF PROBABILITY

Most of us intuitively use or at least encounter the idea of probability every day of our lives. For example, we may listen to the radio weather report and hear that the probability of rain is 20%. On the basis of this information, we may decide not to take an umbrella or raincoat with us, or, if we are more cautious, we may elect to be safe rather than sorry. If we decide to reduce our intake of red meat, it may be because we have heard that the probability of heart disease is lower for people with a low fat intake in their diets.

In other words, we are constantly assessing probabilities, whether we do it consciously or not. Many of our actions are based in part on these assessments—that is, whether we feel an event is likely or unlikely to occur. Our feelings about the probability of an event's occurrence may be based on pure speculation or intuition, on previous experience with similar events, or on a knowledge of theoretical outcomes.

There are times, as seen in the example at the beginning of the chapter, when our intuitive ideas about probability are incorrect. In fact, a sizable body of research has developed on the ways in which people's estimates of probability can go awry and on the factors that influence these estimates. Consider *gambler's fallacy*, the mistaken belief that the probability of a particular event changes with a long string of the same event. For example, suppose an unbiased coin (one in which a head or tail is equally likely to appear on any given flip) is flipped nine times, with a head appearing each time. What is the probability of a tail coming up on the tenth flip? The answer is that the probability of either a head or a tail is exactly the same as it was on the first flip: $\frac{1}{2}$, or .5. The string of heads has in no way increased or decreased the likelihood of a tail appearing, even though we may subjectively feel that this has happened. Coins have no memory. Similarly, after a string of failures, people often say, "I'm due for some good luck." And baseball announcers frequently refer to a batter with a long hitless streak as someone who is "due." These are all examples of gambler's fallacy.

For our purposes, the **probability** of an event is defined as the proportion of times an event would occur if the chances for occurrence were infinite. In other words, the probability of an event is equal to the number of ways *that* event can occur divided by the number of ways *any* event of that type can occur.

To illustrate, let's consider what the probability is of obtaining a head from the toss of an unbiased coin. If the coin were flipped an infinite number of times, on half of the flips a head would appear and on the other half a tail would appear. The ratio of the number of times the event (a head) occurs to the total number of events is $\frac{1}{2}$, or .5, or 50%.

Similarly, suppose we have one die (singular of *dice*). What is the probability of any particular number of spots from 1 to 6 appearing on any particular roll, assuming the die is unbiased? Because the die has six sides and each side is equally likely to appear, the probability of any particular number of spots is $\frac{1}{6}$.

There are two primary rules of probability: the addition rule and the multiplication rule.

The Addition Rule

On any particular flip of an unbiased coin, what is the probability of obtaining either a head *or* a tail? Because there are no other possibilities, the probability is 1, or 100%. That is, we will always observe either a head or a tail when we flip the coin. As you can see, to obtain the probability of either a head *or* a tail on one flip, the probabilities of the two possibilities have been summed:

$$p(H) = .5,$$
$$p(T) = .5,$$
$$p(H \text{ or } T) = .5 + .5 = 1,$$

where $p(H)$ is the probability of a head, $p(T)$ is the probability of a tail, and $p(H$ or $T)$ is the probability of a head or a tail.

What is the probability of getting either 1 or 2 on one roll of our unbiased die? Because the probability of getting either number is $\frac{1}{6}$, the probability of obtaining either a 1 or a 2 is the sum of their individual probabilities:

$$\frac{1}{6} + \frac{1}{6} = \frac{2}{6}, \text{ or } .33.$$

That is, $\frac{1}{3}$ of the time we would get either a 1 or a 2.

One more example: Suppose you're a graduate student doing research with guinea pigs. You have 10 guinea pigs; 4 are cinnamon brown (CB), 3 are black and white (BW), and 3 are all white (AW). The 10 animals are in one large cage, and you've been asked to take one out. What is the probability that you will draw either a BW or an AW? The probability of getting a BW is 3/10; the probability of getting an AW is the same, 3/10. The probability of getting either a BW or an AW is $\frac{3}{10} + \frac{3}{10} = \frac{6}{10}$, or .6.

These simple examples illustrate the **addition rule of probability,** which states that for mutually exclusive random events, the probability of either one event or another event equals the sum of the probabilities of the individual events. This is expressed symbolically in Formula 9-1, where A and B represent two independent events:

FORMULA 9-1   *Addition rule of probability*

$$p(\text{A or B}) = p(\text{A}) + p(\text{B}).$$

The Multiplication Rule

In the previous section we considered what might happen with only one flip of a coin or one roll of a die. What rule of probability can we apply when dealing with a series of events?

For example, suppose we roll one die twice. What is the probability of obtaining a pair of 1s? All of the possible events that we might observe are shown in Figure 9-1. Note that in the 36 possible events, there is only one way for two consecutive rolls of 1 to occur. Thus, the probability is $\frac{1}{36}$. The same result

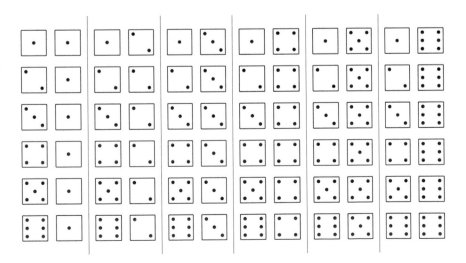

FIGURE 9-1   All possible events that might be observed following two throws of one unbiased die.

could also be obtained by multiplying the individual probabilities. In this case, the probability of obtaining a 1 on the first roll is $\frac{1}{6}$, and the probability of a 1 on the second roll is also $\frac{1}{6}$. The product of the individual probabilities is $\frac{1}{6} \times \frac{1}{6} = \frac{1}{36}$.

As another example, what would be the probability of getting heads in three successive flips of an unbiased coin? Using the multiplication procedure, the product of the individual probabilities would be $\frac{1}{2} \times \frac{1}{2} \times \frac{1}{2} = \frac{1}{8}$. This is the same answer that would be obtained if all the possible events were described. The possible events are HHH, HHT, HTT, TTT, TTH, THH, THT, and HTH. As you can see, there is only one way that three heads can occur out of the eight possibilities for three flips of an unbiased coin, and the probability is $\frac{1}{8}$.

Or what about our cage of guinea pigs? What is the probability of drawing three BW guinea pigs if you put the guinea pig back after each draw—in other words, if you sample with replacement? Again, it is the product of the individual probabilities or $\frac{3}{10} \times \frac{3}{10} \times \frac{3}{10} = 0.3 \times 0.3 \times 0.3 = .027$.

Stated formally, the **multiplication rule of probability** says that the probability of two or more independent events occurring on separate occasions is the product of their individual probabilities. It is expressed symbolically by Formula 9-2, where $p(A, B)$ is the probability of the occurrence of both A and B:

FORMULA 9-2   *Multiplication rule of probability*

$$p(A, B) = p(A) \times p(B).$$

Any number of other independent events could be added to this expression. For example, for three events, we would have

$$p(A, B, C) = p(A) \times p(B) \times p(C).$$

With **independent events,** the occurrence of one event does not alter the probability of any other event. For example, whether or not a head appears on one toss of a coin does not alter the probability of a head appearing on a succeeding toss. Similarly, if there are 10 guinea pigs in a cage, 3 BW, 3 AW, and 4 CB, the probability of selecting a BW is $\frac{3}{10}$ initially. If a BW is selected on the first draw and replaced, the probability of selecting a BW on the second draw is still $\frac{3}{10}$. Sampling with replacement does not change the probabilities for subsequent events.

However, what if we sample without replacement? What if we're dealing with *nonindependent events?* For example, suppose we've drawn a 6 from a deck of cards and have not replaced it. What is the probability of our drawing another 6? The probability of drawing the first 6 was $\frac{4}{52}$, or $\frac{1}{13}$, or .077, but the probability of drawing a second 6 depends on the first draw. That is, after one 6 has been taken from the deck and not replaced, there are now only three 6s left in a 51-card deck, for a probability of $\frac{3}{51}$, or .059. The probability of drawing a pair of 6s in two draws is therefore .077 × .059 = .0045.

This example is an illustration of **conditional probability,** the probability of an event given that another event has already occurred. Conditional probability is expressed symbolically by $p(B|A)$ (read "probability of B given A"). As we have seen, determining the probability for a sequence of events involves the multiplication rule for independent events. The difference here is that the probability of B depends on A. Thus, Formula 9-2 can be modified to reflect nonindependent events:

FORMULA 9-3   *Probability of a sequence of nonindependent events*

$$p(A, B) = p(A) \times p(B | A).$$

For three events, the equation becomes

$$p(A, B, C) = p(A) \times p(B | A) \times p(C | A, B).$$

Let's look at another example that illustrates conditional probability with nonindependent events. Suppose we select an AW guinea pig on the first draw from the cage and do not put it back. What is the probability that we will draw another AW? The probability of drawing the first AW was $\frac{3}{10}$, but the probability of drawing another is $\frac{2}{9}$. Thus, the probability of selecting AW guinea pigs on consecutive draws is

$$p(AW, AW) = p(AW) \times p(AW | AW) = .3 \times .22 = 0.066.$$

The birthday example at the beginning of the chapter illustrates a series of conditional probabilities. The calculations necessary to solve this problem—determining the probability of any 2 people out of 25 having the same birthday—are quite complicated, because we have to compute the probability of the same day (out of 365 days) being named by 2 or more of the 25 people. Nevertheless, the principle of conditional probability is the same.

THE NORMAL PROBABILITY DISTRIBUTION

Probability and Areas Under the Curve

In the previous sections, we introduced probability theory (in an abbreviated form). Now let's take a look back at the normal distribution and review how probability is related to it.

Recall that the normal distribution is often called a probability distribution, and where we discussed percentage areas under the curve, we could just as easily have talked about probabilities. We can convert the percentage areas in the normal curve table to probabilities using Formula 9-4 on the next page.

> **FORMULA 9-4** *Probability from percentage area*
>
> $$p\ (\text{probability}) = \frac{\%\ \text{area}}{100}.$$

For example, if the percentage area under the curve between 2 and 3 standard deviation units of the mean is 2.15, then the probability of someone having a score in this area is

$$\frac{2.15}{100} = .0215.$$

Let's look at a specific problem.

Suppose we were asked to determine the probability that a person picked at random would have an IQ score of 136 or above on the Stanford–Binet intelligence test. After constructing the curve in Figure 9-2, we see that the immediate problem is to determine the percentage area above a score of 136.

As before, the first step is to convert the raw score into a z score. The Stanford–Binet has a mean IQ of 100, with a standard deviation of 16, so we use the z score formula based on population values:

$$z_{136} = \frac{X - \mu}{\sigma} = \frac{136 - 100}{16} = \frac{36}{16} = 2.25.$$

According to the normal curve table, 48.78% of the normal curve lies between the mean and z = 2.25, with only 1.22% of the curve lying beyond that z score. Figure 9-3 is constructed to incorporate the new information.

This area of 1.22% above a score of 136 can be converted to probability with the help of Formula 9-4:

$$p = \frac{1.22}{100} = .0122.$$

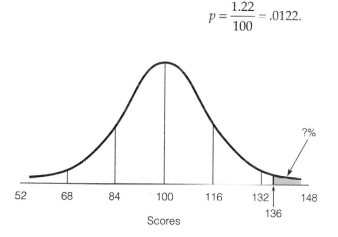

FIGURE 9-2 Normal curve illustrating the problem of finding the probability of an IQ score of 136 or above.

FIGURE 9-3   Normal curve showing the percentage area between the mean and an IQ score of 136 (48.78%) and the area above 136 (1.22%).

Because the range of probability values is from 0 to 1, a value of .0122 expresses a low probability event, one that occurs only a little over 1 time in 100. It is unlikely that we would encounter someone with an IQ score of 136 or higher.

✪ CHECKING YOUR PROGRESS

Remember the 2,000 psychology students from Chapter 7? Their mean score on a test was 73.5, with $s = 9.8$. What is the probability that someone scored 95 or above? 60 or below?

Answer: $p = .0143$, $p = .0838$. The likelihood of any given student scoring 95 or above is .0143, whereas the probability of scoring 60 or below is .0838.

Probability and Deviant Scores

The last type of problem we considered in Chapter 7 involved deviant scores—scores occurring only 10% or 5% or 1% (or whatever) of the time. This type of problem can also be related to probability. Consider the following: What IQ scores are so deviant that the probability of their occurrence is .05 or less? The first step this time, even before drawing the normal curve, is to convert the probability value to a percentage value so that we can use the normal curve table. Thus,

$$p = \frac{\% \text{ area}}{100}$$

$$\% \text{ area} = (p)(100) = (.05)(100) = 5\%.$$

Now that we have a percentage area, we can reword the problem to ask which IQ scores are so deviant that they occur 5% or less of the time. The prob-

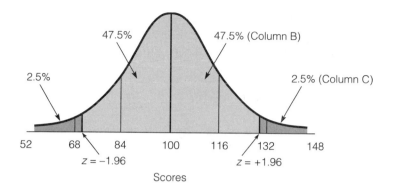

FIGURE 9-4 Normal curve illustrating the problem of finding the scores cutting off the deviant 5% of the distribution (IQs occurring with a probability of .05 or less).

lem is shown graphically in Figure 9-4. As was done in Chapter 7, the deviant 5% has been split, with 2.5% at either end of the curve. Looking for 2.5% in column C of Table A, we find the z score cutting it off to be exactly 1.96 (± 1.96 for both tails). To solve the problem, we now need to convert these z scores to raw scores:

$$X = z\sigma + \mu = (\pm 1.96)(16) + 100 = \pm 31.36 + 100 = 68.64 \text{ and } 131.36.$$

Thus, the IQ scores so unlikely that they occur with a probability of .05 or less are 69 or below and 131 or above.

In sum, the areas under the curve represent probabilities, and as we go further from the mean, the probabilities get smaller and smaller. This is the essence of hypothesis testing, our focus in the next chapter.

---

⑤ CHECKING YOUR PROGRESS

Getting back to our 2,000 psychology students (mean score of 73.5, $s = 9.8$), what scores were so abnormal that their probability of occurrence was .15 or less?

Answer: 59.39 or below, 87.61 or above. Scores of 59 or below and 88 and above occurred with a probability of .15 or less.

SUMMARY

Probability is defined as the proportion of times an event would occur if the chances for occurrence were infinite, or as the ratio of the number of times the event occurs to the total number of events. Gambler's fallacy is the mistaken notion that the probability of a particular event changes with a long string of the same event.

Two simple rules from probability theory are the addition rule and the multiplication rule. The addition rule states that the probability of either one event or another event is equal to the sum of the probabilities of the individual events. It is expressed symbolically as

$$p(A \text{ or } B) = p(A) + p(B).$$

The multiplication rule states that the probability of two or more independent events occurring on separate occasions is the product of their individual probabilities. Its symbolic expression is

$$p(A, B) = p(A) \times p(B).$$

Events are independent if the occurrence of one event does not alter the probability of any other event. Conditional probability is the probability of an event given that another event has already occurred. It is expressed symbolically as $p(B \mid A)$, and the multiplication rule can be modified to reflect nonindependent events:

$$p(A, B) = p(A) \times p(B \mid A).$$

The normal distribution is often called a probability distribution. Percentage areas under the curve can be converted to probabilities simply by dividing them by 100. Problems in which deviant scores are sought can be reworded in terms of probability; for example, what scores are so deviant that their probability of occurrence is .05 or less?

EXERCISES

1. A standard deck of playing cards has 52 cards, so the probability of drawing any particular card is $\frac{1}{52}$. In five consecutive draws (without replacement) from a standard deck of playing cards, what is the probability of obtaining a royal straight flush (10, jack, queen, king, ace) in hearts?

2. Define the following:
   a. gambler's fallacy
   b. addition rule
   c. multiplication rule

3. Toss a coin, roll one die, and draw one card from a standard deck. What is the probability of getting the following combination: tails, 4, king?

4. What is the probability of drawing either an ace or a king on any single draw? What is the probability of drawing either a heart or a spade? What is the probability of drawing an ace and a king on two consecutive draws?

5. What is the probability of drawing four consecutive aces without replacement?

6. The probability of exposure to a virus in a blood transfusion is .001 at a particular hospital. A man who has had a blood transfusion at that hospital is later tested for the presence of the virus, and the test is negative. The probability that the test will result in a false negative (i.e., that it will fail to detect the presence of the virus) is .01. What is the probability that the man was exposed to the virus and that the screening test failed to detect it?

7. On the final exam in a large statistics class, the average score was 76 with a standard deviation of 7. Assuming a normal population, what scores were so deviant that their probability of occurrence was .01 or less? What was the probability of a score of 60 or less?

8. In Exercise 6 in Chapter 7, we noted that the police department of a large city had found that the average height of its officers was 71 inches, with $s = 2.3$ inches. What is the probability of encountering an officer in that city who is 66 inches tall or less?

9. Data collected by the highway patrol indicate that the average speed on a stretch of interstate is 63 mph, with a standard deviation of 7.5. What is the likelihood of observing a vehicle traveling 80 mph? 45 mph? If a police officer observed 1,000 vehicles in an afternoon, how many of them (rounded to the nearest whole vehicle) would be traveling 90 mph or more?

10

Confidence Intervals and Hypothesis Testing

 Eva is watching the news the night before election day. A local television station is reporting the results of a poll it commissioned on voter support for a bond issue to rehabilitate local school buildings. The news anchor reports that 45% of the voters favor the bond issue, 40% are against it, and 15% are undecided. The anchor also reports that there is a margin of error of 3%. Eva thinks she knows how the 45% was determined; registered voters were asked for their position on the bond issue, and 45% said they supported it. But where did the 3% come from? Eva thinks that it probably means that the 45% is an estimate and might be off by 3% either way. But Eva wonders how it was determined that the margin was 3% and not 5% or some other amount.

Many of us, in learning the results of a poll, have had similar experiences. Intuitively, we understand that most of the statistics we are given are only estimates because they are based only on some portion (a sample) of the larger group of interest (population). It also makes sense that estimates may miss the true (population) value by some amount. Rarely will estimates exactly match the population value. In this chapter, we will discuss the process of estimation and how to determine the range within which our estimates should fall.

In Chapter 7, we discussed the properties of the normal distribution and how to use the normal distribution table to find areas under the curve. We also discussed the use of the normal curve table to determine scores associated with particular areas. In this chapter, we will discuss two distributions—the sampling distribution of means and the *t* distribution—that can be used to solve variants of the same two types of problems encountered in Chapter 7 (finding areas when we know scores and finding scores when we know areas). Specifically, we will discuss the use of the new distributions to construct confidence intervals (intervals of values around the sample mean) and to test hypotheses about the population from which our sample was drawn. We look first at the sampling distribution of means.

THE SAMPLING DISTRIBUTION OF MEANS

In the social sciences, the problem most often faced by investigators is one of estimating a population value from a sample value. When we collect our data, we rarely have the luxury of knowing population parameters. For example, if we conduct a study of the effects of a new drug on hypertension, there are no existing population values of the effect of the drug—after all, the drug is new. So we must estimate those population values from our sample. *— NOT EXACT*

In Chapter 5, we said that the mean of a sample is an *unbiased estimate* of the population mean. What do we mean by *unbiased?* In a nutshell, it means that if we draw a sample from a population and calculate the sample mean ($\overline{X}$), it will, on average, be the same as the population mean (μ). *AS ACCURATE AS POSSIBLE*

Sometimes the sample mean will be higher than the population mean, and sometimes it will be lower, but it will never be consistently high or consistently low. It is this property of the sample mean that makes it an unbiased estimate of the population mean.

We also know that the larger the sample we use in estimating the population value, the closer our sample mean is likely to be to the population mean. Let's take the example of coin tosses. Suppose we toss a coin 10 times. Although we expect the mean proportion of heads to be the population mean, 50%, we will not be surprised if the mean is 30% or even 80%. After all, we did the experiment (10 tosses) only once. However, if we do the experiment 100 times, we expect the sample means to cluster much more closely around the population value of 50%—perhaps at 48% or 56%. If we do the experiment 1,000 times, we expect our sample means to be even more accurate estimates of the population value.

The point of this example is to describe the derivation of a new type of distribution, the **sampling distribution of means**. The sampling distribution of means is constructed by drawing a sample of a certain size (say, $N = 20$) calculating the mean, plotting it, then repeating the process for a large number of samples. The resulting distribution of means will be "normal" in shape and have as its mean the population mean. The use of the sampling distribution underlies several inferential statistical techniques. *— AKA DISTRIBUTION OF SAMPLE OF MEANS*

If we arrange the sample means from our coin toss experiment into a frequency distribution and then plot a frequency polygon from the resulting distribution, what are the properties of this frequency polygon?

To begin, we note that the vast majority of sample means differ from each other. In general, it is unlikely that any two successive samples will have precisely equivalent means. Further, any one sample mean is more likely to differ from the population mean than be equal to it. However, and this is the *first property* of the sampling distribution of means, the mean of all the sample means (symbolized by $\mu_{\bar{X}}$, which is read "mu sub ex bar") equals the mean of the population (μ).

The *second property* of this distribution is that the larger the size of each sample selected from the population, the more nearly the sampling distribution of means will approximate the normal curve. This property is a simplified version of the **central limit theorem.**

The *third property* is that the larger the size of each sample selected from the population, the smaller the standard deviation of the sampling distribution of means. The standard deviation of the sampling distribution of means is called the **standard error of the mean;** it is symbolized by $\sigma_{\bar{X}}$, which is read "little sigma sub ex bar." Mathematically, $\sigma_{\bar{X}}$ is equal to the population standard deviation divided by the square root of the sample size:

> **FORMULA 10-1** *Population standard error of the mean*
>
> $$\sigma_{\bar{X}} = \frac{\sigma}{\sqrt{N}}.$$

To understand the third property of the sampling distribution of means, think of it this way. The larger the size of each sample we take from the population, the closer the sample mean will be to the mean of the population. That is, we are more likely with large samples to obtain a distribution of scores that accurately reflects the population situation. With large samples, there is less deviation of the sample means from the population mean—that is, less variability about the population mean. The smaller variability with larger samples is reflected in a smaller standard error.

Why do we call $\sigma_{\bar{X}}$ a standard error? It seems to be a contradiction—"standard" and "error." Remember that a standard deviation is based on deviation scores ($X - \bar{X}$), which are the distances between scores and the mean. In the case of the sampling distribution, these deviation scores are the distances between a sample mean and the population mean. Because $\bar{X}$ is intended to estimate μ, the distance between $\bar{X}$ and μ ($\bar{X} - \mu$) is an "error"; it is the amount by which the sample mean "missed" its mark. However, because these errors are the basis of a "standard" deviation (of the sampling distribution), we call it "standard error."

To summarize, we have imagined the construction of a frequency polygon from the distribution of sample means that were calculated from successive random samples of a given size drawn from a population. This frequency polygon is called the *sampling distribution of means*. The shape of the polygon is symmetrical and is approximately normal with large samples. The mean of the sampling distribution of means ($\mu_{\bar{X}}$) is equal to the population mean (μ), and the standard deviation (called the standard error) becomes smaller as the sample size increases. A pictorial summary of the derivation and properties of the sampling distribution of means is shown in Figure 10-1.

Step 1: Successive random samples of a given size are drawn from a population, and a mean is computed for each sample.

Step 2: A frequency distribution is constructed from the sample means.

X	f
$\overline{X}_1$	1
$\overline{X}_2$	1
$\overline{X}_3$	1
.	.
.	.
.	.

Step 3: A frequency polygon is drawn from the frequency distribution. Two properties are shown—that $\mu_{\overline{x}} = \mu$ and that the distribution is symmetrical.

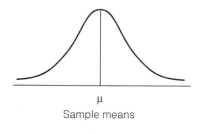

Step 4: Diagram illustrates the property that the standard deviation decreases with increases in N.

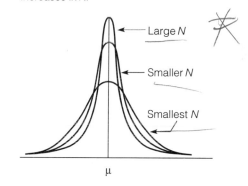

FIGURE 10-1   A sequence of drawings illustrating the derivation and properties of the sampling distribution of means.

Before leaving our discussion of the sampling distribution of means, it will be useful to define a z score for the new distribution. In Chapter 6, a z score was defined as the deviation of a raw score from the mean in standard deviation units, and the formulas were $z = (X - X)/s$ and $z = (X - \mu)/\sigma$. Using the same definition of a z score, we see that each score in this distribution is a sample mean ($\overline{X}$), and the mean of the distribution is the population mean (μ). The standard deviation is the standard error of the mean ($\sigma_{\overline{x}}$). Thus, a z score for the sampling distribution of means is found by the following formula:

FORMULA 10-2   *z score for a sample mean*

$$z_{\overline{X}} = \frac{\overline{X} - \mu}{\sigma_{\overline{X}}}.$$

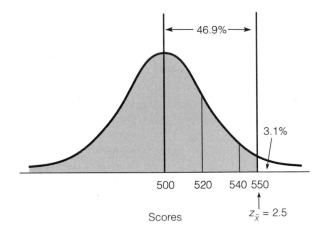

FIGURE 10-2   A normal curve illustrating the problem in which we want to find the percentile rank of a sample mean of 550.

The z score obtained for the mean of a sample can be used in all the ways we used z scores in Chapter 7. The only difference is that we are talking about a sample mean instead of a raw score. For example, a sample of 25 student applicants to a graduate program has a mean verbal GRE score of 550. We know that the verbal GRE has a mean of 500 and a standard deviation of 100. We can find the percentile rank of this sample by following a procedure that parallels the one we used in Chapter 7. First, we draw a curve, as in Figure 10-2, which indicates the information we have and the information we need to know. Second, we find $\sigma_{\bar{X}}$ by using Formula 10-1:

$$\sigma_{\bar{X}} = \frac{\sigma}{\sqrt{N}} = \frac{100}{\sqrt{25}} = \frac{100}{5} = 20.$$

Third, we calculate a z score using Formula 10-2:

$$z_{\bar{X}} = \frac{\bar{X} - \mu}{\sigma_{\bar{X}}} = \frac{550 - 500}{20} = \frac{50}{20} = 2.5.$$

Finally, we refer to Table A in Appendix 4 to find the percentage of scores below a z score of 2.5. Column C gives us 3.1% in the upper tail, but we want all the area below, so we must subtract 3.1% from 100%. Alternatively, we can take 46.9% from column B and add it to 50%. Either way, we find that the percentile rank of a sample mean of 550 is 96.9.

In Chapter 7, we learned to calculate a raw score corresponding to a percentile rank by transforming the z score formula: $\bar{X} = z(\sigma_{\bar{X}}) + \mu$. We can also calculate a value for $\bar{X}$ corresponding to a percentile rank by using Formula 10-3. Notice how it parallels the formula used for the raw scores ($x = z(\sigma) + \mu$).

> **FORMULA 10-3** *Sample mean from population values (computational formula)*
>
> $$\bar{X} = z(\sigma_{\bar{X}}) + \mu.$$

Extending our verbal GRE score example, suppose we wished to find the sample mean value corresponding to the 25th percentile. As with raw scores, we would proceed by first finding the appropriate z score in Table A. We look up 25% in either column B or C and find it associated with $z = .67$ ($-.67$ because it is below the mean). Then we would calculate the value of $\sigma_{\bar{X}}$. In this case, we already know that $\sigma_{\bar{X}} = 20$. Then we simply substitute the values into Formula 10-3:

$$\bar{X} = -.67(20) + 500 = -13.33 + 500 = 486.67.$$

The sample mean verbal GRE score at the 25th percentile is approximately 490.

ESTIMATION AND DEGREES OF FREEDOM

The use of z scores for sample means is appropriate when we know the population mean and population variance. Usually, however, we are missing one (or both) of these values, in which case we must estimate the population values from our sample. For the mean, this is no problem, because we know that the sample mean ($\bar{X}$) is an unbiased estimate of the population mean (μ). However, the sample variance (s^2) is *not* an unbiased estimate of the population variance (σ^2). On average, s^2 underestimates σ^2. The amount of underestimation depends on the size of the sample. With large samples, s^2 more closely approximates σ^2 than with small samples.

To compensate for this bias, we need to introduce a modification in the computational formulas. This modification is to use $N - 1$ instead of N in the denominator of the variance computational formulas. The formula for the **estimated variance** is as follows:

> **FORMULA 10-4** *Estimated population variance*
>
> $$\hat{s}^2 = \frac{SS}{N-1} \text{ where } SS = \Sigma X^2 - \frac{(\Sigma X)^2}{N}.$$

As noted in Chapter 8, the caret ($\hat{}$) over the s indicates an estimated value.

The **estimated standard deviation** is simply the square root of the estimated variance.

> **Formula 10-5** *Estimated standard deviation*
>
> $$\hat{s} = \sqrt{\frac{SS}{N-1}} \quad \text{or} \quad \hat{s} = \sqrt{\hat{s}^2}\,.$$

As mentioned earlier, $N-1$ is a correction we need to make when we are estimating. This is because sample variance underestimates population variance, and sample standard deviation underestimates population standard deviation. Using $N-1$ instead of N slightly increases the estimated values, correcting for the underestimation.

When used for estimating population variance and population standard deviation, $N-1$ is referred to as *degrees of freedom*. **Degrees of freedom (*df*)** is defined as the number of values in a set of scores that are free to vary after certain restrictions are placed on the data. For example, if we are given the sum of 5 scores, only 4 of the scores are "free to vary." Once we have those 4 scores, the fifth one is determined, because we know the sum (the restriction on the data). In this example, $df = 4$.

We can substitute df for $N-1$ in Formula 10-4, giving an alternative formula for estimated population variance:

$$\hat{s}^2 = \frac{SS}{df}$$

We can make the same modification in Formula 10-5 for estimated standard deviation:

$$\hat{s} = \sqrt{\frac{SS}{df}}$$

The reasons for using $N-1$ in these formulas (rather than $N-7$ or $N-19$ or some other number) are complex, and to fully understand them you would have to have more statistical knowledge than we have introduced up to this point. For now, it is more important to understand *when* to use degrees of freedom than to understand *why*. In computing variance and standard deviation, how do you know which formula to use? If you are *estimating* (using the sample as an estimate), then you must use the formulas with degrees of freedom in the denominator (Formulas 10-4 and 10-5). If you are *not* estimating, then you use the computational formulas that do not adjust for degrees of freedom (Formulas 6-12 through 6-18). Remember that you do not need to estimate when you are given or already have population values or when you have scores from all members of the population; in these cases, the mean, variance, and standard deviation can be calculated exactly.

Let's look at an example. Suppose 10 people have done the coin-tossing exercises (10 tosses) and we know the number of times they got heads. We want to know the variance and standard deviation of these scores. Because we are not interested in using these scores to generalize to or estimate for a larger population, we do not need to adjust for degrees of freedom. The scores are as follows:

X	X^2
7	49
8	64
4	16
3	9
5	25
6	36
4	16
5	25
8	64
6	36
$\Sigma X = 56$	$\Sigma X^2 = 340$

Here are our computations:

$$SS = \Sigma X^2 - \frac{(\Sigma X)^2}{N}$$

$$= 340 - \frac{(56)^2}{10}$$

$$= 340 - 313.6 = 26.4,$$

$$s^2 = \frac{SS}{N} = \frac{26.4}{10} = 2.64$$

$$s - \sqrt{s^2} = \sqrt{2.64} = 1.62.$$

These last two values represent the variance and standard deviation of the sample.

If, however, our goal is to use the sample to estimate population variance and population standard deviation, we need to modify our procedure, using degrees of freedom:

$$\hat{s}^2 = \frac{SS}{N-1} = \frac{26.4}{9} = 2.93$$

$$\hat{s} = \sqrt{\hat{s}^2} - \sqrt{2.93} = 1.71.$$

As you can see, we get larger values for variance (2.93) and standard deviation (1.71) when we are estimating.

This problem of estimating also applies to the sampling distribution of means. If we don't know μ and σ, we can't use Formula 10-1 to compute the standard error of the mean. However, as we have already discussed, $\hat{s}$ is an unbiased estimate of σ, so all we need to do is substitute $\hat{s}$ for σ in Formula 10-1. This estimated value is called the **estimated standard error of the mean,** symbolized as $\hat{s}_{\overline{X}}$:

> **FORMULA 10-6**   *Estimated standard error of the mean*
>
> $$\hat{s}_{\overline{X}} = \frac{\hat{s}}{\sqrt{N}}.$$

 see formula 10-5

when you use estimates you cannot use z scores

We can carry this substitution of estimated values for population values one step further. As seen in Formula 10-2, we can compute a z score for a sample mean. Then we can use the z score to find a percentile rank or probability. If we don't have the population value of the standard error, we must once again substitute our unbiased estimate ($\hat{s}_{\overline{X}}$). However, in using the estimated standard error of the mean, we encounter a problem. Remember that estimates contain error. Sometimes the estimates are high, sometimes they are low, but rarely are they identical to the population value. This means that the indices we compute that include $\hat{s}_{\overline{X}}$, such as $\overline{X} - \mu/\hat{s}_{\overline{X}}$, also contain variability, or error, and they no longer conform to the normal (z score) distribution. Instead, they correspond to what is called a **t distribution** and so are called t scores.

Remember that a z score is an exact value, and the normal curve is a distribution of these exact units. However, a t score is an estimate, and a t distribution incorporates the variability, or error, that these estimates contain. The t distribution is the normal distribution with "error added." Because the amount of error contained in an estimate becomes smaller as the sample size becomes larger, the t distribution becomes more and more similar to the normal distribution as sample size increases. A t score is simply an estimated z score. So now we have a new statistic called a t, which can be computed using Formula 10-7:

> **FORMULA 10-7   t score**
>
> $$t_{\overline{X}} = \frac{\overline{X} - \mu}{\hat{s}_{\overline{X}}}.$$

We use t scores in the same way we use z scores. That is, $t_{\overline{X}}$ tells us how far a score ($\overline{X}$) is from the mean (μ) in estimated standard error units.

Now that the sampling distribution of means has been defined and some of its properties discussed, what can we do with it and with the related distribution of t? As in Chapter 7, we will discuss two basic problems: (1) conducting a one-sample t test (analogous to finding areas when we know scores) and (2) constructing a confidence interval (analogous to finding scores when we know an area). Let's begin with confidence intervals.

CONFIDENCE INTERVALS

Suppose an experimental psychologist wants to do a learning study with new-born children to establish the average rate at which a neonate can form a head-turning response to a brief tone followed by a mildly positive stimulus (e.g., a sip of sugar-flavored water). It is impossible to measure the population of neonates, so the scientist randomly selects a sample of 23 infants and assesses their learning skills. The criterion of learning is set at five consecutive head-turning responses, and the score for each child is the number of pairings of the tone with the flavored water before reaching the criterion. From the data collected, a mean number of trials to criterion of 46.33 is computed. What does this figure mean in terms of the population of neonates? If the study were done time and again with random samples of 23 babies, would the results always be similar to this? What is the mean of means, or the population mean (μ)?

Unfortunately, we can't answer the last question. However, one of the things we learned in Chapter 5 was that the mean of a sample, $\overline{X}$, shows no systematic tendencies in relation to the mean of the population, μ, and for this reason it is said to be an unbiased estimate of μ. Thus, we can use the sample mean as an estimate of μ. When we do this, we must realize that it is very unlikely that any given sample $\overline{X}$ will exactly equal μ. Is there any way to increase our chances of capturing the population value? Yes, and it involves designating a range of values rather than only one value in guessing about the location of μ. The range of values is called a confidence interval. A **confidence interval (CI)** is a range of values within which we are reasonably certain the population mean lies. *Margin of error* is one common use of confidence intervals.

In the example at the beginning of the chapter, Eva wondered how pollsters had established a 3% confidence interval (margin of error) for their voter survey. Confidence intervals are useful in establishing a range of scores within which we can safely expect a population value to occur; they are also useful in making decisions about hypotheses.

How confident do we want to be in our guess about the value of μ? Do we want to be 80% sure, or 90%, or 63%, or what? Ninety percent probably sounds pretty good, and most of you would probably balk at anything less than this. Statisticians, however, being very conservative people, have traditionally tended to favor either 95% or 99% certainty. For this reason, we will limit our discussion to the derivation of 95% and 99% confidence intervals. Think of it this way: If we establish a range of values around our sample mean within which we are 95% or 99% sure μ is contained, it is very unlikely—5% or 1%, respectively—that μ will be outside the range. It is not impossible, but highly unlikely.

Now that we have decided how confident we want to be, let's derive a formula for 95% and 99% CIs. To do this, we need to think about one of the last types of problems covered in Chapter 7—finding scores that were so deviant that they occurred less than 5% or 1% of the time. The same problem was also expressed in Chapter 9 as finding the scores that occurred with a probability of .05 (or .01) or less. To find these scores, we first drew a normal curve, divided the 5% (or 1%) in half, and labeled each end of the curve appropriately. We then

FIGURE 10-3 Normal curve showing the problem of finding the scores cutting off the deviant 5% of the distribution , or the scores between which 95% of the curve lies.

looked in the normal curve table to find the z scores cutting off the deviant percentage of the curve and converted these scores to raw scores using the equation $X = zs + \bar{X}$. The problem of finding the deviant scores occurring 5% or less of the time ($p \le .05$) is shown graphically in Figure 10-3.

Note from the graph that while we were seeking the scores cutting off the deviant 5% (or 1%) of the normal curve distribution, we simultaneously found the scores enclosing the central 95% (or 99%) of the distribution. In other words, we already have a technique for finding the 95% or 99% CIs. All we need to do is modify the equations slightly to take into account the new distribution introduced in this chapter, the sampling distribution of means.

Consider the situation where our samples are infinite in size. In this limiting case, the sampling distribution of means is normally distributed and the formulas for finding the 95% and 99% CIs are $X = \pm z\sigma_{\bar{X}} + \mu$ or $X = \pm 1.96\sigma_{\bar{X}} + \mu$ for the 95% CI and $X = \pm 2.58\sigma_{\bar{X}} + \mu$ for the 99% CI. The z scores of ± 1.96 and ± 2.58 are the scores cutting off the deviant 5% and 1% of the normal curve, respectively.

However, the most typical case is the one in which we have to use the estimated standard error of the mean ($\hat{s}_{\bar{X}}$) because we don't know the population value. Because we still don't know either μ or $\sigma_{\bar{X}}$, we will estimate their values with $\bar{X}$ and $\hat{s}_{\bar{X}}$, respectively. The equations just introduced now become $X = \pm t_{.05}\hat{s}_{\bar{X}} + \bar{X}$ for the 95% confidence interval and $X = \pm t_{.01}\hat{s}_{\bar{X}} + \bar{X}$ for the 99% CI. Instead of using the z scores of ± 1.96 and ± 2.58, we need to determine the corresponding values of t.

The values of t are both positive and negative because we are looking for scores on either side of $\bar{X}$. We add the appropriate subscripts, depending on whether we are finding the 95% CI or the 99% CI. The appropriate subscripts with t are $t_{.05}$ (the t scores that cut off the deviant 5% of the distribution or occur with a probability of .05 or less) and $t_{.01}$ (the t scores that cut off the deviant 1% or occur with a probability of .01). Putting all of this together, the formulas for the 95% and 99% CIs are

RUN IT THROUGH TWICE; ONCE AS NEGATIVE ↓ONCE AS NEGATIVE

> **FORMULA 10-8**   *95% confidence interval for the population mean*
>
> $$95\% \text{ CI} = \pm t_{.05}\hat{s}_{\bar{X}} + \bar{X},$$

see. pg. 190, formula 10-6

> **FORMULA 10-9**   *99% confidence interval for the population mean*
>
> $$99\% \text{ CI} = \pm t_{.01}\hat{s}_{\bar{X}} + \bar{X}.$$

Looking at these formulas, we see that we have already encountered two of the three terms needed and shouldn't have any difficulty determining them:

$$\hat{s}_{\bar{X}} = \frac{\hat{s}}{\sqrt{N}} \quad \text{and} \quad \bar{X} = \frac{\Sigma fX}{N}.$$

But where do we get the *t* scores?

To determine the relevant values of *t*, we refer to Table B in Appendix 4, *p. 368* which lists the *t* scores that cut off either the deviant 5% or the deviant 1% of the distribution, depending on sample size. Ordinarily, when we talk about the deviant 5% or 1% of the distribution, we are considering both ends of the distribution. Another way to express this idea is to say that we are considering *both tails* of the distribution of *t* scores. A portion of the table of *t* scores has been reproduced in Table 10-1.

Table 10-1 contains *critical values* of *t*—that is, values of *t* that cut off deviant portions of the distribution. Note the heading "Level of Significance for Two-Tailed Test," with instructions on how to obtain significance levels for a one-tailed test. Next there is a row of four different percentages with appropriate probability values listed below. The numbers in each column below the probabilities are the values of *t* that cut off the deviant percentage of the distribution indicated by the value that heads that column. As with the normal curve table, only the positive half of the curve is given, so that for a two-tailed test, each of the values of *t* in the table is assumed to be both positive and negative.

At the far left of the table there is a column of numbers with the heading "*df*." Remember that the *t* distribution is really a family of distributions that change shape as a function of sample size. This sample size is reflected in degrees of freedom. As mentioned earlier, the concept of degrees of freedom is very complex, and we have only scratched the surface with our discussion. For our purposes, it is sufficient to point out that when we are working with one sample, *df* for *t* is $N - 1$. Because the *t* distribution changes shape with changes in degrees of freedom, we must know *df* to look up the critical value of *t*. For example, if we have a sample of size $N = 46$, $df = N - 1 = 46 - 1 = 45$, and the *t* scores cutting off the deviant 5% of the distribution are ± 2.0141 (from Appendix 4, Table B).

TABLE 10-1

A portion of Table B showing values of t cutting off deviant portions of the sampling distribution of means, depending on the degrees of freedom. The complete table may be found in Appendix 4.

	Level of Significance for Two-Tailed Test (For One-Tailed Test, Halve the Percentages Below)			
df	**10%** **(p = .10)**	**5%** **(p = .05)**	**2%** **(p = .02)**	**1%** **(p = .01)**
1	6.3138	12.7062	31.8207	63.6574
2	2.9200	4.3027	6.9646	9.9248
3	2.3534	3.1824	4.5407	5.8409
4	2.1318	2.7764	3.7469	4.6041
5	2.0150	2.5706	3.3649	4.0322
6	1.9432	2.4469	3.1427	3.7074
7	1.8946	2.3646	2.9980	3.4995
8	1.8595	2.3060	2.8965	3.3554
9	1.8331	2.2622	2.8214	3.2498
10	1.8125	2.2281	2.7638	3.1693

Note. From *Handbook of Statistical Tables* (pp. 28–30), by D. B. Owen, 1962, Reading, MA: Addison-Wesley. Copyright 1962 by Addison-Wesley Publishing Company, Inc. Adapted with permission of Addison-Wesley Longman.

Remember that *t* more closely approximates *z* as sample size increases. As a confirmation, look at the *t* value at the very bottom of the 5% column in Table B and compare it to the corresponding 5% *z* score from Table A. Both are 1.96.

Let's turn now to finding some confidence intervals. At the beginning of this section, we described a learning experiment with newborn children in which the average number of trials to criterion was 46.33 for a sample of size $N = 23$. Suppose that $\hat{s} = 6.51$. What is the 95% CI for μ? We have

$$95\% \text{ CI} = \pm t_{.05}\hat{s}_{\overline{X}} + \overline{X},$$

$$\overline{X} = 46.33,$$

$$\hat{s}_{\overline{X}} = \frac{\hat{s}}{\sqrt{N}} = \frac{6.51}{\sqrt{23}} = \frac{6.51}{4.80} = 1.36.$$

From Table B, the *t* scores cutting off the deviant 5% of the distribution with $df = N - 1 = 23 - 1 = 22$ are ± 2.0739. Thus,

$$95\% \text{ CI} = \pm 2.0739(1.36) + 46.33 = \pm 2.82 + 46.33$$
$$= 43.51 \text{ to } 49.15.$$

The range of values within which we are 95% sure μ is contained is from 43.51 to 49.15. (The CI in this type of equation is often expressed with the mean first—46.33 $\pm$ 2.82—rather than last; either way—43.51 to 49.15 or 46.33 $\pm$ 2.82—is acceptable.) The 99% CI can be obtained in the same way, with the values of t being ±2.8188. The 99% CI is from 42.50 to 50.16.

You can see that the 99% CI is wider (has a greater range of values) than the 95% interval. Why is this? Mathematically, it is because the t scores cutting off the deviant 1% are larger than the scores cutting off the deviant 5%. The deviant 1% of the t distribution is further from the mean than the deviant 5%; hence, it is represented by a larger t score. Also, intuitively, a larger range of values is needed for us to be 99% sure we've captured μ.

Let's try another example. In a study to determine the amount of REM (rapid eye movement) sleep engaged in by young adults, 35 volunteers were monitored in a sleep lab over a 1-week period. The average amount of REM sleep per night was 96 minutes, with an estimated standard deviation of 22 minutes. What is the 95% CI? We have

$$95\% \text{ CI} = \pm t_{.05}\hat{s}_{\overline{X}} + \overline{X},$$

$$\hat{s}_{\overline{X}} = \frac{\hat{s}}{\sqrt{N}} = \frac{22}{\sqrt{35}} = 3.72,$$

$$t_{.05}(df = N - 1 = 35 - 1 = 34) = \pm2.0301,$$

$$95\% \text{ CI} = \pm2.0301(3.72) + 96$$

$$= \pm7.55 + 96$$

$$= 96 \pm 7.55 \text{ or } 88.45 \text{ to } 103.55.$$

[handwritten margin note: $N = 35$, $\overline{X} = 96$, $\hat{s}_x = 22$, $\frac{22}{\sqrt{35}} = 5.916$ *]*

Note that the critical values of t for 34 df are not actually shown in Table B and that the value used was that for $df = 30$. If the sample size is larger than 30, the table is incomplete and the actual value of t may not be given. In this case, we use the value for the most nearly correct df.

For given values of $\overline{X}$ and $\hat{s}$, you will find that the size of a confidence interval is larger with smaller samples. This makes sense intuitively if you consider that the larger the sample, the more sure we are that the sample is an accurate reflection of the population. Hence, we don't need as large a range of values around $\overline{X}$ to be nearly certain we've captured μ. Mathematically, larger samples result in smaller values of $\hat{s}_{\overline{X}}$ and smaller t scores from Table B, both of which result in a narrower range of values for the confidence interval.

Because the distribution of t more and more closely approximates the normal curve as N increases, many instructors use z scores rather than t scores to construct confidence intervals when N is greater than some arbitrary number, such as 50. In our opinion, this results in unnecessary confusion; therefore, we will continue to use t scores, regardless of the size of N.

ᔥ CHECKING YOUR PROGRESS

Suppose the digit span (number of digits a person can hold in short-term memory) of 31 adults has been measured, with the result that $\Sigma X = 220.41$ and $\Sigma X^2 = 1,705.72$. What are the 95% and 99% CIs for μ?

Answer: 95% CI $\doteq$ 6.31 to 7.91; 99% CI = 6.04 to 8.18. We are 95% sure that the adult population digit span is from 6.31 to 7.91 and 99% sure that it is from 6.04 to 8.18.

HYPOTHESIS TESTING: ONE SAMPLE *t* TEST

In our discussion of confidence intervals, we used a distribution that is approximately normal with larger samples in order to establish a range of values within which we have a certain degree of confidence that μ is contained. Another use to which we can put the distribution of t is to test hypotheses about the value of μ.

Let's consider a specific example and develop a testing procedure from it. A researcher is interested in the effect of amphetamine on recent memory. To test this, she has 25 adult volunteers swallow a small dose of amphetamine, wait 30 minutes, and take a digit-span test. The researcher finds that the mean digit span for the subjects is 7.53, with $\hat{s} = 0.97$. Further, she knows on the basis of many previous studies that the average adult digit span is 7. If we assume that $\mu = 7$, what is the probability of selecting a sample of size $N = 25$ from the population (all people taking the small dose of amphetamine) whose mean is as deviant as 7.53?

Using the procedure developed earlier in this chapter for finding the probability of a deviant score, we first calculate a t score for the sample mean of 7.53:

$$\hat{s}_{\overline{X}} = \frac{\hat{s}}{\sqrt{N}} = \frac{0.97}{\sqrt{25}} = \frac{0.97}{5} = 0.194,$$

$$t = \frac{\overline{X} - \mu}{\hat{s}_{\overline{X}}} = \frac{7.53 - 7.00}{0.194} = \frac{0.53}{0.194} = 2.73.$$

This t score of 2.73 indicates that a mean of 7.53 is 2.73 $\hat{s}_{\overline{X}}$ units above a mean of 7 on the sampling distribution of means with $N = 25$. This is shown graphically in Figure 10-4.

Originally, we wanted to know the probability of obtaining an average digit span as deviant as 7.53, assuming that $\mu = 7$. Note that 7.53 is 2.73 estimated standard error units *above* the mean; but the score 2.73 units *below* the mean $[7 - (2.73)(0.194) = 7 - 0.53 = 6.47]$ is equally deviant, and the original problem really asked us to find the area of the curve above 7.53 and below 6.47. We therefore could have added the areas and converted to probability, and we would have determined the probability of obtaining a score as deviant as 7.53, given that $\mu = 7$.

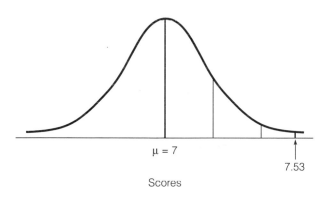

$\mu = 7$

7.53

Scores

FIGURE 10-4 Sampling distribution of means from samples of size $N = 25$ ($df = 24$). Score of 7.53 is 2.73 $s_{\bar{x}}$ units above the mean of 7.

However, because we are dealing with the t distribution, not with the normal curve, we cannot easily determine the exact probability associated with $t = 2.73$. Because there is a family of t distributions, the only way to determine exact probabilities is to have a complete table (similar to Table A in Appendix 4) for each degree of freedom. These tables alone would occupy an entire book. (Books devoted to statistical tables, such as t, can be obtained in most university libraries.)

Table B in Appendix 4 is incomplete. It includes the t values most frequently used in hypothesis testing and the degrees of freedom for which the t distribution differs most from the normal distribution. But this condensed version does not allow us to attach exact probabilities to all t scores. We can, however, compare our computed t score with table values known to cut off the deviant 5% or 1% of the distribution for a given sample size converted to degrees of freedom. The deviant 5% ($p = .05$) and 1% ($p = .01$) levels at which we're testing t are called alpha (α) levels.

For the example we have been considering, we found t to be 2.73 and $df = N - 1 = 25 - 1 = 24$. From Table B, we see that the t scores cutting off the deviant 5% and 1% of the sampling distribution of means when the size of each sample is 25 ($df = 24$) are 2.0639 and 2.7969, respectively. Because our obtained t is more deviant than the critical value at the 5% level (the t score cutting off the deviant 5% of the distribution), the logical thing to do is to reject the assumption that $\mu = 7$. In other words, we reject the assumed value for μ at the $\alpha = .05$, or 5%, level.

Thus, the observed mean of 7.53 is very unlikely if the population mean is 7. The researcher concludes that her treatment had an effect. The average digit span of people who have taken amphetamine is probably not the same as the average digit span of normal adults. She doesn't know what μ is for amphetamine-treated subjects; she just knows that it is probably not 7. Figure 10-5 illustrates what has been done with this problem.

Here is what we have done to this point. A sample has been selected from a population with an assumed mean of 7. The sample mean of 7.53 has been found

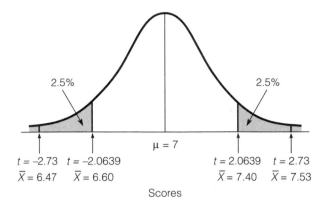

FIGURE 10-5   Drawing showing the region for rejection
of the hypothesis that $\mu = 7$. $t = \pm 2.0639$ cuts off the deviant 5%
(2.5% on either side of μ) of the distribution of t with $N = 25$
($df = 24$). The raw scores corresponding to the t scores are 6.60
and 7.40. $t = 2.73$ ($\overline{X} = 7.53$) is in the region for rejection of μ. To
simplify the drawing, t scores cutting off the deviant 1% have
been omitted.

to be very unlikely given the assumption that $\mu = 7$. We concluded, therefore,
that the sample was probably taken from a population in which μ was not equal
to 7.

The process we have just described is typical of research in the social sciences. Our goal is to reject the assumption that the sample mean is a good estimate of the population mean (that μ falls within a defined confidence interval
around $\overline{X}$). In other words, we hope to reject the hypothesis that $\overline{X} = \mu$. This may
seem like a hopelessly convoluted approach, but there is sound basis for it.

In the experimental approach—in fact, in any empirical approach—nothing
can be proved absolutely true, because we never have all possible data. In experimental work, it is always "possible," no matter how remote, that the next piece of
data will disconfirm our hypothesis. Therefore, hypotheses can never be *proved*
(an absolute term); they can only be *supported* (a relative term). Hypotheses can,
however, be disconfirmed. If properly collected data don't match our hypothesis,
then the hypothesis must be rejected, at least for the conditions and methods
used. In short, scientists cannot prove something to be true; they can only prove
it to be false.

So how do we extricate ourselves from this dilemma? The solution is that we
support our experimental hypotheses by rejecting, or falsifying, alternative
hypotheses. The simplest case, such as in the preceding example, involves two
hypotheses. First, we have an experimental hypothesis that the drug will work,
thus making the mean of the sample different from the mean of the population;
this hypothesis is symbolized by $H_1 = \mu \neq \overline{X}$. Second, we have the competing
hypothesis that the drug will *not* work, in which case we should expect the mean
of the sample to be equal (within an acceptable CI) to the population mean; this

✱ expect no difference

is the **null hypothesis,** symbolized by $H_0 = \mu = \bar{X}$. We cannot prove H_1 to be true; we can only support H_1 by rejecting H_0.

Getting back to our example, if the drug has no effect on memory, then our best prediction is that the mean of the sample equals the mean of the population ($H_0 = \mu = \bar{X}$). This would be a "null" effect; hence the term *null hypothesis.* However, if the drug works, we would expect that the sample mean would reflect this by falling appreciably above or below the population mean ($H_1 = \mu \neq \bar{X}$). Our definition of "appreciably" is determined by the confidence interval. If our sample mean falls outside the 95% CI, then $\bar{X}$ is not a good estimate of μ. That is, $\bar{X}$ cannot be viewed as representative of the population in which μ is the mean. Because the drug is the only thing we have done to the sample that makes it different from the population, we conclude that the drug is responsible for the difference.

The null hypothesis, or H_0, states that a sample mean equals the population parameter:

$$H_0: \mu = \bar{X}.$$

An alternative to the null hypothesis is that the sample mean is not equal to μ, and this is called the **alternative hypothesis,** or H_1. The alternative hypothesis can be either nondirectional or directional. A **nondirectional hypothesis** simply *← doesn't work* says that μ is not equal to $\bar{X}$, but it does not specify in which direction it differs. The nondirectional hypothesis is symbolized by

$$H_1: \mu \neq \bar{X}.$$

This alternative hypothesis is sometimes called bidirectional (i.e., it takes into account both tails of the distribution) because the direction of the difference is not specified.

A **directional hypothesis** states the direction of the difference between μ and *← doesn't work* the sample mean. That is, H_1 may say that $\bar{X}$ is greater than μ or less than μ. Symbolically, the directional hypothesis is

$$H_1: \mu > \bar{X} \qquad \text{or} \qquad H_1: \mu < \bar{X}.$$

In the example we have considered, the sample mean was found to be unlikely given the value assumed for H_0. Thus, we rejected the null hypothesis.

A phrase that is often used in hypothesis testing is "testing for significance." When H_0 is rejected, statisticians say that a **significant** result has been found, corresponding to either the 5% or the 1% level of significance, depending on the α level chosen.

Let's look at another example. Suppose that over a period of several years, a professor has found that the average grade on the final exam for all students taking a course in statistics is 75. One semester, the final exam is given and the grades are found to be slightly lower, with an average of 73.8 for a sample of size $N = 61$. The unbiased standard deviation is 8.3. Assuming $\mu = 75$, what is the

> 95% = SIGNIFICANT; REJECT H_0
< 95% = INSIGNIFICANT

✱ if at .5 level, do not reject H_0

Box 10-1   Steps for Testing the Null Hypothesis

1. Decide on the level at which you will test H_0. That is, choose either the 5% or 1% level of rejection. This is called the alpha (α) level.

2. Make an assumption (usually on the basis of previous research) about the value of μ and state the null hypothesis. Decide whether your alternative hypothesis will be directional or nondirectional, and state it.

3. Determine how far the sample mean deviates from the assumed value of μ in estimated standard error units. In other words, compute a t score with the formula

$$t = \frac{\overline{X} - \mu}{\hat{s}_{\overline{X}}}.$$

4. Determine the critical value of $t(t_{crit})$ from Table B in Appendix 4. To find the appropriate critical value, you need to know both df and α. Alpha was chosen in step 1, and $df = N - 1$ for this test.

5. For a nondirectional test, if the computed $t(t_{comp})$ is equal to or larger in absolute value than the critical value in the table, reject H_0 and conclude that it is very unlikely that the sample came from a population in which μ is what it was assumed to be.

6. For a directional test, t_{comp} should be more extreme but with the same sign as t_{crit}. If you predict $H_1 = \overline{X} < \mu$, then you expect a negative t, and t_{crit} should be negative. If you predict $H_1 = \overline{X} > \mu$, then t_{crit} should be positive.

7. Stated symbolically, the decision rule is as follows:

   For a directional test with t_{crit} positive:

       If $t_{comp} \geq t_{crit}$, reject H_0.
       If $t_{comp} < t_{crit}$, fail to reject H_0.

   For a directional test with t_{crit} negative:

       If $t_{comp} \leq t_{crit}$, reject H_0.
       If $t_{comp} > t_{crit}$, fail to reject H_0.

probability of obtaining a sample with a mean as deviant as 73.8? Is the probability low enough for the professor to reject the null hypothesis and conclude that perhaps a review of teaching and/or testing procedures is in order?

As before, the first step is to choose an α level. For this problem, let's use the 5%, or $p = .05$, level. The next step is to convert our raw score ($\overline{X}$) into a t score.

$$\hat{s}_{\overline{X}} = \frac{\hat{s}}{\sqrt{N}} = \frac{8.3}{\sqrt{61}} = \frac{8.3}{7.81} = 1.06,$$

$$t = \frac{\overline{X} - \mu}{\hat{s}_{\overline{X}}}$$

$$= \frac{73.8 - 75.0}{1.06} = \frac{-1.2}{1.06} = -1.13,$$

$$df = N - 1$$

$$= 61 - 1 = 60.$$

From Table B, the critical value for $df = 60$ is 2.0003 at the 5% level. That is, t scores of ± 2.0003 cut off the deviant 5% of the distribution of t for samples of size $N = 61$ ($df = 60$). Because our t_{comp} is -1.13 (1.13 in absolute value), it is less than the critical value, and we cannot reject H_0. In other words, the probability is quite high of obtaining a sample of size $N = 61$, with a mean of 73.8 from a population in which the mean is 75. Another way we could express our decision (failure to reject H_0) is to write $t(60) = -1.13$, $p > .05$. This is the preferred way to report this result in a research paper. The "$p > .05$" simply means that the probability of the event we observed (sample with $\overline{X} = 73.8$) is greater than the α level we chose for rejecting the null hypothesis.

Continuing to look at Table B, we see that if we have $df = \infty$, the values required for significance are 1.96 at the 5% level and 2.58 at the 1% level. As mentioned earlier, one of the properties of the t distribution is that it approaches the normal curve as sample size increases. You may remember from Chapter 7 that the z scores cutting off the deviant 5% and 1% of the normal curve were ± 1.96 and ± 2.58, respectively.

Finally, note that 1.96 and 2.58 are the smallest values of t that are required for rejection of the null hypothesis for a two-tailed test at the 5% and 1% levels. For this reason, if any computed t is less than 1.96 in absolute value, there is no need to look in the table, because it cannot be significant.

✪ CHECKING YOUR PROGRESS

A new president has been hired at a large university. He has just given his first speech to the general faculty. As the faculty members are leaving, 35 are randomly selected and asked to rate the speech on a scale from 1 to 7, with 1 being poor, 4 average, and 7 outstanding. The average rating is 4.4 with $\hat{s} = 0.93$. Test the hypothesis that the sample was taken from a population where $\mu = 4$.

Answer: $t = 2.50$, $df = 34$, $p < .05$, or $t(34) = 2.50$, $p < .05$. Because $p < .05$, you should reject H_0, and conclude that the president's speech was significantly above average.

Type I and Type II Errors

Hypothesis testing, as it has been discussed in this chapter, involves making an assumption about a population parameter (μ) and then determining whether or not a sample mean differs enough from the assumed value of μ to allow us to reject the null hypothesis. The actual test is performed by computing how far the sample mean deviates from the assumed μ in $\hat{s}_{\overline{X}}$ units (in other words, by computing t). The computed t score is then compared with t scores known to cut off either the deviant 5% or the deviant 1% of the sampling distribution of means for a given value of df. If the absolute value of t_{comp} (computed t) is equal to or larger than the t_{crit} (critical t) at the 5% (or 1%) level of significance, the null hypothesis is rejected. By rejecting H_0, we are concluding that the probability is .05 (.01) or less of obtaining a sample $\overline{X}$ as deviant as the one we obtained from a population with the μ that we assumed. If t_{comp} is smaller than the table values, we do not reject the null hypothesis.

This process of rejecting or failing to reject H_0 is sometimes called "decision making." In statistics, as in life, sometimes we make the wrong decision. Thus, one type of incorrect decision is to reject the null hypothesis when, in fact, it is true. That is, we may conclude on the basis of our sample value that the sample was not taken from a population in which μ was what we assumed it to be when, in fact, the sample was taken from this population.

This type of judgment error is known as a **Type I, or α, error** and is defined as rejecting H_0 when it is true. The levels of significance (5% and 1%) are often called α levels, and the probability of making a Type I error depends directly on α. For example, if $\alpha = .05$, then the probability of rejecting a true H_0 is .05, or 5 times in 100. That is, if we drew 100 samples from a population in which μ is what we have assumed it to be, 5 of those samples would have means deviant enough from μ for us to reject H_0. However, 5 times out of 100 is not very often, and that is why we rejected H_0 initially.

In practice, the $\alpha = .05$ level, or 5% level, of significance is widely used, and most scientists are willing to accept rejection of H_0 at the 5% level as reflecting a true difference from chance. If, however, we want to be more conservative and come closer to ensuring that we don't mistakenly reject a true H_0, we can lower the α level to .01 (1% level of significance) or even to .001, and so on. The problem with the ultraconservative approach is that a true difference may be discarded because it does not quite reach the required critical values caused by the small α. While decreasing the probability of a Type I error, we are simultaneously increasing the probability of a **Type II, or β, error,** which is defined as failing to reject H_0 when it is false. Further, although the probability of a Type I error is determined by the α level, the probability of a Type II error will not be known. Therefore, the investigator must choose the α level that balances Type I and Type II errors. In the social sciences, the 5% level is most often accepted as achieving this balance.

The possible consequences of hypothesis testing as outlined in this chapter are summarized in Figure 10-6. The chart reflects the two possible decisions that can be made: to reject or to fail to reject the null hypothesis, which may be either

rejecting a true null hypotheses

in query

accepting a false hypotheses

FIGURE 10-6 Chart illustrating the possible consequences of decision making in hypothesis testing.

true or false. Rejection of a true H_0 results in an α error, whereas rejection of a false H_0 is correct. Failure to reject a true H_0 is correct, whereas failing to reject a false H_0 leads to a β error.

The Power of a Statistical Test

In the previous section, a Type I, or α, error was defined as rejecting a true null hypothesis, and a Type II, or β, error was defined as failing to reject a false null hypothesis. Further, it was stated that decreasing the likelihood of an α error by lowering α results in an increase in the probability of a β error. That is, by making it less likely that we will mistakenly reject a true null, we are making it increasingly more difficult to reject *any* null hypothesis, even one that is false.

A related concern is the **power** of a test, defined as the probability that our test will detect a false hypothesis. Power may be determined by solving the equation

$$\text{power} = 1 - \beta.$$

in query

Unfortunately, determining the power of a test requires information that we do not have concerning the actual state of affairs in the population. That is, we would need to know exact parameters, which are what we have been estimating from our sample values. Although we cannot determine β (and from it $1 - \beta$), we can discuss some factors that contribute to the power of a test. To better understand these factors, let's consider the distributions shown in Figure 10-7.

In Figure 10-7, there are two partially overlapping distributions designated H_0 and H_1. The distribution called H_0 is what we would expect to observe if H_0 were true, whereas H_1 represents the true state of affairs. Assuming that $\alpha = .05$ and that we are using a one-tailed test (one that considers only one tail of the distribution rather than both tails), a vertical line has been drawn on the graph

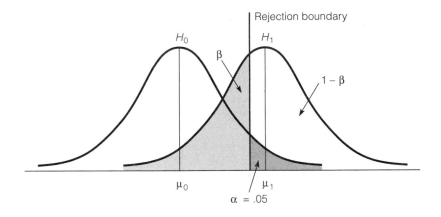

FIGURE 10-7   Illustration of the power of a test. The vertical line represents the lower boundary for rejection of the null hypothesis under H_0. The shaded area under H_1 to the left of the line is β, and the unshaded area to the right is $1 - \beta$, or the power of the test.

illustrating the region of rejection of H_0. That is, any sample mean from H_1 that happened to fall in the unshaded region to the right of the rejection line would enable us to reject H_0. This unshaded portion of the graph is labeled $1 - \beta$, or the power of the test.

However, you can see that a substantial portion of distribution H_1 lies to the left of the rejection line. This portion of H_1 has been shaded and is labeled β. That is, any sample drawn from H_1 with a mean in the shaded portion will not result in the rejection of H_0, which is really false. Thus, observation of a sample in this area will result in a β error. Now let's look at the factors affecting power.

As already mentioned, the value of α affects β, which in turn determines $1 - \beta$. Thus, the smaller we set the α level, the larger β will be, which in turn means that our statistical test will have less power. In constructing the line of rejection shown in Figure 10-7, α was set at .05. Suppose we make $\alpha = .01$ instead. In the new situation, shown in Figure 10-8, we can see that the shaded area β is now larger than it was with $\alpha = .05$, and the power of the test $(1 - \beta)$ has decreased.

A second factor affecting the power of a test is the size of the sample taken from the population. Specifically, the larger the N, the greater the power of the test will be. The reason for this involves one of the properties of the sampling distribution of means: As the size of the sample increases, $\sigma_{\bar{x}}$ decreases. In other words, with larger and larger Ns, the sampling distribution becomes more and more compact. The effect of sample size on the power of a test is shown in Figure 10-9, in which the distributions have been drawn to reflect a larger N than is shown in Figure 10-7. As you can see, although the mean of each distribution is the same as before, the greater compactness results in less overlap, a smaller β, and a larger power.

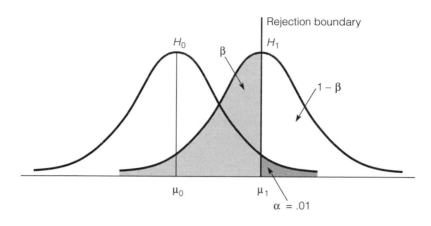

FIGURE 10-8   With $\alpha = .01$ instead of .05, the area of β is increased, with a corresponding decrease in the power of the test $(1 - \beta)$

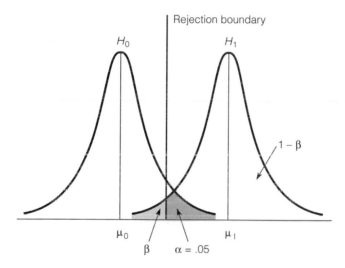

FIGURE 10-9   A larger sample size results in more compact distributions, a smaller region of overlap between H_0 and H_1, and a more powerful test.

A third factor affecting power is the distance between the mean under H_0 and the true mean under H_1. That is, the greater the discrepancy between the hypothesized value and the true value, the greater the power of the test. Figure 10-10 illustrates that power increases when the mean under H_1 is farther away from the mean under H_0 than it was in Figure 10-7.

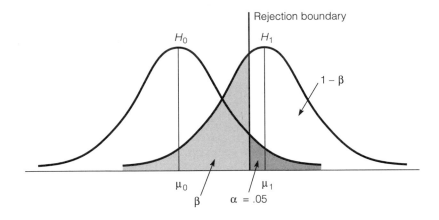

FIGURE 10-10   When the means under H_0 and H_1 are farther apart, β is decreased and $1 - \beta$, or the power of the test, is increased.

STOP HERE

Testing r and r_s for Significance   (*TERMS THAT STATISTICIANS USE*)

It is also possible to test hypotheses for correlation coefficients. We didn't discuss this in Chapter 8 because we first needed to present hypothesis testing and related topics like degrees of freedom. With that discussion complete, we can now discuss testing r for significance.

As discussed in Chapter 8, r measures the degree of relationship between variables X and Y. To test r for significance, we first assume that there is no relationship in the population between the two variables. In other words, we make the assumption that in the population from which our sample was drawn, the two variables are not related. We assume that the underlying population coefficient, represented by ρ, or rho, is 0. This assumption of no relationship in the population is yet another version of the null hypothesis. We then ask: If it is true that the underlying population correlation coefficient is 0, what is the likelihood of obtaining a particular deviant correlation coefficient?

Let's take the example of college student involvement, first introduced in Chapter 8. We found that the correlation between living off campus and being involved in campus activities was −.95. What is the probability of obtaining a sample of size 10 with a correlation coefficient as deviant as .95 from a population in which living off campus and being involved are not related? Most of the samples of size 10 from a population with a zero coefficient would have coefficients pretty close to 0, and only a few samples would have values as extreme as the one we obtained. To actually determine the probability of our sample value, we would need to know the standard deviation of the distribution of sample coefficients or we would have to estimate it. But, as with the t test, the determination of the actual probability is unnecessary.

Instead, we can refer to a table containing correlation coefficients so deviant that they occur less than 5% or 1% of the time in samples of a given size drawn from a population with a zero coefficient. The table is Table C in Appendix 4, for critical values of r, and it contains values of r at the 5% and 1% levels of significance. In other words, if our sample value exceeds the values in the table for the appropriate degrees of freedom, we reject the null hypothesis and conclude that the sample was *not* drawn from a population with a zero correlation coefficient. If the null hypothesis is rejected, we say that a significant relationship exists between the variables in question.

Looking at the table, we see that the left column is labeled "Degrees of Freedom (df)." In the case of r, $df = N - 2$, where N is the number of pairs of scores. The two restrictions placed on r have to do with the fact that r measures the degree of linear relationship between X and Y. Both restrictions are required in fitting a straight line to a sample of score pairs.

In the example we have been considering, $N = 10$ and $df = N - 2 = 10 - 2 = 8$. For $df = 8$, the coefficient required for significance at the 5% level is .632. Because $-.95$ is larger in absolute value than .632, we can reject the null hypothesis at the 5% level and conclude that a relationship probably exists between the two variables. We can also reject the null hypothesis at the 1% level, because $-.95$ is larger in absolute value than .765, the critical table value. In summary, we have found, by referring to a table of critical values for r, that the probability of obtaining a correlation coefficient as large as the one we obtained from a population where $\rho = 0$ is less than .01. (We rejected the null hypothesis at the 1% level, which is the same as saying that the probability is less than .01.) As with t, the correct way to report this result in a research paper is $r(8) = -.95, p < .01$.

Because the probability of our obtained sample value is so small given that the population correlation coefficient is really 0, we conclude that the population coefficient is *not* 0. It is likely that a relationship exists between the variables "off campus" and "involvement." Because we rejected the null hypothesis at the 5% (or 1%) level, does this mean that the population coefficient is not 0? Unfortunately, the answer is not an unequivocal yes. Rejecting the null hypothesis means that it is very unlikely that a coefficient as large as we got would be found in a sample drawn from a population with zero correlation—very unlikely but not impossible. We could obtain a sample with a high correlation coefficient from a population where $\rho = 0$, but in our example the probability was less than .01.

The procedure for testing the significance of r_s parallels that for testing r. The null hypothesis for the significance test of r_s is that no relationship exists between the ranks of the two variables in the population from which the sample was drawn. To test r_s, we merely have to compare its value with critical values in Table D for the appropriate sample size. Note that Table D is constructed using N rather than df. As an example, let's look at the problem in Chapter 8 in which a correlation was found between ratings of anxiety and ratings given for perceived noise level. The sample size in this problem was 10. From Table D we find that the values of r_s at the 5% and 1% levels of significance for samples of size 10 are .648 and .794, respectively. Our obtained r_s of .87 is larger than the value required for rejection of the null hypothesis at the 1% level. Therefore, we reject H_0 and conclude that anxiety level is related to perceived noise level rating.

In summary, here is the procedure for testing the significance of a sample correlation coefficient:

1. Set up the null hypothesis. Make the assumption that the sample was drawn from a population in which the two measured variables have no relationship. That is, assume there is zero correlation between the variables in the population (H_0: $\rho = 0$).

2. Choose a level for rejection of H_0. For most purposes, a reasonable level is the 5% level. If the obtained value of r or r_s is equal to or greater than the value required for rejection at the 1% level, then the lower probability may be reported; that is, $p < .01$.

3. For r ($df = N - 2$), locate the coefficients in Table C necessary for rejecting H_0 at the 5% and 1% levels. For r_s, use N to locate the coefficients in Table D necessary for rejecting H_0 at the 5% and 1% levels.

Compare the sample value with the table values to see whether, in terms of *absolute value*, the sample value is equal to or greater than the table values. If the sample r is less than the value required for significance at the 5% level, do not reject the null hypothesis. If it is equal to or greater than the value required for rejection at the 5% level but less than the value required at the 1% level, reject at the 5% level but not at the 1% level. If it is equal to or greater than the value at the 1% level, reject H_0 at both levels.

SUMMARY

In this chapter, the sampling distribution of means was introduced. The sampling distribution of means was constructed from the means of successive random samples of a given size taken from some population. Here are its properties:

1. It is symmetrical in shape and approaches normality with large samples, even if the population from which the samples are drawn is not normal. This is a simplified version of the central limit theorem.

2. Its mean is equal to the mean of the population (μ).

3. Its standard deviation ($\sigma_{\bar{X}}$, called the standard error of the mean) becomes smaller as the size of the sample becomes larger.

The sample was used to estimate the population values μ, σ, and σ^2. Although $\bar{X}$ is an unbiased estimate of μ, s and s^2 systematically underestimate σ and σ^2. To correct for this underestimation, estimated population variance and standard deviation ($\hat{s}^2$ and $\hat{s}$) are calculated by dividing SS by $N - 1$ instead of by N. $N - 1$ is called degrees of freedom (df), the number of values in a set of scores free to vary after certain restrictions are placed on the data. Standard scores may be calculated using the estimated values, but the scores correspond to a t distribution, not to a z distribution. With large sample size, the t and z distributions become increasingly similar.

The sampling distribution of means was used to construct confidence intervals (defined as a range of values within which we have a certain degree of confidence that μ is contained) and to test hypotheses about the exact value of μ. The two confidence intervals discussed were the 95% CI and the 99% CI. The formula for the 95% CI is

$$95\% \text{ CI} = \pm t_{.05}\hat{s}_{\bar{X}} + \bar{X},$$

where $t_{.05}$ is a value obtained from a table of t scores (Table B in Appendix 4) that cut off the deviant 5% and 1% of the sampling distribution of means. The critical value of t used depends on the degrees of freedom. In the case of t with one sample, $df = N - 1$. The value $\hat{s}_{\bar{X}}$ is an estimate of $\sigma_{\bar{X}}$ and is computed from the formula

$$\hat{s}_{\bar{X}} = \frac{\hat{s}}{\sqrt{N}}.$$

The formula for the 99% CI is

$$99\% \text{ CI} = \pm t_{.01}\hat{s}_{\bar{X}} + \bar{X}.$$

Hypothesis testing involves making an assumption about whether a sample mean is representative of a population with a mean of μ. That is, if the $\bar{X}$ observed is very unlikely given the deviation between $\bar{X}$ and μ, the null hypothesis is rejected. Here are the actual steps:

1. Decide on a level for α, the level at which you will reject or fail to reject the null hypothesis. For most purposes, the 5% level ($p = .05$) is satisfactory.

2. State the null and alternative hypotheses.

3. Determine how far $\bar{X}$ deviates from the assumed value of μ in $\hat{s}_{\bar{X}}$ units. In other words, calculate a t score using the formula

$$t = \frac{\bar{X} - \mu}{\hat{s}_{\bar{X}}}.$$

4. Compare the computed t score with the value of t in Table B with the appropriate df ($N - 1$). For a nondirectional test, if the absolute value of the computed t is equal to or greater than the table value, reject H_0. Otherwise, fail to reject H_0.

5. For a directional test, remember whether you expect t to be positive or negative. If you predict a negative t_{comp}, reject H_0 if $t_{\text{comp}} < t_{\text{crit}}$. If you predict a positive t_{comp}, reject H_0 if $t_{\text{comp}} \geq t_{\text{crit}}$. Otherwise, fail to reject H_0.

Hypothesis testing is also known as testing for significance, and the values of t cutting off the deviant 5% and 1% of the distribution of t define the 5% and 1% levels of significance, respectively.

Two types of errors may be made when testing H_0. The Type I, or α, error is defined as rejection of a true null and has a probability equal to the α level. The

Type II, or β, error is defined as failing to reject a false H_0. The probability of this type of error increases with decreases in α.

The power of a test is defined as the probability of detecting or rejecting a false H_0. Power is determined by the formula

$$\text{power} = 1 - \beta.$$

Three factors affecting power are the α level used, the size of N, and the distance between H_0 and H_1, a true alternative hypothesis.

Significance tests can also be performed for r and for r_S. For r, the null hypothesis is that $\rho = 0$, whereas for r_S it is that the same sample came from a population where there is no relationship between the ranks. To test the hypothesis, compare the computed value to the critical value obtained from Table C for r (remember: $df = N - 2$) and Table D for r_S (remember: use N, not df, for this table). If the absolute value of the computed r or r_S is greater than or equal to the table value, reject H_0. If it is less than the table value, do not reject H_0.

✴✴ Troubleshooting Your Computations

The computations covered in this chapter have, for the most part, been quite simple and require an understanding of what you are trying to find more than mathematical ability. However, there are some questions you should ask yourself after you have worked the problems in this chapter.

First of all, have you obtained a CI that seems reasonable in light of the sample information you have? For example, to be reasonable, the CI should contain the mean of the sample. When you found the t score to plug into the formula for the confidence interval, did you use df or N? You should have used df ($N - 1$) rather than N.

When computing and reporting the t score, did you retain the appropriate sign throughout the computations? That is, if the mean of your sample is less than the value set for μ, your computed t score should be negative.

After making a decision to reject or not to reject the null hypothesis, go back and review the decision-making process. For nondirectional tests, consider whether or not your computed t score was larger in absolute value than the table value of t cutting off the deviant 5% of the distribution of t scores for samples with the df you observed. If so, you should have rejected H_0; if not, you should not have rejected H_0. For directional tests, t_{comp} must be less than or equal to a negative t_{crit} or greater than or equal to a positive t_{crit}.

EXERCISES

1. a.   Given $\bar{X} = 100, \hat{s} = 20$, and $N = 25$, find the 99% CI for μ.

    b.   If $N = 147$, what is the 95% CI for μ? Note that 146 is closer to 120 than it is to ∞.

2. Find the 99% and 95% CIs for each of the following samples:

   a. $\bar{X} = 15, N = 17, \hat{s} = 5$

   b. $\Sigma X = 240, N = 40, \hat{s}_{\bar{X}} = 1.6$

   c. $N = 17, \Sigma X = 1{,}445, \Sigma X^2 = 12{,}343.25$

3. Find the 95% and 99% CIs for μ for the following scores:

X	f	X	f
42	1	22	2
30	2	21	1
26	6	19	2
25	1	18	4
24	1	17	2
23	3		

4. Some data have been collected with the following results:

X	f	X	f
37	1	29	3
36	1	27	2
34	3	26	1
32	1	25	1
31	5	20	1
30	4		

   Find the 95% and 99% CIs for μ.

5. The running time for 137 rats in a 6-foot runway is recorded. The data are $\Sigma X - 1{,}781$ seconds and $\Sigma X'' = 25{,}345$. Assume that $\mu = 11.5$ seconds. Test H_0.

6. A company has developed a training procedure to improve scores on the SAT. Following the training, 100 high school students take the SAT. The average math score is 517, with $\hat{s} = 90$. Assuming $\mu = 500$ for the math SAT, test the null hypothesis. Did the training significantly improve scores ($\alpha = .05$, directional)?

7. Briefly define the following terms:

   a. power of a test

   b. α error

   c. β error

   d. directional hypothesis

8. How was the sampling distribution of means derived, and what are its properties?

9. The brain stem auditory response latency for normal human beings has been found to be 5.68 milliseconds. A random sample of 10 participants is selected, and each subject is asked to go without sleep for 24 hours before a test for brain stem auditory response latency. The average latency is found to be 5.85 milliseconds, with $\hat{s} = 0.14$. Test the hypothesis that lack of sleep has no effect on average latency.

10. A therapist treating clients for communication apprehension (fear of public speaking) assessed the effectiveness of the treatment by giving her clients a standard test at the beginning and at the end of treatment. The difference between the two scores was an indication of change. Here are the scores (a negative score indicates improvement):

X	X
−3	−3
−4	−1
2	4
−8	1
0	−5
−7	−6
6	

If the treatment produced no effect, the change score would be 0, so assume that $\mu = 0$). Test the null hypothesis ($\alpha = .05$, directional). Did the treatment significantly reduce communication apprehension?

11. In the chapter, we discussed the derivation of the sampling distribution of means. Suppose we have a finite population consisting of the scores 1, 3, 5, and 7. All possible samples of size $N = 2$ have been extracted from it and are as follows:

1, 1	5, 1	3, 5	5, 5
1, 3	1, 7	5, 3	5, 7
3, 1	7, 1	3, 7	7, 5
1, 5	3, 3	7, 3	7, 7

From these samples, construct the sampling distribution of means and show that the mean of the distribution is equal to μ. Demonstrate that $\sigma_{\bar{x}} = \sigma/\sqrt{N}$.

12. Exercises 2, 6, 8, and 10 in Chapter 8 involved the calculation of r or r_s. For each of the correlations computed in those exercises, find the critical value at 5% α and test the null hypothesis.

13. Exercises 1, 3, 7, 9, and 11 in Chapter 8 involved the calculation of r or r_s. For each of the correlations computed in those exercises, find the critical value at 5% α and test the null hypothesis.

CHAPTER 11

Significance of the Difference Between Two Sample Means

 Dr. Baxter tried a new approach to the treatment of panic disorder on a few clients, and they appeared to show more improvement than the clients with panic disorder she treated conventionally. When she spoke to her colleagues about the new technique, they seemed interested but unconvinced. Dr. Baxter knew that she and her colleagues needed better evidence to determine the worth of the new treatment.

Dr. Baxter had a large practice, with many panic disorder clients, so she decided that it would be possible to design an experiment to test the effectiveness of her new approach formally. It had been several years since her last statistics and research design course, but it seemed to her that she could devise a simple design with two independent groups that should serve the purpose.

Dr. Baxter collected the files of 25 clients with panic disorder who were all in the early stages of treatment, and by tossing a coin, she randomly assigned 13 clients to a "conventional" treatment group and 12 clients to an "experimental" treatment group. She then administered the appropriate treatment over a period of 8 weeks, which she thought was sufficient time for her patients to show some improvement.

At the end of this time, Dr. Baxter administered a standard assessment to the clients in both groups to determine their level of panic disorder. She listed the scores of the two groups, performed some calculations, and in a few minutes had her answer. The mean of the experimental group ($\bar{X} = 6.6$) was indeed lower than the mean of the conventional treatment group ($\bar{X} = 9.8$). Note that a lower score indicates less panic.

But after all that time and effort, Dr. Baxter was still not satisfied. There was an average difference of 3.2 points, but it didn't seem very impressive. Would her colleagues be convinced by it? How could she clarify her findings? Was there a statistical procedure that could help her determine if the groups differed significantly in their remaining symptoms?

Indeed, there is a statistical test that Dr. Baxter could use. It is called the independent t test, and it is one of the statistical procedures we will discuss in this chapter. The independent t test is used in situations such as the one created by Dr. Baxter, where two separate groups are compared.

Chapter 10 presented the one-sample t test as a means of evaluating the validity of a hypothesis about the population mean on the basis of a sample value. The material in this chapter is really just an extension of what was covered in Chapter 10. However, rather than consider one sample extracted from a population at a time, we will consider two samples taken simultaneously.

In a one-sample t test, a sample mean is compared with a population mean $(\bar{X} - \mu)$. The population mean is known at the outset, either because it is defined theoretically or because it has been established in previous research. Additionally, the population mean is a constant—it is a value that does not change. Thus, the one-sample t test compares a sample mean with a known constant (the population mean).

In practice, one-sample t tests are rarely used because we usually don't know the population mean. When the population mean is unknown, we typically draw two samples. One sample receives the treatment, just as in the one-sample t test. The second sample, often called the **control group,** is used to estimate the population mean. So instead of using the distance between a sample mean and a population mean $(\bar{X} - \mu)$ to test the significance of our treatment, we use the distance between two sample means $(\bar{X}_1 - \bar{X}_2)$. The important difference is that both sample means can vary, because both are estimates. Therefore, we can no longer use the sampling distribution of means as our reference distribution. Instead, we must use a new distribution—the *sampling distribution of the mean differences.*

THE SAMPLING DISTRIBUTION OF THE DIFFERENCES BETWEEN SAMPLE MEANS

Research designs such as that employed by Dr. Baxter use a test of the difference between independent sample means. By **independent samples,** we mean samples in which the behavior of the members of one sample is not related to the behavior of the members of the other. Practically speaking, we will assume that conditions for independence have been satisfied as long as subjects are selected at random from a large group and are assigned randomly to the different treatment conditions.

In Chapter 10, to introduce the sampling distribution of means, we first considered a population. From this population we drew single random samples, all with the same size N, and computed a mean for each sample. The sampling

Step 1: Pairs of random samples are drawn from a population.

Step 2: The mean for some behavioral measure is found for each sample, and the difference is found for each pair of samples.

$\overline{X}$ of 1st sample		$\overline{X}$ of 2nd sample		Difference
$\overline{X}_1$	−	$\overline{X}_2$	=	d_1
$\overline{X}_3$	−	$\overline{X}_4$	=	d_2
•		•		•
•		•		•
•		•		•

Step 3: The frequency polygon of the difference scores is plotted.

$$\mu_{\overline{x}_1 - \overline{x}_2} = 0$$

Difference scores $(\overline{X}_1 - \overline{X}_2)$

FIGURE 11-1 Development of the sampling distribution of mean differences.

distribution of means was constructed from the frequency distribution of the sample means.

Now, suppose that instead of drawing single samples from the population, we draw *pairs* of random samples. As before, we calculate the mean for some behavioral measure for each sample, but this time we take the *difference* between the pair of sample means. For any pair of samples drawn at random from the same population, it is unlikely, because of sampling error, that each would have the same mean.

What do we have at this point? We have a population from which we have drawn pairs of samples, we have the means that we have calculated for each sample of a pair, and we have the difference between the means for each pair of samples. We can now make a frequency distribution based on the differences between sample means and use the distribution to plot a frequency polygon. The shape of the resulting polygon will be symmetrical and, if the samples are large enough, approximately normal. The procedure outlined thus far is shown in Figure 11-1.

The scores plotted along the X axis of the frequency polygon are differences between pairs of sample means, so the distribution is called the **sampling distribution of the mean differences.** In Chapter 10, we talked about three important properties of the sampling distribution of means. The sampling distribution of differences also has three important properties; two of these are the same as corresponding properties of the sampling distribution of means. But to begin, let's discuss the different property.

In the previous chapter, we saw that the mean of the sampling distribution of means was equal to the population mean, or μ. The mean of the sampling distribution of mean differences, on the other hand, is 0. Why is this?

Remember that all samples are assumed to be drawn from the same population. Because of sampling error, we would expect that in some cases, the mean of the first sample of a pair chosen would be larger than the second mean, resulting in a positive difference. In other cases, the mean of the second sample would be the larger, resulting in a negative difference. Then, when the mean of all the differences was calculated, the positive differences would be canceled by the negative differences, resulting in a mean of 0.

The remaining properties of the sampling distribution of differences involve the shape of the distribution and are the same as corresponding properties of the sampling distribution of means. Specifically, the larger the size of the samples chosen from the population, the closer the sampling distribution of differences approximates the normal curve. Also, the larger the size of the samples drawn from the population, the smaller will be the standard deviation of the sampling distribution of differences. The standard deviation of the new distribution is called the **standard error of the difference between means** and is symbolized by $\sigma_{\bar{X}_1 - \bar{X}_2}$ (read "little sigma sub X-bar sub 1 minus X-bar sub 2"). The formula for the standard error of the difference between means is

FORMULA 11-1   *Standard error of the difference between means*

$$\sigma_{\bar{X}_1 - \bar{X}_2} = \sqrt{\sigma_{\bar{X}_1}^2 + \sigma_{\bar{X}_2}^2},$$

where $\sigma_{\bar{X}}^2 = \sigma^2 / N$.

The last property—that the standard error of the difference between means decreases with increases in sample size—may be appreciated if you note that the larger the size of each sample, the closer the mean of the sample is likely to be to the population mean. In turn, the closer the mean of each sample of a pair is to the population value, the closer the sample means will be to each other. If the means of a pair of samples are close to each other, then the difference between their means will be small (i.e., close to 0). Finally, if the differences are close to 0, their variability around the mean of the sampling distribution of differences will be small.

To summarize, here are the properties of the sampling distribution of mean differences:

1. The mean of the distribution is 0.

2. The larger the sample sizes, the more the distribution approximates the normal curve.

3. The larger the sample sizes, the smaller is the standard error of the differences.

Remember that only rarely do we know the population value of $\sigma^2_{\bar{X}_1}$ and $\sigma^2_{\bar{X}_2}$, so there aren't many occasions when we will be able to use Formula 11-1 to calculate the standard error of the differences. However, we can estimate it with $\hat{s}_{\bar{X}_1-\bar{X}_2}$, which we call the **estimated standard error of the mean differences.** Here is the definitional formula:

FORMULA 11-2 *Estimated standard error of the mean differences for independent samples (definitional formula)*

$$\hat{s}_{\bar{X}_1-\bar{X}_2} = \sqrt{\hat{s}^2_{\bar{X}_1} + \hat{s}^2_{\bar{X}_2}} \text{ where } \hat{s}^2_{\bar{X}} = \frac{\hat{s}^2}{N}.$$

see p.190

Unfortunately, Formula 11-2 can be used only if the samples have equal N. For this reason, we now introduce a computational formula that can be used with equal or unequal N:

FORMULA 11-3 *Estimated standard error of the mean differences for independent samples (computational formula)*

$$\hat{s}_{\bar{X}_1-\bar{X}_2} = \sqrt{\left(\frac{(N_1-1)\hat{s}^2_1 + (N_2-1)\hat{s}^2_2}{N_1 + N_2 - 2}\right)\left(\frac{1}{N_1} + \frac{1}{N_2}\right)},$$

where N_1 and N_2 are the number of subjects in the first and second samples, respectively, and the variances of the samples are symbolized by $\hat{s}^2_1$ and $\hat{s}^2_2$. Here is a variation of Formula 11-3 that is even easier to use:

FORMULA 11-4 *Estimated standard error of the mean differences for independent samples (alternative raw-score computational formula)*

$$\hat{s}_{\bar{X}_1-\bar{X}_2} = \sqrt{\left(\frac{SS_1 + SS_2}{N_1 + N_2 - 2}\right)\left(\frac{1}{N_1} + \frac{1}{N_2}\right)} \text{ where } SS = \Sigma X^2 - \frac{(\Sigma X)^2}{N}.$$

We are now in a position to determine whether two samples differ significantly—that is, whether they come from different populations with different means. We can do this in the same way that we tested hypotheses about μ in Chapter 10. As you will recall, we first determined, in $\hat{s}_{\bar{X}}$ units, how far our sample mean was from the hypothesized μ. In other words, we computed a t score and then compared our computed value with critical values of t from Table B in Appendix 4.

Hypothesis testing is the same whether we are considering pairs of samples or only one. Again, the first step is to determine how far, in $\hat{s}_{\overline{X}_1-\overline{X}_2}$ units, our observed difference in sample means deviates from the mean of the sampling distribution of differences. In other words, we will compute a t score just as we did in the last chapter. The formula for t is just another variation on the basic formula for a standard score, or z score.

A z score was defined as the deviation of a raw score from the mean in standard deviation units, or

$$z \text{ score} = \frac{\text{score} - \text{mean}}{\text{standard deviation}}.$$

If we apply this formula to the sampling distribution of differences, the result is

FORMULA 11-5 z score for the sampling distribution of differences

$$z_{\overline{X}_1-\overline{X}_2} = \frac{(\overline{X}_1 - \overline{X}_2) - (\mu_1 - \mu_2)}{\sigma_{\overline{X}_1-\overline{X}_2}},$$

where $(\overline{X}_1 - \overline{X}_2)$ is a score in the distribution, $(\mu_1 - \mu_2)$ is the mean of the distribution, and $\sigma_{\overline{X}_1-\overline{X}_2}$ is the standard deviation of the distribution.

Because we cannot determine $\sigma_{\overline{X}_1-\overline{X}_2}$, we use $\hat{s}_{\overline{X}_1-\overline{X}_2}$ to estimate it. Substituting this value into the equation for z gives us

FORMULA 11-6 t score for the sampling distribution of differences

$$t_{\overline{X}_1-\overline{X}_2} = \frac{(\overline{X}_1 - \overline{X}_2) - (\mu_1 - \mu_2)}{\hat{s}_{\overline{X}_1-\overline{X}_2}}.$$

Because $\mu_1 - \mu_2 = 0$, the formula for t is usually written

FORMULA 11-7   *Two-sample t test for independent samples (definitional formula)*

$$t_{\overline{X}_1-\overline{X}_2} = \frac{(\overline{X}_1 - \overline{X}_2)}{\hat{s}_{\overline{X}_1-\overline{X}_2}}.$$

After our raw score (difference between a pair of sample means) has been converted to a t score, the computed t is compared with t scores known to cut off the deviant 5% and 1% of the sampling distribution of differences. As in the previous chapter, sample size is converted to degrees of freedom, and the critical values of t are located in the same table as before, Table B.

Now that we have discussed how the t test is performed, let's consider an actual problem, compute t, and determine whether or not the samples were drawn from the same population.

COMPUTING t: INDEPENDENT SAMPLES

Tennis coach Tom Robson decided to try a new technique to help the members of his team improve their serves. He showed the entire team a videotape of the proper serving technique. Then Tom divided the team at random into two groups. One group would imagine the proper serving form for 10 minutes before each practice, and the other group would read a pamphlet on proper serving technique. After 1 week, Tom observed each team member's serving skills. On the basis of the difference between sample means that he observed, were the two groups drawn from the same population with the same mean, or did they come from different populations with different means? Let's see.

Tom found that the average number of good serves for the "imagining" group was 27.6 and the average number for the "reading" group was 22.1. There were 10 team members in each group. Assuming that the variance for the first group was 25.4 and the variance for the second group was 22.2, let's compute a t score using the $\alpha = .05$ level for the test.

If we combine Formulas 11-3 and 11-7, we have the following formula for t:

> **FORMULA 11-8** *Two-sample* **t** *test for independent samples (computational formula)*
>
> $$t_{\overline{X}_1 - \overline{X}_2} = \frac{\overline{X}_1 - \overline{X}_2}{\sqrt{\left(\frac{(N_1 - 1)\hat{s}_1^2 + (N_2 - 1)\hat{s}_2^2}{N_1 + N_2 - 2}\right)\left(\frac{1}{N_1} + \frac{1}{N_2}\right)}}$$

[handwritten note: ✻ KEY FORMULA]

Notice that in the denominator of Formula 11-8, $(N_1 - 1)\hat{s}_1^2$ is SS_1 and $(N_2 - 1)\hat{s}_2^2$ is SS_2. These terms can be used to construct a more concise computational formula for the independent t combines Formulas 11-4 and 11-8:

> **FORMULA 11-9** *Two-sample* **t** *test for independent samples (alternative computational formula)*
>
> $$t_{\overline{X}_1 - \overline{X}_2} = \frac{\overline{X}_1 - \overline{X}_2}{\sqrt{\left(\frac{SS_1 + SS_2}{N_1 + N_2 - 2}\right)\left(\frac{1}{N_1} + \frac{1}{N_2}\right)}}$$

Examining Formula 11-9, we see that we need values for each of the following: $\overline{X}_1$, $\overline{X}_2$, N_1, N_2, SS_1, and SS_2. Since $SS_1 = (N_1 - 1)\hat{s}_1^2$, and $SS_2 = (N_2 - 1)\hat{s}_2^2$, $SS_1 = (10 - 1)25.4 = 228.6$. (Thus, the values we require are $\overline{X}_1 = 27.6$, $\overline{X}_2 = 22.1$, $N_1 = N_2 = 10$, $SS_1 = 228.6$, $SS_2 = 199.8$. It's time to compute t:

$$
t_{\overline{X}_1 - \overline{X}_2} = \frac{\overline{X}_1 - \overline{X}_2}{\sqrt{\left(\dfrac{SS_1 + SS_2}{N_1 + N_2 - 2}\right)\left(\dfrac{1}{N_1} + \dfrac{1}{N_2}\right)}}
$$

$$
= \frac{27.6 - 22.1}{\sqrt{\left(\dfrac{228.6 + 199.8}{10 + 10 - 2}\right)\left(\dfrac{1}{10} + \dfrac{1}{10}\right)}}
$$

$$
= \frac{5.5}{\sqrt{\left(\dfrac{428.4}{18}\right)(.2)}} = \frac{5.5}{\sqrt{4.76}} = \frac{5.5}{2.18} = 2.52.
$$

What we have found is that a difference in sample means as large as we observed ($27.6 - 22.1 = 5.5$) is 2.52 estimated standard error units away from a mean of 0. Can we reject the null hypothesis or not?

The null hypothesis is that both samples were drawn from the same population and that the mean of the sampling distribution of differences is 0. This is often symbolized by

$$H_0: \mu_1 - \mu_2 = 0 \quad \text{or} \quad H_0: \mu_1 = \mu_2.$$

To use Table B, which contains critical values of t, we need to know a value for df. For the single samples we considered in the previous chapter, $df = N - 1$. For pairs of independent samples, $df = N - 1$ for each sample, which gives us

$$(N_1 - 1) + (N_2 - 1) = N_1 + N_2 - 2,$$

which is part of the denominator of the t ratio. For the example we have been considering, $df = 10 + 10 - 2 = 18$, and the critical values of t from Table B are 2.1009 at the 5% level and 2.8784 at the 1% level. Thus, for $df = 18$, t scores of ± 2.1009 cut off the deviant 5% of the sampling distribution, and t scores of ± 2.8784 cut off the deviant 1% for a two-tailed test.

The t ratio we observed was 2.52, which is larger than the table value required for significance (for rejection of H_0) at the 5% level but is less than the value required for rejection at the 1% level. We conclude, therefore, that the probability is less than .05 of obtaining a difference in sample means as large as we observed if the samples are both drawn from the same population. In other words, there is a significant difference between the groups, and, in this study at least, imagining the correct serve does improve performance relative to just reading about it. As mentioned earlier, the correct way to report this information in a research paper is $t(18) = 2.52$, $p < .05$.

One-Tailed Versus Two-Tailed Tests

Although we mentioned one-tailed and two-tailed tests in Chapter 10, when we introduced Table B, we didn't go into much detail at that time. In fact, we suggested or implied that most tests of significance were two-tailed tests. This section should clarify the issue.

A **two-tailed test** is one that considers both ends of the distribution, whether it is the normal curve distribution, the sampling distribution of means, the sampling distribution of differences, or whatever. With a two-tailed test, we make no predictions about where our observed score will lie on the sampling distribution. That is, with the two-tailed test, a negative value of t is just as meaningful for our test as a positive t, because we are looking at both ends of the sampling distribution. In summary, then, a two-tailed test is one where we are interested in both tails of the distribution and where we are not required to make any guesses about possible outcomes before beginning the experiment.

There are some situations, however, in which we can make a prediction about the possible outcome of an experiment before conducting it. For example, suppose a researcher wants to do a study to determine the effects of marijuana on time estimation. On the basis of anecdotal evidence and previous research, the experimenter decides he can predict the direction of the experiment's outcome, and he states at the outset that he expects to find that users overestimate the passage of time. That is, if the marijuana group is the first group in the study and the control group is the second and time estimation is the dependent variable, the experimenter predicts that the first group will have a larger mean than the second. This outcome would result in a positive value for t, because the difference in sample means would be positive. Because of his prediction, the experimenter can focus on the upper half of the sampling distribution of differences, ignoring the lower half. For his significance test, the researcher can employ a one-tailed test.

The **one-tailed test** considers only one end of the sampling distribution—the end predicted by the experimenter. The researcher should have a good reason for his or her prediction, preferably a reason based on previous research, anecdotal evidence, or logic. Because only one end, or tail, of the distribution is considered, the one-tailed test is a more powerful test if the prediction comes true and the experimental result is in the desired direction. By more powerful, we mean that it will be easier for the experimenter to reject the null hypothesis. That is, the value required for significance in the table is lower for the one-tailed test than it is for the two-tailed test at the same level of significance. For example, with infinite degrees of freedom, the critical value of t at the 5% level for a two-tailed test is 1.9600. For a one-tailed test, the corresponding critical value is taken from the 10% column, following the instructions to halve the percentages for a one-tailed test. Thus, the critical value for a one-tailed test at the 5% level with infinite degrees of freedom is 1.6449.

There is a danger in using the one-tailed test, however. Remember, we must make a prediction about the outcome of the experiment *before* doing the study. What if our prediction is wrong and we observe a large difference in means in the direction *opposite* to our prediction? Because we are looking at the wrong tail with our one-tailed test, we will not be able to reject the null hypothesis; use of a two-tailed test would have permitted rejection. In other words, a one-tailed test is a more powerful test only if our prediction is accurate. For this reason and also because experimenters tend to acknowledge a rationale for the one-tailed test *after* the data are in, many statisticians argue against the use of the one-tailed test for any reason. Our position is that if we can reasonably predict the outcome's direction before data collection, then use of the more sensitive test is warranted. If we can legitimately apply a one-tailed test to our data, we halve the probability values in Table B to determine a critical value of t.

Another Example of the *t* Test for Independent Samples

Let's return to the example at the beginning of the chapter. Dr. Baxter was trying to demonstrate the effectiveness of a new form of therapy for panic disorder. Twelve clients with panic disorder received the experimental treatment and 13 received the conventional treatment. After 8 weeks, the clients' panic disorder was assessed using a standard scale of panic disorder. Here are the scores:

	Experimental				Conventional		
X_1	f	fX_1	fX_1^2	X_2	f	fX_2	fX_2^2
10	1	10	100	14	1	14	196
9	2	18	162	13	3	39	507
8	1	8	64	12	2	24	288
7	3	21	147	11	0	0	0
6	2	12	72	10	1	10	100
5	1	5	25	9	0	0	0
4	0	0	0	8	2	16	128
3	1	3	9	7	2	14	98
2	1	2	8	6	0	0	0
	$N_1 = 12$	$\Sigma fX_1 = 79$	$\Sigma fX_1^2 = 587$	5	2	10	50
					$N_2 = 13$	$\Sigma fX_2 = 127$	$\Sigma fX_2^2 = 1,367$

The first thing we should do is write Formula 11-9 and study it to see what we have to determine. We have

$$t = \frac{\overline{X}_1 - \overline{X}_2}{\sqrt{\left(\dfrac{SS_1 + SS_2}{N_1 + N_2 - 2}\right)\left(\dfrac{1}{N_1} + \dfrac{1}{N_2}\right)}}.$$

We need to know six things: N_1, N_2, $\overline{X}_1$, $\overline{X}_2$, SS_1, and SS_2. To find the means and sums of squares, we will need to use ΣfX and ΣfX^2.

The means and sums of squares are computed as follows:

- Experimental Therapy:

$$\overline{X}_1 = \frac{\Sigma f X_1}{N_1} = \frac{79}{12} = 6.58,$$

$$SS_1 = \Sigma f X_1^2 - \frac{(\Sigma f X_1)^2}{N_1} = 587 - \frac{(79)^2}{12} = 587 - 520.08 = 66.92.$$

- Conventional Therapy:

$$\overline{X}_2 = \frac{\Sigma f X_2}{N_2} = \frac{127}{13} = 9.77,$$

$$SS_2 = \Sigma f X_2^2 - \frac{(\Sigma f X_2)^2}{N_2} = 1,367 - \frac{(127)^2}{13} = 1,367 - 1,240.69 = 126.31.$$

We now have all the values we need to compute the t score:

$$t = \frac{6.58 - 9.77}{\sqrt{\left(\dfrac{66.92 + 126.31}{12 + 13 - 2}\right)\left(\dfrac{1}{12} + \dfrac{1}{13}\right)}} = \frac{-3.19}{\sqrt{\left(\dfrac{193.23}{23}\right)(.083 + .077)}}$$

$$= \frac{-3.19}{\sqrt{\left(\dfrac{193.23}{23}\right)(.16)}} = \frac{-3.19}{\sqrt{8.40(.16)}} = \frac{-3.19}{\sqrt{1.344}} = \frac{-3.19}{1.159} = -2.75,$$

with $df = N_1 + N_2 - 2 = 12 + 13 - 2 = 23$.

The negative value of t (−2.75) indicates that the mean of the first group (experimental treatment) is smaller than the mean of the second group (conventional treatment). Because we will apply a two-tailed test, we are interested in the absolute value of the t score in our comparison with critical table values. Remember that for the two-tailed test, it really doesn't matter whether the t score is positive or not; the sign simply tells us the direction of the difference in sample means.

If we had predicted at the beginning of the study that the experimentally treated clients would perform better than the conventionally treated clients, then for a one-tailed test the t score would have to be negative. Under these conditions, a positive t could never lead to rejection of H_0, no matter how large it was.

Looking in Table B for the critical values of t when $df = 23$, we see that 2.0687 is required for significance at the 5% level, and 2.7969 is required at the 1% level. Because our computed t of −2.75 is larger in absolute value than the 5% table value, we reject the null hypothesis that the two samples were drawn from the same population at the 5% level but not at the 1% level. Another way to express this rejection of H_0 is to say that the difference in means that we observed has a probability less than .05. Alternatively, we can say that the two groups differ significantly at the 5% level. That is, when we reject H_0 at the 5% level, we are in effect saying that the groups differ significantly, because the probability of their mean difference is less than .05 if both groups were really taken from the same population. Again, if you are reporting these results in a research paper, the correct format is $t(23) = -2.75$, $p < .05$. We conclude from these results that the clients receiving the experimental treatment improved more than the clients treated conventionally.

↺ CHECKING YOUR PROGRESS

A group of researchers is studying the genetics of obesity. They have a group of 20 rats that are naturally obese because of the presence of two copies of a mutant gene referred to as the "obese gene." The researchers inject half of the rats (experimental group) with a protein believed to reduce appetite and stimulate exercise (energy use). The other half receive an injection of saline solution (control group). Both groups are allowed to eat as much as they want for 4 weeks. At the end of 4 weeks, all the rats are weighed. Their weights, in grams, are as follows:

Control Group	Experimental Group
437	383
455	355
483	313
392	410
455	289
469	344
513	418
452	400
444	344
410	310

Determine whether or not the protein injection had an effect on weight.

Answer: $t(18) = 5.28$, $p < .01$. The experimental protein injections resulted in less weight gain than the saline injections.

Assumptions of the Two-Sample *t* Test

To use the sampling distribution of differences for tests of significance between sample means, two assumptions must be made. First, we must assume *normal distribution* of the dependent variable in the populations from which we drew our samples. Second, we must assume **homogeneity of variance**—that is, that population variances are the same. We assume that $\sigma_1^2 = \sigma_2^2$, where σ_1^2 and σ_2^2 are the variances of the dependent variable in the populations from which we are sampling.

Fortunately, both assumptions can apparently be violated with little effect on the conclusions made from the t test. Of the two assumptions, normal distribution is considered less important than homogeneity of variance. As long as sample sizes are fairly large, even large deviations from normality seem to make little difference in the conclusions. Because of this, if we have reason to suspect that the population distributions are badly skewed, we should use large samples in our experiments.

The assumption of homogeneity of variance is considered more important. In fact, in some texts, a test for homogeneity of variance is performed before t is computed. However, most authorities agree that such a test is not worth the effort. As long as samples of equal size are used, a relatively great departure from homogeneity will have little effect on conclusions drawn from the t test. The moral is: If in doubt about homogeneity, use samples of equal size.

COMPUTING t: DEPENDENT SAMPLES

In testing H_0, the most desired outcome is rejection of the null hypothesis. Although this seems odd to most students, the reason for it is that if we don't reject H_0, we can never be sure that it is true. It may be that we just didn't do the experiment properly—our samples may have been too small, the variability within the groups may have obscured the difference in sample means, and so on. Thus, any procedure that increases the power of the test (makes rejection of H_0 more likely) is desirable. Using dependent samples is one such procedure.

Obtaining Dependent Samples

Dependent samples might be obtained in a number of ways. For example, we could form **matched pairs** of unrelated individuals. That is, subject pairs could be selected in which behavioral or physiological characteristics relevant to the dependent variable are as closely matched as possible. Then one member of each pair would be assigned to one treatment group, and the other member to the other group. Another way to obtain matched pairs is to use people who are related either by blood or by marriage. Thus, we might select wife-husband pairs or pairs of siblings from the population and then assign the members of each pair randomly to one or the other of our pair of samples. Yet another dependent-group experiment involves **within-subject comparisons.** This is the situation in which the same individuals are subjected to each of two treatments; that is, each subject is his or her own control. Because each subject is given both treatments, this type of experiment is sometimes called a **repeated measures design.**

How does the dependent-samples design help us to reject H_0 (increase the power of the test)? It helps by reducing the variability between the samples. That is, the more similar we can make the groups before administering the independent variable, the more we reduce variability from individual differences. Using matched pairs or a repeated measures design reduces variability relative to randomly selecting subjects that we randomly assign to treatment conditions.

At the beginning of this chapter, we constructed the sampling distribution of differences by extracting pairs of random samples from a population. Further, we assumed that the pairs were independent of (unrelated to) each other. Let's look at how the sampling distribution of differences might be altered if, instead of having independent samples, we have samples that are dependent, or related to each other.

Earlier we found that the sampling distribution of differences was composed of difference scores between pairs of sample means. People who are related to each other (or are matched) are likely to be more similar to each other on a variety of measures than are unrelated individuals selected at random from the population. Of course, the similarity is even greater when each subject appears in both samples (within-subject comparison). The result of this greater similarity between related samples is that the scores that make up the sampling distribution of differences for related samples are relatively small. They will be closer to the mean of the distribution, which is 0. Thus, the scores deviate less from the mean with related samples. The major difference in the sampling distribution of differences between related samples is that the standard deviation of the distribution (the standard error of the mean differences, $\sigma_{\overline{D}}$, estimated by $\hat{s}_{\overline{D}}$) is smaller.

We won't be able to compute $\sigma_{\overline{D}}$, so let's go straight to the formula for $\hat{s}_{\overline{D}}$:

FORMULA 11-10   *Estimated standard error of the mean differences*

$$\hat{s}_{\overline{D}} = \sqrt{\hat{s}_{\overline{X}_1}^2 + \hat{s}_{\overline{X}_2}^2 - 2r\hat{s}_{\overline{X}_1 - \overline{X}_2}}\ .$$

The formula is identical to the formula for $\hat{s}_{\overline{X}_1 - \overline{X}_2}$, except for the expression $-2r\hat{s}_{\overline{X}_1}\hat{s}_{\overline{X}_2}$. Recall from Chapter 8 that the correlation coefficient r is a measure of the degree of relationship between pairs of scores in a pair of samples. What happens if the samples are independent and $r = 0$? In this case, the final expression drops out and

$$\hat{s}_{\overline{D}} = \sqrt{\hat{s}_{\overline{X}_1}^2 + \hat{s}_{\overline{X}_2}^2} = \hat{s}_{\overline{X}_1 - \overline{X}_2}\ .$$

However, with dependent samples, r is not 0, and $\hat{s}_{\overline{X}_1 - \overline{X}_2}$ is reduced by the amount of $\sqrt{2r\hat{s}_{\overline{X}_1}\hat{s}_{\overline{X}_2}}$. Thus, $\hat{s}_{\overline{D}}$ will be smaller than $\hat{s}_{\overline{X}_1 - \overline{X}_2}$.

Again, the t ratio consists of the difference between sample means divided by the estimated standard error, which in this case is $\hat{s}_{\overline{D}}$. The relatively small value of the denominator results in a relatively large value for t and makes rejection of the null hypothesis more likely. This, then, is one of the main reasons for using matched or related samples in an experiment; such samples decrease the estimated standard error and result in a larger t score.

The formula for the t test with related samples is

FORMULA 11-11 *t test for dependent samples (definitional formula)*

$$t = \frac{\overline{X}_1 - \overline{X}_2}{\hat{s}_{\overline{D}}},$$

---

where $\hat{s}_{\overline{D}} = \sqrt{\hat{s}_{\overline{X}_1}^2 + \hat{s}_{\overline{X}_2}^2 - 2r\hat{s}_{\overline{X}_1}\hat{s}_{\overline{X}_2}}$.

However, computation of the t ratio for dependent samples is quite tedious using Formula 11-11 and for this reason, we turn now to a technique known as the direct difference method.

The Direct Difference Method

To discuss the direct difference method, let's consider a specific problem. A pharmaceutical company hires a psychologist to test the effectiveness of Painfree, a new painkiller they have manufactured. The experimenter decides to test the analgesic, or pain-reducing, effect of Painfree on a pain other than headache. Volunteer subjects are asked to immerse their hands in a pail of ice water. The response measure (the dependent variable) is the length of time each subject can tolerate the immersion.

Twelve persons are selected at random; half the group receives a dose of Painfree and the other half a placebo. After a delay of 10 minutes to allow the drug to take effect, each person is asked to place the preferred hand in the water and to keep it there until the pain becomes unbearable. The next day, the subjects return to be tested again, but this time they receive a drug other than the one they were given for the first test. This procedure is called **counterbalancing** and is done to control for the possibility that order of drug presentation will affect the experimental result. A **double-blind** technique of drug presentation is employed; that is, neither the administrator nor the subject knows which drug is being given before a particular test.

The results of the experiment appear on the following page.

Subject	Painfree (Time in Seconds)	Placebo (Time in Seconds)
1	60	45
2	20	15
3	47	49
4	63	50
5	53	56
6	90	70
7	76	55
8	28	14
9	90	65
10	16	10
11	32	16
12	86	57

From this problem, we can see another advantage of the repeated measures, or within-subject, design. The number of subjects required to do the study is halved. The same study employing a matched-pairs design would require 24 subjects, 12 with each drug. Using each subject as his or her own control is obviously more efficient.

We have 12 pairs of scores. To use the direct difference method, we first subtract the second of the pair of scores from the first and call this the difference (D). All further calculations are based on the difference between each pair of scores rather than on the scores themselves.

The formulas for the t ratio for the direct difference method are

> **FORMULA 11-12 t test for dependent samples (*computational formulas*)**
>
> $$t = \frac{\overline{X}_D}{\hat{s}_{\overline{X}_D}} \qquad \text{or} \qquad t = \frac{\overline{X}_D \sqrt{N}}{\hat{s}_D}$$
>
> $$\text{because } \hat{s}_{\overline{X}_D} = \frac{\hat{s}_D}{\sqrt{N}} \text{ and } t = \frac{\overline{X}_D}{\frac{\hat{s}_D}{\sqrt{N}}} = \frac{\overline{X}_D \sqrt{N}}{\hat{s}_D}.$$

In essence, we divide the mean of the differences by the estimated standard error of the differences. The mean of the differences, or $\overline{X}_D$, is defined as the *algebraic* sum of the differences divided by the number of pairs of scores, or N. Because the sum of the differences is algebraic, we must remember to take the sign of the difference into account when summing. The estimated standard error of the differences is found by dividing the estimated standard deviation of the differences by the square root of the sample size (Formula 11-13).

> **FORMULA 11-13** *Estimated standard error of the mean difference (computational formula)*
>
> $$\hat{s}_{\overline{X}_D} = \frac{\hat{s}_D}{\sqrt{N}}.$$

Remember that N is the number of differences, which is half the total number of scores. Also, $\overline{X}_D$ is equivalent to $\overline{X}_1 - \overline{X}_2$. Computing $\overline{X}_1 - \overline{X}_2$ can be used as a check to see if $\overline{X}_D$ has been calculated correctly.

Now that the formula for t has been described, let's go back to the original problem, find the difference scores, and from them determine the mean and standard deviation of the differences. This has been done here:

Subject	Painfree (Time in Seconds)	Placebo (Time in Seconds)	Difference (D)	D^2
1	60	45	15	225
2	20	15	5	25
3	47	49	−2	4
4	63	50	13	169
5	53	56	−3	9
6	90	70	20	400
7	76	55	21	441
8	28	14	14	196
9	90	65	25	625
10	16	10	6	36
11	32	16	16	256
12	86	57	29	841
			$\Sigma D = 159$	$\Sigma D^2 = 3{,}227$

$$\overline{X}_D = \frac{\Sigma D}{N} = \frac{159}{12} = 13.25,$$

$$SS_D = \Sigma D^2 - \frac{(\Sigma D)^2}{N} = 3{,}227 - \frac{(159)^2}{12} = 3{,}227 - 2{,}106.75 = 1{,}120.25,$$

$$\hat{s}_D^2 = \frac{SS_D}{N-1} = \frac{1{,}120.25}{11} = 101.84,$$

$$\hat{s}_D - \sqrt{\hat{s}_D^2} = \sqrt{101.84} = 10.09,$$

$$\hat{s}_{\overline{X}_D} = \frac{\hat{s}_D}{\sqrt{N}} = \frac{10.09}{\sqrt{12}} = \frac{10.09}{3.46} = 2.92,$$

and finally,

$$t = \frac{\overline{X}_D}{\hat{s}_{\overline{X}_D}} = \frac{13.25}{2.92} = 4.54.$$

Alternatively,

$$t = \frac{\overline{X}_D \sqrt{N}}{\hat{s}_D} = \frac{13.25\sqrt{12}}{10.09} = \frac{45.85}{10.09} = 4.54.$$

For degrees of freedom, we know that $df = N - 1$, where N is the number of pairs of scores. In this case, $df = 12 - 1 = 11$. With $df = 11$, the values of t that cut off the deviant 5% and 1% are 2.2010 and 3.1058, respectively. Our computed t score is 4.54, which is larger than either of the critical values from Table B, or $t(11) = 4.54$, $p < .01$. Therefore, we reject the null hypothesis that both groups come from the same population. Painfree is significantly more effective than a placebo in the treatment of a pain other than headache.

Let's look at another example. Ten pairs of individuals, matched as carefully as possible in terms of age, sex, education, and IQ, have been exposed either to a sedative or to a placebo in the form of a cookie. After 30 minutes, each subject is tested on a simple task requiring the crossing out of all the letters a on a sheet of paper containing a random assortment of letters. The number of errors (letters not crossed out) made by each subject in a 2-minute test is shown here, along with the computation of a dependent t score:

Pair	Sedative	Placebo	D	D²
1	15	12	3	9
2	13	14	−1	1
3	16	13	3	9
4	22	16	6	36
5	8	7	1	1
6	13	10	3	9
7	12	14	−2	4
8	9	7	2	4
9	5	4	1	1
10	6	3	3	9
			$\Sigma D = 19$	$\Sigma D^2 = 83$

$$\overline{X}_D = \frac{\Sigma D}{N} = \frac{19}{10} = 1.9,$$

$$SS_D = \Sigma D^2 - \frac{(\Sigma D)^2}{N} = 83 - \frac{(19)^2}{10} = 46.9,$$

$$\hat{s}_D = \sqrt{\frac{SS_D}{N-1}} = \sqrt{\frac{46.9}{9}} = \sqrt{5.21} = 2.28,$$

$$\hat{s}_{\overline{X}_D} = \frac{\hat{s}_D}{\sqrt{N}} = \frac{2.28}{\sqrt{10}} = 0.72,$$

$$t = \frac{\overline{X}_D}{\hat{s}_{\overline{X}_D}} = \frac{1.9}{0.72} = 2.64,$$

with $df = N - 1 = 10 - 1 = 9$. From Table B, the critical value of t at the 5% level for $df = 9$ is 2.2622. The computed t of 2.64 is larger than the critical t, so we reject the null hypothesis. That is, $t(9) = 2.64$, $p < .05$. On the basis of this study, we can conclude that the ingestion of this sedative results in significantly more errors on the letter-crossing task.

⟲ CHECKING YOUR PROGRESS

To fulfill the requirements for a class in experimental psychology, 10 students are given a 1-minute test on a mirror-tracing task in which the knowledge they receive about their efforts comes from their mirror reflection. A comparison is made of the average time spent in accurately tracing a star with the preferred and nonpreferred hands. The results of the experiment are shown here. The experimental question is whether or not the hand used affects the accuracy of mirror tracing. Compute a t score by the direct difference method and test it for significance.

Student	Preferred Hand (Average Time in Seconds)	Nonpreferred Hand (Average Time in Seconds)
John	35	37
Vanessa	22	18
Doug	43	32
Vikram	15	17
Robin	31	25
Laura	25	29
Moira	38	31
Mike	26	29
Jack	33	33
Susan	10	5

Answer: $t = 1.37$, which for $df = 9$ is not significant ($p > .05$), or $t(9) = 1.37$, $p > .05$. Using the preferred hand did not result in superior mirror tracing relative to using the nonpreferred hand.

SUMMARY

This chapter has discussed a technique that allows us to make a comparison of the results from two independent samples and from two dependent samples. The technique is called the t test because we first convert our observed difference in sample means into a t score. The t score is an estimated version of a z score. In this chapter, the t score is a standard score on the X axis of the sampling distribution of the differences. The null hypothesis tested is that the two samples come from the same population. Thus, if the computed t score is very unlikely given the null hypothesis, we reject H_0 and conclude that the samples probably come from different populations with different means.

The computational formula for the t test based on independent (unrelated) samples is

$$t = \frac{\overline{X}_1 - \overline{X}_2}{\sqrt{\left(\dfrac{SS_1 + SS_2}{N_1 + N_2 - 2}\right)\left(\dfrac{1}{N_1} + \dfrac{1}{N_2}\right)}}, \quad \text{or} \quad t = \frac{\overline{X}_1 - \overline{X}_2}{\sqrt{\dfrac{\left((N_1 - 1)s_1^2 + (N_2 - 1)s_2^2\right)\left(\dfrac{1}{N_1} + \dfrac{1}{N_2}\right)}{N_1 + N_2 - 2}}}$$

where N_1 and N_2 are the numbers of subjects in the first and second samples, $\overline{X}_1$ and $\overline{X}_2$ are the means of the first and second samples, and SS_1 and SS_2 are the sums of squares of the first and second samples, respectively, and S_1^2 and S_2^2 are the variances of the first and second samples, respectively.

For the test of significance, the computed value of t is compared with the critical values in Table B using the appropriate degrees of freedom ($N_1 + N_2 - 2$). If t_{comp} is equal to or larger in absolute value than the critical value at the 5% level, the null hypothesis is rejected for a nondirectional test. For a directional test, the sign of the predicted t must be considered. If the predicted t is positive, then H_0 is rejected when $t_{\text{comp}} \geq t_{\text{crit}}$. If the predicted t is negative, then H_0 is rejected when $t_{\text{comp}} \leq t_{\text{crit}}$.

Experiments are often performed in which matched, or related, samples are used, because such samples increase the power of the test. That is, by reducing the size of the standard error, we increase t which makes it more likely that the null hypothesis will be rejected. Dependent samples can be constructed by matching pairs of subjects and then assigning each member of a pair to one or the other of the experimental treatments or by using each subject as her or his own control (within-subject comparison).

The direct difference method is used to compute a t score for dependent samples. The formula is

$$t = \frac{\overline{X}_D}{\hat{s}_{\overline{X}_D}} \quad \text{or} \quad t = \frac{\overline{X}_D \sqrt{N}}{\hat{s}_D},$$

where $\overline{X}_D$ is the mean of the differences, $\hat{s}_{\overline{X}_D}$ is the estimated standard error, and $\hat{s}_D$ is the estimated standard deviation of the differences. The t score obtained by the direct difference method is compared with critical values in Table B, with $df =$

$N - 1$. The rejection of H_0 for directional and nondirectional tests is determined in the same manner as for independent t tests.

We briefly discussed the difference between one-tailed and two-tailed tests of significance. If the direction of the difference in means can be predicted before the data have been collected for an experiment, then the one-tailed test is appropriate. The one-tailed test is a more powerful test than the two-tailed test, because only one tail of the sampling distribution is considered. With the two-tailed test, both ends of the distribution are considered.

Two assumptions for the two-sample t test are that the populations from which the samples are taken are normally distributed and that the population variances are homogeneous. Both assumptions may be violated with little effect on the conclusions drawn with the t test. It is often recommended that large and equal-sized samples be used if violation of the assumptions is suspected.

✳✳ Troubleshooting Your Computations

In this chapter, we have considered two methods for comparing sample means. One method was used when the samples were independent of, or unrelated to, each other, and the other method was used with related, or dependent, samples. When choosing the form of the t test to apply, be careful to select the one appropriate to your data. If you have collected data on matched pairs or you are comparing two behaviors from the same individuals, the t test for dependent samples will be the correct choice. However, if your subjects have been selected at random from a population and randomly assigned to the two groups, you will need to apply the t test for independent samples.

Because of the complexity of the computational formula for the t test for independent samples, a number of errors can be made. For example, occasionally students compute $\hat{s}_{\bar{X}_1 - \bar{X}_2}$ and report its value for t. Additionally, be sure that the value under the square root sign for $\hat{s}_{\bar{X}_1 - \bar{X}_2}$ is positive; a negative value indicates a computational error.

Don't forget about the term

$$\frac{1}{N_1} + \frac{1}{N_2}$$

in the formula for $\hat{s}_{\bar{X}_1 - \bar{X}_2}$. Some students omit it entirely by mistake. The easiest way to compute it is to first change the fractions to decimals and then add.

Be sure that the final t score you compute has the correct sign. It's easy to lose a negative sign in the last few steps, so be careful. Remember, if the mean of the first group is smaller than the mean of the second group, t will be negative.

In computing the t score for dependent samples, remember that all computations are performed on the difference scores rather than on the raw scores. Be careful as you add the difference scores algebraically; that is, remember to take the signs into account. One check on the accuracy of your computation of $\bar{X}_D$ is to compute $\bar{X}_1$ and $\bar{X}_2$ and find the difference between them. It should be $\bar{X}_D$.

Remember the decision rule: For a nondirectional test, if the absolute value of your computed t is equal to or larger than the critical value of t from Table B, reject H_0. Otherwise, fail to reject.

Also remember to consider the sign of the predicted t for a directional test. If the predicted t is positive, then H_0 is rejected when $t_{comp} \geq t_{crit}$. If the predicted t is negative, then H_0 is rejected when $t_{comp} \leq t_{crit}$.

EXERCISES

1. An experiment was performed to measure the effect of sleep deprivation on cognitive performance. Twenty college juniors were randomly selected from a group of volunteers and arbitrarily assigned either to a sleep deprivation group or to a control group. The subjects in the sleep deprivation group were kept awake for 24 hours; the members of the control group had a normal night's sleep. Participants were then asked to perform a simple mental arithmetic task, and the time it took each participant to complete the task was recorded. The results were as follows:

Sleep Deprivation Group (Time in Seconds)	Control Group (No Sleep Deprivation) (Time in Seconds)
10	13
15	8
13	14
5	11
27	8
7	7
16	2
20	2
21	17
13	5

Determine whether or not the groups differ significantly. If you reject the null hypothesis, tell what it means in the context of the problem. Give the table values required for significance.

2. The members of 13 pairs of identical twins were randomly assigned to one of two treatment conditions. One group learned a list of nonsense syllables while a tape of a speech by former President A was playing. The second group learned the same list of syllables while a tape of a speech by President B was playing. The number of presentations of the list before an errorless recital was as follows:

Twin Pair	President A	President B
1	26	23
2	13	16
3	10	6
4	24	19
5	24	25
6	25	21
7	23	25
8	20	17
9	16	17
10	13	5
11	15	10
12	19	15
13	22	20

Determine which president's speech was more distracting and whether or not the difference is significant. Tell what your result means in the context of the problem. Give table values required for significance.

3. Assume that the data in Exercise 2 was actually collected from independent samples. That is, a randomly assigned group of 13 participants heard former President A, and a different group of 13 heard President B. Perform an independent t test on the data. Which president's speech was more distracting? Compare the results of the two t tests. What are the similarities and differences?

4. In a study of modeling, one group of 20 children saw an adult acting aggressively on videotape. Another group of 20 children saw the same adult acting aggressively in real life. Later, each child was placed in a room where he or she was given the opportunity to behave aggressively toward a Bobo doll (a humanlike dummy). The researchers recorded the number of aggressive acts toward the Bobo doll by each child in a 15-minute period. Here are the results:

Real-Life Model		Video Model	
X	f	X	f
37	1	25	1
35	2	23	3
34	3	22	2
30	2	21	5
27	4	19	4
22	3	18	2
19	2	17	2
18	3	10	1

Compare the two groups in terms of the aggressiveness displayed. If you reject the null hypothesis, tell what it means in the context of the problem.

5. A group of 10 rats is first trained on a brightness discrimination task to a criterion of 9 correct responses in 10 trials. Following this, the same animals are trained on a pattern discrimination task to the same criterion. Compare the results to see if one task was easier to learn than the other. Scores shown are the number of errors made before achieving the criterion:

Rat No.	Brightness Discrimination	Pattern Discrimination
1	22	14
2	16	8
3	10	5
4	15	7
5	25	13
6	33	15
7	8	10
8	26	15
9	18	11
10	13	14

Why do you think one task was easier to learn in this study?

6. Ten people learned two lists of nonsense syllables. Both lists were of equal difficulty. Test to see whether the order of learning had an effect on the number of trials to learn. If you reject the null hypothesis, tell what it means in the context of the problem.

Person No.	List A	List B
1	13	8
2	11	12
3	15	10
4	7	4
5	10	7
6	16	14
7	4	5
8	9	5
9	9	6
10	8	9

7. In a study of the relationship between violent pornography and aggression toward women, 18 male volunteers are selected and randomly assigned to

one of two groups. One group views a violent, sexually explicit film, and the other group sees a nature film. A test to measure aggressive feelings toward women is then administered to all participants. The scores are shown here (high scores = high aggressiveness). Did viewing the film significantly increase aggressive feelings toward women? If you reject the null hypothesis, tell what it means in the context of the problem.

Nature Film	Explicit Film
4	6
5	8
7	5
9	11
6	10
4	7
2	7
3	4
5	5

8. In another study of the effect of violent, sexually explicit material on aggression, the same researchers use a within-subject design rather than independent groups (as in Exercise 7). They test the aggressiveness of 9 volunteers, expose them to a violent, sexually explicit film, and then retest their aggressiveness. The data are shown here. Did viewing the film increase aggressiveness?

Subject #	Pretest	Posttest
1	4	6
2	5	8
3	7	5
4	9	11
5	6	10
6	4	7
7	2	7
8	3	4
9	5	5

Notice that the scores for Exercise 7 are identical to the scores in this exercise. Compare the t values and conclusions you would draw in each case.

9. What are the assumptions for the two-sample t test? Why is so little space devoted to their discussion?

10. Using the definition of a z score, demonstrate that the definitional formula for a two-sample t score is just another variation on the basic formula for z.

11. A study is performed to determine how alcohol affects the brain's response to sound. Using appropriate control procedures, the researchers measure brain responses in 6 participants both before and after the subjects drink an alcoholic beverage. The results are as follows:

Person No.	Before	After
1	5.80	5.90
2	5.88	6.05
3	5.38	5.64
4	5.40	5.58
5	5.90	6.05
6	5.71	5.87

Determine whether or not alcohol ingestion affects brain response to sound.

12. Forty students are randomly assigned to two different groups. One group learns a list of nonsense syllables with high association value (each syllable elicits many associations), and the other group learns syllables with low association value. The number of repetitions before an errorless recitation of the syllables is recorded for each student. The results are shown here. Compare the groups.

High Association Value		Low Association Value	
No. of Repetitions	f	No. of Repetitions	f
23	1	35	1
21	3	33	2
20	2	31	1
19	3	28	3
18	5	25	4
16	1	22	1
15	2	21	1
14	1	20	3
10	1	18	2
8	1	17	2

If you reject the null hypothesis, tell what it means in the context of the problem.

13. An experiment is designed to test the "bystander effect"—the tendency of a person to respond to an emergency more slowly if other people are present. Thirty students from a social psychology class are equally and randomly assigned to one of two treatment conditions. In condition A, a student is asked to fill out a questionnaire in a small room by him- or herself. After 5

minutes, artificial smoke is piped under the door of the room, and the student is timed to see how long it takes him or her to respond to the "emergency." In condition B, a student is asked to fill out a questionnaire in a room in which 3 other students (confederates of the experimenter) are seated. Again, artificial smoke is piped under the door and the subject's reaction time is recorded. From the following data, compute a t score and test it for significance:

- Condition A: $N = 15, \Sigma X = 1,695, \Sigma X^2 = 250,685$
- Condition B: $N = 15, \Sigma X = 3,645, \Sigma X^2 = 975,335$

If you reject the null hypothesis, tell what it means in the context of the problem.

CHAPTER 12

One-Way Analysis of Variance

Dr. Baxter was excited about the new treatment for panic disorder she had developed (remember Dr. Baxter from Chapter 11). She hoped that her new approach would revolutionize the treatment of this disabling condition. She felt that if she could convince her colleagues of the effectiveness of this new approach, she could make a real contribution to the field.

Knowing that the first step was to get her work published, Dr. Baxter submitted a paper detailing her work to the most prestigious journal in her field. The paper included the data and statistics from her comparison of patients treated conventionally and patients receiving her experimental treatment. Her numbers clearly supported the effectiveness of the new treatment.

To her surprise, however, she received a rejection letter from the journal. The editor wrote that although the work was interesting and promising, there were fundamental flaws in the design used to evaluate the treatments. The editor encouraged Dr. Baxter to correct the problems and resubmit the paper.

In considering the problem, Dr. Baxter realized that she needed to include a group of untreated panic disorder patients to establish a baseline for comparison of the two treatment groups. As the editor had pointed out, the observed difference between Dr. Baxter's two groups might have resulted from the conventional treatment making the clients worse. If the experimental treatment simply left the patients unaffected, there would still be a group difference. In this case, the difference would mean that the new treatment was superior to the old, but it would not demonstrate that the new treatment was better than no treatment at all.

The solution for Dr. Baxter was to collect more data, this time including patients who were not treated. She needed to measure the panic disorder levels of this untreated group during the same time period she was administering treatment to the other two groups.

So Dr. Baxter once again collected data, but this time from three groups of 10 patients. When she was ready to analyze the data, she realized that using *t* tests to compare two groups at a time would require three separate analyses and unnecessary effort. She also realized that *t* tests wouldn't determine if there was an overall difference, considering all the groups simultaneously. Leafing through her statistics book, she found that the test she needed now was one called analysis of variance.

In Chapter 11, we used the *t* test to compare the results from two samples to see if they differed significantly—that is, were drawn from different populations. As you probably realize, there are often occasions when we will want to compare more than two groups at a time. The most widely used test for this purpose in behavioral science is called **analysis of variance,** or **ANOVA** (ANalysis Of VAriance). The name of the test describes what we are actually going to do: develop a way to analyze the variance in our experimental groups.

One reason for preferring ANOVA over the independent *t* test is that computing multiple *t* tests is very tedious (unless you're using a computer). To analyze the results from a study with only three groups—A, B, and C—would require at least three separate *t*-score computations. We would have to compare Groups A and B, Groups A and C, and Groups B and C. The addition of only one more group, D, would necessitate three more *t* scores: A and D, B and D, and C and D. But there's a more important reason for not doing multiple *t* tests. The more tests you do on the same data, the more likely it becomes that you will get a spurious significant difference—that is, that you will reject a true null hypothesis (commit a Type I, or α, error). Using ANOVA helps prevent such errors.

There are numerous applications of ANOVA in the social sciences. It is a technique that transcends the limits of *t* tests. However, like the *t* test, it has two versions: a between-subjects ANOVA, which parallels an independent *t*, and a repeated measures ANOVA, sometimes referred to as within-subjects ANOVA, which is similar to a dependent *t* test. In terms of experimental design, one-way ANOVA is a simple extension of the *t* test in that it examines the effect of one independent variable—thus the name *one-way ANOVA*. (We examine two-way ANOVA, which analyzes the effect of two independent variables, in Chapter 14.) However, instead of comparing only two groups, ANOVA allows for the comparison of two, three, or more groups or the same group at different points in time. For example, an educational psychologist might be interested in evaluating the effectiveness of a new teaching method. Students might be tested before receiving a new form of instruction, immediately after the instruction, and at a 6-month follow-up. Similarly, a psychopharmacologist might be interested in the effect of a new drug on depression. The depression levels of a group of patients before and at several points during treatment could be compared. Or a social psychologist might want to look at the effect of the number of witnesses on witness response in an emergency. To study the phenomenon, she could create groups consisting of one person, two people, four people, and so on, and expose each group to a simulated emergency. In all these cases, ANOVA is appropriate.

The between-subjects ANOVA, like the independent t test, assumes independent groups of participants. The repeated measures ANOVA, like the dependent t test, "repeatedly measures" the same group of participants. The same individuals receive all levels of the treatment. The same concepts of variability apply to both types of ANOVA, between-subjects and repeated measures. We begin this chapter with between-subjects ANOVA and discuss variability and other topics in this section. Later in the chapter, we introduce repeated measures ANOVA, noting that much of the discussion under between-subjects ANOVA also applies to repeated measures ANOVA.

BETWEEN-SUBJECTS ANOVA

As already mentioned, analysis of variance is a simple extension of the t test. Remember that the t test is actually a measure of distance—the distance of a group mean from a population mean or of a group mean from another group mean in standard-score terms. So a t score is basically a standard deviation, and a standard deviation is the square root of variance.

As we will show, one of the ways to compare more than two groups is to move from a statistic that is a measure of standard deviation to a statistic based on variance. Variance can be used to determine whether groups differ, but it is not limited to two groups. One of the reasons variance is not limited to two groups is that it has the property of additivity: The variance of a sum (or difference) of scores is equal to the sum of the variances of the parts, as long as the parts are independent of each other. The number of parts makes no difference. This property of additivity is expressed in Formula 12-1.

FORMULA 12-1   *Variance of a sum of scores from independent groups*

$$\sigma^2_{X_1+X_2} = \sigma^2_{X_1} + \sigma^2_{X_2}$$

Analysis of variance capitalizes on the property of additivity. We can take a set of scores and find a total variance in the entire set. Then, if we know that this total set of scores is composed of a number of subgroups corresponding to our treatment groups, we can divide this total variability into its component parts. One part would be the amount of variability in scores resulting from differences among the groups. Another part would be the inherent variability in the scores independent of the treatment—that is, within-groups variability. Finally, we can compare the relative sizes of the component parts to determine whether the variability stemming from differences among groups is large relative to the amount of inherent variability in the scores. Thus, ANOVA is a procedure that first finds a total variance, then breaks it down into its component parts and compares the parts.

Let's consider an example. Suppose a psychiatrist suspects that certain psychoactive drugs (drugs known to have an effect on behavior) may be beneficial in the treatment of phobias. To test this idea, the psychiatrist designs an experiment in which consenting patients are given one of three different substances: (1) a placebo, (2) a mild tranquilizer, or (3) a drug reported to cause mild hallucinations.

The participants in the experiment have been selected on the basis of their fear of snakes, as determined by the distance they maintain between themselves and a live snake in an aquarium. Only patients who will not approach nearer than 10 feet in a preliminary test are used in the study.

In the experiment, each participant is given a capsule containing one of the three substances. Ten minutes later, each participant is tested a second time for approach to the feared object. The distance from the participant to the aquarium in the second test is the dependent variable. Here are the data:

Group 1	Group 2	Group 3
10	6	11
8	5	12
9	4	10
7	2	10
5	1	9
3	0	8
$\Sigma X = 42$	$\Sigma X = 18$	$\Sigma X = 60$

The group means are as follows:

- Group 1 $\quad \overline{X}_1 = \dfrac{\Sigma X}{N} = \dfrac{42}{6} = 7$

- Group 2 $\quad \overline{X}_2 = \dfrac{18}{6} = 3$

- Group 3 $\quad \overline{X}_3 = \dfrac{60}{6} = 10$

The total mean is $(42 + 18 + 60)/18 = 120/18 = 6.67$.

Remember that we are interested in analyzing the variance in this chapter. What are the sources of variance in the data?

To begin, we can see that each of the 18 scores differs from the total, or overall, mean of 6.67. This source of variability is called the **total variability** and is related to the deviation of each score (X) from the total mean ($\overline{X}_{tot}$), or

$$X - \overline{X}_{tot}.$$

Further, the total variability has two components. One component is the variability within each group, or the **within-groups variability.** For example, in Group 1, the mean is 7, but only one participant actually had this score; the rest of the group members deviated from the mean. We first encountered variability within a group in Chapter 6, where we learned that it is based on the deviation between each score in a group and the group's mean. This deviation is symbolized by

$$X_g - \bar{X}_g,$$

where X_g is a score within a group and $\bar{X}_g$ is the mean of the group.

What is the origin of the variability within groups? If each member of a group has the same treatment, why is there a difference between the scores? Basically, there are two sources of the variability: individual differences and experimental error.

Each of our experimental participants is a unique individual, with particular abilities, motives, background, and so forth. Thus, each individual is different from the others and is likely to act differently in response to the experimental treatment. This is what is meant by **individual differences.**

Experimental error may also contribute to the differences in scores within a group. By **experimental error,** we mean such things as imprecise measuring equipment, momentary changes in experimenter and participant attention, and slight changes in background conditions during data collection (fluctuations in temperature, lighting, sound level, etc.). Because of individual differences and experimental error, it is highly unlikely that all participants within a treatment will have the same score.

In addition to the variability within each group, there is also variability between groups, or **between-groups variability.** Because the total mean ($\bar{X}_{tot}$) is 6.67, you can see that each of the group means (7, 3, 10) deviates from it. The variability between groups is based on the deviation of each group mean from the total mean:

$$\bar{X}_g - \bar{X}_{tot}.$$

Why do the group means differ from the total mean? Why is there variability between groups? This time there are three potential sources of variability: individual differences, experimental error, and treatment effects.

Because our treatment groups contain different individuals, individual differences can be expected to play a role in the variability between groups as well as within them. Similarly, experimental error acts across groups as well as within them to produce differing scores and differing group means. **Treatment effect** is the third potential source of variability between groups. That is, we have applied different treatments to each of our groups in the hope that the manipulations will produce behavioral changes. For example, if the mean of Group 2 differs from the mean of Group 1, it may be because the tranquilizer's active ingredient affects performance on the behavioral avoidance test.

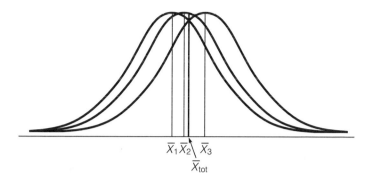

FIGURE 12-1 Graph showing the degree of overlap of three samples drawn from the same population.

In summary, the total variability contained in two or more groups is the sum of the variability between groups and the variability within each group. The test of significance based on the analysis of variance considers which of the two components of variability (between or within) contributes most to the total variability.

Suppose we have selected three large samples from the *same* population. The distribution of scores based on measurement of some behavioral characteristic might resemble the graph in Figure 12-1. From a study of the graph, note that the variability between groups based on the deviation of each group mean from the total mean is small relative to the variability within each group. That is, there is a lot of spread of scores around each group mean, and the difference between each $\overline{X}_g$ and $\overline{X}_{tot}$ is small.

But what about the situation where one or more of the samples is taken from *different* populations? Assuming that the variability within each group is the same as before, the variability between groups will be large relative to the within-groups variability. A hypothetical situation is shown in Figure 12-2.

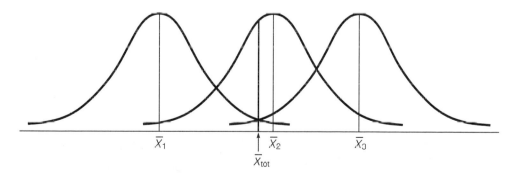

FIGURE 12-2 Graph illustrating the large amount of variability between groups when one or more of the groups come from different populations.

The significance test assesses the relative contribution of the two components of variability, assuming that the samples come from the same population. If this assumption is true, then the ratio of the variability between groups to the variability within groups (the *F* ratio) will be relatively small. Why is this? If we assume that the samples come from the same population, we are assuming that the different treatments are without effect; that is, there is no treatment effect. If this is the case, then the sources of variability within and between groups—individual differences and experimental error—are identical. Hence, the *F* ratio will have a value close to 1.00.

However, if the assumption is not true, then the *F* ratio will be relatively large because of the added source of variability (treatment effect) contributing to the between-groups differences. In this case, we will conclude that the samples come from different populations. The question at this point is, How do we measure the variability?

Measuring Variability: The Sum of Squares

The main component of the measure of variability is the *sum of squares*, which we introduced in Chapter 6. At that time, we said that the numerator of the formula for the sample variance was sometimes called the sum of squares. We will need to compute three sums of squares: total, within groups, and between groups.

The **total sum of squares** (SS_{tot}) is the sum of the squared deviation of each score from the total mean, or

> **FORMULA 12-2**   *Total sum of squares (definitional formula)*
>
> $$SS_{tot} = \Sigma(X - \bar{X}_{tot})^2.$$

Note the similarity between this formula and Formula 6-10.

We also said that the variability within each group is based on the deviation between each score in a group and the mean of the group. Thus, the *sum of squares within each group* (SS_w) is the sum of the squared deviations of each score in a group from its group mean, and the deviations are summed across groups. The definitional formula is

> **FORMULA 12-3**   *Within-groups sum of squares (definitional formula)*
>
> $$SS_w = \sum_g (X_g - \bar{X}_g)^2.$$

The little g under the large sigma means that the deviations are summed across groups.

Finally, we have the *sum of squares between groups* (SS_b), based on the deviation between each group mean and the total mean. The definitional formula is

> **FORMULA 12-4**   *Between-groups sum of squares (definitional formula)*
>
> $$SS_b = \sum_g N_g (\overline{X}_g - \overline{X}_{tot})^2.$$

The definitional formula for SS_b says to square the deviation between each group mean and the total mean [$(\overline{X}_g - \overline{X}_{tot})^2$], to multiply by the number of subjects in a particular group (N_g), and to sum over groups (Σ_g).

As usual, we will not use the definitional formulas to compute the sums of squares. Instead, we will use computational, or raw-score, formulas. To begin, the equation for the total sum of squares is

> **FORMULA 12-5**   *Total sum of squares (computational formula)*
>
> $$SS_{tot} = \Sigma X^2 - \frac{(\Sigma X)^2}{N}.$$

If Formula 12-5 looks familiar, it is because it is the sum of squares. To compute the total sum of squares, we first square each score and then add all the squared scores together (ΣX^2). Next we add all the scores, square the sum, and divide by N, or the total number of scores. Subtracting the last value from the first gives us SS_{tot}.

The computational formula for the within-groups sum of squares is

> **FORMULA 12-6**   *Within-groups sum of squares (computational formula)*
>
> $$SS_w = \sum_g \left[\Sigma X_g^2 - \frac{(\Sigma X_g)^2}{N_g} \right].$$

Look carefully at Formula 12-6 and you will see that it is almost the same as the formula for the total sum of squares. The difference is that the computations are performed for each group separately and then summed across groups instead of being done on *all* the scores. The formula tells us to sum the squared scores within each group (ΣX_g^2), to subtract from the total the sum of the scores within a group squared and divided by the number of subjects within the group [$(\Sigma X_g)^2 / N_g$], and to sum the totals for each group.

The computational formula for finding the between-groups sum of squares is

FORMULA 12-7 *Between-groups sum of squares (computational formula)*

$$SS_b = \sum_g \left[\frac{(\Sigma X_g)^2}{N_g} \right] - \frac{(\Sigma X)^2}{N}.$$

The formula tells us first to sum the scores within a group, square the sum, and divide by the number within the group $[(\Sigma X_g)^2/N_g]$. Next, we sum the totals across groups (Σ_g). From this total we subtract the sum of all the scores squared divided by the total number of scores $[(\Sigma X)^2/N]$.

Computing the Sums of Squares

Even with the computational formulas, computing the sums of squares is quite tedious. However, there is one thing we can do to simplify the task considerably. The secret is to compute the sum of the scores in each of the groups (ΣX_g), then compute the sum of the squared scores in each group (ΣX_g^2), and finally note the number of subjects in each group (N_g). From these values we can easily determine the sum of all the scores (ΣX), the sum of all the squared scores (ΣX^2), and the total N. Let's go back to our example about snake phobias and compute the sums of squares:

Group 1	Group 2	Group 3
10	6	11
8	5	12
9	4	10
7	2	10
5	1	9
3	0	8

	ΣX_g	ΣX_g^2	N_g
Group 1 (X_1)	42	328	6
Group 2 (X_2)	18	82	6
Group 3 (X_3)	60	610	6
Totals	$\Sigma X = 120$	$\Sigma X^2 = 1{,}020$	$N = 18$

We have computed the sum of the scores for each group, and this is shown below the heading ΣX_g. For example, the sum of X_1 is found by adding $10 + 8 + \cdots + 3 = 42$. Similarly, $\Sigma X_2 = 18$ and $\Sigma X_3 = 60$.

To find the sum of the squared scores in each group, we square each of the scores in the group and add. For example, ΣX_1^2 is obtained by adding $10^2 + 8^2 + \cdots + 3^2 = 328$. Also, $\Sigma X_2^2 = 82$ and $\Sigma X_3^2 = 610$.

The totals are found by adding each column in the summary table; ΣX is found by summing $\Sigma X_1 + \Sigma X_2 + \Sigma X_3 - 42 + 18 + 60 = 120$. Similarly, ΣX^2 is found by adding the sums of the squared scores: $328 + 82 + 610 = 1,020$. The number of subjects in each group is 6, and the total N is 18. We are now ready to compute the sums of squares:

$$SS_{tot} = \Sigma X^2 - \frac{(\Sigma X)^2}{N}$$

$$= 1,020 - \frac{(120)^2}{18} = 1,020 - \frac{14,400}{18}$$

$$= 1,020 - 800 = 220,$$

$$SS_b = \sum_g \left[\frac{(\Sigma X_g)^2}{N_g} \right] - \frac{(\Sigma X)^2}{N} = \left[\frac{(\Sigma X_1)^2}{N_1} + \frac{(\Sigma X_2)^2}{N_2} + \frac{(\Sigma X_3)^2}{N_3} \right] - \frac{(\Sigma X)^2}{N}$$

$$= \left(\frac{42^2}{6} + \frac{18^2}{6} + \frac{60^2}{6} \right) - \frac{120^2}{18}$$

$$= \left(\frac{1,764}{6} + \frac{324}{6} + \frac{3,600}{6} \right) - \frac{14,400}{18}$$

$$= (294 + 54 + 600) - 800$$

$$= 948 - 800 = 148,$$

$$SS_w = \sum_g \left[\Sigma X_g^2 - \frac{(\Sigma X_g)^2}{N_g} \right]$$

$$= \left[\Sigma X_1^2 - \frac{(\Sigma X_1)^2}{N_1} \right] + \left[\Sigma X_2^2 - \frac{(\Sigma X_2)^2}{N_2} \right] + \left[\Sigma X_3^2 - \frac{(\Sigma X_3)^2}{N_3} \right]$$

$$= \left(328 - \frac{42^2}{6} \right) + \left(82 - \frac{18^2}{6} \right) + \left(610 - \frac{60^2}{6} \right)$$

$$= \left(328 - \frac{1,764}{6} \right) + \left(82 - \frac{324}{6} \right) + \left(610 - \frac{3,600}{6} \right)$$

$$= (328 - 294) + (82 - 54) + (610 - 600)$$

$$= 34 + 28 + 10 = 72.$$

We have now determined the total sum of squares (220), the between-groups sum of squares (148), and the within-groups sum of squares (72). To check our computations, we can see if the between-groups and within-groups sums total SS_{tot}. And they do: $148 + 72 = 220$.

Although the sums of squares computations appear quite tedious, the amount of work is considerably lessened with the aid of the memory function on a pocket calculator. Try several of these computations for practice. You will find that they take less and less time the more you do them.

There is another approach to the computations that shortens the process considerably. Remember additivity? In the one-way between-groups ANOVA we have been illustrating, there are two components in the total sum of squares: between-groups sum of squares and within-groups sum of squares. Once we have calculated the SS_{tot} and one of the components (SS_b or SS_w), we can find the other component by subtraction. Thus, $SS_w = SS_{tot} - SS_b$ and $SS_b = SS_{tot} - SS_w$. This procedure does not provide the built-in check of our calculations that computing each source of variance separately provides. However, it is much faster.

Now that we have the sums of squares, what do we do with them? The formulas for the sums of squares are very similar to the numerator of the formula for sample variance. We now need to define the denominator for each of the sums of squares so that we can compute a variance. It will simplify proceedings at this point if we introduce the analysis of variance *summary table*.

The Analysis of Variance Summary Table

The **ANOVA summary table** is a convenient place to summarize the values we have calculated and those we still need to determine. The table takes the following form:

ANOVA Summary Table

Source	SS	df	MS	F
Between groups				
Within groups				
Total				

Examination of the summary table reveals some items we have not yet discussed. First, note that there are places for the sums of squares (between groups, within groups, and total). Next, we see places for degrees of freedom, or *df*, which we have not identified for ANOVA. The *df* column is followed by a column labeled *MS*, the abbreviation for mean square, which will be discussed in the next paragraph. Finally, there is a heading at the end of the table labeled *F*. Under *F* we put the number indicating the relative contribution of the two sources of variability. The size of *F* determines whether or not we conclude that the samples were drawn from the same population.

The **mean square** (*MS*) is really the variance we want to analyze. It is determined by dividing the sums of squares by the appropriate degrees of freedom. All we need to do, then, is determine *df*, and *MS* will be easy to compute.

The between-groups *df* is equal to $K - 1$, where K is the number of groups we are comparing. For our specific example, $df_b = 2$, because we are comparing 3 groups and $K - 1 = 3 - 1 = 2$. The within-groups *df* equals $N - K$, which for our example is $18 - 3 = 15$. Finally, the total *df* equals $N - 1$, or $18 - 1 = 17$. Here again, the total is equal to the sum of the parts, just as it was for the sum of squares. Thus,

$$df_{\text{tot}} = df_b + df_w,$$

or

$$N - 1 = (K - 1) + (N - K),$$
$$N - 1 - N - 1 + K \quad K,$$
$$N - 1 = N - 1.$$

Summarizing the formulas for *df*, we have the following:

> **FORMULA 12-8** *Between-groups degrees of freedom*
>
> $$df_h = K - 1,$$

> **FORMULA 12-9** *Within-groups degrees of freedom*
>
> $$df_w = N - K,$$

> **FORMULA 12-10** *Total degrees of freedom*
>
> $$df_{\text{tot}} = N - 1.$$

As already noted, the mean squares are found by dividing the sums of squares by the appropriate degrees of freedom. Thus, we have the following formulas:

> **FORMULA 12-11** *Between-groups mean square*
>
> $$MS_b = \frac{SS_b}{df_b},$$

> **FORMULA 12-12**   *Within-groups mean square*
>
> $$MS_w = \frac{SS_w}{df_w}.$$

The final term we need for the summary table is F, which is the ratio of MS_b to MS_w (the **F ratio**):

> **FORMULA 12-13**   **F** *ratio*
>
> $$F = \frac{MS_b}{MS_w}.$$

Here is the completed summary table for the problem we have been considering:

ANOVA Summary Table

Source	SS	df	MS	F
Between groups	148	$K - 1 = 2$	$\dfrac{SS_b}{df_b} = \dfrac{148}{2} = 74$	$F = \dfrac{MS_b}{MS_w}$
Within groups	72	$N - K = 15$	$\dfrac{SS_w}{df_w} = \dfrac{72}{15} = 4.8$	$= \dfrac{74}{4.8}$
Total	220	$N - 1 = 17$		$= 15.42$

At the end of the summary table, the F ratio has been computed; for our example, it is 15.42. What does this mean? Were the groups drawn from different populations or did they come from the same population? As noted earlier, if the groups are actually drawn from the same population, then there should not be very much difference between the group means; that is, there should be a small treatment effect. With little treatment effect contributing to the variability between groups, the F ratio will be close to 1.00. However, our computed F ratio is obviously much larger than 1.00.

As in the two previous chapters, our significance test will require a comparison of the computed statistic with critical values found in a table. Table E in Appendix 4 contains critical values of F based on the F distribution. The F distribution is a family of curves whose shapes depend on both sample sizes and the number of samples being compared. Instead of being symmetrical, like t distributions, F distributions are positively skewed with a peak around 1.00.

A portion of Table E is shown in Table 12-1. The critical values in the table are F ratios cutting off either the upper 5% or the upper 1% of a particular F distribu-

TABLE 12-1

A Portion of Table E Showing Critical Values of F

df Associated with the Denominator (*df*$_w$)		*df* Associated with the Numerator (*df*$_b$)								
		1	2	3	4	5	6	7	8	9
1	5%	161	200	216	225	230	234	238	239	241
	1%	4052	5000	5403	5625	5764	5859	5928	5981	6022
2	5%	18.5	19.0	19.2	19.2	19.3	19.3	19.4	19.4	19.4
	1%	98.5	99.0	99.2	99.2	99.3	99.3	99.4	99.4	99.4
3	5%	10.1	9.55	9.28	9.12	9.01	8.97	8.89	8.85	8.81
	1%	34.1	30.8	29.5	28.7	28.2	27.9	27.7	27.5	27.3
4	5%	7.71	6.94	6.59	6.39	6.26	6.16	6.09	6.04	6.00
	1%	21.2	18.0	16.7	16.0	15.5	15.2	15.0	14.8	14.7
5	5%	6.61	5.79	5.41	5.19	5.05	4.95	4.88	4.82	4.77
	1%	16.3	13.3	12.1	11.4	11.0	10.7	10.5	10.3	10.2
6	5%	5.99	5.14	4.76	4.53	4.39	4.28	4.21	4.15	4.10
	1%	13.7	10.9	9.78	9.15	8.75	8.47	8.26	8.10	7.98
7	5%	5.59	4.74	4.35	4.12	3.97	3.87	3.79	3.73	3.68
	1%	12.2	9.55	8.45	7.85	7.46	7.19	6.99	6.84	6.72
8	5%	5.32	4.46	4.07	3.84	3.69	3.58	3.50	3.44	3.39
	1%	11.3	8.65	7.59	7.01	6.63	6.37	6.18	6.03	5.91
9	5%	5.12	4.26	3.86	3.63	3.48	3.37	3.29	3.23	3.18
	1%	10.6	8.02	6.99	6.42	6.06	5.80	5.61	5.47	5.35
10	5%	4.96	4.10	3.71	3.48	3.33	3.22	3.14	3.07	3.02
	1%	10.0	7.56	6.55	5.99	5.64	5.39	5.20	5.06	4.94
11	5%	4.84	3.98	3.59	3.36	3.20	3.09	3.01	2.95	2.90
	1%	9.65	7.21	6.22	5.67	5.32	5.07	4.89	4.74	4.63
12	5%	4.75	3.89	3.49	3.26	3.11	3.00	2.91	2.85	2.80
	1%	9.33	6.93	5.95	5.41	5.06	4.82	4.64	4.50	4.39
13	5%	4.67	3.81	3.41	3.18	3.03	2.92	2.83	2.77	2.71
	1%	9.07	6.70	5.74	5.21	4.86	4.62	4.44	4.30	4.19
14	5%	4.60	3.74	3.34	3.11	2.96	2.85	2.76	2.70	2.65
	1%	8.86	6.51	5.56	5.04	4.70	4.46	4.28	4.14	4.03
15	5%	4.54	3.68	3.29	3.06	2.90	2.79	2.71	2.64	2.59
	1%	8.68	6.36	5.42	4.89	4.56	4.32	4.14	4.00	3.89

Note. The entire table may be found in Appendix 4. From "Tables of Percentage Points of the Inverted Beta (*F*) Distribution," by M. Merrington & C. M. Thompson, 1943, *Biometrika, 33*, pp. 73–88. Reprinted with permission of the Biometrika Trustees.

tion. If our computed *F* ratio equals or exceeds an appropriate critical value, we will reject the null hypothesis.

Under the table's title is the heading "*df* Associated with the Numerator (*df*$_b$)"; below this are the numbers 1 through 9 in a row. To the left is a column of numbers from 1 to 15 (in the appendix there are additional numbers, up to 120). The heading over this column is "*df* Associated with the Denominator (df_w)." The terms *numerator* and *denominator* refer to relevant portions of the *F* ratio. The numerator of the *F* ratio is MS_b, and its *df* is df_b. The denominator of the *F* ratio is MS_w, whose *df* is df_w.

For the problem we have been considering, $df = 2$ for the numerator and $df = 15$ for the denominator. Thus, to find the critical values for the test of our computed *F* ratio, we read down the row of numbers in the left margin of the table until we come to 15, and then across the columns of numbers to the column headed by 2. The critical values are 3.68 at the 5% level and 6.36 at the 1% level. Because our computed *F* of 15.42 is larger than either of the two critical values, we reject the null hypothesis that the groups came from the same population; $F(2, 15) = 15.42, p < .01$. Based on this fictitious study, we conclude that the drugs tested had an effect on the behavioral avoidance test in the phobic patients.

The *F* test does not tell us which of the possible group comparisons is actually significant. All we know at this point is that there are significant differences somewhere in the data we have analyzed. We might perform *t* tests on the groups that we feel, from looking at the means, might be significantly different. However, remember that ANOVA was introduced as an alternative to multiple *t* tests. Fortunately, there are several **post-ANOVA tests**—tests that follow the analysis of variance—that we can use to analyze the data further. Some examples are the Scheffé test, the Tukey HSD test, the Fisher LSD test, the Newman–Keuls test, and the Duncan test. We will consider the HSD and LSD tests in the next chapter.

Another Between-Subjects ANOVA Example

Let's perform the ANOVA for the example about treatments for panic disorder at the beginning of the chapter. The data are as follows:

Experimental	Conventional	Untreated
10	14	16
9	13	14
6	12	10
5	7	10
11	12	6
2	7	13
7	13	9
3	8	17
9	5	15
7	13	11
80	100	120

Box 12-1	Summary of the Procedure for Calculating F

1. For each separate group, determine the number of subjects or observations in the group (N_g). Then add all the scores in the group (ΣX_g). Finally, square each of the scores and add the squared scores in the group (ΣX_g^2).

2. Use the values calculated in step 1 to determine N, the sum of all N_g's; ΣX, the sum of all ΣX_gs; and ΣX^2, the sum of all ΣX_g^2s.

3. Use Formula 12-5 to compute SS_{tot}.

4. Use Formula 12-6 to compute SS_w.

5. Use Formula 12-7 to compute SS_b; alternatively SS_b or SS_w may be determined by subtraction once SS_{tot} and one or the other of the components has been computed. That is, $SS_b = SS_{tot} - SS_w$ and $SS_w = SS_{tot} - SS_b$.

6. After the sums of squares have been determined, construct and fill in the ANOVA summary table.

ANOVA Summary Table

Source	SS	df	MS	F
Between groups		$K-1$	$\dfrac{SS_b}{df_b}$	$F = \dfrac{MS_b}{MS_w}$
Within groups		$N-K$	$\dfrac{SS_w}{df_w}$	
Total		$N-1$		

7. Once the summary table is properly completed, compare the computed value of F, symbolized by F_{comp}, with critical values of F, symbolized by F_{crit}, from Table E for the appropriate degrees of freedom. The degrees of freedom for the F test are the degrees of freedom associated with the numerator of the F ratio (df_b) and the degrees of freedom associated with the denominator (df_w). If the computed F is larger than the critical value at the 5% level (1% if you need to be more conservative), reject the null hypothesis and conclude that the samples were drawn from different populations. A significant F ratio indicates that one or more of the groups came from different populations, but it doesn't tell you which. Further testing is needed to determine exactly where the significant differences lie.

First of all, we need to determine the sum of the scores in each group, the sum of the squared scores in each group, the total sum of scores, and the total sum of squared scores. We will also note the number of subjects per group and total N. This has been done in the following chart, but check the computations:

	ΣX_g	ΣX_g^2	N_g
Experimental	80	690	10
Conventional	100	1,082	10
Untreated	120	1,540	10
Totals	$\Sigma X = 300$	$\Sigma X^2 = 3,312$	$N = 30$

It's time to compute the sums of squares:

$$SS_{tot} = \Sigma X^2 - \frac{(\Sigma X)^2}{N} = 3,312 - \frac{(300)^2}{30}$$
$$= 3,312 - 3,000 = 312,$$

$$SS_w = \sum_g \left[\Sigma X_g^2 - \frac{(\Sigma X_g)^2}{N_g} \right] = \left(690 - \frac{80^2}{10} \right) + \left(1,082 - \frac{100^2}{10} \right) + \left(1,540 - \frac{120^2}{10} \right)$$
$$= (690 - 640) + (1,082 - 1,000) + (1,540 - 1,440)$$
$$= 50 + 82 + 100 = 232,$$

$$SS_b = \sum_g \left[\frac{(\Sigma X_g)^2}{N_g} \right] - \frac{(\Sigma X)^2}{N} = \left(\frac{80^2}{10} + \frac{100^2}{10} + \frac{120^2}{10} \right) - \frac{300^2}{30}$$
$$= (640 + 1,000 + 1,440) - 3,000$$
$$= 3,080 - 3,000 = 80.$$

Now that the sums of squares have been computed, let's fill in the ANOVA summary table:

ANOVA Summary Table

Source	SS	df	MS	F
Between groups	80.0	2	40.0	4.66
Within groups	232.0	27	8.59	
Total	312.0	29		

Here are our computations:

$$df_b = K - 1 = 3 - 1 = 2,$$

$$df_w = N - K = 30 - 3 = 27,$$

$$df_{tot} = N - 1 = 30 - 1 = 29,$$

$$MS_b = \frac{SS_b}{df_b} = \frac{80.0}{2} = 40.0,$$

$$MS_w = \frac{SS_w}{df_w} = \frac{232.0}{27} = 8.59,$$

$$F = \frac{MS_b}{MS_w} = \frac{40.0}{8.59} = 4.66.$$

The final result is $F = 4.66$ with $df = 2, 27$. According to Table E, the critical values for 2 and 27 df are 3.35 at the 5% level and 5.49 at the 1% level. Because the computed F is larger than the critical value at the 5% level, we reject the null hypothesis that the samples came from the same population and conclude that the treatments varied in their effectiveness; $F(2, 27) = 4.66$, $p < .05$. Further analysis of these data must await the discussion in the next chapter.

ᕫ CHECKING YOUR PROGRESS

Suppose we are interested in nonsense syllable learning. We select three groups of participants, each of which learns a list of nonsense syllables under different conditions. The first group learns the list in a normally lighted room; the second group learns the list in a darkened room lit only by a small lamp placed near the memory drum (a rotating device with a small window where each nonsense syllable appears briefly); the third group learns the list in a room with flashing lights. We record the number of repetitions of the list each participant requires before he or she has an errorless repetition. We intended to have the same N in each group, but one of the participants was unable to complete training and her data were discarded. The data are as follows:

Group X_1 (Normal Room)	Group X_2 (Dark Room)	Group X_3 (Flashing Lights)
5	3	10
7	4	11
6	5	20
10	10	13
15	7	10
11	6	8
8	2	7
7	4	12
	5	12

Compute F and test it for significance.

Answer: $F = 9.02$, which for 2 and 23 df is significant ($p < .01$); $F(2, 23) = 9.02$, $p < .01$. One or more of the groups came from different populations.

REPEATED MEASURES ANOVA

The analysis of variance situation just discussed uses independent groups of participants at each level of the treatment. That is, the scores in each treatment group are based on different participants. This between-subjects ANOVA design extends the independent t test, which also uses independent groups.

As discussed in Chapter 11, there are also instances in which the same participants are tested repeatedly. If there are only two occasions for measurement, the appropriate analysis is the dependent t test. However, investigators often wish to measure the same participants on more than two occasions, most commonly in studies designed to examine the effectiveness of programs or interventions. These studies might, for example, include a pretest, a test administered after some period of treatment, another test administered at the end of treatment, and perhaps one or more follow-up tests. The advantage of a repeated measures (or within-subjects) design is that it allows us not only to follow the same people to determine if a particular treatment is effective but also to see if the treatment effect persists.

Recall from Chapter 11 that one of the main advantages of the dependent t test is that it reduces the error variability in the scores. Each participant is used as his or her own control (baseline). In other words, for the same scores, the denominator of a dependent t test is smaller than it is for an independent t test. However, the numerator is identical, so the reduction in the size of the denominator makes it more likely that the statistic will be significant. The same situation holds in one-way repeated measures ANOVA. By using each person as his or her own control, we are able to extract some of the variability from our scores.

Earlier in this chapter, we discussed the within-groups sum of squares (SS_w). We indicated that there are two sources of variability that contribute to SS_w: experimental error (SS_{error}) and the inherent variability in subjects (SS_{subj}). Thus, we can represent SS_w as being composed of SS_{subj} and SS_{error}:

> **FORMULA 12-14** *Within-groups sum of squares in one-way repeated measures ANOVA (definitional formula)*
>
> $$SS_w = SS_{subj} + SS_{error}.$$

The one-way repeated measures ANOVA allows us to remove the variance caused by variability in subjects. That is, we can estimate SS caused by individual differences and remove it from SS_w. We are left with SS caused by experimental error. It is this SS_{error} that we will use as the denominator in computing our F value.

Note that once again, the principle of additivity applies. We are simply breaking SS_{tot} into its component parts. For a one-way repeated measures ANOVA, this involves estimating one more component than we found in the one-way between-subjects ANOVA. The formula is

> **FORMULA 12-15** *Total sum of squares in one-way repeated measures ANOVA (definitional formula)*
>
> $$SS_{tot} = SS_b + SS_{subj} + SS_{error}.$$

A sample problem will help illustrate the steps involved in the one-way repeated measures analysis of variance. Suppose we are interested in the effect of practice on the ability to solve algebra problems. First we test 6 participants in algebra performance before practice, recording the number of problems they solve correctly out of 10 problems. We then provide the participants with practice on algebra problems and retest their performance. We want to know whether the effects of practice persist, so we retest our participants after 1 day and again after 1 week following the practice session. Here are their scores:

	Pretest	Retest	1 Day After	1 Week After
Sarah	2	4	4	5
Marcus	4	7	6	6
Courtney	3	5	8	9
Ari	6	8	9	7
Joy	1	3	5	6
Margaret	5	6	7	3

In the first steps of the problem, we proceed exactly as in one-way between-subjects ANOVA. We calculate SS_{tot} and SS_b as before:

	ΣX_g	ΣX_g^2	N_g
Pretest (X_1)	21	91	6
Retest (X_2)	33	199	6
1 Day After (X_3)	39	271	6
1 Week After (X_4)	36	236	6
Totals	$\Sigma X = 129$	$\Sigma X^2 = 797$	$N = 24$

$$SS_{tot} = \Sigma X^2 - \frac{(\Sigma X)^2}{N} = 797 - \frac{(129)^2}{24} = 797 - 693.75 = 103.25,$$

$$SS_b = \sum_g \left[\frac{(\Sigma X_g)^2}{N_g} \right] - \frac{(\Sigma X)^2}{N} = \left(\frac{21^2}{6} + \frac{33^2}{6} + \frac{39^2}{6} + \frac{36^2}{6} \right) - \frac{129^2}{24}$$

$$= 724.5 - 693.75 = 30.75.$$

But now we have an additional step: We must compute SS_{subj}. To do this, we first find a total for each subject. It is helpful to construct a table, such as the one for treatments. In a sense, subjects are dealt with as another treatment factor. Notice the similarity in the formulas for obtaining SS_{subj} and SS_b:

FORMULA 12-16   *Within-subjects sum of squares in one-way repeated measures ANOVA (computational formula)*

$$SS_{subj} = \sum_s \left[\frac{(\Sigma X_m)^2}{T} \right] - \frac{(\Sigma X)^2}{N},$$

where T = number of treatments and m refers to each subject. Here are our data and the computations:

	ΣX_m	T
Sarah	15	4
Marcus	23	4
Courtney	25	4
Ari	30	4
Joy	15	4
Margaret	21	4
Totals	$\Sigma X = 129$	$N = 24$

$$SS_{subj} = \sum_s \left[\frac{(\Sigma X_m)^2}{T_m} \right] - \frac{(\Sigma X)^2}{N} = \left(\frac{15^2}{4} + \frac{23^2}{4} + \frac{25^2}{4} + \frac{30^2}{4} + \frac{15^2}{4} + \frac{21^2}{4} \right) - \frac{129^2}{24}$$

$$= (56.25 + 132.25 + 156.25 + 225 + 56.25 + 110.25) - 693.75$$

$$= 736.25 - 693.75 = 42.5.$$

Once we have found SS_{subj}, we can determine SS_{error} by subtraction:

FORMULA 12-17   *Error sum of squares in one-way repeated measures ANOVA (computational formula)*

$$SS_{error} = SS_{tot} - SS_b - SS_{subj}.$$

For our data, $SS_{error} = SS_{tot} - SS_b - SS_{subj} = 103.25 - 30.75 - 42.5 = 30.0$.

The last step is to construct a summary table. It is similar to the summary table for the one-way between-subjects ANOVA except that our SS_{tot} is composed of three parts instead of two. First we fill in the appropriate SS for each of the sources:

ANOVA Summary Table

Source	SS	df	MS	F
Between groups	30.75	$K - 1 = 3$	$\dfrac{SS_b}{df_b} = \dfrac{30.75}{3} = 10.25$	$F = \dfrac{MS_b}{MS_{error}}$
Subjects	42.50	$S - 1 = 5$		$= \dfrac{10.25}{2.00}$ $= 5.125$
Error	30.00	$(K-1)(S-1) = 3 \times 5 = 15$	$\dfrac{SS_{error}}{df_{error}} = \dfrac{30}{15} = 2.00$	
Totals	103.25	$N - 1 = 23$		

Our next step is to find df for each source. Note that df_b corresponds to the number of levels of the treatment minus 1 ($K - 1$), just as in one-way between-subjects ANOVA. For subjects, degrees of freedom are found by subtracting 1 from the number of subjects ($S - 1$). Degrees of freedom for error is the product of df_b and df_{subj}, as shown in Formula 12-18:

FORMULA 12-18 Error degrees of freedom

$$df_{error} = (K - 1)(S - 1).$$

Alternatively, df_{error} can be found by subtracting df_b and df_{subj} from df_{tot}:

$$df_{error} = df_{tot} - df_b - df_{subj}.$$

Next, we find MS_b as in one-way between-subjects ANOVA and MS_{error} using Formula 12-19:

FORMULA 12-19 Mean square error in one-way repeated measures ANOVA (computational formula)

$$MS_{error} = \frac{SS_{error}}{df_{error}}.$$

Finally, the F ratio for our treatment is found by dividing MS_b by MS_{error}, as indicated in Formula 12-20:

**FORMULA 12-20 F *ratio in one-way repeated measures ANOVA*
(*computational formula*)**

$$F = \frac{MS_b}{MS_{error}}.$$

Once we have computed the F value, we use Table E to find the critical value for F. Remember to use the correct degrees of freedom—df corresponding to the numerator and denominator used in calculating F (df_b and df_{error}, respectively). In this example, $F_{comp} = 5.125$ and $F_{crit} = 3.29$ at the 5% level; $F(3, 15) = 5.125$, $p < .05$. Thus, we reject the null hypothesis. We can conclude that practice did improve algebra performance.

Normally, an F value for subjects is not computed, although it could be. The reason for this is that an F value for subjects doesn't tell us anything useful in our research. We know that people differ on the dimension employed. Our primary purpose is to statistically remove the contribution of individual differences to the variability in our scores.

ᔐ CHECKING YOUR PROGRESS

Suppose we are interested in the effect of practice on public speaking anxiety. We recruit eight volunteers and pretest them on public speaking anxiety on a standardized test. We then provide the volunteers with several practice sessions in giving speeches and test them again. To see if the practice causes a lasting change in their anxiety, we administer a follow-up test 6 months later. Here are the data (higher scores indicate higher anxiety):

	Pretest	Posttest	Follow-Up
Volunteer 1	8	6	7
Volunteer 2	6	4	5
Volunteer 3	5	5	7
Volunteer 4	7	7	2
Volunteer 5	7	4	5
Volunteer 6	3	1	2
Volunteer 7	10	6	4
Volunteer 8	10	7	8

Compute F and test it for significance.

Answer: $F = 4.65$, which for 2 and 14 *df* is significant ($p < .05$); $F(2, 14) = 4.65$, $p < .05$. One or more of the groups (testing situations) came from different populations. We can conclude that practice was effective in reducing public speaking anxiety, at least for these volunteers.

SUMMARY

In this chapter, we covered a technique that allows us to perform a significance test on the results of comparing two or more levels of an independent variable. The test is called the one-way analysis of variance, or ANOVA. There are two types of one-way ANOVA. Between-subjects ANOVA is used when independent groups receive each level of the treatment; repeated measures ANOVA is used when the same individuals receive all levels of the treatment. The analysis of variance results in computation of an *F* ratio, which is compared with critical values from Table E.

The determination of *F* begins with the calculation of the sums of squares. We first compute the total sum of squares using the formula

$$SS_{\text{tot}} = \Sigma X^2 - \frac{(\Sigma X)^2}{N}.$$

The total sum of squares is divided into the between-groups sum of squares and the within-groups sum of squares, which are computed from the formulas

$$SS_b - \sum_g \left[\frac{(\Sigma X_g)^2}{N_g} \right] - \frac{(\Sigma X)^2}{N}$$

and

$$SS_w = \sum_g \left[\Sigma X_g^2 - \frac{(\Sigma X_g)^2}{N_g} \right].$$

The mean square (*MS*) is found by dividing each sum of squares by the appropriate degrees of freedom. In the case of SS_b, $df = K - 1$, where *K* is the number of groups being compared. The *df* for SS_w is $N - K$, where *N* is the total number of subjects. The total degrees of freedom is $df_{\text{tot}} = N - 1$.

The *F* ratio is calculated by dividing MS_b by MS_w. Using the degrees of freedom associated with the numerator of the ratio (df_b) and the degrees of freedom associated with the denominator (df_w), we can locate critical values of *F* in Table E. If the computed value is equal to or larger than the critical value at the 5% level, we reject the null hypothesis (that all groups came from the same population).

One-way repeated measures ANOVA is identical to one-way between-subjects ANOVA in the computation of SS_{tot} and SS_b. However, SS_w is divided into SS_{subj} and SS_{error} using the following formulas:

$$SS_{subj} = \sum_s \left[\frac{(\Sigma X_m)^2}{T} \right] - \frac{(\Sigma X)^2}{N},$$

and

$$SS_{error} = SS_{tot} - SS_b - SS_{subj}.$$

As in one-way between-subjects ANOVA, mean squares are found by dividing each SS by the appropriate df. For SS_b, $df = K - 1$. Degrees of freedom for subjects is $S - 1$, where S is the number of subjects. Degrees of freedom for error is $(K - 1)(S - 1)$. The F value is found by dividing MS_b by MS_{error}. The critical value for F is found in Table E using df_b and df_{error}. If the computed F is greater than or equal to the 5% critical value, we reject the null hypothesis. Ordinarily, an F value for subjects is not computed.

For either type of ANOVA, if the F ratio is significant, further analysis of the data may be performed with tests found in the next chapter.

�礼 *Troubleshooting Your Computations*

Using formulas as complex as the ones discussed in this chapter increases the possibility of computational error. Two obvious signs of trouble when computing the sums of squares are a negative value for any sum of squares and the failure of $SS_b + SS_w$ or $SS_b + SS_{subj} + SS_{error}$ to total SS_{tot}. If either of these occurs, 99% of the time the error will be in the original computations—a failure to compute correctly one or more of the sums of scores or the sums of squared scores. Prevention is always preferable to treatment, and we suggest you check all your original computations twice as you do them to be sure you aren't making a mistake that will haunt you later.

If your mistake is not in the original summing of the scores and of the squared scores, check your formulas to see that they have been copied correctly. Then be sure that you substituted the correct number for the appropriate symbol in the equations. If you have unequal N_g values, be sure you noted this in substituting in the SS_b and SS_w equations.

The most common error in filling in the summary table is to determine df incorrectly. Remember that $df_b = K - 1$, where K is the number of groups you are comparing; that $df_w = N - K$; that $df_{subj} = S - 1$, where S is the number of subjects; and that df_{error} is $(K - 1)(S - 1)$. Also, $df_{tot} = df_b + df_w = df_b + df_{error} + df_{subj} = N - 1$.

EXERCISES

1. We know that some people are more susceptible to hypnosis than others and that people who are highly suggestible have a vivid imagination and fantasy life. This leads us to hypothesize that the ability to recall dreams will also be affected by hypnotic susceptibility (HS). Using the Stanford Scale of Hypnotic Susceptibility, we create low, medium, and high susceptibility groups by selecting from volunteers who took the scale. We then ask the volunteers to keep a dream diary for 1 month. At the end of the month, we collect the diaries and count the number of dreams recalled for each person:

Low HS	Medium HS	High HS
4	14	22
9	12	26
6	3	13
8	26	20
14	15	27
16	19	19
8	17	16
10	5	14

Compare the groups on dream recall.

2. An experiment is performed to determine the effects of taking a statistics class on the ability to perform simple algebra problems. Ten statistics students are given a 20-item algebra test at the beginning of a statistics course, after completing the course, and 6 months after the course. Here are the data, which represent the number of problems completed correctly:

Student	Before	After	6 Months After
1	10	11	10
2	12	14	14
3	14	20	15
4	6	10	11
5	15	16	14
6	12	14	16
7	12	15	13
8	2	7	7
9	9	10	10
10	8	18	15

Did experience with a statistics course affect algebra performance?

3. An investigator in child development research is studying the development of object permanence—the understanding that an object still exists even if it is out of sight. She tests three groups of infants—10 9-month-olds, 10 12-month-olds, and 10 15-month-olds. She presents each of the 30 infants with 10 trials. On each trial, a toy is first shown to the child and then covered with a piece of cloth. The infant demonstrates object permanence if he or she looks for the object or shows signs of distress when it is covered. Each infant is given a score for the number of trials (out of 10) on which he or she shows object permanence. Here are the scores:

9 Months	12 Months	15 Months
8	10	10
3	5	8
4	6	9
6	7	9
5	6	8
4	5	7
9	10	9
2	3	6
0	3	6
1	3	8

Determine whether there were group differences in object permanence.

4. Trauma victims frequently suffer from intrusive memories and images of the traumatic event. We are interested in the effectiveness of a new therapeutic technique that uses structured recall of the traumatic event in conjunction with a cognitive restructuring of the experience. We have seven trauma patients record their intrusive thoughts for a 1-week period before receiving the therapy (0 months), after 2 months of therapy (2 months), at termination (4 months), and again 2 months after completing therapy (6 months). Here are the data:

Patient #	0 Months	2 Months	4 Months	6 Months
1	14	10	9	10
2	10	8	5	6
3	8	7	5	2
4	16	12	8	10
5	12	11	10	9
6	9	8	5	5
7	8	7	7	7

Did the new therapy significantly affect intrusive memories in these patients?

5. In a study of the effect of fatigue on performance of simple tasks, volunteers were instructed to perform a data entry task as rapidly and as accurately as possible. The number of errors committed during four 15-minute time periods was recorded:

Person	1st 15 Min.	2nd 15 Min.	3rd 15 Min.	4th 15 Min.
1	4	2	8	10
2	5	5	12	10
3	11	11	14	20
4	16	18	15	23
5	4	4	11	17

Did fatigue influence performance?

6. Several student volunteers were deprived of sleep for varying periods, and their performance on a pursuit rotor task was measured. The object of the pursuit rotor task is to keep a stylus in contact with a spot on a rotating turntable. It is primarily a measure of hand-eye coordination and should be sensitive to the effects of sleep deprivation. The length of the deprivation and the amount of time during a 1-minute test each student could keep the stylus in contact with the target are shown here. Determine whether lack of sleep affected performance on the task. People scoring 0 often fell asleep at the start of a session.

Sleep Deprivation

0 Hr.	24 Hr.	48 Hr.	72 Hr.
30	10	5	5
45	10	10	3
15	5	5	5
20	15	5	0
30	20	0	0
35	10	20	6

7. Assume that the data shown in Exercise 3 have been collected from the same 10 infants on three different occasions—at 9 months, 12 months, and 15 months. Perform the appropriate analysis to determine if object permanence changed over time. Compare the summary table to that obtained in Exercise 3.

8. An experiment has been done to investigate the effect of alcohol on reaction time of adult males. Reaction time was measured in a simulated driver's seat from the moment a picture of a stop sign appeared until the subject applied force to a brake. Forty subjects were selected and randomly assigned to one of four treatment groups: Group 1, placebo; Group 2, 0.5 ounce of alcohol; Group 3, 1.0 ounce; Group 4, 2.0 ounces. Testing was conducted 30 minutes after alcohol ingestion. Here are the data:

Reaction Time in Seconds

0 Oz.	0.5 Oz.	1.0 Oz.	2.0 Oz.
0.8	1.1	1.5	2.0
1.2	1.5	1.3	1.8
0.7	0.9	1.2	1.7
0.9	1.6	1.4	1.5
1.1	1.4	1.6	1.8
1.5	1.3	0.9	1.7
0.6	1.4	1.1	1.6
0.8	0.9	1.8	1.7
1.0	1.1	1.5	1.5
1.1	1.2	1.4	2.1

Determine whether there were group differences.

9. In Exercise 4, the same 7 patients were asked to report their intrusive thoughts at four different times. What if the data had been collected from four different groups of patients? Reanalyze the data in Exercise 4, assuming that the data have been collected from 28 trauma patients assigned to one of four groups based on their position in the therapy process. Compare your results to those obtained in Exercise 4. What are the similarities and differences in the summary tables?

CHAPTER 13

Post Hoc Comparisons

✳ The data analysis was complete, and Dr. Baxter was pleased (remember Dr. Baxter from Chapters 11 and 12). The one-way ANOVA comparing her treatment groups had yielded a significant F value. Now she could make the necessary changes to her paper and resubmit it to the journal. She had only to add some interpretation of her findings to the manuscript and she would be finished.

So what did her results mean? Overall, Dr. Baxter could see that the mean of the group receiving the experimental treatment was 2.0 points better than the mean of the group receiving the conventional treatment, which was 2.0 points better than the untreated group. These findings meant that the experimental treatment group was 4.0 points better than the untreated group. However, the pattern wasn't as clear as Dr. Baxter expected. She realized that to make sense of the differences among the groups, she would have to use a different test—a post hoc comparison.

In Chapter 12 we said that finding a significant F ratio is not sufficient to tell us which group or treatment comparisons might actually differ significantly. Suppose, for example, a one-way ANOVA includes four groups (A, B, C, D). A significant F value would not specify which groups or combination of groups is significantly different from which other group or groups. Group A might differ from groups B, C, and D, but B, C, and D might not differ from each other. Alternatively, group A might not differ from B, but might differ from C and D. Group B might differ from D but not C—and the possibilities go on. A significant F is only a first step. Further analysis is necessary to determine the exact pattern of differences involved.

Remember that one of the main reasons for not doing multiple *t* tests initially was that there was an increased risk of committing a Type I, or alpha (α), error (rejecting a true null). Many **a posteriori** (after the fact) or **post hoc tests** avoid the problem of inflation of an alpha error by increasing the critical value needed to reject the null hypothesis. In this chapter, we consider two post hoc or multiple comparison tests: the Tukey HSD and the Fisher LSD. The tests could also be called post-ANOVA tests because they follow ANOVA.

In addition to the post hoc or a posteriori tests, there are also **a priori tests,** or tests designed to look at specific hypotheses before the experiment is performed. A priori tests perform planned comparisons, in contrast to post hoc tests, which perform unplanned comparisons. The logic and computational procedures for a priori tests are beyond the scope of this text. Therefore, we restrict our discussion in this chapter to post hoc tests, which are conducted when the experimenter cannot predict the patterning of means before the research is performed.

THE TUKEY HSD

The first of the post hoc tests we will examine is the **Tukey HSD (honestly significant difference) test,** or simply the **HSD test.** It is a good place to begin because it is often used by behavioral scientists and because the required computation is simple. Although the HSD test can be used for more complex comparisons, we will use it when we have equal numbers per group for making all pairwise comparisons of the data. Actually, the HSD test can be done with unequal group sizes, but the computations are much more complicated.

By pairwise comparisons, we mean that we make all possible comparisons between groups by looking at one pair of groups at a time. For example, if we have three groups labeled A, B, and C, then we will compare Groups A and B, Groups A and C, and Groups B and C. We will not use the HSD test to compare Group A with the combination of Groups B and C, for example, as this would not be a pairwise comparison.

The technique is simple. The difference between two sample means is significant if it is greater than HSD, which is found by the following equation:

> **FORMULA 13-1** *Honestly significant difference (HSD) between pairs of means (computational formula)*
>
> $$\text{HSD}_\alpha = q_\alpha \sqrt{\frac{MS_w}{N_g}}.$$

As before, α is the level of significance—that is, either the 5% ($p = .05$) or the 1% ($p = .01$) level. The value of q is obtained from the distribution of the studentized range statistic found in Table F. (The studentized range statistic is sometimes used instead of the F statistic for making group comparisons. It is generally a less powerful test than the F test.) To determine the value of q from the table, we need to know two things: the df_w (degrees of freedom within groups) and K (the number of groups, treatments, or means).

Using the Tukey HSD

Let's look at a specific example. In Chapter 12 we worked with some data from a hypothetical experiment in which snake avoidance was measured after one of three different treatments. The group means were these: Group 1 (placebo), $\bar{X}_1 = 7$; Group 2 (mild tranquilizer), $\bar{X}_2 = 3$; Group 3 (mild hallucinogen), $\bar{X}_3 = 10$. The analysis of variance summary table is repeated here:

ANOVA Summary Table

Source	SS	df	MS	F
Between groups	148	2	74	F = 15.42
Within groups	72	15	4.8	
Total	220	17		

The first step is to define all the pairwise comparisons we are going to make and to find the difference in the means for each comparison. The possible pairwise comparisons are as follows: Group 1 and Group 2, Group 1 and Group 3, and Group 2 and Group 3. Subtracting the smaller mean from the larger for each comparison, we observe the following differences:

$$\bar{X}_1 - \bar{X}_2 = 7 - 3 = 4,$$
$$\bar{X}_3 - \bar{X}_1 = 10 - 7 = 3,$$
$$\bar{X}_3 - \bar{X}_2 = 10 - 3 = 7.$$

Equivalently, we could have subtracted in the order originally specified (that is, $\bar{X}_1 - \bar{X}_2$, $\bar{X}_1 - \bar{X}_3$, $\bar{X}_2 - \bar{X}_3$) and then used the absolute value of the differences in the comparison with HSD.

The next step is to determine HSD_α. Again, the formula for HSD_α is

$$HSD_\alpha = q_\alpha \sqrt{\frac{MS_w}{N_g}}.$$

With three groups and $df_w = 15$, the value of $q_{.05}$ from Table D is 3.67. The value of

Box 13-1   Computational Steps for Tukey HSD

1. Compute the mean for each of the treatment groups.
2. Determine the differences between means for each pairwise comparison. Either subtract to get a positive difference or use the absolute value of the difference.
3. Compute HSD for the 5% and 1% levels from the formula

$$\text{HSD}_\alpha = q_\alpha \sqrt{\frac{MS_w}{N_g}},$$

   where q_α is a value from Table D. In repeated measures ANOVA, use MS_{error} instead of MS_w.
4. Compare the computed HSD values with the mean differences from step 2. If the difference in means is equal to or larger than $\text{HSD}_{.05}$, reject the null hypothesis for the comparison. That is, conclude that the groups came from different populations.

$q_{.01} = 4.84$. As $MS_w = 4.8$ from the summary table and $N_g = 6$,

$$\text{HSD}_{.05} = 3.67 \sqrt{\frac{4.8}{6}} = 3.67\sqrt{0.8} = 3.67(0.89) = 3.27,$$

$$\text{HSD}_{.01} = 4.84(0.89) = 4.31.$$

Now that the values for HSD have been computed, we can compare them with the mean differences computed earlier. The result is that two differences are larger than $\text{HSD}_{.05}$ and one is larger than $\text{HSD}_{.01}$. Specifically, the difference between the means for Group 1 and Group 2 was 4, which is larger than the HSD of 3.27 required for significance at the 5% level. Additionally, the difference of 7 between Groups 2 and 3 is larger than the HSD at the 1% level (4.31). The difference between Groups 1 and 3 (3) was less than $\text{HSD}_{.05}$.

In summary, the F test in Chapter 12 indicated that a significant difference(s) existed in the data. The Tukey HSD test revealed that the difference between the first and second groups (placebo and mild tranquilizer) was significant and that the difference between the second and third groups (tranquilizer and mild hallucinogen) was also significant. In other words, the tranquilizer was more effective than either the placebo or the mild hallucinogen in reducing the snake phobia. However, the hallucinogen was not significantly better than the placebo.

Another Tukey HSD Example

Let's help Dr. Baxter answer the question by applying the Tukey HSD test to the data from her study. The information we need from Chapter 12 is as follows.

- (Experimental treatment) $\bar{X}_1 = 8.00$
- (Conventional treatment) $\bar{X}_2 = 10.00$
- (No treatment) $\bar{X}_3 = 12.00$
- $MS_W = 8.59$, $N_g = 10$

As we already have the means, the first step is to find the differences for all pairwise comparisons. The possible comparisons are $\bar{X}_1$ with $\bar{X}_2$, $\bar{X}_1$ with $\bar{X}_3$, and $\bar{X}_2$ with $\bar{X}_3$. Subtracting to obtain positive differences, we have the following:

$$\bar{X}_2 - \bar{X}_1 = 10 - 8 = 2,$$
$$\bar{X}_3 - \bar{X}_1 = 12 - 8 = 4,$$
$$\bar{X}_3 - \bar{X}_2 = 12 - 10 = 2.$$

We then compute the HSD:

$$HSD_\alpha = q_\alpha \sqrt{\frac{MS_w}{N_g}}.$$

Because Table D has no entries for $df_w = 27$, we will take the conservative approach and use the values for $df_w = 24$.

$$HSD_{.05} = 3.53\sqrt{\frac{8.59}{10}} = 3.53\sqrt{.859} = 3.53(0.93) = 3.27,$$
$$HSD_{.01} = 3.96(0.93) = 3.65.$$

Now we can compare our computed HSD values with the mean differences. If any difference is equal to or larger than the HSD at the 5% level (3.27), we will reject the null hypothesis for the comparison. The differences are listed again below, this time with the decisions indicated by probability values. If $p < .05$, the difference is significant (the null hypothesis has been rejected); if $p > .05$, the difference is not significant, at least with the Tukey HSD test.

$$\bar{X}_2 - \bar{X}_1 = 10 - 8 = 2, p > .05,$$
$$\bar{X}_3 - \bar{X}_1 = 12 - 8 = 4, \ p < .05 \text{ and } p < .01,$$
$$X_3 - X_2 = 12 - 10 = 2, \ p > .05.$$

Another way to summarize the results of our HSD test is shown in Table 13-1. In the table the group means are listed from lowest to highest. The differences in means for each possible comparison are readily apparent, and asterisks are used to show the significant comparisons.

In summary, the experimental treatment group was significantly different from the untreated group but not from the conventionally treated group. The conventionally treated group did not differ significantly from the untreated group. Although Dr. Baxter can be confident that her new treatment for panic disorder is more effective than no treatment, she can't say that it is better than conventional treatment. This pattern is often observed in research. The pattern

TABLE 13-1

HSD Tests on Differences Between Pairs of Means

		Groups		
		3 **Experimental** **Treatment**	**2** **Conventional** **Treatment**	**1** **Untreated**
	Means	8.00	10.00	12.00
Group 3	8.00	—	2.0	4.0**
Group 2	10.00		—	2.0
Group 1	12.00			—

$$\text{HSD}_{.05} = 3.27$$
$$\text{HSD}_{.01} = 3.65$$

*$p < .05$
**$p < .01$

of means is consistent with predictions, but post hoc comparisons indicate that not all the expected differences are actually significant. The problem in these instances is usually one of statistical power. The experimental design was not sufficiently powerful to discern the differences that are probably there. The most obvious solution is to rerun the research with a larger sample.

ᔕ CHECKING YOUR PROGRESS

In Exercise 4 of Chapter 12, an experiment was described in which 7 trauma victims were tested for different amounts of intrusive imagery at different points in therapy. An F test performed on the data results in a significant F ratio, and the appropriate summary table is shown below, along with the other information needed to perform the HSD test. Make all pairwise comparisons.

ANOVA Summary Table

Source	SS	df	MS	F
Between groups	77	3	25.67	$F = 3.85$ $df = 3, 24$
Within groups	160	24	6.67	
Total	237	27		

$$N_g = 7, \quad \Sigma X_1 = 77, \quad \Sigma X_2 = 63, \quad \Sigma X_3 = 49, \quad \Sigma X_4 = 49.$$

Answer: $HSD_{.05} = 3.80$ and $HSD_{.01} = 4.79$. Groups 3 and 4 (patients at 4 months of treatment—termination—and at 6 months—follow-up) differed significantly from Group 1 (patients at 0 months—pretreatment); that is, patients at the end of treatment and after 2 months reported fewer incidents of intrusive imagery than they had reported before treatment. No other groups were significantly different.

THE FISHER LSD

Like the Tukey HSD, the **Fisher LSD (least significant difference) test,** or simply **LSD test,** is easy to compute and is used to make all pairwise comparisons of group means. One advantage of the LSD for our purposes is that it doesn't require equal sample sizes. Another advantage is that it is a more powerful test; that is, we are more likely to be able to reject the null hypothesis with it than with the HSD. As experimenters, we would rather reject a few true nulls than fail to reject false hypotheses. In other words, the Type II (β) error is considered to be more serious than the α error.

The LSD test is sometimes called a **protected t test** because it follows a significant F test. If we used the t test to do all pairwise comparisons *before* the F test, the probability of committing an α error would be greater than α. However, by applying a form of the t test after the F test has revealed at least one significant comparison, the error rate (probability of α error) is protected.

Each pair of means is tested with the formula

FORMULA 13-2   *Least significant difference (LSD) between pairs of group means (computational formula)*

$$LSD = \frac{\overline{X}_1 - \overline{X}_2}{\sqrt{MS_w \left(\dfrac{1}{N_1} + \dfrac{1}{N_2} \right)}},$$

where $\overline{X}_1$ and $\overline{X}_2$ are the means for the groups being compared and N_1 and N_2 are the sample sizes for the two groups. If the LSD is being performed on data in a repeated measures design, substitute MS_{error} and df_{error} for MS_w and df_w in the formula.

The computed t score is compared with critical t scores from Table B with $df = N - K$ (df_w). If the absolute value of the computed t is equal to or greater than the critical value at the 5% level, the null hypothesis should be rejected.

Using the Fisher LSD

Let's use the Fisher LSD to analyze some data after a significant F ratio. A study was performed to test the effect of attractiveness on perceived happiness. Three groups of participants were presented with photos of a very attractive person, a moderately attractive person, or an unattractive person. The participants then used a standardized scale to rate how happy they judged the person in the photo to be. The data are as follows:

Very Attractive	Moderately Attractive	Unattractive
6	5	4
8	6	3
8	8	3
10	9	6
7	7	2

The problem is to determine whether there is a significant overall result and, if there is, to determine which groups differ significantly. We won't go through all the computations resulting in F (treat this example as another review exercise); the summary table is as follows:

ANOVA Summary Table

Source	SS	df	MS	F
Between groups	49.7	2	24.85	$F = 10.67$,
				$df = 2, 12$, or
Within groups	28.0	12	2.33	$F(2, 12) = 10.67, p < .01$
Total	77.7	14		

$$N_g = 5, \quad \overline{X}_1 = \frac{39}{5} = 7.8, \quad \overline{X}_2 = \frac{35}{5} = 7, \quad \overline{X}_3 = \frac{18}{5} = 3.6.$$

Using these data, let's compute the Fisher LSD for each pairwise comparison:

$$LSD_{1,2} = \frac{7.8 - 7}{\sqrt{2.33\left(\frac{1}{5} + \frac{1}{5}\right)}} = \frac{0.8}{\sqrt{2.33(0.4)}} = \frac{0.8}{\sqrt{0.93}}$$

$$= \frac{0.8}{0.96} = 0.83.$$

Because the denominator stays the same, we need to compute it only once:

$$\text{LSD}_{1,3} = \frac{7.8 - 3.6}{0.96} = \frac{4.2}{0.96} = 4.38,$$

$$\text{LSD}_{2,3} = \frac{7 - 3.6}{0.96} = \frac{3.4}{0.96} = 3.54.$$

For $df = 12$, the critical t scores from Table B are 2.1788 at the 5% level and 3.0545 at the 1% level. Based on the LSD test, Groups Very Attractive and Moderately Attractive do not differ significantly ($p > .05$). Both Group Very Attractive and Group Moderately Attractive differ from Group Unattractive at the 1% level, as the resulting LSD scores are larger than the critical value of 3.0545. That is, both very attractive and moderately attractive people are perceived to be happier than unattractive people.

Another Fisher LSD Example

Let's use the Fisher LSD test to reanalyze the data from the study of trauma victims and intrusive imagery. As before, we have $N_g = 7$, $MS_w = 6.67$, $df_w = 24$, $\overline{X}_1 = 11.0$, $\overline{X}_2 = 9.0$, $\overline{X}_3 = 7.0$, $\overline{X}_4 = 7.0$. From our previous computation, we have the difference in means for each pairwise comparison:

$$\text{LSD}_{1,2} = \frac{\overline{X}_2 - \overline{X}_1}{\sqrt{MS_w\left(\frac{1}{N_1} + \frac{1}{N_2}\right)}} = \frac{11 - 9}{\sqrt{6.67\left(\frac{1}{7} + \frac{1}{7}\right)}} = \frac{2}{\sqrt{6.67(0.286)}} = \frac{2}{\sqrt{1.90}} = \frac{2}{1.38} = 1.45,$$

$$\text{LSD}_{1,3} \text{ and } \text{LSD}_{1,4} = \frac{4}{1.38} = 2.9,$$

$$\text{LSD}_{2,3} \text{ and } \text{LSD}_{2,4} = \frac{2}{1.38} = 1.45,$$

$$\text{LSD}_{3,4} = \frac{0}{1.38} = 0.0.$$

From Table B, with $df = 35$, the critical values of t are 2.0639 at the 5% level and 2.7969 at the 1% level. With the Fisher LSD test, Group 1 differs significantly from Groups 3 and 4 at the 1% level; that is, the termination and follow-up groups had less intrusive imagery than they did before they began treatment. No other comparisons are significant.

Table 13-2 summarizes the LSD test in a format similar to that introduced in Table 13-1. Instead of mean differences, the LSD values are shown for each comparison.

TABLE 13-2

Summary of LSD Comparisons of Pairs of Means

		Groups			
		1 **0 months**	**2** **2 months**	**3** **4 months**	**4** **6 months**
Group	1	—	1.45	2.90**	2.90**
Group	2		—	1.45	1.45
Group	3			—	0.00
Group	4				—

$t_{.05} = 2.0639$
$t_{.01} = 2.7969$

*$p < .05$
**$p < .01$

---

⑤ CHECKING YOUR PROGRESS

In a "Checking Your Progress" problem in Chapter 12 (p. 257), you were asked to compute and test an F ratio based on data from people learning nonsense syllables under three different conditions. Because the sample sizes were unequal, you could not use the Tukey HSD test to analyze the data further. However, you can apply the Fisher LSD test. Here is the information you need:

$$\Sigma X_1 = 69, \quad N_1 = 8, \quad \Sigma X_2 = 46, \quad N_2 = 9,$$
$$\Sigma X_3 = 103, \quad N_3 = 9,$$
$$MS_w = 10.04, \quad df_w = 23.$$

Answer: For the comparison between Groups 1 and 2, LSD = 2.27, $p < .05$; Groups 1 and 3, LSD = 1.81, $p > .05$; Groups 2 and 3, LSD = 4.25, $p < .01$. Performance in the normal room and the room with flashing lights did not differ significantly, but it was easier to learn the nonsense syllables in the dark room than in either of the other rooms.

SUMMARY

When a significant F ratio is obtained, a variety of post hoc tests are available for further analysis of the data. One such test is the Tukey HSD. The value of HSD is computed from the following formula:

$$HSD_\alpha = q_\alpha \sqrt{\frac{MS_w}{N_g}}.$$

The value for q_a is taken from Table F using the appropriate K (number of groups, treatments, or means) and df_w. If absolute differences between any pair of group means is equal to or larger than $HSD_{.05}$ or $HSD_{.01}$, the null hypothesis is rejected. The HSD test may be used to make all pairwise comparisons between group means when the sample sizes are the same for all groups.

Also called the protected t test, the Fisher LSD is another post hoc test that can be used to make all pairwise comparisons. It is a more powerful test than the HSD, and, as presented in this chapter, it can be used to compare groups with unequal numbers. For each pairwise comparison, a value of LSD is computed with the formula

$$LSD = \frac{\overline{X}_1 - \overline{X}_2}{\sqrt{MS_w\left(\frac{1}{N_1} + \frac{1}{N_2}\right)}},$$

where $\overline{X}_1$ and $\overline{X}_2$ are the means of the samples being compared and N_1 and N_2 are their sample sizes.

Using $df = N - K$ (df_w), critical values of t are found in Table B. If the absolute value of a computed LSD is equal to or larger than the critical t score at the 5% level (1% for a more conservative test), the null hypothesis is rejected for the comparison.

⁂ *Troubleshooting Your Computations*

The most common error made in calculating HSD is to use N instead of N_g in the expression under the radical sign. Another error is using a critical F ratio from Table E rather than the q value from Table F. Also, remember that after you compute HSD, you compare it to the difference in means that you have calculated. If the difference in means is larger than $HSD_{.05}$, you reject the null hypothesis for that comparison and conclude that there is a significant difference between the means (that they were drawn from different populations).

The Fisher LSD is really just a two-sample t test with a simplified formula. Remember to consider the absolute value of the computed LSD when you're making a decision and to use df_w to locate the critical t scores from Table B. A common error is to use the critical F from Table E for significance comparison rather than the critical t, as the test requires.

EXERCISES

1. In Exercise 1 of Chapter 12, people differing in level of hypnotic susceptibility were asked to recall dreams. The data resulted in a significant F ratio, so further analysis would be worthwhile. Using the following information,

perform all pairwise comparisons with the techniques presented in this chapter (HSD and LSD):

$$\Sigma X_1 = 75, \quad \Sigma X_2 = 111, \quad \Sigma X_3 = 157, \quad N_g = 8, \quad MS_w = 33.55.$$

2. In Exercise 2 of Chapter 12, the effects of taking a statistics class on students' ability to solve simple algebra problems was investigated. The analysis resulted in a significant F ratio, so further analysis would be appropriate. Using the following information, perform all pairwise comparisons using the techniques presented in this chapter.

$$\Sigma X_1 = 110, \quad \Sigma X_2 = 135, \quad \Sigma X_3 = 120, \quad N_g = 10, \quad MS_{error} = 2.14.$$

3. In Exercise 3 from Chapter 12, some data were presented from a study of the development of object permanence in children. As the data resulted in a significant F ratio, further analysis would be worthwhile. Using the following information, perform all pairwise comparisons with the techniques presented in this chapter.

$$\Sigma X_1 = 42, \quad \Sigma X_2 = 58, \quad \Sigma X_3 = 80, \quad N_g = 10, \quad MS_w = 5.67.$$

4. In Exercise 5 from Chapter 12, the effect of fatigue on task performance was studied. Data were collected during four consecutive time periods. The F ratio was significant. Perform the appropriate post hoc tests using the following information.

$$\Sigma X_1 = 40, \quad \Sigma X_2 = 40, \quad \Sigma X_3 = 60, \quad \Sigma X_4 = 80, \quad N_g = 5, \quad MS_{error} = 3.58.$$

5. In Exercise 6 from Chapter 12, the effects of sleep deprivation on hand-eye coordination were assessed and the F ratio was significant. Use the following information and the appropriate post hoc tests to make all pairwise comparisons.

$$\Sigma X_1 = 175, \quad \Sigma X_2 = 70, \quad \Sigma X_3 = 45, \quad \Sigma X_4 = 19, \quad N_g = 6, \quad MS_w = 48.83.$$

6. A study of alcohol and reaction time in Exercise 8 of Chapter 12 resulted in a significant F ratio. Use the following information and the LSD and HSD tests to perform all pairwise comparisons.

$$\Sigma X_1 = 9.7, \quad \Sigma X_2 = 12.4, \quad \Sigma X_3 = 13.7, \quad \Sigma X_4 = 17.4, \quad N_g = 10, \quad MS_w = 0.0586.$$

7. Sixteen guinea pigs have been randomly assigned to four groups. Within each group, each guinea pig is given 10 trials with a particular type of food.

The response measure is the number of pieces of food eaten by each subject. The scores are shown here.

Lettuce Pieces	Carrot Pieces	Alfalfa Pellets	Strawberry Pieces
10	8	5	1
9	8	5	1
9	9	4	2
10	7	6	1

Perform an overall test of significance. If the test is significant, make all pairwise comparisons.

8. We know that the presence of others often interferes with an individual's complex problem solving. Two-digit multiplication problems with answers are presented to participants on a computer screen. Their task is to respond "correct" or "incorrect" as quickly as possible. Response latencies (time taken to respond) are recorded by the computer. Participants perform the task alone (1-person group), in the presence of another person (2-person group), or in the presence of three other people (4-person group). In the 4-person group, a computer failure led to the loss of one participant's data. Perform an overall test of significance. If the test is significant, do all pairwise comparisons.

1-Person Group	2-Person Group	4-Person Group
0.55	1.55	3.28
1.23	2.69	2.15
0.25	1.10	5.63
0.36	0.85	1.18
1.16	0.75	4.75
0.15	1.25	2.65
0.80	3.16	

14

Two-Way Analysis of Variance

 Dr. Baxter (remember Dr. Baxter from Chapters 11, 12, and 13) was attending a convention of psychotherapists. She was pleased with the interest of her colleagues in the development of her new approach to the treatment of panic disorder.

While having coffee in the lobby of the convention hotel one morning, she was approached by Dr. Salinger, a representative of a well-known and respected drug company. Dr. Salinger informed Dr. Baxter that he had a proposal to make that might be mutually beneficial. He asked if she had ever considered including psychoactive drugs in her work. His company, he told her, had recently developed a new drug (Panic-EA) specifically for sufferers of panic attack. Based on what he had read about Dr. Baxter's work, he felt that the new drug would be particularly effective when used in conjunction with a psychotherapeutic approach like that developed by Dr. Baxter. Dr. Salinger's proposal was that if Dr. Baxter included Panic-EA in her next treatment study, his company would fund the research.

The drug company was interested in the same basic research design used by Dr. Baxter in the first study but wanted to add a second factor: Panic-EA. That is, Dr. Baxter would once again collect data on panic attack patients receiving no treatment, conventional treatment, or experimental treatment. However, half of each treatment group would receive a placebo and the other half would receive Panic-EA. Dr. Salinger drew a diagram of the research design he had in mind.

Psychotherapy

	No Treatment	Conventional Treatment	Experimental Treatment
Placebo			
Panic-EA			

Drug

Dr. Baxter asked for some time to consider the proposal. Later that night she thought about the research design and realized that a one-way ANOVA would not be suitable. She needed a statistical test that could accommodate more complex data. She needed a different kind of ANOVA.

In Chapter 12, the one-way analysis of variance, or ANOVA, was introduced as a method for analyzing data that result from the administration of two or more levels of an independent variable. In this chapter, we look at an additional complication: the introduction of another independent variable. When we have more than one independent variable, we use a test called the **two-way analysis of variance,** or **two-way ANOVA.** The variables in this type of test are called **factors.** In Dr. Baxter's new study, the two factors are type of treatment and drug. Let's look at some additional examples of experiments with two-factor ANOVA designs.

Suppose an experimenter wants to examine the effects of task difficulty and anxiety level on problem-solving behavior. She decides to have three levels of task difficulty (easy, moderate, hard) and three levels of anxiety as determined by scores on the Taylor Manifest Anxiety Scale (low, medium, high). The dependent variable is the average time to solve 10 word problems. Because there are three levels of each independent variable (task difficulty, anxiety level), the resulting experiment is called a 3 × 3 **factorial design.** Nine groups are required: Subjects with low anxiety are given easy, moderate, or hard problems to solve; subjects with medium anxiety are given easy, moderate, or hard problems; and subjects with high anxiety are given easy, moderate, or hard problems.

In another example, a social psychologist might be interested in the effects of subjects' thrill-seeking tendency and alcohol intake on their performance on a simulated driving task. He first administers a test that measures a tendency for thrill seeking and divides his subject pool into two categories: low and high. Volunteers from each category are given no alcohol, a low dose of alcohol, or a high dose, and their performance is scored on the driving task. This illustrates a 2 × 3 factorial design, as there are two levels of thrill seeking and three levels of alcohol.

Of course, each of the studies we've described has exemplified a two factor ANOVA design. Theoretically, there's nothing to prevent us from adding other independent variables. In each of the studies outlined, gender could be an additional independent variable, resulting in a three-factor design, which would be analyzed by a three-way ANOVA.

MAIN EFFECTS AND EFFECTS OF INTERACTION

In a two-factor experiment, the effect of each independent variable, considered by itself, is called a **main effect.** Returning to Dr. Baxter's study, let's call Panic-EA factor A (row variable) and type of treatment factor B (column variable). If we looked at the effect of the drug while ignoring the type of treatment received, we would be looking at the main effect of factor A. Similarly, an examination of the effect of type of treatment without considering the drug would be an examination of the main effect of factor B. Thus, it is possible to look at the data from a two-factor experiment as though we had two separate single-factor studies.

In addition to the main effects in a two-factor experiment, there is the possibility of interaction. **Interaction** is related to the joint effect of the two independent variables. An interaction occurs when two factors work together to produce an effect that neither factor by itself produces. If an interaction effect exists, the effect of one factor *depends* on the levels of the second factor.

Consider the prediction made by Dr. Salinger for the effect of Panic-EA. He thought the drug would be especially effective for patients receiving the experimental treatment. In other words, the effects of the drug were not expected to be uniform across all levels of the treatment. So if asked what the predicted effects of Panic-EA were, Dr. Salinger would say, "It depends." It depends on whether you are talking about the untreated, conventionally treated, or experimentally treated patients. Panic-EA was expected to reduce panic in all patients, but the reduction should be most marked in the patients receiving Dr. Baxter's experimental treatment.

One way to look at interaction or lack of it in a factorial study is to graph the results. A typical graph shows the mean dependent variable scores for factor B plotted over levels of factor A. The observed data for Salinger's predictions and some hypothetical alternative results are graphed in Figure 14-1.

If there is no interaction between factors, the graph of the data will show essentially parallel lines or lines that are approximately equidistant at each data point. An example of this is shown in the middle graph of the figure. Here, the placebo patients have a higher mean than patients receiving Panic-EA at each level of factor B.

Interaction between factors is revealed graphically when the lines are not parallel, especially when they converge or cross, and this is what we have in the top and bottom graphs. At the top is the graph of Dr. Salinger's predictions. Analysis of the data would probably reveal a significant main effect for treatment, a significant effect for drug, and a significant effect for interaction. The bottom graph shows another hypothetical result, one in which Panic-EA scores decrease across levels of factor A. Again, an analysis would probably result in significance for both main effects and the interaction.

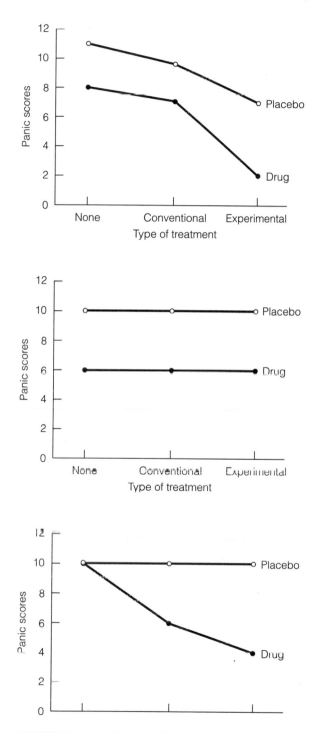

FIGURE 14-1 Graphs of Dr. Salinger's predictions and alternative results.

Note that we're given some probable results of the analysis of the data shown in the graphs. How did we arrive at these interpretations?

To interpret a graph of cell means, where levels of factor A are shown on the X-axis and levels of factor B are plotted as different lines, the following "rules" are beneficial:

1. If the averages of the points above each level of factor A are unequal, there may be a significant main effect for factor A.
2. If the averages of the points used to plot the lines are unequal, there may be a significant main effect for factor B.
3. If the lines converge or cross—that is, are not parallel—there may be a significant interaction.

Note that for each of the "rules," there *may* be a significant main effect or a significant interaction. That is, as in the one-way ANOVA, the two-way ANOVA involves the computation of F ratios. Whether an F ratio is large enough to allow us to reject a null hypothesis depends in large part on variability within each group (MS_w). Although there may be a great deal of separation between treatment means on the graph, if there is a lot of variability *within* each treatment condition, the appropriate F ratio will be small. By the same token, it is quite possible for plotted lines to cross or converge without a significant interaction occurring. The "rules" are clues to look for in trying to interpret results; the computed F ratios determine whether the main effects or interactions are significant.

Assume that for each of the graphs in Figure 14-1, MS_w is small enough that any apparent difference will be significant. Let's apply the "rules" to each of the graphs. In the top graph of Figure 14-1, the averages of the points above each level of factor A are different. Above None (No Treatment, or NT), the average is 9.5; above Conventional (CT), the average is 8.5; above Experimental (ET), the average is 4.5. In other words, we would find a significant main effect for treatment. The averages of the points used to plot the lines are also different: $\bar{X}_{placebo} = 9.3$ [(11 + 10 + 7)/3 = 9.3]; $\bar{X}_{drug} = 5.67$ [(8 + 7 + 2)/3 = 5.7]. Thus, the main effect for the drug is significant. Finally, the lines are not the same distance apart at all treatment levels, indicating a significant interaction. Notice that there is a 5.5-point difference for the experimental treatment, but only a 3-point difference at the other two treatment levels.

In the middle graph, the averages of the points above each level of factor A are the same—8 at each treatment level—leading us to conclude that there is not a significant treatment effect. However, there is a drug effect, as the points used to plot the lines average 10 for the placebo and 6 for the drug. The lines are parallel, so the interaction would not be significant.

In the bottom graph, there are different averages of the points above each treatment. For NT, $\bar{X} = 10.0$; for CT, $\bar{X} = 8.0$; and for ET, $\bar{X} = 7.0$. Thus, the effect of treatment may be significant. Similarly, the averages of the points used to plot the line are different ($\bar{X}_{placebo} = 10$, $\bar{X}_{drug} = 6.7$), suggesting a significant drug effect. The lines are not parallel, so there is also a significant interaction effect.

ADVANTAGES OF THE TWO-FACTOR DESIGN

Are there advantages to incorporating both independent variables in the same study? What does the two-factor ANOVA design add that could not be learned with two separate one-factor ANOVA experiments?

The main advantage of the two-factor design is that we can test for the presence of an *interaction* between the factors. If we did Dr. Baxter's study first with a placebo and then later with Panic-EA, we could test to see whether the treatment was effective without the drug, and we could test to see whether the treatment was effective with the drug, but there would be no way to do a significance test on the interaction of the drug and the treatment.

A second advantage of the two-factor design is that it allows a *savings in the number of subjects* we need for our study. Suppose Dr. Baxter had decided to do her study without Panic-EA and wanted to have 20 patients at each treatment level. With three levels of treatment, she would need 60 patients. Repeating the study with Panic-EA would require another 60 patients. Thus, doing the study as two one-factor ANOVAs requires 120 subjects.

But suppose Dr. Baxter actually does the study as a two-factor design with 20 subjects tested under each treatment. In this case, she will need only 60 subjects—30 receiving the placebo and 30 receiving Panic-EA, with 10 of each receiving each type of treatment. Exactly half the number of subjects is needed for the two-factor design as is needed for two one-factor designs.

A third advantage of the two-factor design is an *increase in power* of the statistical tests on the main effects, power defined as the likelihood of rejecting a false null. That is, the two-factor ANOVA design usually has greater power than two separate one-factor designs. This is because we are separating the total variance into more parts. In doing so, we are removing variance from MS_w. This makes it more likely that we will find a significant effect, because the obtained F value will be larger.

Yet another advantage of the two-factor design is *greater generalizability*. For example, in Dr. Baxter's study we know the effects of one factor for either two or three levels of the other factor. This information is not available with two separate one-way ANOVAs. We know how different treatments affect both patients given the placebo and patients given Panic-EA. We can generalize to more conditions than we could if we had done two one-way ANOVAs.

LOGIC OF THE TWO-WAY ANOVA

Although the equations and the computations are more complicated with the two-way ANOVA than with the one-way ANOVA, the underlying rationale for the tests is the same as that encountered in Chapter 12. The two-factor ANOVA results in three hypothesis tests rather than only one as before. The three tests are as follows at the top of the next page.

1. A test of the main effect of factor A. The null hypothesis for the test is that there are no population mean differences among the different levels of factor A.

2. A test of the main effect of factor B. The null hypothesis for the test is that there are no population mean differences among the different levels of factor B.

3. A test of the interaction of factors A and B. The null hypothesis is that there is no interaction.

Analysis of the data results in three F ratios, each having the same general form we encountered in Chapter 12. That is, each consists of the variance between treatments (for factor A, for factor B, or for the A $\times$ B interaction) divided by the variance within treatments. The same error term, variance within treatments, or MS_w, is used for each of the F ratios.

As before, the variance between treatments is assumed to be caused by individual differences, experimental error, and a treatment effect, and the variance within treatments is caused by individual differences and experimental error. Thus, a value of the F ratio close to 1.00 indicates the lack of a treatment effect, and a value much larger than 1.00 suggests a valid treatment effect.

INTERPRETATION OF RESULTS

Basically, interpretation of the two-way ANOVA depends on whether the interaction is significant. If the interaction is not significant, a significant main effect can be analyzed with post hoc tests such as the ones discussed in Chapter 13. For example, suppose Dr. Baxter found that the effect of treatment was significant but the drug and the treatment by drug interaction were not. She could then do pairwise comparisons of the different treatments with either the Tukey HSD or the Fisher LSD or with some other test not discussed in this text.

Unfortunately, the main advantage of the two-factor ANOVA, the ability to test an interaction effect, is a mixed blessing. Although such a test provides important additional information about a study, a positive result—that is, a significant interaction—may complicate the study's interpretation considerably. If Dr. Baxter found a significant interaction between the drug and the type of treatment, her interpretation of a main effect for the drug would be more complicated. The interaction would mean that the effect of the drug would differ from treatment to treatment. Remember that Dr. Baxter and Dr. Salinger predicted that Panic-EA would have a stronger effect when paired with the experimental psychotherapy.

The first step in interpreting a significant interaction is to plot the group means. The resulting graph will indicate by its crossing or converging lines where the interaction is occurring. Further interpretation involves individual group comparisons.

The main point here is that a significant interaction effect indicates that interpretation may not be completely straightforward. That is, the action of one factor is not uniform across all levels of the other factor.

A LOOK AT TWO-WAY ANOVA COMPUTATIONS

Although the main goal of this chapter is to offer a basic overview of two-way ANOVA, in this section we present a greatly simplified look at the computations required by the analysis. Let's analyze Dr. Baxter's data, assuming the scores in each treatment condition or group are as shown below. The sums of scores and squared scores are shown in each group, along with row and column totals.

	Placebo	Drug	Row Totals
No treatment	12, 10, 14, 8, 15, 10, 9, 7, 12, 13 $\Sigma X = 110$ $\Sigma X^2 = 1,272$	7, 8, 12, 10, 10, 10, 8, 7, 5, 13 $\Sigma X = 90$ $\Sigma X^2 = 864$	$\Sigma X = 200$ $\Sigma X^2 = 2,136$
Conventional treatment	9, 10, 12, 8, 12, 10, 9, 10, 12, 8 $\Sigma X = 100$ $\Sigma X^2 = 1,022$	8, 9, 4, 3, 10, 4, 6, 5, 8, 3 $\Sigma X = 60$ $\Sigma X^2 = 420$	$\Sigma X = 160$ $\Sigma X^2 = 1,442$
Experimental treatment	10, 12, 10, 12, 9, 8, 7, 6, 8, 8 $\Sigma X = 90$ $\Sigma X^2 = 846$	0, 4, 3, 2, 6, 1, 2, 4, 5, 3 $\Sigma X = 30$ $\Sigma X^2 = 120$	$\Sigma X = 120$ $\Sigma X^2 = 966$
Column totals	$\Sigma X = 300$ $\Sigma X^2 = 3,140$	$\Sigma X = 180$ $\Sigma X^2 = 1,404$	$\Sigma X = 480$ $\Sigma X^2 = 4,544$

k = levels of factor A (treatment) = 3
m = levels of factor B (drug) = 2
N_g = number of patients per group = 10
N = total number of subjects = 60
ΣX^2 = sum of *all* squared scores
ΣX = sum of *all* scores
ΣX_R^2 = sum of squared scores in a given row; row variable is factor A, or treatment
ΣX_R = sum of scores in a given row
ΣX_C^2 = sum of squared scores in a column; column variable is factor B, or drug
ΣX_C = sum of scores in a column

There are six sums of squares to compute for the analysis, two can be found by subtraction. The following are the simplified equations for the *SS* that we need:

$$SS_{tot} = \Sigma X^2 - \frac{(\Sigma X)^2}{N}$$

$$SS_b = \sum_g \left[\frac{(\Sigma X_g)^2}{N_g} \right] - \frac{(\Sigma X)^2}{N} \qquad \text{between-groups } SS$$

$$SS_A = \sum_R \left[\frac{(\Sigma X_R)^2}{(N_g)(m)} \right] - \frac{(\Sigma X)^2}{N} \qquad SS \text{ for factor A}$$

$$SS_B = \sum_C \left[\frac{(\Sigma X_C)^2}{(N_g)(k)} \right] - \frac{(\Sigma X)^2}{N} \qquad SS \text{ for factor B}$$

$$SS_{AB} = SS_b - SS_A - SS_B \qquad \text{interaction } SS$$

$$SS_w = SS_{tot} - SS_b \qquad \text{within-groups } SS, \text{ or the error term}$$

SS_w can be computed directly from the following equation:

$$SS_w = \sum_g \left[\sum X_g^2 - \frac{(\Sigma X_g)^2}{N_g} \right]$$

Now let's compute the sums of squares:

$$SS_{tot} = 4,544 - \frac{(480)^2}{60} = 4,544 - 3,840 = 704,$$

$$SS_b = \left(\frac{(110)^2}{10} + \frac{(100)^2}{10} + \frac{(90)^2}{10} + \frac{(90)^2}{10} + \frac{(60)^2}{10} + \frac{(30)^2}{10} \right) - \frac{(480)^2}{60}$$

$$= (1,210 + 1,000 + 810 + 810 + 360 + 90) - 3,840 = 4,280 - 3,840 = 440,$$

$$SS_A = \left(\frac{(200)^2}{20} + \frac{(160)^2}{20} + \frac{(120)^2}{20} \right) - \frac{(480)^2}{60} = (2,000 + 1,280 + 720) - 3,840$$

$$= 4,000 - 3,840 = 160,$$

$$SS_B = \left(\frac{(300)^2}{30} + \frac{(180)^2}{30} \right) - \frac{(480)^2}{60} = (3,000 + 1,080) - 3,840$$

$$= 4,080 - 3,840 = 240,$$

$$SS_{AB} = SS_b - SS_A - SS_B = 440 - 160 - 240 = 40,$$

$$SS_w = SS_{tot} - SS_b = 704 - 440 = 264.$$

Alternatively, we could compute SS_w directly, as follows:

$$SS_w = \left(1,272 - \frac{(110)^2}{10}\right) + \left(846 - \frac{(90)^2}{10}\right) + \left(1,022 - \frac{(100)^2}{10}\right) + \left(420 - \frac{(60)^2}{10}\right)$$

$$+ \left(864 - \frac{(90)^2}{10}\right) + \left(120 - \frac{(30)^2}{10}\right) = 264.$$

As with the one-way ANOVA, computing the sums of squares is just the first step in analyzing the variance. We must now determine degrees of freedom for each SS and use df to compute the mean squares.

$$df_{tot} = N - 1 = 60 - 1 = 59,$$
$$df_b = (k \times m) - 1 = (3 \times 2) - 1 = 5,$$
$$df_A = k - 1 = 3 - 1 = 2,$$
$$df_B = m - 1 = 2 - 1 = 1,$$
$$df_{AB} = df_b - df_A - df_B = 5 - 2 - 1 = 2, \quad \text{or}$$
$$df_{AB} = df_A \times df_B = 2 \times 1 = 2,$$
$$df_w = df_{tot} - df_b = 59 - 5 = 54,$$
$$MS_A = \frac{SS_A}{df_A} = \frac{160}{2} = 80,$$
$$MS_B = \frac{SS_B}{df_B} = \frac{240}{1} = 240,$$
$$MS_{AB} = \frac{SS_{AB}}{df_{AB}} = \frac{40}{2} = 20,$$
$$MS_w = \frac{SS_w}{df_w} = \frac{264}{54} = 4.89.$$

There are also three F ratios to compute, as shown below.

$$F_A = \frac{MS_A}{MS_w} = \frac{80}{4.89} = 16.36,$$

$$F_B = \frac{MS_B}{MS_w} = \frac{240}{4.89} = 49.08,$$

$$F_{AB} = \frac{MS_{AB}}{MS_w} = \frac{20}{4.89} = 4.09.$$

As before, we can summarize our results in a table.

Two-Way ANOVA Summary Table

Source	SS	df	MS	F	p
Between groups	440	5	88		
A (treatment)	160	2	80	16.36 < .01 (df = 2, 54)	
B (drug)	240	1	240	49.08 < .01 (df = 1, 54)	
A × B (treatment × drug)	40	2	20	4.09 < .05 (df = 2, 54)	
Within groups	264	54	4.89		
Total	704	59			

For $df = 2, 60$, the critical values from Table C in Appendix 4 are 3.15 at the 5% level and 4.98 at the 1% level. These df, $df = 2, 60$, are the closest df in the table to the df we had in the study for the treatment comparison and for the test of the interaction (treatment by drug). For more conservative tests, we could use the critical F values for $df = 2, 40$. Either way, the result would be the same: We reject the null hypothesis at the 1% level ($p < .01$) for the treatment and drug main effects at the 5% level ($p < .05$) for the interaction.

Our conclusion: All effects were significant, indicating that both the type of treatment and the drug reduced panic. The significant interaction confirmed the prediction that the combination of Panic-EA and experimental treatment was especially effective. Post hoc comparisons would be needed to confirm the statistical significance of each of these cell differences.

SUMMARY

This chapter has presented the simplest of the factorial designs: the two-factor or two-way analysis of variance. The two-factor design differs from the one-way ANOVA discussed in Chapter 12 by having different levels of two independent variables rather than only one.

A test of the effect of each of the independent variables, considered in isolation, is called a main effect. The row variable is called factor A, and the column variable is called factor B. The joint effect of the two variables or factors is called interaction.

A typical graph of data from a two-factor study shows the mean dependent variable scores for factor B plotted over levels of factor A. Unequal averages of the points above each level of factor A indicate a significant main effect for factor A. If the averages of the points used to plot the lines are unequal, there is probably a significant factor B main effect. A significant interaction between factors is shown by converging or crossing lines on the graph.

The two-factor ANOVA results in three hypothesis tests or F ratios: one for the main effect of factor A, one for the main effect of factor B, and a ratio for the interaction of A and B. As in Chapter 12, if an F ratio has a value much above 1.00, the null hypothesis for the test will probably be rejected.

The main advantage of the two-factor ANOVA design is the test for an interaction between the factors. Unfortunately, a significant interaction makes interpretation of the results more difficult. Other advantages include a savings in the number of subjects required, greater generalizability, and an increase in the power of the tests on the main effects. If there is no interaction, interpretation of a significant main effect is the same as it was in Chapters 12 and 13.

EXERCISES

1. For each of the following graphs, tell the probable outcome of each of the significance tests:

a.

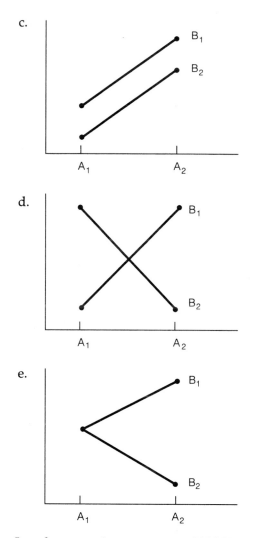

2. In what way is a two-way ANOVA more economical than two one-way ANOVAs on the same variables?

3. What is the main advantage of the two-factor design over the one-factor design? Why is the advantage a mixed blessing?

4. What is the first step in interpreting a significant interaction?

5. How is a significant interaction revealed graphically?

CHAPTER 15

Chi-Square

Jackie worked at the admissions desk of a health clinic. Part of her job was to screen patients as they came in for treatment. This included taking a health history, checking insurance forms, and completing all paper work. As the latest patient described his symptoms, Jackie was struck by the realization that he was yet another person who lived near the industrial park and who was reporting respiratory symptoms. The clinic was always busy, and only a small portion of patients sought treatment for respiratory problems, but it still seemed to Jackie that of the patients reporting respiratory symptoms, an unusually large proportion lived in the area near the industrial park.

Part of Jackie's job was to be alert to trends in admissions so that staffing and resources at the clinic could be properly distributed. But Jackie wasn't certain her observation was correct. Was there an unusual number of patients with respiratory symptoms from the industrial park area, or was she imagining this relationship?

She decided to see what the record showed. She examined the files of patients seen at the clinic in the past week and classified them by neighborhood (industrial park vs. nonindustrial park) and type of symptoms (respiratory vs. nonrespiratory). She found that 120 patients had been seen. Eighty patients had nonrespiratory symptoms and 40 had respiratory symptoms. Sixteen of the patients were from the industrial park area and 104 were from other neighborhoods. Jackie tabulated her data as shown below.

	Industrial Park	Nonindustrial Park	Row Totals
Nonrespiratory symptoms	4	76	80
Respiratory symptoms	8	32	40
Column totals	12	108	120

Jackie knew that 10% of the clinic patients typically came from the industrial park area and 90% came from elsewhere. She also knew that 33% of the clinic patients had respiratory symptoms and 67% didn't. Thus, she would expect that 12 of the 120 patients (10%) would come from the industrial park. Of these 12, 4 (33%) would be expected to have respiratory symptoms and 8 (67%) would be expected to have nonrespiratory symptoms. (This can be continued to get expected values for the patients who were not from the industrial park.) She used these proportions to determine the number of patients with respiratory symptoms who should come from each residential area. She found that 4 patients from the industrial park area and 36 patients from other areas could be expected to have respiratory problems. Eight residents of the industrial park area and 72 patients from other residential areas could be expected to report nonrespiratory symptoms. Jackie added this information to her table.

	Industrial Park	Nonindustrial Park	Row Totals
Nonrespiratory symptoms	4 (8)	76 (72)	80
Respiratory symptoms	8 (4)	32 (36)	40
Column totals	12	108	120

Note. Expected values are in parentheses.

The trends seemed clear enough to Jackie, but what would a statistician say about these data?

Jackie's problem is a common one in the social sciences. She has a set of observed frequencies of an outcome and a set of expected frequencies. However, her data are nominal (frequencies) rather than interval or ratio. Therefore, she cannot legitimately perform statistical procedures that involve certain arithmetic operations, such as averaging scores, and that make assumptions about the underlying distribution of scores. In this chapter we discuss a statistic for testing data of the sort collected by Jackie.

NONPARAMETRIC TESTS

In previous chapters, we have considered two powerful inferential tests: the t test and the F test. The t test and the F test are examples of **parametric tests**—tests designed to test hypotheses about population parameters. For example, when we used the one-sample t test, the null hypothesis was that our sample was drawn from a population in which the mean had a particular value. That is, we assumed a certain value for a population parameter, the mean (or μ). Another assumption we made in using the t test and the F test was that there was a normal distribution of the variable we measured in the population from which our sample(s) was obtained. These tests also require interval or ratio data, which we often don't have.

In this chapter and the next, we study tests that don't require normality assumptions and that don't test hypotheses about population parameters. Because population parameters are not considered, the tests are sometimes called **nonparametric tests.** Because the tests don't assume any particular distribution, they are also called **distribution-free tests.** Before discussing the first of the nonparametric tests, chi-square, let's review a topic encountered in Chapter 2: scaling.

In Chapter 2, we defined four different measurement scales: nominal, ordinal, interval, and ratio. The nominal scale is used for labeling only; we cannot specify the interval between values nor the ranking or ordering of the values. We can only record frequencies of occurrence—the number of subjects falling under a particular label or name. But that's exactly the kind of data generated by Jackie. She counted the number of clinic patients with and without respiratory symptoms who came from the industrial park area and from other areas.

How can we analyze Jackie's data? The inferential tests (t and F) that we studied previously required at least interval scale data, and the data analyzed with t and F were scores, not frequencies of occurrence. Now we need a new test, something appropriate with categorical data: the **chi-square test,** symbolized by χ^2 (read "ki-square," with a long i).

THE CHI-SQUARE GOODNESS-OF-FIT TEST

Actually there are two different chi-square tests—one in which we have different levels of a *single* categorical variable and one in which we have different levels of *two* categorical variables. A chi-square test on a single categorical variable is called a **chi-square goodness-of-fit test.** Let's look at an example of data involving a single categorical variable.

A professional test constructor is interested in whether the items on a recently constructed 20-item ability test are uniformly difficult throughout the test. She doesn't want difficult or easy items concentrated in any one area of the test. As a check, she has 20 people take the test; she then plots their errors for each 5-item segment of the test. She finds that 39 errors occur in the first segment, 15 in the second, 28 in the third, and 18 in the fourth. The data can be summarized as follows:

	Item #				
	1–5	6–10	11–15	16–20	Total
Frequency within segment	39	15	28	18	100

If the errors were no more likely to occur in one segment than another, she should have observed 25 errors in each segment. That is, there were 100 errors, and there were four different segments: $\frac{100}{4} = 25$. How well do the observed data fit what was expected? How good is the fit? It's time to apply the chi-square goodness-of-fit test.

The formula for the test is very simple:

FORMULA 15-1   *Chi-square*

$$\chi^2 = \Sigma \frac{(O - E)^2}{E},$$

where O stands for the *observed* frequency and E stands for the *expected* frequency.

The observed frequencies—39, 15, 28, and 18—are what the test constructor actually saw in her study. As noted above, assuming an equal distribution of frequencies in the test segments, each of the expected frequencies is 25. Computation of χ^2 then is as follows:

$$\chi^2 = \Sigma \frac{(O - E)^2}{E} = \frac{(39 - 25)^2}{25} + \frac{(15 - 25)^2}{25} + \frac{(28 - 25)^2}{25} + \frac{(18 - 25)^2}{25}$$

$$= \frac{196}{25} + \frac{100}{25} + \frac{9}{25} + \frac{49}{25}$$

$$= 7.84 + 4.00 + 0.36 + 1.96 = 14.16.$$

For the goodness-of-fit test, the degrees of freedom are determined by $K - 1$, where K is the number of categories. Thus, for this problem, $df = 3$, because there are four segments and the sum of the frequencies is fixed. Three values are free to vary, because the values in the first three segments could have been any numbers less than 100, and the value of the fourth segment would be determined by the frequencies in the first three segments.

As before, to determine whether to reject the null hypothesis, we consult a table of critical values of the test statistic, in this case Table G. For $df = 3$, the critical values are 7.82 at the 5% level and 11.34 at the 1% level. Because 14.16 is larger than the table value at the 1% level, we reject the idea that errors were evenly distributed across the four segments.

In this example, the expected frequencies were found by dividing the total number of observations by the number of segments. In other words, we assumed equal distribution of observations across categories.

The goodness-of-fit test can also be used when the expected frequencies are not assumed to be equally distributed. For example, in one study, a personality test called the Myers–Briggs Type Indicator (MBTI) was administered to a sample of 93 people with diagnosed and treated heart disease. The rationale for the study was to learn whether heart patients differ in personality characteristic(s) as measured by the MBTI from comparable persons without heart disease. If personality types are associated with heart disease, it might be possible to modify the personality characteristics that place a person most at risk. The MBTI assigns a score on each of four paired dimensions: extraversion–introversion, or E–I; sensing–intuition, or S–N; thinking–feeling, or T–F, judging–perceiving, or J–P. That is, a given individual may be classified as ISTJ or ENFP or as any other of 16 different types based on the four-letter combinations.

Let's look at the results from just the E–I scale. For the sample of 93 heart patients, there were 38 extraverts and 55 introverts. But what would the researchers have expected to observe in normal people, people without diagnosed heart disease?

Based on data gathered by the Center for Applied Psychological Type (CAPT) in Florida, 55% of the people of ages similar to the ages of the sample are introverts and 45% are extraverts. In other words, in a sample of 93 normal people there should be 51 introverts (93 × 55%) and 42 extraverts (93 × 45%). The data are summarized here with expected values in parentheses:

	MBTI Designation		
	Extravert (E)	Introvert (I)	Total
Frequency within category	38 (42)	55 (51)	93

Chi-square is computed as before.

$$\chi^2 = \Sigma \frac{(O-E)^2}{E} = \frac{(55-51)^2}{51} + \frac{(38-42)^2}{42}$$

$$= 0.31 + 0.38 = 0.69.$$

With $df = K - 1 = 2 - 1 = 1$, the critical value of chi-square at the 5% level (from Table G) is 3.84, or $\chi^2(1, N = 93) = 0.69$, $p > .05$. Thus, the null hypothesis is not rejected; there's no reason to believe from this sample that people with known heart disease differ on the E–I scale of the MBTI from what would be predicted based on data from CAPT.

ᕫ CHECKING YOUR PROGRESS

Let's look at performance by the heart disease sample on another MBTI scale. On the S–N scale, 79 heart disease patients were classified as S and 14 as N. The prediction from the CAPT data is that there will be 60% Ss and 40% Ns. Use the chi-square goodness-of-fit test to test the null hypothesis.

Answer: $\chi^2(1, N = 79) = 23.75$, $p < .01$. Heart patients were more likely to be Ss than would be expected from the proportion of Ss in the population.

THE CHI-SQUARE TEST OF INDEPENDENCE

The chi-square test based on two categorical variables is called variously the **chi-square test of independence,** the *two-sample chi-square test*, and the *chi-square test of significance*. With this test, we want to determine whether the two categorical variables are independent. That is, we want to see whether the distribution of frequencies across the levels of one variable is the same for all levels of the other variable. We assume the frequencies are the same and reject the null hypothesis if the test shows they probably are not.

Let's look at some examples. First, the problem introduced in the story at the beginning of the chapter was a two-variable problem. The two categorical variables (respiratory symptoms, neighborhood) form a frequency table called a **contingency table,** which is repeated here.

	Industrial Park	Nonindustrial Park	Row Totals
Nonrespiratory symptoms	4 (8)	76 (72)	80
Respiratory symptoms	8 (4)	32 (36)	40
Column totals	12	108	120

Note. Expected values are in parentheses.

The table is called a 2 × 2 contingency table because there are two rows and two columns (the totals don't count as rows and columns). If there were no difference in the proportion of patients with respiratory and nonrespiratory symptoms from the two different neighborhoods, we would expect to see similar percentages of the total frequency of respiratory symptoms in patients from each neighborhood. Obviously, this is not the case; a greater than expected proportion of patients with respiratory symptoms are from the industrial park area, and a smaller than expected proportion of patients with nonrespiratory symptoms are from the industrial park area. But is the difference great enough for us to conclude that there is a lack of independence in the groups, that the likelihood of having respiratory symptoms is contingent on where a person lives?

The formula for the chi-square test of independence is the same as the one introduced for the goodness-of-fit test—that is, Formula 15-1. The formula is repeated here:

$$\chi^2 = \Sigma \frac{(O-E)^2}{E}.$$

All we have to do is determine the expected frequency for each cell in the 2 × 2 table, subtract it from the observed frequency in the cell, square the result and divide it by the expected frequency, and add together the results from each cell to get chi-square. Remember that Jackie had calculated the expected frequencies in each cell by using the proportion of patients who came from each neighborhood and the proportions of respiratory and nonrespiratory patients examined at the clinic. These values are in parentheses in the table. We are now ready to use Formula 15-1 to calculate chi-square.

$$\chi^2 = \Sigma \frac{(O-E)^2}{E} = \frac{(4-8)^2}{8} + \frac{(76-72)^2}{72} + \frac{(8-4)^2}{4} + \frac{(32-36)^2}{36}$$

$$= \frac{-4^2}{8} + \frac{4^2}{72} + \frac{4^2}{4} + \frac{-4^2}{36} = 2 + 0.22 + 4 + 0.44$$

$$= 6.66.$$

With $df = 1$, the value required for significance at the 5% level is 3.84 and at the 1% level is 6.64, or $\chi^2(1, N = 120) = 6.66$, $p < .01$. From this calculation we can conclude that a significantly higher than expected number of patients with respiratory symptoms came from the industrial park area.

An Alternative Method for Finding Expected Values

Most of the time we do not have information from previous research or theory that allows us to establish expected values a priori. In these instances, we can calculate expected values by multiplying the marginal totals for a particular cell and dividing the result by the overall total. Doing this gives us Formula 15-2,

> **FORMULA 15-2**   *Expected frequencies for the chi-square test of independence*
>
> $$E = \frac{RT \times CT}{N},$$

where RT stands for row total and CT stands for column total. N is the total number of observations.

Using our original example, let's assume that we don't know proportions of patients from each neighborhood. In that case, we would have to use the formula to find the expected frequency of patients with nonrespiratory symptoms from the industrial park area. The row total for the cell of interest is 80, and the column total is 12. We compute E as follows:

$$E = \frac{(80)(12)}{120} = \frac{960}{120} = 8.$$

The expected frequencies for a given row or column must sum to the row or column total, so for a 2 × 2 table we have to calculate only one of the Es; we can determine the rest by subtraction. Thus, the expected number of patients with nonrespiratory symptoms from neighborhoods other than the industrial park area is $80 - 8 = 72$; E for patients for respiratory symptoms from the industrial park area is $12 - 8 = 4$; and E for patients with respiratory symptoms from neighborhoods other than the industrial park area is $40 - 4 = 36$. Note that our new method for determining expected frequencies results in precisely the same values as before.

Let's consider another example to illustrate the use of Formula 15-2 for computing expected frequencies.

A medical researcher is interested in the effect of a new drug treatment for Parkinson's disease, a progressively debilitating motor disorder. Seventy-five patients with early symptoms of Parkinson's receive either the new drug treatment or a placebo, and the dependent variable is whether or not the disease progressed to debility (e.g., need for a wheelchair) before the end of the study's 2-year time period. A contingency table of the results is shown below.

		Treatment		Row Totals
		Drug	Placebo	
Disease course	Progressed to debility	10	20	30
	Didn't progress to debility	28	17	45
	Column Totals	38	37	75

Using Formula 15-2, we can compute the expected frequency for the first cell in the table, the one showing the number of patients who progressed to debility while taking the new drug. The row total for the cell is 30 and the column total is 38. E is computed as follows:

$$E = \frac{(30)(38)}{75} = \frac{1,140}{75} = 15.2.$$

Because the expected frequencies for a given row or column must sum to the row or column total, we can determine the rest of the Es by subtraction. Thus, E for the number of placebo patients who progressed to debility is the row total (30) minus the E we just computed, or 14.8. The expected value for the number of drug patients who didn't progress is $38 - 15.2 = 22.8$; E for the number of placebo patients who didn't progress is $45 - 22.8 = 22.2$. The E values are shown in parentheses in the following contingency table:

| | | Treatment | | |
		Drug	Placebo	Row Totals
Disease course	Progressed to debility	10 (15.2)	20 (14.8)	30
	Didn't progress to debility	28 (22.8)	17 (22.2)	45
	Column Totals	38	37	75

We are now ready to compute chi-square.

$$\chi^2 = \Sigma \frac{(O-E)^2}{E}$$

$$= \frac{(10-15.2)^2}{15.2} + \frac{(20-14.8)^2}{14.8} + \frac{(28-22.8)^2}{22.8} + \frac{(17-22.2)^2}{22.2}$$

$$= \frac{(-5.2)^2}{15.2} + \frac{(5.2)^2}{14.8} + \frac{(5.2)^2}{22.8} + \frac{(-5.2)^2}{22.2}$$

$$= 1.78 + 1.83 + 1.19 + 1.22 = 6.02.$$

Again, we need to know degrees of freedom in order to use Table G for our test of significance. Recall that degrees of freedom was defined as the number of values free to vary after certain restrictions are placed on the data. For the chi-square test of independence, the restriction on the data is that the row and column totals are fixed.

Now, how many expected frequencies did we actually have to compute? The answer is 1, because the others were obtained by subtraction. Thus, degrees of freedom for a 2 × 2 contingency table will always be 1, as this is the number of values free to vary with the row and column totals fixed. A formula to determine the degrees of freedom is as follows:

FORMULA 15-3   *Degrees of freedom for the chi-square test of independence*

$$df = (R - 1)(C - 1),$$

where R is the number of rows and C the number of columns.

In our example, both R and C were 2, and $df = (2 - 1)(2 - 1) = (1)(1) = 1$. With $df = 1$, the value required for significance at the 5% level is 3.84 and at the 1% level is 6.64, or $\chi^2(1, N = 75) = 6.02$, $p < .05$. The new drug appears to offer early Parkinson's patients some protection against progression to a debilitating state.

Another Chi-Square Test of Independence Example

Another example of the chi-square test of independence may be instructive. A social psychologist was interested in learning whether the presence of others influenced people's helping behavior. He approached people on a city street who were either walking alone or walking with one or two others. He showed the person (the potential helper) his camera and asked if he or she would be willing to take his (the investigator's) photo. The number of people in each condition who complied with the request have been summarized in the following 2 × 2 contingency table.

	Complied	Refused	Row Totals
Group	6	74	80
Alone	25	55	80
Column totals	31	129	160

The first step is to determine the expected frequencies, and we can use Formula 15-2 to do this. How many helpers should we have observed if the groups were independent?

$$E = \frac{RT \times CT}{N} = \frac{(80)(31)}{160} = \frac{2,480}{160} = 15.5.$$

Box 15-1	Logic of Determining Expected Frequencies

Let's look at the logic behind the determination of the expected frequencies for the two-sample chi-square test. Let's again use the example of the patients with respiratory and nonrespiratory symptoms.

First, what is the probability that a person coming to the clinic will have symptoms of something other than a respiratory problem? In Chapter 9, we said that the probability of an event was the ratio of the number of times the event occurred to the total number of events. Jackie screened 80 patients with nonrespiratory symptoms out of a total sample of 120. The probability is $80/120 = .67$.

Now, what is the probability that a patient will be from the industrial park area? There were 12 such patients in the 120 total, giving a probability of $12/120 = .10$.

Finally, what is the probability that a patient will have nonrespiratory symptoms *and* be from the industrial park area? Here we need to refer to the multiplication rule from Chapter 9. The rule is that the probability that both events A and B will occur is the product of their individual probabilities. In other words, the probability of a patient's having nonrespiratory symptoms and being from the industrial park area is

$$(.67)(.10) = .067$$

We would expect about 6.7% of the 120 patients—8.04—to have both characteristics. This number is quite close to the 8 we obtained with Formula 15-2. However, the number obtained with Formula 15-2 is more accurate, because there is no rounding.

The remaining expected frequencies can be found by subtraction and are shown in parentheses in the completed contingency table.

	Complied	Refused	Row Totals
Group	6 (15.5)	74 (64.5)	80
Alone	25 (15.5)	55 (64.5)	80
Column totals	31	129	160

Having determined the expected frequencies, let's now compute chi-square.

$$\chi^2 = \Sigma \frac{(O-E)^2}{E} = \frac{(6-15.5)^2}{15.5} + \frac{(74-64.5)^2}{64.5} + \frac{(25-15.5)^2}{15.5} + \frac{(55-64.5)^2}{64.5}$$

$$= \frac{(-9.5)^2}{15.5} + \frac{(9.5)^2}{64.5} + \frac{(9.5)^2}{15.5} + \frac{(-9.5)^2}{64.5}$$

$$= \frac{90.25}{15.5} + \frac{90.25}{64.5} + \frac{90.25}{15.5} + \frac{90.25}{64.5}$$

$$= 5.82 + 1.40 + 5.82 + 1.40 = 14.44.$$

For $df = 1$, the critical values from Table G are 3.84 at the 5% level and 6.64 at the 1% level, or $\chi^2(1, N = 160) = 14.44$, $p < .01$. As 14.44 is larger than the critical value at the 1% level, we reject the null hypothesis of independence between the variables and conclude that people are more likely to comply with a request for assistance when they are alone than when they are with one or two others.

⟳ CHECKING YOUR PROGRESS

Based on teacher assessments, an experimenter has divided 100 students into two groups, one judged to have high self-esteem and one judged to have low self-esteem. The experimenter administers a survey of common fears to the two groups of students. She has arbitrarily decided that a score of 1 to 10 on the scale indicates a low number of fears, 11 to 20 a moderate number of fears, and 21 to 30 a high number of fears. For the low self-esteem group, she finds that 10 fall into the low category, 15 fall into the moderate category, and 25 fall into the high category. The results for the high self-esteem group are just the opposite: 25 students are in the low category, 15 in the moderate category, and 10 in the high category. Perform a chi-square test of independence to see whether high and low self-esteem students differ on the fear survey.

Answer: $\chi^2(2, N = 100) = 12.86$, $p < .01$, indicating that students in the low self-esteem group have more fears than students in the high self-esteem group.

RESTRICTIONS ON CHI-SQUARE

A number of conditions must be met for chi-square to be applied. First, *chi-square can be used only with frequency data*. In practice, this is no problem as it is possible to convert whatever data we have into frequency data by selecting different categories and counting the number of scores that fall into each one. This is exactly what was done in the example about test item difficulty. The 20-item test was divided into four segments, and the number of errors was determined for each segment. The primary danger in converting measurement data into frequency data is that chi-square is a less sensitive test than others we might apply.

A second restriction that must be placed on chi-square is that *the individual events or observations that constitute the data must be independent of each other*. This would not be true, for example, if we asked each subject multiple questions and then treated each of the responses as though it was independent of the others. Similarly, if we were dealing with wife–husband pairs, we should not expect their responses to be independent of each other.

The third restriction is that *we must have in the data both the frequency of occurrence and the frequency of nonoccurrence if we are recording whether or not an event occurs*. This restriction is necessary for the sums of the observed and expected frequencies to be the same.

The fourth restriction placed on chi-square is that *no expected frequencies should be less than 5*. If any expected frequencies are less than 5, the distribution of chi-square may have different values from those shown in Table G. There are ways to circumvent this rule, however. First, the rule may be relaxed if there are more than four cells and only a few of them have expected frequencies less than 5. Second, if we have a 2 × 2 table and expected frequencies less than 5, an alternative to chi-square is the *Fisher exact probability test*. One source for this test is *Nonparametric Statistics for the Behavioral Sciences*, 2d ed., by S. Siegel and N. J. Castellan, Jr. (New York: McGraw-Hill, 1988). Finally, we can always test more subjects so that the expected frequencies are larger.

SUMMARY

A nonparametric test is a test that doesn't examine hypotheses about population parameters and doesn't require normality assumptions. Nonparametric tests are sometimes called distribution-free tests. This chapter considered one nonparametric test: the chi-square test.

The chi-square test is applied when the measurement scale is nominal and the data consist of frequency counts. A chi-square test on a single categorical variable is called a goodness-of-fit test; a test on two categorical variables is called a chi-square test of independence, a two-sample chi-square test, or a chi-square test of significance.

The formula for chi-square is

$$\chi^2 = \Sigma \frac{(O - E)^2}{E},$$

where O is the observed frequency and E is the expected frequency. For the goodness-of-fit test, the expected frequencies are determined either by equally distributing the total number of observations across categories or by assigning the frequencies on the basis of percentages obtained from previous research. For the chi-square test of independence, the expected frequencies for a given cell in a contingency table may be found by solving the following equation:

$$E = \frac{RT \times CT}{N},$$

where RT stands for row total, CT stands for column total, and N is the total number of observations. Because the expected frequencies for a given row or column must sum to the row or column total, most of the expected frequencies may be obtained by subtraction. Another way to determine the expected frequencies is to base them on known proportions when these are available.

The computed value of chi-square is compared with the values in Table G with the appropriate degrees of freedom. For the goodness-of-fit test, $df = K - 1$, where K is the number of categories; for the chi-square test of independence, $df = (R - 1)(C - 1)$ where R is the number of rows and C is the number of columns. If the computed chi-square is equal to or larger than the appropriate table value at the 5% level, we reject the null hypothesis.

There are certain restrictions on the use of chi-square that must always be considered:

1. Chi-square can be used only with frequency data.
2. The individual events or observations that constitute the data must be independent of each other.
3. The data on which chi-square is computed must contain both the frequency of occurrence and the frequency of nonoccurrence if both have been recorded.
4. No expected frequencies should be less than 5. This rule may be relaxed if there are more than four cells and only a few have expected frequencies less than 5. An alternative to chi-square with a 2 × 2 table and small expected frequencies is the *Fisher exact probability test*. As a last alternative, more observations can be made to increase the expected frequencies.

❊ *Troubleshooting Your Computations*

The computations for chi-square usually cause little trouble, but there are a few things to remember. First, practice computing E for the test of significance and watch your subtraction if you're using this approach to determine E for a particular cell. Both the expected frequencies and the observed frequencies must sum to give you a row or column total. Also, because you are squaring each of the differences between O and E for a cell before you divide by E, be sure no negative signs creep in for a cell total. Finally, be careful in computing degrees of freedom for the test of significance; it would be unfortunate if you computed chi-square correctly only to make the wrong decision because of incorrect degrees of freedom.

EXERCISES

1. As voters leave a polling place, they are asked whether they consider themselves conservative, moderate, or liberal. They are then asked whether they
   voted for or against a tax to fund an experimental program in the schools.
   The frequencies are below.

	Conservative	Moderate	Liberal
For	36	63	81
Against	45	27	18

   Determine whether political orientation is related to support for the tax.

2. A professor wants to determine whether college algebra should be kept as a
   prerequisite for the course entitled Introductory Psychological Statistics.
   Accordingly, some students are allowed to register for the course on a
   pass–fail basis regardless of whether they have had the prerequisite. Of the
   70 students in the class, 40 have had algebra and 30 have not. At the end of
   the semester, the professor compares the number of students passing or failing the course with whether they had algebra. The results are summarized
   here:

	Pass	Fail
Algebra	34	6
No Algebra	12	18

   Determine whether having studied algebra is related to student success in
   the statistics course.

3. In a social psychology experiment, 56 students are asked to wait individually
   outside a closed door. While they are sitting outside the room waiting their
   turn, a person who is either well dressed or shabbily dressed walks toward
   them carrying a large notebook filled with loose papers. Under the pretext of
   stumbling, the person drops the notebook, spilling a large number of papers
   onto the floor. The experiment is designed to find whether there is a difference in willingness to aid a stranger as a function of whether the stranger is
   well or shabbily dressed.
       Of the 26 participants exposed to the well-dressed clumsy person, 20
   helped and 6 continued to wait their turn in the experiment. Of the 30 participants exposed to the shabbily dressed clumsy person, 10 helped. Construct
   the appropriate 2 × 2 table and apply the chi-square test.

4. There is some evidence for asymmetry in the size of the left and right hemi-spheres of the human brain. In a study of 100 brains, the left hemisphere was found to be larger in 60, the right hemisphere in 15, and 25 had left and right hemispheres equal in size. Perform a chi-square goodness-of-fit test on the data to see whether there is evidence for asymmetry. Assume there is none and that the expected frequencies are evenly distributed.

5. A test of need for affiliation has been given to 50 first-born and 40 later-born students. The results, put into three categories of need for affiliation—high, medium, and low—are shown below.

	High	Medium	Low
Later born	10	24	16
First born	26	8	6

Perform a test of significance to see whether the frequencies are evenly dis-tributed.

6. The student population of a local college is approximately one-third blond and two-thirds other hair color. Over a 2-day period the hair color of each student entering the student union building is tallied, with the following results: blonds, 452; others, 1,548. Determine whether blonds and others are as likely to enter the union as would be predicted on the basis of their per-centage in the student population.

7. A researcher administers a survey to 25 randomly selected persons from a rural community and finds that 16 of them demonstrate conservative politi-cal preferences. In a randomly selected group of 25 persons from an urban region, he finds that 7 demonstrate conservative political preferences. Do the two groups differ significantly?

8. In a study of intraspecific aggression (aggression directed toward other members of the same species), an experimenter finds that 16 of 23 animals tested in Species A exhibit aggression, but only 6 of 25 are aggressive in Species B. Do the two species differ significantly in terms of intraspecific aggression?

9. In a voter survey, people of different religious affiliations were asked whether they had voted for a Republican or for a Democrat in the last presi-dential election. The results are shown here:

	Baptist	Catholic	Methodist	Episcopal
Republican	27	24	10	2
Democrat	9	15	33	14

Determine whether religious affiliation had anything to do with the way people voted.

10. A chimpanzee was trained to make same-different judgments about pairs of stimuli. For pictures of objects, the animal's score was 23/24 correct. As each question had two choices (same-different), the expected value was 12/24. Perform a chi-square goodness-of-fit test on the animal's correct-incorrect responses.

11. In a study of the effectiveness of an antipsychotic drug, patients treated with the drug were compared to patients receiving a placebo. In terms of the number relapsing, 698 of 1,068 patients relapsed after taking the placebo, whereas 639 of 2,127 patients relapsed after taking the antipsychotic drug. Was the antipsychotic effective in preventing relapse?

16

Alternatives to *t* and *F*

✳ Brad was working on his honors dissertation in psychology. He wanted to study the effect of different schedules of reinforcement on the rate of extinction of a response. He hypothesized that a more complex reinforcement schedule would result in slower extinction than a simpler reinforcement schedule.

Brad randomly assigned 20 rats to one of two groups. In both groups, the rats were rewarded with a food pellet on a variable-interval (VI) schedule for bar-pressing behavior. In one group, the rats received a reward approximately every 30 seconds; this was the Simple VI schedule. In the other group, the range of intervals was much greater, although the average was still about 30 seconds; this was the Complex VI schedule.

Brad trained the rats until their responding stabilized. He then switched to extinction: The rats no longer received a reward pellet for pressing the bar. However, before he got to this phase of his experiment, Brad had to eliminate four rats from the study (three from the Simple group and one from the Complex group) because they developed respiratory infections.

Brad kept track of the number of days it took for the rats to stop responding. Two rats from the Complex group, however, continued to respond, and it looked as though they might go on forever. After consulting with his advisor, Brad decided to cut off the study at some arbitrary point. He chose twice the number of sessions it took the longest-responding rat in the Simple group to stop responding. So after 24 days, he terminated the experiment, with two of the animals in the Complex group still bar-pressing for no reward.

Brad's results were as follows:

Days to Extinction

Group Simple	Group Complex
12	24*
12	24*
11	16
8	15
7	14
6	12
6	11
	10
	9

*Arbitrary cut-off score; animal still responding.

Brad had planned to analyze his data with a *t* test, but he realized now that his samples were too small and uneven. Additionally, two of the rats had never achieved the criterion, and he'd had to cut them off arbitrarily; he really didn't know what their scores would have been if they had been allowed to continue. To compute the means and variances and to generate estimated population parameters, he needed *all* the scores.

Brad knew there were several nonparametric alternatives to the *t* and *F* tests; now he had to decide which one would be most suitable for his data.

In the last chapter, we studied chi-square, an example of a nonparametric or distribution-free test. A nonparametric test is one in which population parameters such as μ and σ are not involved; such a test is distribution free because no particular distribution is assumed. In this chapter, we examine three more nonparametric methods: the Mann–Whitney *U* test, the Wilcoxon test, and the Kruskal–Wallis test.

When should nonparametric alternatives to *t* and *F* be used? Part of the answer to this question involves scaling, the topic discussed in Chapter 2; parametric statistics assume at least interval scale measurement. If our level of measurement is nominal scale—that is, if we have frequency data—we use chi-square for a test of significance, as we saw in Chapter 15. With scores on an ordinal scale (data are rank ordered although intervals between them may not be equal), we can use a variety of nonparametric techniques, including the ones in this chapter.

An experimenter may elect to use a nonparametric test even when the parametric method would also be appropriate. However, when both parametric and nonparametric tests are appropriate, the parametric test is recommended because the power of parametric tests is generally greater. That is, all things being equal, we will be more likely to reject the null hypothesis with a parametric than with a nonparametric test.

Remember that the parametric tests assume normality in the population from which we take our sample(s). If our sample is badly skewed, we may feel uncomfortable with this assumption of normality. In this case, the nonparametric test may be preferable.

From our experience as researchers, we have found nonparametric tests to be most useful when a study involves small samples with unequal numbers of subjects. Small samples often have a few extreme scores that contribute a disproportionate amount to the sample's variability. In test statistics such as t and F, the denominator is a measure of variability; hence, the greater the variability, the smaller is the statistic and the less likely we are to be able to reject the null hypothesis. Because it avoids the measure of variability, the nonparametric alternative may result in rejection of the null hypothesis when this would not occur with t or F.

THE MANN–WHITNEY U TEST

The **Mann–Whitney (M–W) U test** is a powerful alternative to the t test for independent samples. It is used in two major instances:

1. When the level of measurement is ordinal scale and the best we can do with the numbers is to rank them from highest to lowest, and
2. When the assumption of normality in the population from which the samples were drawn cannot be made.

The Mann–Whitney test can also be applied when the level of measurement is interval scale and when other assumptions of the t test are met. However, the t test is preferable in situations where both tests are appropriate, as mentioned earlier.

The assumptions required by the Mann–Whitney test are that the samples are independent, that there is an underlying continuous scale of measurement, and that the measurement scale is at least ordinal. The hypothesis tested is that the populations from which the samples are drawn are identical.

The rationale for the test is based on the null hypothesis being tested. That is, assuming that the populations being sampled are identical, if we rank the combined observations from our two samples, we would expect to find the scores from the two samples rather evenly mixed in our combined ranking. If the scores are not evenly mixed in the combined ranking (that is, most of the scores from one sample have lower ranks than most of the scores in the other sample), then they probably come from different populations. The test is based on a determination of how evenly mixed the scores are from the two samples.

Let's consider a type of problem for which the Mann–Whitney test is appropriate: Brad's response extinction study. The data are repeated on the next page.

Group Simple	Group Complex
12	24
12	24
11	16
8	15
7	14
6	12
6	11
	10
	9

There are at least two reasons for not applying the *t* test to Brad's data. First, a parametric test is inappropriate—we should not compute the mean of the samples because some of the animals were eliminated from the study before achieving the criterion of extinction. In Chapter 5, we said that $\bar{X}$ should not be calculated when there are arbitrary cut-off points in the data.

Second, the sample sizes are small and the samples are oddly distributed. They are so oddly distributed, in fact, that it would be difficult to justify the assumption of normality in the population from which they came. Let's apply the Mann–Whitney *U* test, for which the formula is

---

FORMULA 16-1 *Mann–Whitney* **U** *test (computational formula)*

$$U = N_1 N_2 + \frac{N_1(N_1 + 1)}{2} - R_1.$$

---

where R_1 is the sum of the ranks of the scores in the first group, N_1 is the number of subjects in the first group, and N_2 is the number of subjects in the second group. The Mann–Whitney *U* test involves computing both *U* and *U'* (pronounced "you-prime").

The procedure for computing and testing *U* for significance is as follows:

1. Rank the scores from both groups combined from the lowest to the highest, with the smallest score receiving the rank of 1. Give tied scores the average of the tied ranks.

2. Sum the ranks for the first sample and call it R_1.

3. Once you obtain R_1, compute *U* using Formula 16-1.

4. After computing *U*, calculate *U'* from the following equation:

FORMULA 16-2   U'

$$U' = N_1 N_2 - U.$$

The *lower* value, either U or U', is used for the significance test.

5. The null hypothesis is that the two samples are drawn from identical populations. The alternative to this is that the two populations are different.

6. Compare U or U' to values in Table H. Use of Table H depends on the size of the samples and will be explained when we have a U (or U') to test.

Let's compute U for Brad's experiment and test it for significance. The first step is to rank the two sets of scores; the result of this ranking is as follows:

Group Simple	Rank	Group Complex	Rank
12	10	24	15.5
12	10	24	15.5
11	7.5	16	14
8	4	15	13
7	3	14	12
6	1.5	12	10
6	1.5	11	7.5
		10	6
		9	5
	$R_1 = \overline{37.5}$		$R_2 = 98.5$

As you can see, the scores have been ranked with the smallest score receiving the lowest rank. In this case, there were two scores of 6, so each 6 received the average of the tied ranks (1 and 2: average = 1.5). The next lowest score, 7, received the next rank, or 3, the 8 received a rank of 4, and so on until the highest scores, 24, received the average of their tied ranks, or 15.5.

After the combined scores in the two groups were ranked, the sum of the ranks for the first group was found and called R_1. We are now ready to compute U, using the values $N_1 = 7$, $N_2 = 9$, and $R_1 = 37.5$.

$$U = N_1 N_2 + \frac{N_1(N_1 + 1)}{2} - R_1$$

$$= (7)(9) + \frac{7(7 + 1)}{2} - 37.5$$

$$= 63 + 28 - 37.5 = 53.5,$$

$$U' = N_1 N_2 - U = (7)(9) - 53.5 = 63 - 53.5 = 9.5.$$

U' (the smaller of U and U') is compared with critical values in Table H. With $N_1 = 7$ and $N_2 = 9$, the critical value for a two-tailed test at the 5% level is 12. The decision rule is this: If U or U' is equal to or *less* than the table value, we reject the null hypothesis. Our computed value (9.5) is less than the table value, so we reject the null hypothesis and conclude that the two groups differ significantly. That is, we conclude that rats trained on the Complex VI schedule of reinforcement require more time to extinguish a response than rats trained on the Simple VI schedule. Note that the computed value must be equal to or *less* than the table value, not more than the critical value, as in the parametric tests we have studied.

Let's look at another example. An investigator is interested in the effect of "speed" instructions on memory. Fifteen students are asked to memorize a list of 4-digit numbers. Seven of the students are told to memorize as quickly as possible. The other 8 are told to work at their own pace. One week later, the 15 students are retrained on the list, this time without instructions to hurry. A percentage savings score is computed for each student. Any student requiring more than twice as many trials to relearn the list as were needed to learn it originally is assigned a score of –100% and testing is discontinued. The savings scores are as follows:

Speed Instructions	Own Pace Instructions
40	70
35	68
10	65
–20	55
–50	50
–100	–10
–100	–30
	–100

We have arbitrary cut-off scores and uneven groups with a lot of variability, so the M–W test is indicated. As before, we need to rank the scores from the combined groups, sum the ranks for each sample, and compute U and U'. The ranked scores and the summed ranks are as follows:

Speed	Rank	Own Pace	Rank
40	10	70	15
35	9	68	14
10	8	65	13
–20	6	55	12
–50	4	50	11
–100	2	–10	7
–100	2	–30	5
		–100	2
	$R_1 = \overline{41}$		$R_2 = \overline{79}$

As you can see, the scores have been ranked algebraically, with the largest negative score having the lowest rank. At the bottom are three scores of –100, which are tied for the ranks of 1, 2, and 3. Each of the three is assigned the average of the tied ranks:

$$\frac{1+2+3}{3} = \frac{6}{3} = 2.$$

Next lowest is a score of –50, which is assigned the rank of 4 (1, 2, and 3 have already been used); next is –30, with the rank of 5; and so on until the highest score is ranked. After the scores are ranked, we sum the ranks and find $R_1 = 41$ and $R_2 = 79$. We are now ready to compute U, using the values $N_1 = 7$, $N_2 = 8$, and $R_1 = 41$:

$$U = N_1 N_2 + \frac{N_1(N_1 + 1)}{2} - R_1$$

$$= (7)(8) + \frac{7(7 + 1)}{2} - 41$$

$$= 56 + 28 - 41 = 43,$$

$$U' = N_1 N_2 - U = (7)(8) - 43$$

$$= 56 - 43$$

$$= 13 \text{ (the smaller of } U \text{ and } U')$$

U' is compared with critical values in Table H. With $N_1 = 7$ and $N_2 = 8$, the critical value for a one-tailed test at the 5% level is 13. Our computed value is equal to the table value, so we reject the null hypothesis and conclude that the two groups differ significantly. In terms of this study, we conclude that students who learned the list at their own pace had better memory of the 4-digit numbers than students who learned under speed conditions.

It is also possible to compute U' directly, with a slight change in the equation for U. The equation for U' is

FORMULA 16-3 U'

$$U' = N_1 N_2 + \frac{N_2(N_2 + 1)}{2} - R_2.$$

Applying this equation to the previous problem, we have

$$U' = (7)(8) + \frac{8(8 + 1)}{2} - 79 = 56 + 36 - 79$$

$$= 92 - 79 = 13.$$

As you can see, solving Formula 16-3 is a useful check on the accuracy of the original computations.

The Mann–Whitney U test may also be used for comparing groups larger than $N = 20$. The procedure is the same except that after U (or U') has been computed, it is converted to a z score using the following equation:

FORMULA 16-4   *z score for large-sample* U

$$z = \frac{U - \dfrac{N_1 N_2}{2}}{\sqrt{\dfrac{(N_1)(N_2)(N_1 + N_2 + 1)}{12}}}.$$

If the z score obtained is equal to or larger than 1.96 (two-tailed test, 5% level) or 1.64 (one-tailed test, 5% level), the null hypothesis is rejected. As the M–W test is most useful for small samples, further examples illustrating its use with large samples will not be shown in this text. One final note: Either U or U' will result in the same absolute value for z. Only the sign will differ.

⑤ CHECKING YOUR PROGRESS

An experimenter predicted that extraverted children would display more social motivation than introverted children would. To test this idea, she had a teacher divide the 22 children in her class into two groups, introverts and extraverts. Each child was shown five pictures of people engaged in various activities and was asked to make up a story about each picture. The stories were then read by a trained judge who rated each story for affiliative images as an indication of social motivation. Each story received a score from 0 (no affiliative imagery) to 20 (consistent, high affiliative imagery). The total scores for the five stories are as follows:

Introverts	Extraverts
21	63
15	57
10	55
9	54
8	49
7	48
6	45
5	43
4	42
4	20
	14
	11

Using the M–W U test, compare the two groups.

Answer: $U' = 5$, $p < .01$, two-tailed test, indicating that extraverts showed significantly more social motivation than introverts.

THE WILCOXON MATCHED-PAIRS SIGNED-RANKS TEST

In Chapter 11, we discussed the t tests for both independent and dependent samples. In this chapter we have so far examined the Mann–Whitney test, which is a nonparametric alternative to the t test for independent samples. Now let's look at the **Wilcoxon matched-pairs signed-ranks test,** which is an alternative to the t test for dependent or related samples.

As an example, suppose we want to test the effectiveness of an analgesic agent (Painfree) on a pain other than headache. We conduct the experiment as described in Chapter 11 except that, instead of measuring the length of time each volunteer subject can tolerate the immersion of his or her hand in ice water, we have each subject rate the subjective quality of his or her pain on a scale of 0 to 20 after the hand has been immersed in ice water for a set period of time. The results are as follows:

Subject	Placebo	Painfree
A	15	10
B	17	15
C	10	11
D	8	8
E	14	13
F	13	7
G	10	5
H	8	5

As you can see, we have eight subjects, and each has been tested with both Painfree and the placebo, resulting in eight pairs of scores. Our level of measurement is no better than ordinal because of the subjectiveness of the ratings, and so we will use the Wilcoxon test.

The assumptions of the test are that the subjects must be randomly and independently selected, that the scale of measurement must be at least ordinal, and that we must be able to rank-order the difference scores. The null hypothesis is that the distributions of the populations under each condition are identical.

Computation of the test is simple. We first find the difference (d) between each pair of scores, discarding pairs with 0 differences. Next, we rank-order the difference scores in terms of absolute magnitude, retaining the appropriate sign.

Finally, we sum the ranks with the less frequently occurring sign and compare this value with table values in a test of significance.

If the distributions of the populations under each condition are identical, there will usually be about the same number of positive and negative differences, and the sums of the ranks for the positive and negative differences will not vary to any great extent. However, if the population distributions are not the same, then we could expect to see many more differences of one sign than of the other. Thus, the smaller the sum of the less frequently occurring ranks, the more likely it is that the population distributions under each condition are different.

Let's go back to the problem and solve it.

Subject	Placebo	Painfree	d	Rank of d	Rank with Less Frequent Sign
A	15	10	5	5.5	
B	17	15	2	3	
C	10	11	−1	−1.5	1.5
D	8	8	0		
E	14	13	1	1.5	
F	13	7	6	7	
G	10	5	5	5.5	
H	8	5	3	4	
					$T = \overline{1.5}$

The differences (d) have been found and the absolute values ranked. Ranking is performed as before, with the smallest difference having the first rank and so on until all the differences have been ranked. Tied scores are given the average rank; for example, in absolute value, two differences had a magnitude of 1 and each received the average of ranks 1 and 2, or 1.5. In the last column, the ranks with the less frequent sign are entered. In our example, only one negative difference occurred and the rank of this difference, 1.5, appears. Finally, the ranks (rank in this case) with the less frequent sign are summed and called T. Thus, our obtained $T = 1.5$. For comparative purposes the sum of the positive ranks is 26.5. Remember that if the population distributions are really identical, the sums of the positive and negative ranks will not be very different.

The obtained T of 1.5 is compared with the appropriate values in Table 1. The table's title tells us that it contains critical values of T. Thus, for $N = 7$, a T of 2 or *less* is required for rejection of the null hypothesis at the 5% level, two-tailed test. Incidentally, although we had eight pairs of scores originally, differences were found between only seven of them, and the pair having no difference was discarded. Our obtained T was 1.5, so we reject the null hypothesis. The participants' subjective rating of pain following use of Painfree was lower than after the administration of a placebo.

Let's look at another example of the use of the Wilcoxon test. A teacher was interested in the effect of public speaking training on the quality of speeches given by her students. Ten students gave speeches, and their quality was rated on a 30-point scale. The students then received training in public speaking and were asked to give another speech, which was also rated on a 30-point scale. The before and after training scores are as follows:

Student	Before	After	d	Rank of d	Rank with Less Frequent Sign
A	27	29	−2	−3	3
B	22	14	8	8	
C	5	5	0		
D	9	7	2	3	
E	17	18	−1	−1	1
F	35	21	14	9	
G	14	7	7	7	
H	3	5	−2	−3	3
I	8	5	3	5	
J	7	3	4	6	

$$T = \overline{7}$$

The difference is found for each pair of scores, and then the differences are ranked without regard to sign. Student C did not change and her data are discarded. Finally, the ranks with the less frequent sign are summed, giving a T of 7. In Table I, with $N = 9$, we see that a T of 6 or less is required for rejection at the 5% level of significance with a two-tailed test. We conclude that our observed result is not different enough from chance to enable us to reject the null hypothesis. In this study, training did not cause a statistically significant change in speech quality.

Table I cannot be used with samples greater than 25. However, as we've discovered with a number of other test statistics, with large samples the distribution of T is approximately normal. Thus, we can convert our T score to a z score using the formula

> **FORMULA 16-5**   *z score for large-sample* **T**
>
> $$z = \frac{T - \dfrac{N(N+1)}{4}}{\sqrt{\dfrac{N(N+1)(2N+1)}{24}}}.$$

If the value computed for z is 1.96 or larger (1.64 for a one-tailed test), the null hypothesis is rejected at the 5% level, two-tailed test.

⑤ CHECKING YOUR PROGRESS

An experiment has been performed to study the effects of movie depiction of altruism on expressed attitudes toward helping. Each member of 12 pairs of identical twins has been randomly assigned to one of two treatment conditions. One member of each pair watches scenes from a movie showing altruistic behavior and self-sacrifice. The other member watches neutral scenes from the same movie. Each subject is then given a self-rating scale designed to elicit attitudes about helping behavior. High scores represent a low threshold for the expression of helping. The results are as follows:

Twin Pair Number	Group Altruism	Group Neutral
1	23	15
2	13	15
3	15	12
4	17	17
5	19	15
6	23	19
7	25	19
8	10	10
9	16	17
10	8	5
11	7	2
12	12	11

Test the null hypothesis.

Answer: $T = 4.5$, which has a $p < .02$ for a two-tailed test. Exposure to the movie scenes of altruism and self-sacrifice produced significantly lower thresholds for the expression of helping than did exposure to the neutral scenes.

THE KRUSKAL–WALLIS ONE-WAY ANOVA

The **Kruskal–Wallis (K–W) one-way analysis of variance by ranks test** is a useful technique for comparing more than two groups when we have at least ordinal scale measurement and the assumptions of the one-way analysis of variance test cannot be met. In other words, it is used in situations similar to those we discussed favoring the M–W U test except that more than two independent groups are compared.

The K–W test is actually an extension of the M–W test and again requires that we rank the scores from the combined groups. The null hypothesis tested is that the samples have identical population distributions. If the distributions from which we draw our samples are identical, the sums of the ranks of each sample should be similar. Very different sums suggest that the samples come from different populations and result in rejection of the null hypothesis. Let's consider a problem for which the K–W test is appropriate.

The head of the anthropology department at a local college has three candidates in his department for an excellence in teaching award, and he wants to select the candidate with the best teaching skills. Each candidate currently teaches a section of Anthro 101. The department head develops an evaluation form and asks five students from each of the three sections to fill it out. On the form, students are asked to rate their current instructor on a scale of 1–30 for such qualities as command of the material, ability to explain difficult concepts, and availability to students outside of class. The ratings are as follows:

Instructor A	Instructor B	Instructor C
26	17	30
23	15	25
19	14	20
17	12	18
15	10	16

Obviously there are some differences in the ratings given to the three instructors, but are the differences great enough for us to conclude that the samples come from different populations? The K–W test is appropriate here because of the level of measurement used; that is, the ratings of the instructors constitute an ordinal level of measurement. The formula for the test is

FORMULA 16-6   *Kruskal–Wallis test (computational formula)*

$$H = \frac{12}{N(N+1)} \sum \frac{R_i^2}{N_i} - 3(N+1),$$

where N_i = the number of observations in a particular sample,
N = the total number of observations in all samples combined,
R_i = the sum of the ranks for a particular sample.

The large summation sign tells us to sum the squared ranks divided by the N in a group over all groups. With three groups and at least five subjects in each group, H is distributed approximately as chi-square, and we can use Table G with $df = K - 1$ (K is the number of samples) to evaluate H. However, with three groups and fewer than five subjects in any group, H is sufficiently deviant from chi-square that Table G cannot be used. An appropriate table may be found in *Nonparametric Statistics for the Behavioral Sciences*, 2d ed., by S. Siegel and N. J. Castellan, Jr. (New York: McGraw-Hill, 1988).

Let's find H. As with the M–W test, the first step is to rank the combined scores from the lowest to the highest and then to sum the ranks for each sample.

Instructor A	Rank	Instructor B	Rank	Instructor C	Rank
26	14	17	7.5	30	15
23	12	15	4.5	25	13
19	10	14	3	20	11
17	7.5	12	2	18	9
15	4.5	10	1	16	6
	$R_1 = 48$		$R_2 = 18$		$R_3 = 54$

The lowest rating in the combined groups is 10, and this is assigned a rank of 1. The same instructor also received a rating of 12, which is given the rank of 2. The ranking is continued until the highest score, 30, is reached, and this receives a rank of 15. As before, tied scores receive the average of the tied ranks. Finally, the sum of the ranks for each instructor is found: R_1 (the sum of the ranks of Instructor A) is 48, $R_2 = 18$, and $R_3 = 54$.

We're now ready to compute H.

$$H = \frac{12}{N(N+1)} \sum \frac{R_i^2}{N_i} - 3(N+1)$$

$$= \frac{12}{15(15+1)} \left(\frac{48^2}{5} + \frac{18^2}{5} + \frac{54^2}{5} \right) - 3(15+1)$$

$$= \frac{12}{(15)(16)} \left(\frac{2,304}{5} + \frac{324}{5} + \frac{2,916}{5} \right) - 3(16)$$

$$= \frac{12}{240} (460.8 + 64.8 + 583.2) - 48$$

$$= 0.05(1,108.8) - 48 = 55.44 - 48 = 7.44.$$

With $df = K - 1 = 3 - 1 = 2$, the critical value at the 5% level from Table G is 5.99. As our observed $H = 7.44$, we reject the null hypothesis and conclude that the samples come from different populations. In other words, the three instructors differ in their ratings. Just looking at the scores, it appears that Instructors A and C received higher ratings than Instructor B. Further testing will be needed to determine which differences are significant.

Let's consider another example. Recruiters from a national hotel chain were interviewing college seniors majoring in psychology, history, business, and sociology for management training positions. Two interviewers evaluated each candidate on a scale of acceptability from 0 (unacceptable) to 7 (highly desirable). The ratings of the two interviewers were summed to give an overall rating. The interviewers were interested in whether students from some majors received higher ratings than students from other majors. To answer the question, they analyzed the data using a Kruskal–Wallis one-way ANOVA.

Psychology	History	Business	Sociology
13	14	12	10
12	7	11	8
11	7	10	8
10	7	8	6
7	6	6	6
6	5	5	5
6	5	5	5
4	2	4	1

As before, the first step is to rank the combined scores. Once this has been done, we can sum the ranks for each sample and compute H. The computations are as follows:

Psychology	Rank	History	Rank	Business	Rank	Sociology	Rank
13	31	14	32	12	29.5	10	25
12	29.5	7	18.5	11	27.5	8	22
11	27.5	7	18.5	10	25	8	22
10	25	7	18.5	8	22	6	13.5
7	18.5	6	13.5	6	13.5	6	13.5
6	13.5	5	7.5	5	7.5	5	7.5
6	13.5	5	7.5	5	7.5	5	7.5
4	3.5	2	2	4	3.5	1	1
	$R_1 = 162$		$R_2 = 118$		$R_3 = 136$		$R_4 = 112$

$$H = \frac{12}{N(N+1)} \sum \frac{R_i^2}{N_i} - 3(N+1)$$

$$= \frac{12}{32(32+1)} \left(\frac{162^2}{8} + \frac{118^2}{8} + \frac{136^2}{8} + \frac{112^2}{8} \right) - 3(32+1)$$

$$= \frac{12}{1,056} (3,280.5 + 1,740.5 + 2,312 + 1,568) - 99$$

$$= 0.01136(8,901) - 99 = 101.12 - 99 = 2.12.$$

Note that the fraction $12/1,056$ has been carried out to five decimal places rather than being rounded to hundredths. If we use 0.01, the final answer will have a negative value (–9.99), which is impossible. It would be slightly more accurate to multiply the numerator of the fraction by 8,901 [(12)(8,901) = 106,812] and divide the result by 1,056 (106,812/1,056 = 101.15). Then the final answer would be $H = 2.15$.

Do you notice that there are quite a few tied scores? Actually, the value of H is affected by ties; for this reason, there is a procedure to correct for them. However, the correction is minor, and it would be worth applying only in a situation where the H value computed was slightly below that required for significance. For this problem, the H value corrected for ties is 2.16 even though there were eight sets of tied scores including almost all of the 32 scores in the four samples. Because the difference is negligible, the correction procedure will not be presented. (For further details of the procedure, consult *Nonparametric Statistics for the Behavioral Sciences*, 2d ed., by Siegel and Castellan.)

From Table E we find that the critical values for chi-square with $df = 3$ ($K - 1 = 4 - 1 = 3$) are 7.82 and 11.34 at the 5% and 1% levels, respectively. Our H value, corrected or uncorrected, is much less than the value at the 5% level, and we cannot reject the null hypothesis. Thus, there is no reason to believe that students from some majors received higher ratings than students from other majors.

---

⑤ CHECKING YOUR PROGRESS

Research has suggested that birth order influences people's social competence. To verify this finding, 21 students were categorized as first-born, second-born, or later-born, and then rated by their classmates on the amount of their class participation. The score for each student is the sum of the student's ratings. The scores are shown here:

First-born	Second-born	Later-born
25	28	14
24	27	12
23	26	10
20	18	7
19	15	5
18	15	5
15	14	
	12	

Compute H and test it for significance.

Answer: $H = 11.49$, $p < .01$, suggesting that first-born and second-born students engage in significantly more class participation than later-born students do.

FURTHER TESTING AFTER A SIGNIFICANT *H*

What happens when a significant *H* value is obtained? Does this tell us which group comparisons are significant? The answer is no, just as it was with the *F* test. In this case, individual comparisons can be made with a test we've already discussed in this chapter, the Mann–Whitney *U* test. Recall that the K–W is an extension of the M–W.

To illustrate, let's reconsider the first example of the K–W we solved—the ratings of the three anthropology instructors. Suppose that, after finding differences among the instructors the department head wanted to compare the ratings obtained by Instructors A and B. Computation of the M–W test is as follows:

Instructor A	Rank	Instructor B	Rank
26	10	17	6.5
23	9	15	4.5
19	8	14	3
17	6.5	12	2
15	4.5	10	1
	$R_1 = 38$		$R_2 = 17$

$$U = N_1 N_2 + \frac{N_1(N_1 + 1)}{2} - R_1$$

$$= (5)(5) + \frac{5(5 + 1)}{2} - 38$$

$$= 25 + 15 - 38 = 40 - 38 = 2,$$

$$U' = N_1 N_2 - U = (5)(5) - 2 = 25 - 2 = 23.$$

The smaller of *U* and *U'* is *U* = 2, and this is the value we will test for significance. From Table H we find that 2 is the critical value for a two-tailed test at the .05 level (for a one-tailed test at the .025 level). Thus, we reject the null hypothesis for the comparison between Instructors A and B. Instructor A received higher ratings than Instructor B.

⤴ CHECKING YOUR PROGRESS

To check your progress, compare Instructors A and C and Instructors B and C.

Answer: $U' = 10$, $p > .05$ for the comparison between Instructors A and C; $U' = 1$, $p = .02$, two-tailed test, for the comparison between Instructors B and C. Instructor C received higher ratings than Instructor B but did not differ from Instructor A.

SUMMARY

The techniques studied in this chapter—the Mann–Whitney U test, the Wilcoxon matched-pairs signed-ranks test, and the Kruskal–Wallis H test—are valuable alternatives to the t test and the one-way ANOVA. Instead of being based on a comparison of the means of independent samples or on a comparison of the variances, the M–W and the K–W tests compare the ranks of the sample scores. The Wilcoxon test studies the ranks of the difference scores. The tests are nonparametric and are used primarily for comparing data generated by an ordinal scale—that is, rank-ordered data.

The M–W test is used to compare two independent samples. The procedure is as follows:

1. Rank the scores from the combined samples from the lowest to the highest, giving the lowest score the rank of 1. Give tied scores the average of the tied ranks.

2. Find the sum of the ranks for each sample.

3. Compute the statistic U using the formula

$$U = N_1 N_2 + \frac{N_1(N_1 + 1)}{2} - R_1,$$

where N_1 is the number of observations in the first sample, N_2 is the number of observations in the second sample, and R_1 is the sum of the ranks in the first sample.

4. Compute U' from the equation

$$U' = N_1 N_2 - U.$$

Use the smaller of U or U' in the significance test.

5. Compare the smaller of U or U' with table values from Table H for the appropriate sample sizes. If U or U' is smaller than the critical table value, reject the null hypothesis.

6. For samples larger than $N = 20$, convert U or U' to a z score using the formula

$$z = \frac{U - \frac{N_1 N_2}{2}}{\sqrt{\frac{(N_1)(N_2)(N_1 + N_2 + 1)}{12}}}.$$

If the absolute value of the z score is equal to or larger than 1.96, reject the null hypothesis.

The Wilcoxon test is useful as an alternative to the t test for dependent samples when the assumptions for t cannot be met. The difference between pairs of scores is found and ranked without regard to sign. The sum of the ranks with the less frequently occurring sign is found, and if N is 25 or less, the resulting T is compared with values in Table I. If T is equal to or *less* than critical values in the table, the null hypothesis is rejected. For samples larger than 25, the distribution of T is approximately normal and z is computed from the equation

$$z = \frac{T - \dfrac{N(N+1)}{4}}{\sqrt{\dfrac{N(N+1)(2N+1)}{24}}}.$$

If the z score is 1.96 or larger, the null hypothesis is rejected at the 5% level.

The K–W test is an extension of the M–W test for situations in which three or more samples are to be compared. As with the M–W test, the combined scores from the groups are first ranked and then the sum of the ranks for each sample is found. A statistic H is computed from the formula

$$H = \frac{12}{N(N+1)} \sum \frac{R_i^2}{N_i} - 3(N+1),$$

where N_i is the number of observations for a particular sample, N is the total number of observations for the combined groups, and R_i is the sum of the ranks for a particular sample.

With sample sizes of at least 5 and at least 3 samples, H is distributed approximately as chi-square; Table G is used to evaluate H, with $df = K - 1$, where K is the number of samples.

❈ Troubleshooting Your Computations

Although the techniques discussed in this chapter are fairly simple to apply, there are some possible problem areas and warnings that something has gone awry in your proceedings. For example, both the K–W test and the M–W test require ranking of the *combined* scores in the groups from the lowest to the highest. The rank of the highest score should be equal to N unless the highest scores are tied. If the highest score doesn't receive a rank of N, you should go back to the beginning of the ranking procedure and be sure you haven't skipped a rank somewhere along the way.

The value you obtain for either U or H should be a positive number. If it is not, check the sum of the ranks to be sure you haven't made an error there.

If you are using the M–W U test, be sure to compute U' as well as U, and be sure to use the smaller of the two values in the significance test. Also, when using Table H, be sure to remember that the value of U or U' is significant if it is *less* than the appropriate table value, not greater, as in the other tests we have considered.

When using the Wilcoxon test be sure to discard all zero differences. Also, the difference scores are ranked in terms of absolute value—that is, without regard to sign. To be significant, the obtained *T* must be equal to or *less* than the table value.

EXERCISES

1. Ten monkeys, five reared with a surrogate (artificial) mother and five reared normally, have been observed over a 10-day period in a group play area. The number of self-directed behaviors has been scored for each animal during a 20-minute daily test session. The summed scores for each animal are as follows:

Reared with Surrogate Mother	Normally Reared
255	173
241	150
213	142
185	131
151	75

    Compute the M–W *U* and test it for significance.

2. The Myers–Briggs Type Indicator (MBTI) has been administered to a large number of people to determine their personality types. On the basis of this test, a number of persons have been designated as either thinking or feeling types and have been given a questionnaire concerning their attitudes toward extrasensory perception. Each person receives a score on the questionnaire reflecting the degree of his or her belief in ESP, with higher scores reflecting more positive attitudes about ESP. The scores are as follows:

Group Thinking	Group Feeling
8	20
7	18
7	15
5	15
3	14
1	12
0	6
0	5
	4
	1

    Compare the groups.

3. In situations where both parametric and nonparametric tests could be used, why is the parametric test usually preferable?

4. The quality of articles from the most recent issue of four different professional sociology journals has been rated, with higher numbers representing higher ratings. The results were as follows:

Journal A	Journal B	Journal C	Journal D
12	45	20	37
10	43	13	35
9	42	11	28
9	41	8	27
8	36	6	20
7	25	5	13
3	23	4	10
2	15	1	
	10		

Determine whether the differences are significant. Note: Carry the division of $12/[N(N + 1)]$ to at least 5 decimal places.

5. Perform all pairwise comparisons for Exercise 4.

6. What does it mean to call a test nonparametric?

7. Using the MBTI mentioned in Exercise 3, researchers have identified a large number of students classified as feeling types. From this group, 14 persons expressing strong belief in ESP on a questionnaire have been shown a film presenting a very negative view of ESP's validity. Before and after scores on the ESP questionnaire are listed here:

Student	Before the Film	After the Film	Student	Before the Film	After the Film
1	20	22	8	25	28
2	18	13	9	10	10
3	15	15	10	12	13
4	15	18	11	17	23
5	17	16	12	15	11
6	16	14	13	13	17
7	14	10	14	10	10

Test the null hypothesis.

8. An identical procedure to that followed in Exercise 7 has been performed, except that 13 thinking types have been selected for low belief in ESP. The students are shown a biased film presenting ESP in a favorable light. Before and after scores on the ESP questionnaire were as follows on the next page.

Student	Before the Film	After the Film
1	7	7
2	5	8
3	0	5
4	3	7
5	2	4
6	1	3
7	4	10
8	4	12
9	5	4
10	7	4
11	8	8
12	5	15
13	2	11

Test the null hypothesis.

9. An investigator wants to learn whether there are occupational differences in self-ratings on a scale of sociability. Ten salespeople and eight delivery people rate themselves on a 20-item scale of sociability. The ratings are as follows:

Sales	Delivery
15	16
14	3
12	10
17	5
13	15
10	18
5	14
4	11
	9
	10

Compare salespeople and delivery people on the sociability ratings.

1

Brief Math–Algebra Review

Let's face it: There's a lot of variability in the mathematical sophistication under-graduates bring to their first statistics course. From our experience, preparation ranges from avoidance of any college math to completion of an advanced college calculus course. If your background qualifies you for the calculus end of the range, read no further; this appendix is not for you. On the other hand, if you've avoided college math before this, read on. The material in this appendix is designed to refresh your memory of topics long forgotten and to prepare you for the very basic mathematics presented elsewhere in this text.

SYMBOLS

Symbol	Read	Example
$=$	equals	$7 = 7$
$\neq$	is not equal to	$6 \neq 37$
$>$	greater than	$5 > 2$
$<$	less than	$2 < 5$
$\geq$	greater than or equal to	$p \geq .05$
$\leq$	less than or equal to	$p \leq .01$
$+$	plus	$3 + 3 = 6$
$-$	minus	$3 - 3 = 0$
$\times$ or $(\ )(\ )$ or $\cdot$	times	$3 \times 3 = 9$
		$(3)(3) = 9$
		$3 \cdot 3 = 9$
$\div$ or $/$	divided by	$6 \div 3 = 2$

Symbol	Read	Example
( )²	square	$(3)^2 = 3^2 = 9$
√	square root	$\sqrt{4} = 2$
| |	absolute value of (the number without regard to sign)	$\|-5\| = 5$ $\|5\| = 5$
±	plus or minus	6 ± 5 is $6 + 5 = 11$ and $6 - 5 = 1$

ARITHMETIC OPERATIONS

Addition

Numbers may be added in any order or combination.

Example:

$$8 + 4 + 3 = 3 + 4 + 8 = (3 + 4) + 8 = 15$$

Addition of Negative Numbers

Add as though the numbers were positive; then put a negative sign before the result.

Example:

$$(-1) + (-3) + (-5) + (-7) = -(1 + 3 + 5 + 7) = -16$$

Subtraction

Subtraction is equivalent to the addition of a negative number.

Example:

$$12 - 3 = 12 + (-3) = 9$$

As with addition, numbers may be subtracted in any order or combination.

Example:

$$27 - 4 - 12 = 27 + (-4) + (-12) = 27 + [(-4) + (-12)]$$
$$= -4 + (-12) + 27 = 11$$

Adding a Combination of Positive and Negative Numbers

Sum the positive and negative numbers separately; take the difference between the sums; then put the sign of the larger sum on the result.

Examples:

$$(+5) + (+3) + (+6) + (-2) + (-5) + (-15)$$

$$= +14 + (-22) = -8 \quad \text{(The difference between 22 and 14 is 8,}$$
$$\text{and the sign of the larger difference is } -.)$$

$$(+5) + (+10) + (-3) + (-5) = +15 + (-8) = 7$$

Subtracting Negative Numbers

Change the sign of the negative number to be subtracted and add.

Examples:

$$10 - (-5) = 10 + 5 = 15$$
$$-15 - (-6) = -15 + 6 = -9$$

MULTIPLICATION AND DIVISION

In multiplication and division, the result is positive if all of the terms are positive or if there is an even number of negative terms. The result is negative if there is an odd number of negative terms.

Examples:

$$(6)(3) = +18$$
$$(-6)(-3) = +18$$
$$(-6)(3) = -18 \quad \text{or} \quad (6)(-3) = -18$$
$$\frac{-6}{-3} = +2$$
$$\frac{6}{3} = +2$$
$$\frac{6}{-3} = -2$$
$$\frac{-6}{3} = -2$$

As with addition and subtraction, order of computation makes no difference.

Example:

$$(6)(-3)(-4) = (-4)(-3)(6) = 72$$

ORDER OF OPERATIONS

Work from the inside out; that is, do everything inside parentheses or brackets first. Within an expression, follow the order of operations summarized in the mnemonic "Follow My Dear Aunt Sally."

1. Follow = Functional operations such as square or square root
2. My Dear = Multiplication and Division
3. Aunt Sally = Addition and Subtraction

Example 1:

$$6(5 - 2^2) + \frac{13\sqrt{25}}{8} = 6(5 - 4) + \frac{(13)(5)}{8}$$

$$= 6(1) + \frac{65}{8} = 6 + 8.13 = 14.13$$

Example 2:

$$\left[\frac{(0.9)(5)}{4}\right]X - \left[\frac{(0.9)(5)}{4}\right](12) + 20$$

Do everything inside parentheses or brackets first. Multiply; then divide:

$$\left(\frac{4.5}{4}\right)X - \left(\frac{4.5}{4}\right)(12) + 20$$

$$1.13X - (1.13)(12) + 20$$

Multiply before adding:

$$1.13X - 13.56 + 20 = 1.13X + 6.44$$

In adding −13.56 and +20, take the difference between the numbers and give the sign of the larger number to the result.

WORKING WITH FRACTIONS

In these days of the pocket calculator, the simplest way to work with fractions is to convert them to decimals and carry out the operations specified by the equation. To convert a fraction to a decimal, divide the numerator (top part of the fraction) by the denominator (bottom part of the fraction).

Examples:

$$\frac{1}{15} + \frac{1}{17} = 0.07 + 0.06 = 0.13$$

$$\left(\frac{3}{19}\right)\left(\frac{7}{16}\right) = (0.16)(0.44) = 0.07$$

Nevertheless, there are times when it is more convenient or it is necessary (such as when your calculator breaks) to work with fractions. In these situations, there are several rules, specific to fractions, that must be followed.

Addition or Subtraction of Fractions

In adding or subtracting fractions, first express each fraction in terms of the least common denominator. Then add (or subtract) the numerators and place the result over the common denominator.

Examples:

$$\frac{1}{8} + \frac{1}{2} + \frac{1}{4} = \frac{1}{8} + \frac{4}{8} + \frac{2}{8} = \frac{7}{8}$$

$$\frac{11}{12} - \frac{1}{6} - \frac{1}{3} = \frac{11}{12} - \frac{2}{12} - \frac{4}{12} = \frac{5}{12}$$

Multiplication of Fractions

In multiplying fractions, find the product of the numerators and divide by the product of the denominators.

Examples:

$$\frac{2}{3} \times \frac{3}{5} = \frac{2 \times 3}{3 \times 5} = \frac{6}{15}$$

$$\frac{1}{2} \times \frac{3}{7} \times \frac{3}{5} = \frac{1 \times 3 \times 3}{2 \times 7 \times 5} = \frac{9}{70}$$

Multipying a Whole Number by a Fraction

In multiplying fractions and whole numbers, multiply the numerator of the fraction(s) by the whole number(s) and divide by the denominator.

Examples:

$$\left(\frac{1}{9}\right)(5) = \frac{(1)(5)}{9} = \frac{5}{9}$$

$$\left(\frac{1}{7}\right)(4)(3) = \frac{(1)(4)(3)}{7} = \frac{12}{7}$$

$$\left(\frac{4}{5}\right)\left(\frac{1}{3}\right)(7) = \frac{(4)(1)(7)}{(5)(3)} = \frac{28}{15}$$

SOLVING EQUATIONS WITH ONE UNKNOWN

You will frequently be required to solve equations with one unknown. These are quite simple and usually involve performing arithmetic steps to isolate the unknown on one side of the equation and then simplifying the other side of the equation. The specific steps required are different for each problem. The principle to remember is that whatever you do on one side of the equation must also be done on the other side of the equation. Examples of the basic types of problems you may encounter should illustrate the procedures involved.

Solving for X by addition:

$$X - 7 = 4$$
$$X - 7 + 7 = 4 + 7 \quad \text{(add 7 to both sides)}$$
$$X = 11$$

Solving for X by subtraction:

$$X + 6 = 10$$
$$X + 6 - 6 = 10 - 6 \quad \text{(subtract 6 from both sides)}$$
$$X = 4$$

Solving for X by division:

$$3X = 15$$

$$\frac{3X}{3} = \frac{15}{3} \qquad \text{(divide both sides by 3)}$$

$$X = 5$$

Solving for X by multiplication:

$$\frac{X}{7} = 4$$

$$(7)\frac{X}{7} = (4)7 \qquad \text{(multiply both sides by 7)}$$

$$X = 28$$

Solving for X by a combination of procedures:

$$4X + 2 = 18$$

$$4X + 2 - 2 = 18 - 2 \qquad \text{(subtract 2 from both sides)}$$

$$4X = 16$$

$$\frac{4X}{4} = \frac{16}{4} \qquad \text{(divide both sides by 4)}$$

$$X = 4$$

$$\frac{X - 10}{3} = 2$$

$$(3)\left(\frac{X - 10}{3}\right) = 2(3) \qquad \text{(multiply both sides by 3)}$$

$$X - 10 = 6$$

$$X - 10 + 10 = 6 + 10 \qquad \text{(add 10 to both sides)}$$

$$X = 16$$

EXERCISES

1. $\dfrac{3 + (13 - 3^2)}{(4)(6 - 3)(5 + 2^2)} = ?$

2. $\dfrac{1}{10} + \dfrac{5}{17} + \left(\dfrac{6}{23}\right)\left(\dfrac{5}{11}\right) = ?$

3. $\left(\dfrac{15}{27}\right)\left(\dfrac{3^2}{13^2}\right) = ?$

4. $13 + (-7) + 14 + (-3^2) = ?$

5. $15 - (-10) = ?$

6. $|-27| = ?$

7. $(-11)^2 = ?$

8. $(-10)(13) = ?$

9. $\dfrac{10\sqrt{5}}{\sqrt{\dfrac{275}{12} - 4^2}} = ?$

10. $\dfrac{(8)(7^2) + 1/3(7 + 6^2)}{(10 + 11 - 2)(6 - 3)} = ?$

11. $\dfrac{17}{10 - 15} = ?$

12. $\dfrac{3X + 14}{5} = 10 \qquad X = ?$

13. $\dfrac{2}{3}X \quad 3 = 11 \qquad X = ?$

14. $\dfrac{3(X + 2)}{7} = 6 \qquad X = ?$

15. $7X - 15 = -1 \qquad X = ?$

Glossary of Statistical Terms

abscissa   the horizontal axis, or X axis

absolute value   value of a number without regard to sign

addition rule of probability   for mutually exclusive random events, the probability of either one event or another event equals the sum of the probabilities of the individual events

additivity   the property of variance that, for individual samples, the variance of a sum of parts is equal to the sum of the variances of the parts

alternative hypothesis (H_1)   in hypothesis testing, the hypothesis that the value of a population parameter is something other than what we have assumed it to be

analysis of variance (ANOVA)   parametric inferential technique designed to test for significant differences among two or more different groups

ANOVA summary table   table used to summarize the results of the analysis of variance; contains values for SS, df, MS, and the F ratio

a posteriori tests   unplanned comparisons following a significant F ratio; also called post-ANOVA or post hoc tests

apparent limits   limits of class intervals with gaps between them

a priori tests   tests designed to look at specific hypotheses before the experiment is done

average deviation (AD)   average amount that each score in a distribution deviates from the distribution's mean

bar graph   type of histogram used to graph nominal scale or categorical data; each bar is separated from its neighbors

between-group variability   part of the ANOVA test based on the deviation between each group mean and the total mean; variability between the groups

biased sample   sample that is not representative of the population of interest

bimodal   referring to a distribution with two modes

central limit theorem   a simplified version is that as sample size increases, the resulting sampling distribution of means more closely approximates the normal distribution

central tendency   tendency for a distribution's scores to be concentrated near the middle of the distribution

chi-square goodness-of-fit test   chi-square test on different levels of a single categorical variable

chi-square test   nonparametric test for nominal scale data

chi-square test of independence   chi-square test on different levels of two categorical variables; also called chi-square test of significance and the two-sample chi-square test

class interval (ci)   interval of scores in a grouped frequency distribution

coefficient of determination (r^2)   amount of variability in one variable explained by variability in another

conditional probability   the probability of an event given that another event has already occurred

confidence interval (CI)   range of values within which we are reasonably confident the population mean lies

contingency table   tabular presentation of frequencies by category

continuous variable   variable whose measurement can assume an infinite number of values

control group   group of subjects not subjected to experimental treatment, but like the experimental group(s) in all other ways. The purpose of the control group is to provide a base against which to measure any change in the experimental group(s)

correlation   degree of relationship between two or more variables

counterbalancing   method to control for order effects in a repeated measures design by including all orders of treatment presentation

cumulative frequency curve, or **cumulative frequency polygon**   polygon created from a cumulative frequency distribution

cumulative frequency distribution   frequency distribution in which the frequencies are accumulated from the lowest score or class interval to the highest score or class interval

cumulative percentage distribution   frequency distribution in which the percentage frequencies are accumulated from the lowest score or class interval to the highest score or class interval

cumulative percentage polygon   curve plotted from a cumulative percentage distribution

data   numbers; the results of measurement

degrees of freedom (*df*)   number of values free to vary after certain restrictions are placed on the data

dependent variable   in behavioral science, the measurement of behavior

descriptive statistics   statistical techniques used to illustrate or describe data

deviations   differences of scores from a standard or reference value; usually refers to differences between a score and the mean

directional hypothesis   alternative hypothesis that states the direction of the difference between a population parameter and the value assumed by H_0

discrete variables   variables capable of assuming only a finite number of values

dispersion   spread of scores around the mean

distribution-free tests   see *nonparametric tests*

double-blind   referring to an experimental design often used in drug research in which neither the subject nor the treatment administrator knows the subject's group designation

estimated population variance ($\hat{s}^2$)   the unbiased sample estimate of the population variance

estimated standard deviation ($\hat{s}$)   the unbiased sample estimate of the population standard deviation

estimated standard error of the differences ($\hat{s}_{\overline{X}_1 - \overline{X}_2}$)   estimated standard deviation of the sampling distribution of the differences

estimated standard error of the mean ($\hat{s}_{\overline{X}}$)   estimated standard deviation of the sampling distribution of means

experimental error   source of variability in data caused by such things as imprecise measuring equipment, momentary changes in experimenter and subject attention, and slight changes in background conditions during data collection

factorial design   experimental design in which there are two or more independent variables

factors   designation for variables when there are two or more

Fisher LSD (least significant difference) test   powerful post-ANOVA test that computes a *t* score for each between-group comparison; also called the protected *t* test

F ratio   ratio of the variability between groups to the variability within groups; test statistic for the ANOVA test

frequency   number of times a score occurs

frequency distribution   listing of scores from highest to lowest (or lowest to highest) with each score's frequency beside it

frequency polygon   graphic representation of a frequency distribution, in which scores are plotted on the X axis and frequencies are plotted on the Y axis

grouped frequency distribution   frequency distribution in which the range of scores is divided into a number of mutually exclusive intervals

histogram   graph of a frequency distribution in which a rectangular bar is drawn over each score value on the X axis

homogeneity of variance   condition in which the population variances are the same

HSD test   see *Tukey HSD (honestly significant difference) test*

independent events   events for which occurrence of one event doesn't alter the probability of any other event

independent samples   samples in which the behavior of the members of one sample is not related to the behavior of the members of the other

independent sampling   sampling such that the selection of one person or object has no effect on the probability of another person or object being selected; see also *random sampling*

independent *t* test   test for situations in which two separate and independent groups are compared

independent variable   variable controlled or manipulated by the experimenter

indices   the summary numbers that result from an analysis of data

individual differences   differences between subjects in an experiment because of different subject backgrounds, experiences, abilities, motives, and so on

inferential statistics   statistical techniques that allow you to make conclusions about a larger group based on results from some portion of it

interaction   joint effect of two independent variables on behavior

interval scale   measurement scale with equal intervals between the scores in addition to the properties of naming and ranking of objects or events

Kruskal–Wallis (K–W)   one-way analysis of variance by ranks test; nonparametric alternative to the one-way ANOVA

least squares line   line generated by the regression equation

linear correlation   degree to which a straight line best describes the relationship between two variables

line graph   type of graph in which an independent variable is plotted on the X axis and some measure of the dependent variable is plotted on the Y axis

LSD test   see *Fisher LSD (least significant difference) test*

main effect   in a factorial experiment, the effect of each independent variable, considered by itself

Mann–Whitney (M–W) *U* test   nonparametric alternative to the *t* test for independent samples

matched pairs   dependent samples in which subject pairs are as closely matched as possible on some characteristic(s) relevant to the dependent variable

mean ($\bar{X}$, μ)   the sum of the scores divided by the number of scores; the arithmetic average

mean square (*MS*)   the analyzed variance in the ANOVA test, found by dividing each sum of squares by the appropriate *df*

median (*Md*)   point on the score scale separating the top 50% of the scores from the bottom 50%; the score at the 50th percentile

mode (*Mo*)   most frequently occurring score(s) in a distribution

multimodal   referring to a distribution with two or more modes

multiplication rule of probability   the probability of two or more independent events occurring on separate occasions is the product of their individual probabilities

negative correlation   inverse relationship between two variables; high scores on one variable are associated with low scores on the other variable

negatively skewed curve   skewed curve whose tail is to the left end of the X axis

nominal scale   measurement scale assigning a name, or label, to different objects or events

nondirectional hypothesis   an alternative to H_0 that states that the population parameter is not equal to the value specified by the null hypothesis

nonindependent events   events for which the occurrence of one event alters the probability of any other event

nonparametric, or **distribution-free, tests**   tests that do not test hypotheses about population parameters and do not assume any particular distribution; examples are the chi-square test, the Mann–Whitney test, the Wilcoxon test, and the Kruskal–Wallis test

normal curve   symmetrical, bell-shaped curve whose tails never reach the X axis and whose measures of central tendency are identical

normal distribution   distribution of the normal curve

null hypothesis (H_0)   in hypothesis testing, the hypothesis that assumes a particular value for a population parameter

one-tailed test   signficance test that considers only one end of the distribution, the end predicted by the experimenter

ordinal scale   measurement scale in which numbers both name objects or events and allow the objects or events to be ranked

ordinate   the vertical axis, or Y axis

parameters   numerical summary characteristics of populations

parametric tests   statistical tests designed to test hypotheses about population parameters

Pearson product-moment correlation coefficient, or **Pearson *r***   mean of the z-score products of the X and Y variables

percentage frequencies   frequencies of occurrence presented as percentages of the total sample

percentile   score at or below which a given percentage of the scores lie

percentile rank   percentage of cases up to, and including, the one in which we're interested; total percentage of the distribution below a score

population   complete collection of something

positive correlation   direct relationship between two variables; high scores are associated with high scores, and low scores with low scores

positively skewed curve   skewed curve whose tail is to the right end of the X axis

post-ANOVA tests   see *a posteriori tests*

post hoc tests   see *a posteriori tests*

power   probability that the inferential test will detect a false null hypothesis

probability   the proportion of times an event would occur if the chances for occurrence were infinite

probability density distribution   the probabilities associated with scores in addition to the scores themselves

protected *t* test   see *Fisher LSD test*

randomized sampling   sampling in which all available subjects are assigned at random to the different experimental conditions

random sampling, or random and independent sampling   sampling method in which each population member has an equal chance of being selected

range   difference between the highest score and the lowest score in a distribution

ranking, or rank ordering   placing objects or events in order, usually from highest to lowest

ratio scale   interval scale with a true zero

real limits   limits of class intervals without gaps between them

regression coefficient   the slope of the regression line

regression equation   equation for the straight line that best describes the linear relationship between two variables

repeated measures design   experimental design in which each subject experiences all levels of the independent variable; also known as within-subjects comparisons

sample   portion or subset of the population

sampling   the process of selecting a sample from a population

sampling distribution   distribution whose scores are sample statistics computed from an infinite number of samples drawn from some population

sampling distribution of means   distribution whose scores are means of samples drawn from some population

sampling distribution of the mean differences   distribution whose scores are differences between pairs of sample means

sampling without replacement   sampling in which each chosen individual is not returned to the population before the next selection

sampling with replacement   sampling in which each selected individual is returned to the population before the next selection

scales, or **scales of measurement**   rules used for assigning numbers to objects or events

scaling   assigning numbers or categories to objects or events

scatterplot   graphical representation of correlation in which pairs of scores are plotted, with the scores on one variable plotted on the X axis and the scores on the other variable plotted on the Y axis

score   data point, symbolized by X

significant   in statistics, a term indicating rejection of the null hypothesis

skewed curve   curve in which a large number of scores are piled at one end or the other with a tail at the opposite end

Spearman rank order correlation coefficient (r_s)   nonparametric, easily computed alternative to the Pearson r

standard deviation (s, σ)   square root of the average squared deviation; square root of the variance

standard error of the difference between means ($\sigma_{\bar{X}_1 - \bar{X}_2}$)   standard deviation of the sampling distribution of the mean differences

standard error of the mean ($\sigma_{\bar{X}}$)   standard deviation of the sampling distribution of the means

standard normal curve   normal, or bell-shaped, curve with a mean of 0 and a standard deviation of 1

standard score   deviation of a raw score from the mean in standard deviation units; also known as a z score

statistic   numerical summary characteristic of a sample

statistical hypotheses   predictions about a population based on sample results

statistics   a set of tools and procedures concerned with the collection, organization, and analysis of data

stem-and-leaf plot   data display created by splitting each score into a stem and a leaf, listing the different stems from lowest to highest, and putting each leaf beside its stem

stratified random sampling   sampling in which the population is divided into relevant groups (strata) and random samples are taken from each group

sum of squares (SS_X)   sum of the squared deviations of the scores from the mean; one of the main components of the analysis of variance

t distribution   probability distribution of t scores, which are estimated z scores

total sum of squares (SS_{tot})   sum of the squared deviation of each score from the total mean in the analysis of variance

total variability   variability in data based on the deviation between each score and the overall, or total, mean

treatment effect   variability in data caused by administration of the independent variable

Tukey HSD (honestly significant difference) test post-ANOVA test that compares each mean difference with a computed HSD or honestly significant difference

two-tailed test significance test that considers both ends of the distribution

two-way analysis of variance, or **two-way ANOVA** ANOVA technique used for analyzing data resulting from the administration of two or more levels of two independent variables

Type I, or α, **error** rejecting a true null hypothesis

Type II, or β, **error** failing to reject a false null hypothesis

unbiased estimate statistic that shows no systematic tendencies in relation to the estimated parameter

unbiased sample sample that accurately reflects the population from which it was drawn

variable anything that may take on different values or amounts

variance (s^2, σ^2) average squared deviation

Wilcoxon test nonparametric alternative to the t test for dependent samples

within-groups variability part of the ANOVA test based on the deviation between each score in a group and the group mean; variability within a group

within-subjects comparisions the same individuals are subjected to each of two treatment conditions; each subject is his or her own control

zero correlation no relationship between two variables

z score deviation of a raw score from the mean in standard deviation units; also called a standard score

Symbol Glossary and Glossary of Computational Formulas

CHAPTER 3: THE FREQUENCY DISTRIBUTION

Symbols

Symbol	Stands For
X	a score
f	frequency of a score
ci	class interval
i	width of a class interval
R	range of scores
N	sum of the frequencies, or total sample size
Cum f	cumulative frequency

Formulas

Formula 3-1. Width of class intervals

$$i = \frac{R}{\text{number of ci}}$$

Formula 3-2. Percentage from frequency

$$\%\text{age (percentage)} = \frac{f}{N}(100)$$

Formula 3-3. Cumulative percentage from cumulative frequency

$$\text{Cum \%age (cumulative percentage)} = \frac{\text{Cum } f}{N}(100)$$

CHAPTER 4: GRAPHING DATA

Symbols

Symbol	Stands For
MP	midpoint of a class interval

CHAPTER 5: MEASURES OF CENTRAL TENDENCY

Symbols

Symbol	Stands For
Mo	mode
Md	median
LRL	lower real limit of an interval
$\overline{X}$	sample mean
Σ	capital sigma, means to sum what follows
$X - \overline{X}$	deviation of a score from the mean
μ	population mean, read "mu"

Formulas

Formula 5-1. Median for a frequency distribution

$$Md = \text{LRL} + i\left(\frac{N/2 - \text{Cum } f}{f}\right)$$

Formula 5-2. Mean

$$\overline{X} = \frac{\Sigma X}{N}$$

Formula 5-3. Mean for a frequency distribution

$$\overline{X} = \frac{\Sigma fX}{N}$$

CHAPTER 6: MEASURES OF DISPERSION AND STANDARD SCORES

Symbols

Symbol	Stands For
R	range of a set of scores
AD	average deviation
σ^2	population variance
s^2	sample variance
σ	population standard deviation
s	sample standard deviation
SS_X	sum of squares for the X variable
z	standard score, or z score

Formulas

Formula 6-3. Average deviation for a frequency distribution

$$AD = \frac{\Sigma f|X - \overline{X}|}{N}$$

Formula 6-8 and 6-9. Sample variance

$$s^2 = \frac{\Sigma X^2 - \frac{(\Sigma X)^2}{N}}{N} \quad \text{or} \quad \frac{\Sigma fX^2 - \frac{(\Sigma fX)^2}{N}}{N}$$

Formula 6-11. Sum of squares

$$SS_X = \Sigma X^2 - \frac{(\Sigma X)^2}{N} \left[\Sigma fX^2 - \frac{(\Sigma fX)^2}{N} \text{ for a frequency distribution} \right]$$

Formula 6-12. Sample variance using sum of squares

$$s^2 = \frac{SS}{N}$$

Formula 6-17. Sample standard deviation when $f = 1$

$$s = \sqrt{\frac{\Sigma X^2 - \frac{(\Sigma X)^2}{N}}{N}} \quad \text{or} \quad \sqrt{\frac{SS}{N}}$$

Formula 6-18. Sample standard deviation for a frequency distribution

$$s = \sqrt{\frac{\Sigma f X^2 - \frac{(\Sigma f X)^2}{N}}{N}} \quad \text{or} \quad \sqrt{\frac{SS}{N}}$$

Formula 6-20. z score from a raw score using sample statistics

$$z = \frac{X - \overline{X}}{s}$$

Formula 6-22. Raw score from a z score using sample statistics

$$X = zs + \overline{X}$$

CHAPTER 8: CORRELATION AND REGRESSION

Symbols

Symbol	Stands For
r	Pearson r, Pearson product-moment correlation coefficient
z_X, z_Y	z scores for the X and Y variables, respectively
ρ	rho, the population correlation coefficient
$\hat{Y}$ or $\hat{X}$	Y caret or X caret: predicted values for Y or X based on the regression equation
s_Y, s_X	standard deviation of the Y and X variables, respectively
r^2	coefficient of determination
r_S	Spearman rank order correlation coefficient
d	difference between the ranks
b	regression coefficient
a	Y intercept of the regression line

Formulas

Formula 8-2. Pearson r

$$r = \frac{N\Sigma XY - \Sigma X \Sigma Y}{\sqrt{\left[N\Sigma X^2 - (\Sigma X)^2\right]\left[N\Sigma Y^2 - (\Sigma Y)^2\right]}}$$

Formula 8-3. Cross products

$$CP = \Sigma XY - \frac{\Sigma X \Sigma Y}{N}$$

Formula 8-4. Pearson r (alternative)

$$r = \frac{CP}{\sqrt{(SS_X)(SS_Y)}}$$

Formula 8-5. Y predicted from X

$$\hat{Y} = \left(\frac{rs_Y}{s_X}\right)X - \left(\frac{rs_Y}{s_X}\right)(\overline{X}) + \overline{Y}$$

Formula 8-6. Regression coefficient

$$b = \frac{CP}{SS_X}$$

Formula 8-7. Y intercept of the regression line

$$a = \overline{Y} - b\overline{X}$$

Formula 8-8. Coefficient of determination

$$\text{coefficient of determination} = \frac{\text{explained variation}}{\text{total variation}} = r^2$$

Formula 8-9. Spearman rank order correlation coefficient

$$r_s = 1 - \frac{6\Sigma d^2}{N(N^2 - 1)}$$

CHAPTER 9: PROBABILITY

Symbols

Symbol	Stands For
$p(A)$	probability of event A
$p(A \text{ or } B)$	probability of event A or event B
$p(A, B)$	probability of both A and B
$p(A \mid B)$	probability of event B given that event A has occurred

Formulas

Formula 9-1. Addition rule of probability

$$p(A \text{ or } B) = p(A) + p(B)$$

Formula 9-2. Multiplication rule of probability

$$p(A, B) = p(A) \times p(B)$$

Formula 9-3. Probability of a sequence of nonindependent events

$$p(A, B) = p(A) \times p(B \mid A)$$

Formula 9-4. Probability from percentage area

$$p(\text{probability}) = \frac{\% \, \text{area}}{100}$$

CHAPTER 10: CONFIDENCE INTERVALS AND HYPOTHESIS TESTING

Symbols

Symbol	Stands For
$\sigma_{\overline{X}}$	standard error of the mean
$\mu_{\overline{X}}$	mean of the sampling distribution of means
$\hat{s}_{\overline{X}}$	estimated standard error of the mean

(continued)

Symbol	*Stands For*
$t_{\overline{X}}$ or t	t score, which is an estimate of a z score
CI	confidence interval
df	degrees of freedom
$t_{.05}$ or $t_{.01}$	t scores from Table B cutting off deviant 5% or 1% of the distribution [occur with probability of .05(.01) or less]
H_0	null hypothesis
α	alpha level, level at which we test H_0
H_1	alternative hypothesis
t_{comp}	computed t score
t_{crit}	critical t score from Table B
Type I or α error	rejecting true H_0
Type II or β error	failing to reject false H_0

Formulas

Formula 10-3. Sample mean from population values

$$\overline{X} = z(\sigma_{\overline{X}}) + \mu$$

Formula 10-4. Estimated population variance

$$\hat{s}^2 = \frac{SS}{N-1} \quad \text{where} \quad SS = \Sigma X^2 - \frac{(\Sigma X)^2}{N}$$

Formula 10-5. Estimated standard deviation

$$\hat{s} = \sqrt{\frac{SS}{N-1}} \qquad \text{or} \qquad \hat{s} = \sqrt{\hat{s}^2}$$

Formula 10-6. Estimated standard error of the mean

$$\hat{s}_{\overline{X}} = \frac{\hat{s}}{\sqrt{N}}$$

Formula 10-7. t score

$$t_{\overline{X}} = \frac{\overline{X} - \mu}{\hat{s}_{\overline{X}}}$$

Formula 10-8 and 10-9. Confidence intervals for the population mean

$$95\% \text{ CI} = \pm t_{.05}\hat{s}_{\overline{X}} + \overline{X} \qquad 99\% \text{ CI} = \pm t_{.01}\hat{s}_{\overline{X}} + \overline{X}$$

CHAPTER 11: SIGNIFICANCE OF THE DIFFERENCE BETWEEN TWO SAMPLE MEANS

Symbols

Symbol	Stands For
$\sigma_{\overline{X}_1 - \overline{X}_2}$	standard error of the difference between means
$\hat{s}_{\overline{X}_1 - \overline{X}_2}$	estimated standard error of the differences
$\overline{X}_1 - \overline{X}_2$	score in the sampling distribution of the differences
$\mu_1 - \mu_2$	mean of the sampling distribution of the differences
$z_{\overline{X}_1 - \overline{X}_2}$	z score based on the sampling distribution of the differences
$t_{\overline{X}_1 - \overline{X}_2}$	t score based on the sampling distribution of the differences
$\sigma_{\overline{D}}$	standard error of the mean differences
$\hat{s}_{\overline{D}}$	estimated standard error of the mean differences
r	correlation coefficient
$\overline{X}_D$	mean of the differences
$\hat{s}_{\overline{X}_D}$	estimated standard error of the differences
$\hat{s}_D$	estimated standard deviation of the differences
D	difference between a pair of scores

Formulas

Formula 11-3. Estimated standard error of mean differences for independent samples

$$\hat{s}_{\overline{X}_1 - \overline{X}_2} = \sqrt{\left(\frac{(N_1 - 1)\hat{s}_1^2 + (N_2 - 1)\hat{s}_2^2}{N_1 + N_2 - 2}\right)\left(\frac{1}{N_1} + \frac{1}{N_2}\right)}$$

Formula 11-4. Estimated standard error of mean differences for independent samples (alternative raw-score formula)

$$\hat{s}_{\overline{X}_1 - \overline{X}_2} = \sqrt{\left(\frac{SS_1 + SS_2}{N_1 + N_2 - 2}\right)\left(\frac{1}{N_1} + \frac{1}{N_2}\right)} \text{ where } SS = \Sigma X^2 - \frac{(\Sigma X)^2}{N}$$

Formula 11-7 and 11-8. Two-sample t test for independent samples

$$t_{\overline{X}_1-\overline{X}_2} = \frac{\overline{X}_1 - \overline{X}_2}{\hat{s}_{\overline{X}_1-\overline{X}_2}} \quad \text{or} \quad \frac{\overline{X}_1 - \overline{X}_2}{\sqrt{\left(\frac{(N_1-1)\hat{s}_1^2 + (N_2-1)\hat{s}_2^2}{N_1 + N_2 - 2}\right)\left(\frac{1}{N_1} + \frac{1}{N_2}\right)}}$$

Formula 11-9. Two-sample t test for independent samples (alternative computational formula)

$$t_{\overline{X}_1-\overline{X}_2} = \frac{\overline{X}_1 - \overline{X}_2}{\sqrt{\left(\frac{SS_1 + SS_2}{N_1 + N_2 - 2}\right)\left(\frac{1}{N_1} + \frac{1}{N_2}\right)}}$$

Formula 11-12. t test for dependent samples

$$t = \frac{\overline{X}_D}{\hat{s}_{\overline{X}_D}} \quad \text{or} \quad \frac{\overline{X}_D\sqrt{N}}{\hat{s}_D}$$

Formula 11-13. Estimated standard error of the mean difference

$$\hat{s}_{\overline{X}_D} = \frac{\hat{s}_D}{\sqrt{N}}$$

CHAPTER 12: ONE-WAY ANALYSIS OF VARIANCE

Symbols

Symbol	Stands For
$\overline{X}_{tot}$	total mean
X_g	score within a group
$\overline{X}_g$	mean of a group
SS_{tot}	total sum of squares
SS_w	sum of squares within a group
SS_b	sum of squares between groups
N_g	number of subjects within a group
N	total number of subjects
$\sum_g$	sum over or across groups

Symbol	Stands For
MS_b	mean square between groups
MS_w	mean square within groups
df_b	degrees of freedom between groups
K	number of groups
df_w	degrees of freedom within groups
df_{tot}	total degrees of freedom
F	F ratio, ANOVA test

Formulas

Formula 12-5. Total sum of squares

$$SS_{tot} = \Sigma X^2 - \frac{(\Sigma X)^2}{N}$$

Formula 12-6. Within-groups sum of squares

$$SS_w = \sum_g \left[\Sigma X_g^2 - \frac{(\Sigma X_g)^2}{N_g} \right]$$

Formula 12-7. Between-groups sum of squares

$$SS_b = \sum_g \left[\frac{(\Sigma X_g)^2}{N_g} \right] - \frac{(\Sigma X)^2}{N}$$

Formula 12-8, 12-9, and 12-10. Between groups degrees of freedom, within groups degrees of freedom, and total degrees of freedom, respectively

$$df_b = K - 1 \qquad df_w = N - K \qquad df_{tot} = N - 1$$

Formula 12-11. Between-groups mean square

$$MS_b = \frac{SS_b}{df_b}$$

Formula 12-12. Within-groups mean square

$$MS_w = \frac{SS_w}{df_w}$$

Formula 12-13. *F* ratio

$$F = \frac{MS_b}{MS_w}$$

Formula 12-14. Within-groups sum of squares in one-way repeated measures ANOVA

$$SS_w = SS_{subj} + SS_{error}$$

Formula 12-15. Total sum of squares in one-way repeated measures ANOVA

$$SS_{tot} = SS_b + SS_{subj} + SS_{error}$$

Formula 12-16. Within-subjects sum of squares in one-way repeated measures ANOVA

$$SS_{subj} = \sum_s \left[\frac{(\Sigma X_m)^2}{T} \right] - \frac{(\Sigma X)^2}{N}$$

Formula 12-17. Error sum of squares in one-way repeated measures ANOVA

$$SS_{error} = SS_{tot} - SS_b - SS_{subj}$$

Formula 12-18. Error degrees of freedom

$$df_{error} = (K - 1)(S - 1)$$

Formula 12-19. Mean square error in one-way repeated measures ANOVA

$$MS_{error} = \frac{SS_{error}}{df_{error}}$$

Formula 12-20. *F* ratio in one-way repeated measures ANOVA

$$F = \frac{MS_b}{MS_{error}}$$

CHAPTER 13: POST HOC COMPARISONS

Symbols

Symbol	Stands For
HSD	honestly significant differences
LSD	least significant differences
q	studentized range statistic
$HSD_{.05}$, $HSD_{.01}$	honestly significant difference at the 5% or 1% level, respectively

Formulas

Formula 13-1. Honestly significant difference (HSD) between pairs of means

$$HSD_\alpha = q_\alpha \sqrt{\frac{MS_w}{N_g}}$$

Formula 13-2. Least significant difference (LSD) between pairs of group means

$$LSD = \frac{\overline{X}_1 - \overline{X}_2}{\sqrt{MS_w\left(\frac{1}{N_1} + \frac{1}{N_2}\right)}}$$

CHAPTER 14: TWO-WAY ANALYSIS OF VARIANCE

Symbols

Many new symbols and formulas were introduced in an example in this chapter. Because the goal of the chapter was to provide an intuitive look at two-way ANOVA, this material may be bypassed.

CHAPTER 15: CHI-SQUARE

Symbols

Symbol	Stands For
χ^2	chi-square
O	observed frequency

(continued)

Symbol	Stands For
E	expected frequency
K	number of categories
RT	row total
CT	column total
R	number of rows
C	number of columns

Formulas

Formula 15-1. Chi-square

$$\chi^2 = \Sigma \frac{(O - E)^2}{E}$$

Formula 15-2. Expected frequencies for the chi-square test of independence

$$E = \frac{RT \times CT}{N}$$

Formula 15-3. Degrees of freedom for the chi-square test of independence

$$df = (R - 1)(C - 1)$$

CHAPTER 16: ALTERNATIVES TO t AND F

Symbols

Symbol	Stands For
U or M–W U or U'	statistic computed for the Mann–Whiney (M–W) test of significance
N_1, N_2	number of subjects in the first and second groups, respectively
R_1, R_2	rank of the scores in the first and second groups, respectively
d	differences between pairs of scores in the Wilcoxon test
T	sum of the ranks of the scores with the less frequent sign (Wilcoxon test)

(continued)

Symbol	Stands For
H or K–W H	statistic computed for the Kruskal–Wallis (K–W) test
N_i	number of observations in a particular sample
R_i	sum of the ranks for a particular sample
K	number of samples

Formulas

Formula 16-1. Mann–Whitney U test

$$U = N_1 N_2 + \frac{N_1(N_1 + 1)}{2} - R_1$$

Formula 16-2. U'

$$U' = N_1 N_2 - U$$

Formula 16-4. z score for large-sample U

$$z = \frac{U - \dfrac{N_1 N_2}{2}}{\sqrt{\dfrac{(N_1)(N_2)(N_1 + N_2 + 1)}{12}}}$$

Formula 16-5. z score for large-sample T

$$z = \frac{T - \dfrac{N(N + 1)}{4}}{\sqrt{\dfrac{N(N + 1)(2N + 1)}{24}}}$$

Formula 16-6. Kruskal–Wallis test

$$H = \frac{12}{N(N + 1)} \sum \frac{R_i^2}{N_i} - 3(N + 1)$$

4

Tables for Inferential Tests

TABLE A

Areas under the right half (positive z scores) of the standard normal curve ($\mu = 0$, $\sigma = 1$)

(A)	(B)	(C)		(A)	(B)	(C)		(A)	(B)	(C)
	area between mean and	area beyond			area between mean and	area beyond			area between mean and	area beyond
z	z	z		z	z	z		z	z	z
0.00	00.00	50.00		0.40	15.54	34.46		0.80	28.81	21.19
0.01	00.40	49.60		0.41	15.91	34.09		0.81	29.10	20.90
0.02	00.80	49.20		0.42	16.28	33.72		0.82	29.39	20.61
0.03	01.20	48.80		0.43	16.64	33.36		0.83	29.67	20.33
0.04	01.60	48.40		0.44	17.00	33.00		0.84	29.95	20.05
0.05	01.99	48.01		0.45	17.36	32.64		0.85	30.23	19.77
0.06	02.39	47.61		0.46	17.72	32.28		0.86	30.51	19.49
0.07	02.79	47.21		0.47	18.08	31.92		0.87	30.78	19.22
0.08	03.19	46.81		0.48	18.44	31.56		0.88	31.06	18.94
0.09	03.59	46.41		0.49	18.79	31.21		0.89	31.33	18.67
0.10	03.98	46.02		0.50	19.15	30.85		0.90	31.59	18.41
0.11	04.38	45.62		0.51	19.50	30.50		0.91	31.86	18.14
0.12	04.78	45.22		0.52	19.85	30.15		0.92	32.12	17.88
0.13	05.17	44.83		0.53	20.19	29.81		0.93	32.38	17.62
0.14	05.57	44.43		0.54	20.54	29.46		0.94	32.64	17.36
0.15	05.96	44.04		0.55	20.88	29.12		0.95	32.89	17.11
0.16	06.36	43.64		0.56	21.23	28.77		0.96	33.15	16.85
0.17	06.75	43.25		0.57	21.57	28.43		0.97	33.40	16.60
0.18	07.14	42.86		0.58	21.90	28.10		0.98	33.65	16.35
0.19	07.53	42.47		0.59	22.24	27.76		0.99	33.89	16.11
0.20	07.93	42.07		0.60	22.57	27.43		1.00	34.13	15.87
0.21	08.32	41.68		0.61	22.91	27.09		1.01	34.38	15.62
0.22	08.71	41.29		0.62	23.24	26.76		1.02	34.61	15.39
0.23	09.10	40.90		0.63	23.57	26.43		1.03	34.85	15.15
0.24	09.48	40.52		0.64	23.89	26.11		1.04	35.08	14.92
0.25	09.87	40.13		0.65	24.22	25.78		1.05	35.31	14.69
0.26	10.26	39.74		0.66	24.54	25.46		1.06	35.54	14.46
0.27	10.64	39.36		0.67	24.86	25.14		1.07	35.77	14.23
0.28	11.03	38.97		0.68	25.17	24.83		1.08	35.99	14.01
0.29	11.41	38.59		0.69	25.49	24.51		1.09	36.21	13.79
0.30	11.79	38.21		0.70	25.80	24.20		1.10	36.43	13.57
0.31	12.17	37.83		0.71	26.11	23.89		1.11	36.65	13.35
0.32	12.55	37.45		0.72	26.42	23.58		1.12	36.86	13.14
0.33	12.93	37.07		0.73	26.73	23.27		1.13	37.08	12.92
0.34	13.31	36.69		0.74	27.04	22.96		1.14	37.29	12.71
0.35	13.68	36.32		0.75	27.34	22.66		1.15	37.49	12.51
0.36	14.06	35.94		0.76	27.64	22.36		1.16	37.70	12.30
0.37	14.43	35.57		0.77	27.94	22.06		1.17	37.90	12.10
0.38	14.80	35.20		0.78	28.23	21.77		1.18	38.10	11.90
0.39	15.17	34.83		0.79	28.52	21.48		1.19	38.30	11.70

(continued)

TABLE A

continued

(A)	(B)	(C)		(A)	(B)	(C)		(A)	(B)	(C)
	area between mean and	area beyond			area between mean and	area beyond			area between mean and	area beyond
z	z	z		z	z	z		z	z	z
1.20	38.49	11.51		1.60	44.52	05.48		2.00	47.72	02.28
1.21	38.69	11.31		1.61	44.63	05.37		2.01	47.78	02.22
1.22	38.88	11.12		1.62	44.74	05.26		2.02	47.83	02.17
1.23	39.07	10.93		1.63	44.84	05.16		2.03	47.88	02.12
1.24	39.25	10.75		1.64	44.95	05.05		2.04	47.93	02.07
1.25	39.44	10.56		1.65	45.05	04.95		2.05	47.98	02.02
1.26	39.62	10.38		1.66	45.15	04.85		2.06	48.03	01.97
1.27	39.80	10.20		1.67	45.25	04.75		2.07	48.08	01.92
1.28	39.97	10.03		1.68	45.35	04.65		2.08	48.12	01.88
1.29	40.15	09.85		1.69	45.45	04.55		2.09	48.17	01.83
1.30	40.32	09.68		1.70	45.54	04.46		2.10	48.21	01.79
1.31	40.49	09.51		1.71	45.64	04.36		2.11	48.26	01.74
1.32	40.66	09.34		1.72	45.73	04.27		2.12	48.30	01.70
1.33	40.82	09.18		1.73	45.82	04.18		2.13	48.34	01.66
1.34	40.99	09.01		1.74	45.91	04.09		2.14	48.38	01.62
1.35	41.15	08.85		1.75	45.99	04.01		2.15	48.42	01.58
1.36	41.31	08.69		1.76	46.08	03.92		2.16	48.46	01.54
1.37	41.47	08.53		1.77	46.16	03.84		2.17	48.50	01.50
1.38	41.62	08.38		1.78	46.25	03.75		2.18	48.54	01.46
1.39	41.77	08.23		1.79	46.33	03.67		2.19	48.57	01.43
1.40	41.92	08.08		1.80	46.41	03.59		2.20	48.61	01.39
1.41	42.07	07.93		1.81	46.49	03.51		2.21	48.64	01.36
1.42	42.22	07.78		1.82	46.56	03.44		2.22	48.68	01.32
1.43	42.36	07.64		1.83	46.64	03.36		2.23	48.71	01.29
1.44	42.51	07.49		1.84	46.71	03.29		2.24	48.75	01.25
1.45	42.65	07.35		1.85	46.78	03.22		2.25	48.78	01.22
1.46	42.79	07.21		1.86	46.86	03.14		2.26	48.81	01.19
1.47	42.92	07.08		1.87	46.93	03.07		2.27	48.84	01.16
1.48	43.06	06.94		1.88	46.99	03.01		2.28	48.87	01.13
1.49	43.19	06.81		1.89	47.06	02.94		2.29	48.90	01.10
1.50	43.32	06.68		1.90	47.13	02.87		2.30	48.93	01.07
1.51	43.45	06.55		1.91	47.19	02.81		2.31	48.96	01.04
1.52	43.57	06.43		1.92	47.26	02.74		2.32	48.98	01.02
1.53	43.70	06.30		1.93	47.32	02.68		2.33	49.01	00.99
1.54	43.82	06.18		1.94	47.38	02.62		2.34	49.04	00.96
1.55	43.94	06.06		1.95	47.44	02.56		2.35	49.06	00.94
1.56	44.06	05.94		1.96	47.50	02.50		2.36	49.09	00.91
1.57	44.18	05.82		1.97	47.56	02.44		2.37	49.11	00.89
1.58	44.29	05.71		1.98	47.61	02.39		2.38	49.13	00.87
1.59	44.41	05.59		1.99	47.67	02.33		2.39	49.16	00.84

(continued)

TABLE A

continued

(A)	(B)	(C)		(A)	(B)	(C)		(A)	(B)	(C)
	area between mean and	area beyond			area between mean and	area beyond			area between mean and	area beyond
z	z	z		z	z	z		z	z	z
2.40	49.18	00.82		2.80	49.74	00.26		3.20	49.93	00.07
2.41	49.20	00.80		2.81	49.75	00.25		3.21	49.93	00.07
2.42	49.22	00.78		2.82	49.76	00.24		3.22	49.94	00.06
2.43	49.25	00.75		2.83	49.77	00.23		3.23	49.94	00.06
2.44	49.27	00.73		2.84	49.77	00.23		3.24	49.94	00.06
2.45	49.29	00.71		2.85	49.78	00.22		3.25	49.94	00.06
2.46	49.31	00.69		2.86	49.79	00.21		3.30	49.95	00.05
2.47	49.32	00.68		2.87	49.79	00.21		3.35	49.96	00.04
2.48	49.34	00.66		2.88	49.80	00.20		3.40	49.97	00.03
2.49	49.36	00.64		2.89	49.81	00.19		3.45	49.97	00.03
2.50	49.38	00.62		2.90	49.81	00.19		3.50	49.98	00.02
2.51	49.40	00.60		2.91	49.82	00.18		3.60	49.98	00.02
2.52	49.41	00.59		2.92	49.82	00.18		3.70	49.99	00.01
2.53	49.43	00.57		2.93	49.83	00.17		3.80	49.99	00.01
2.54	49.45	00.55		2.94	49.84	00.16		3.90	49.995	00.005
2.55	49.46	00.54		2.95	49.84	00.16		4.00	49.997	00.003
2.56	49.48	00.52		2.96	49.85	00.15				
2.57	49.49	00.51		2.97	49.85	00.15				
2.58	49.51	00.49		2.98	49.86	00.14				
2.59	49.52	00.48		2.99	49.86	00.14				
2.60	49.53	00.47		3.00	49.87	00.13				
2.61	49.55	00.45		3.01	49.87	00.13				
2.62	49.56	00.44		3.02	49.87	00.13				
2.63	49.57	00.43		3.03	49.88	00.12				
2.64	49.59	00.41		3.04	49.88	00.12				
2.65	49.60	00.40		3.05	49.89	00.11				
2.66	49.61	00.39		3.06	49.89	00.11				
2.67	49.62	00.38		3.07	49.89	00.11				
2.68	49.63	00.37		3.08	49.90	00.10				
2.69	49.64	00.36		3.09	49.90	00.10				
2.70	49.65	00.35		3.10	49.90	00.10				
2.71	49.66	00.34		3.11	49.91	00.09				
2.72	49.67	00.33		3.12	49.91	00.09				
2.73	49.68	00.32		3.13	49.91	00.09				
2.74	49.69	00.31		3.14	49.92	00.08				
2.75	49.70	00.30		3.15	49.92	00.08				
2.76	49.71	00.29		3.16	49.92	00.08				
2.77	49.72	00.28		3.17	49.92	00.08				
2.78	49.73	00.27		3.18	49.93	00.07				
2.79	49.74	00.26		3.19	49.93	00.07				

Source: This table is from Runyon, R. P. and Haber, A. *Fundamentals of Behavioral Statistics* (Third Edition), Addison-Wesley, 1976, pp. 377–379. Copyright © 1976 by Addison-Wesley. Reprinted with permission of Random House, Inc.

peep. 188

TABLE B

Critical values of t

df = N − 1 for one-sample t *test, confidence intervals, and for the* t *test for dependent samples*

df = N_1 + N_2 − 2 for two-sample t *test*   N/A

	Level of Significance for Two-Tailed Test (For one-tailed test, halve the percentages below)			
	10%	5%	2%	1%
df	(*p* = .10)	(*p* = .05)	(*p* = .02)	(*p* = .01)
1	6.3138	12.7062	31.8207	63.6574
2	2.9200	4.3027	6.9646	9.9248
3	2.3534	3.1824	4.5407	5.8409
4	2.1318	2.7764	3.7469	4.6041
5	2.0150	2.5706	3.3649	4.0322
6	1.9432	2.4469	3.1427	3.7074
7	1.8946	2.3646	2.9980	3.4995
8	1.8595	2.3060	2.8965	3.3554
9	1.8331	2.2622	2.8214	3.2498
10	1.8125	2.2281	2.7638	3.1693
11	1.7959	2.2010	2.7181	3.1058
12	1.7823	2.1788	2.6810	3.0545
13	1.7709	2.1604	2.6503	3.0123
14	1.7613	2.1448	2.6245	2.9768
15	1.7531	2.1315	2.6025	2.9467
16	1.7459	2.1199	2.5835	2.9208
17	1.7396	2.1098	2.5669	2.8982
18	1.7341	2.1009	2.5524	2.8784
19	1.7291	2.0930	2.5395	2.8609
20	1.7247	2.0860	2.5280	2.8453
21	1.7207	2.0796	2.5177	2.8314
22	1.7171	2.0739	2.5083	2.8188
23	1.7139	2.0687	2.4999	2.8073
24	1.7109	2.0639	2.4922	2.7969
25	1.7081	2.0595	2.4851	2.7874
26	1.7056	2.0555	2.4786	2.7787
27	1.7033	2.0518	2.4727	2.7707
28	1.7011	2.0484	2.4671	2.7633
29	1.6991	2.0452	2.4620	2.7564
30	1.6973	2.0423	2.4573	2.7500
35	1.6869	2.0301	2.4377	2.7238
40	1.6839	2.0211	2.4233	2.7045
45	1.6794	2.0141	2.4121	2.6896
50	1.6759	2.0086	2.4033	2.6778
60	1.6706	2.0003	2.3901	2.6603
70	1.6669	1.9944	2.3808	2.6479
80	1.6641	1.9901	2.3739	2.6387
90	1.6620	1.9867	2.3685	2.6316
100	1.6602	1.9840	2.3642	2.6259
110	1.6588	1.9818	2.3607	2.6213
120	1.6577	1.9799	2.3598	2.6174
∞	1.6449	1.9600	2.3263	2.5758

N = 121 ← 120

Source: This table is from Owen, D. B., *Handbook of Statistical Tables,* Addison-Wesley, 1962, pp. 28–30.
Copyright © 1962 by Addison Wesley Publishing Company, Inc. Reprinted with permission of Addison Wesley Longman.

TABLE C

Critical values of r

$df = N - 2$, *where* N *is the number of pairs of scores*

Degrees of Freedom (*df*)	5%	1%	Degrees of Freedom (*df*)	5%	1%
1	.997	1.000	24	.388	.496
2	.950	.990	25	.381	.487
3	.878	.959	26	.374	.478
4	.811	.917	27	.367	.470
5	.754	.874	28	.361	.463
6	.707	.834	29	.355	.456
7	.666	.798	30	.349	.449
8	.632	.765	35	.325	.418
9	.602	.735	40	.304	.393
10	.576	.708	45	.288	.372
11	.553	.684	50	.273	.354
12	.532	.661	60	.250	.325
13	.514	.641	70	.232	.302
14	.497	.623	80	.217	.283
15	.482	.606	90	.205	.267
16	.468	.590	100	.195	.254
17	.456	.575	125	.174	.228
18	.444	.561	150	.159	.208
19	.433	.549	200	.138	.181
20	.423	.537	300	.113	.148
21	.413	.526	400	.098	.128
22	.404	.515	500	.088	.115
23	.396	.505	1000	.062	.081

Source: This table is from Table VII of Fisher and Yates: *Statistical Tables for Biological, Agricultural and Medical Research,* published by Longman Group Ltd., London (previously published by Oliver & Boyd, Edinburgh). Reprinted by permission of Addison Wesley Longman.

TABLE D

Critical values of r_s

N	5%	1%	N	5%	1%
5	1.000	—	16	.506	.665
6	.886	1.000	18	.475	.625
7	.786	.929	20	.450	.591
8	.738	.881	22	.428	.562
9	.683	.833	24	.409	.537
10	.648	.794	26	.392	.515
12	.591	.777	28	.377	.496
14	.544	714	30	.364	.478

Source: This table is adapted from Olds, E. G., Distribution of sums of squares of rank differences for small samples, *Annals of Mathematical Statistics,* 1938, 9, 133–148, and, the 5% significance levels for sums of squares of rank differences and a correction, *Annals of Mathematical Statistics,* 1949, 20, 117–118, with permission of the editor.

TABLE E

Critical Values of F

df Associated with the Denominator (*df*w)		*df* Associated with the Numerator (*df*b)								
		1	2	3	4	5	6	7	8	9
1	5%	161	200	216	225	230	234	238	239	241
	1%	4052	5000	5403	5625	5764	5859	5928	5982	6022
2	5%	18.5	19.0	19.2	19.2	19.3	19.3	19.4	19.4	19.4
	1%	98.5	99.0	99.2	99.2	99.3	99.3	99.4	99.4	99.4
3	5%	10.1	9.55	9.28	9.12	9.01	8.97	8.89	8.85	8.81
	1%	34.1	30.8	29.5	28.7	28.2	27.9	27.7	27.5	27.3
4	5%	7.71	6.94	6.59	6.39	6.26	6.16	6.09	6.04	6.00
	1%	21.2	18.0	16.7	16.0	15.5	15.2	15.0	14.8	14.7
5	5%	6.61	5.79	5.41	5.19	5.05	4.95	4.88	4.82	4.77
	1%	16.3	13.3	12.1	11.4	11.0	10.7	10.5	10.3	10.2
6	5%	5.99	5.14	4.76	4.53	4.39	4.28	4.21	4.15	4.10
	1%	13.7	10.9	9.78	9.15	8.75	8.47	8.26	8.10	7.98
7	5%	5.59	4.74	4.35	4.12	3.97	3.87	3.79	3.73	3.68
	1%	12.2	9.55	8.45	7.85	7.46	7.19	6.99	6.84	6.72
8	5%	5.32	4.46	4.07	3.84	3.69	3.58	3.50	3.44	3.39
	1%	11.3	8.65	7.59	7.01	6.63	6.37	6.18	6.03	5.91
9	5%	5.12	4.26	3.86	3.63	3.48	3.37	3.29	3.23	3.18
	1%	10.6	8.02	6.99	6.42	6.06	5.80	5.61	5.47	5.35
10	5%	4.96	4.10	3.71	3.48	3.33	3.22	3.14	3.07	3.02
	1%	10.0	7.56	6.55	5.99	5.64	5.39	5.20	5.06	4.94
11	5%	4.84	3.98	3.59	3.36	3.20	3.09	3.01	2.95	2.90
	1%	9.65	7.21	6.22	5.67	5.32	5.07	4.89	4.74	4.63
12	5%	4.75	3.89	3.49	3.26	3.11	3.00	2.91	2.85	2.80
	1%	9.33	6.93	5.95	5.41	5.06	4.82	4.64	4.50	4.39
13	5%	4.67	3.81	3.41	3.18	3.03	2.92	2.83	2.77	2.71
	1%	9.07	6.70	5.74	5.21	4.86	4.62	4.44	4.30	4.19
14	5%	4.60	3.74	3.34	3.11	2.96	2.85	2.76	2.70	2.65
	1%	8.86	6.51	5.56	5.04	4.70	4.46	4.28	4.14	4.03
15	5%	4.54	3.68	3.29	3.06	2.90	2.79	2.71	2.64	2.59
	1%	8.68	6.36	5.42	4.89	4.56	4.32	4.14	4.00	3.89
16	5%	4.49	3.63	3.24	3.01	2.85	2.74	2.66	2.59	2.54
	1%	8.53	6.23	5.29	4.77	4.44	4.20	4.03	3.89	3.78
17	5%	4.45	3.59	3.20	2.96	2.81	2.70	2.61	2.55	2.49
	1%	8.40	6.11	5.18	4.67	.434	4.10	3.93	3.79	3.68

(continued)

TABLE E

continued

df Associated with the Denominator (df_w)		df Associated with the Numerator (df_b)								
		1	2	3	4	5	6	7	8	9
18	5%	4.41	3.55	3.16	2.93	2.77	2.66	2.58	2.51	2.46
	1%	8.29	6.01	5.09	4.58	4.25	4.01	3.84	3.71	3.60
19	5%	4.38	3.52	3.13	2.90	2.74	2.63	2.54	2.48	2.42
	1%	8.18	5.93	5.01	4.50	4.17	3.94	3.77	3.63	3.52
20	5%	4.35	3.49	3.10	2.87	2.71	2.60	2.51	2.45	2.39
	1%	8.10	5.85	4.94	4.43	4.10	3.87	3.70	3.56	3.46
21	5%	4.32	3.47	3.07	2.84	2.68	2.57	2.49	2.42	2.37
	1%	8.02	5.78	4.87	4.37	4.04	3.81	3.64	3.51	3.40
22	5%	4.30	3.44	3.05	2.82	2.66	2.55	2.46	2.40	2.34
	1%	7.95	5.72	4.82	4.31	3.99	3.76	3.59	3.45	3.35
23	5%	4.28	3.42	3.03	2.80	2.64	2.54	2.44	2.37	2.32
	1%	7.88	5.66	4.76	4.26	3.94	3.71	3.54	3.41	3.30
24	5%	4.26	3.40	3.01	2.78	2.62	2.51	2.42	2.36	2.30
	1%	7.82	5.61	4.72	4.22	3.90	3.67	3.50	3.36	3.26
25	5%	4.24	3.39	2.29	2.76	2.60	2.49	2.40	2.34	2.28
	1%	7.77	5.57	4.68	4.18	3.86	3.63	3.46	3.32	3.22
26	5%	4.23	3.37	2.98	2.74	2.59	2.47	2.39	2.32	2.27
	1%	7.72	5.53	4.64	4.14	3.82	3.59	3.42	3.29	3.18
27	5%	4.21	3.35	2.96	2.73	2.57	2.46	2.37	2.31	2.25
	1%	7.68	5.49	4.60	4.11	3.78	3.56	3.39	3.26	3.15
28	5%	4.20	3.34	2.95	2.71	2.56	2.45	2.36	2.29	2.24
	1%	7.64	5.45	4.57	4.07	3.75	3.53	3.36	3.23	3.12
29	5%	4.18	3.33	2.93	2.70	2.55	2.43	2.35	2.28	2.22
	1%	7.60	5.42	4.54	4.04	3.73	3.50	3.33	3.20	3.09
30	5%	4.17	3.32	2.92	2.69	2.53	2.42	2.33	2.27	2.21
	1%	7.56	5.39	4.51	4.02	3.70	3.47	3.30	3.17	3.07
40	5%	4.08	3.23	2.84	2.61	2.45	2.34	2.25	2.18	2.12
	1%	7.31	5.18	4.31	3.83	3.51	3.29	3.12	2.99	2.89
60	5%	4.00	3.15	2.76	2.53	2.37	2.25	2.17	2.10	2.04
	1%	7.08	4.98	4.13	3.65	3.34	3.12	2.95	2.82	2.72
120	5%	3.92	3.07	2.68	2.45	2.29	2.18	2.09	2.02	1.96
	1%	6.85	4.79	3.95	3.48	3.17	2.96	2.79	2.66	2.56

Source: This table is adapted from Merrington, M., & Thompson, C. M., Tables of percentage points of the inverted beta (*F*) distribution, *Biometrika*, 1943, *33*, 73–88. Reprinted with permission of the Biometrika Trustees.

TABLE F

Critical Values of q_α

(df_w)	α	2	3	4	5	6	7	8	9	10
		\multicolumn{9}{c	}{K = Number of Groups (Means)}
1	.05	17.97	26.98	32.82	37.08	40.41	43.12	45.40	47.36	49.07
	.01	90.03	135.00	164.30	185.60	202.20	215.80	227.20	237.00	245.60
2	.05	6.08	8.33	9.80	10.88	11.74	12.44	13.03	13.54	13.99
	.01	14.04	19.02	232.29	24.72	26.63	28.20	29.53	30.68	31.69
3	.05	4.50	5.91	6.82	7.50	8.04	8.48	8.85	9.18	9.46
	.01	8.26	10.62	12.17	13.33	14.24	15.00	15.64	16.20	16.69
4	.05	3.93	5.04	5.76	6.29	6.71	7.05	7.35	7.60	7.83
	.01	6.51	8.12	9.17	9.96	10.58	11.10	11.55	11.93	12.27
5	.05	3.64	4.60	5.22	5.67	6.03	6.33	6.58	6.80	6.99
	.01	5.70	6.98	7.80	8.42	8.91	9.32	9.67	9.97	10.24
6	.05	3.46	4.34	4.90	5.30	5.63	5.90	6.12	6.32	6.49
	.01	5.24	6.33	7.03	7.56	7.97	8.32	8.61	8.87	9.10
7	.05	3.34	4.16	4.68	5.06	5.36	5.61	5.82	6.00	6.16
	.01	4.95	5.92	6.54	7.01	7.37	7.68	7.94	8.17	8.37
8	.05	3.26	4.04	4.53	4.89	5.17	5.40	5.60	5.77	5.92
	.01	4.75	5.64	6.20	6.62	6.96	7.24	7.47	7.68	7.86
9	.05	3.20	3.95	4.41	4.76	5.02	5.24	5.43	5.59	5.74
	.01	4.60	5.43	5.96	6.35	6.66	6.91	7.13	7.33	7.49
10	.05	3.15	3.88	4.33	4.65	4.91	5.12	5.30	5.46	5.60
	.01	4.48	5.27	5.77	6.14	6.43	6.67	6.87	7.05	7.21
11	.05	3.11	3.82	4.26	4.57	4.82	5.03	5.20	5.35	5.49
	.01	4.39	5.15	5.62	5.97	6.25	6.48	6.67	6.84	6.99
12	.05	3.08	3.77	4.20	4.51	4.75	4.95	5.12	5.27	5.39
	.01	4.32	5.05	5.50	5.84	6.10	6.32	6.51	6.67	6.81
13	.05	3.06	3.73	4.15	4.45	4.69	4.88	5.05	5.19	5.32
	.01	4.26	4.96	5.40	5.73	5.98	6.19	6.37	6.53	6.67
14	.05	3.03	3.70	4.11	4.41	4.64	4.83	4.99	5.13	5.25
	.01	4.21	4.89	5.32	5.63	5.88	6.08	6.26	6.41	6.54
15	.05	3.01	3.67	4.08	4.37	4.59	4.78	4.94	5.08	5.20
	.01	4.17	4.84	5.25	5.56	5.80	5.99	6.16	6.31	6.44
16	.05	3.00	3.65	4.05	4.33	4.56	4.74	4.90	5.03	5.15
	.01	4.13	4.79	5.19	5.49	5.72	5.92	6.08	6.22	6.35
17	.05	2.98	3.63	4.02	4.30	4.52	4.70	4.86	4.99	5.11
	.01	4.10	4.74	5.14	5.43	5.66	5.85	6.01	6.15	6.27
18	.05	2.97	3.61	4.00	4.28	4.49	4.67	4.82	4.96	5.07
	.01	4.07	4.70	5.09	5.38	5.60	5.79	5.94	6.08	6.20
19	.05	2.96	3.59	3.98	4.25	4.47	4.65	4.79	4.92	5.04
	.01	4.05	4.67	5.05	5.33	5.55	5.73	5.89	6.02	6.14
20	.05	2.95	3.58	3.96	4.23	4.45	4.62	4.77	4.90	5.01
	.01	4.02	4.64	5.02	5.29	5.51	5.69	5.84	5.97	6.09

(continued)

TABLE F

continued

(df_w)	α	2	3	4	5	6	7	8	9	10
					K = Number of Groups (Means)					
24	.05	2.92	3.53	3.90	4.17	4.37	4.54	4.68	4.81	4.92
	.01	3.96	4.55	4.91	5.17	5.37	5.54	5.69	5.81	5.92
30	.05	2.89	3.49	3.85	4.10	4.30	4.46	4.60	4.72	4.82
	.01	3.89	4.45	4.80	5.05	5.24	5.40	5.54	5.65	5.76
40	.05	2.86	3.44	3.79	4.04	4.23	4.39	4.52	4.63	4.73
	.01	3.82	4.37	4.70	4.93	5.11	5.26	5.39	5.50	5.60
60	.05	2.83	3.40	3.74	3.98	4.16	4.31	4.44	4.55	4.65
	.01	3.76	4.28	4.59	4.82	4.99	5.13	5.25	5.36	5.45
120	.05	2.80	3.36	3.68	3.92	4.10	4.24	4.36	4.47	4.56
	.01	3.70	4.20	4.50	4.71	4.87	5.01	5.12	5.21	5.30
∞	.05	2.77	3.31	3.63	3.86	4.03	4.17	4.29	4.39	4.47
	.01	3.64	4.12	4.40	4.60	4.76	4.88	4.99	5.08	5.16

TABLE G

Critical Values of χ^2

$df = C - 1$ *for the chi-square goodness-of-fit test.* C *is the number of columns.*

$df = (R - 1)(C - 1)$ *for the chi-square test of independence.* R *is the number of rows.*

Degrees of Freedom (df)	5%	1%	Degrees of Freedom (df)	5%	1%
1	3.84	6.64	16	26.30	32.00
2	5.99	9.21	17	27.59	33.41
3	7.82	11.34	18	28.87	34.80
4	9.49	13.28	19	30.14	36.19
5	11.07	15.09	20	31.41	37.57
6	12.59	16.81	21	32.67	38.93
7	14.07	18.48	22	33.92	40.29
8	15.51	20.09	23	35.17	41.64
9	16.92	21.67	24	36.42	42.98
10	18.31	23.21	25	37.65	44.31
11	19.68	24.72	26	38.88	45.64
12	21.03	26.22	27	40.11	46.96
13	22.36	27.69	28	41.34	48.28
14	23.68	29.14	29	42.56	49.59
15	25.00	30.58	30	43.77	50.89

TABLE H

Critical Values for the Mann–Whitney U

For a two-tailed test at the 10% level (roman type, α = 0.10) and at the 5% level (boldface type, α = 0.05). For a one-tailed test, halve the probabilities.

Dashes in the body of the table mean that no decision is possible at the given α.

N_2 \ N_1	1	2	3	4	5	6	7	8	9	10	11	12	13	14	15	16	17	18	19	20
1	—	—	—	—	—	—	—	—	—	—	—	—	—	—	—	—	—	—	0	0
																			—	
2	—	—	—	—	0	0	0	1	1	1	1	2	2	2	3	3	3	4	4	4
					—	—	—	**0**	**0**	**0**	**0**	**1**	**1**	**1**	**1**	**1**	**2**	**2**	**2**	**2**
3	—	—	0	0	1	2	2	3	3	4	5	5	6	7	7	8	9	9	10	11
	—	—	—	—	**0**	**1**	**1**	**2**	**2**	**3**	**3**	**4**	**4**	**5**	**5**	**6**	**6**	**7**	**7**	**8**
4	—	—	0	1	2	3	4	5	6	7	8	9	10	11	12	14	15	16	17	18
	—	—	—	**0**	**1**	**2**	**3**	**4**	**4**	**5**	**6**	**7**	**8**	**9**	**10**	**11**	**11**	**12**	**13**	**13**
5	—	0	1	2	4	5	6	8	9	11	12	13	15	16	18	19	20	22	23	25
	—	—	**0**	**1**	**2**	**3**	**5**	**6**	**7**	**8**	**9**	**11**	**12**	**13**	**14**	**15**	**17**	**18**	**19**	**20**
6	—	0	2	3	5	7	8	10	12	14	16	17	19	21	23	25	26	28	30	32
	—	—	**1**	**2**	**3**	**5**	**6**	**8**	**10**	**11**	**13**	**14**	**16**	**17**	**19**	**21**	**22**	**24**	**25**	**27**
7	—	0	2	4	6	8	11	13	15	17	19	21	24	26	28	30	33	35	37	39
	—	—	**1**	**3**	**5**	**6**	**8**	**10**	**12**	**14**	**16**	**18**	**20**	**22**	**24**	**26**	**28**	**30**	**32**	**34**
8	—	1	3	5	8	10	13	15	18	20	23	26	28	31	33	36	39	41	44	47
	—	**0**	**2**	**4**	**6**	**8**	**10**	**13**	**15**	**17**	**19**	**22**	**24**	**26**	**29**	**31**	**34**	**36**	**38**	**41**
9	—	1	3	6	9	12	15	18	21	24	27	30	33	36	39	42	45	48	51	54
	—	**0**	**2**	**4**	**7**	**10**	**12**	**15**	**17**	**20**	**23**	**26**	**28**	**31**	**34**	**37**	**39**	**42**	**45**	**48**
10	—	1	4	7	11	14	17	20	24	27	31	34	37	41	44	48	51	55	58	62
	—	**0**	**3**	**5**	**8**	**11**	**14**	**17**	**20**	**23**	**26**	**29**	**33**	**36**	**39**	**42**	**45**	**48**	**52**	**55**
11	—	1	5	8	12	16	19	23	27	31	34	38	42	46	50	54	57	61	65	69
	—	**0**	**3**	**6**	**9**	**13**	**16**	**19**	**23**	**26**	**30**	**33**	**37**	**40**	**44**	**47**	**51**	**55**	**58**	**62**
12	—	2	5	9	13	17	21	26	30	34	38	42	47	51	55	60	64	68	72	77
	—	**1**	**4**	**7**	**11**	**14**	**18**	**22**	**26**	**29**	**33**	**37**	**41**	**45**	**49**	**53**	**57**	**61**	**65**	**69**
13	—	2	6	10	15	19	24	28	33	37	42	47	51	56	61	65	70	75	80	84
	—	**1**	**4**	**8**	**12**	**16**	**20**	**24**	**28**	**33**	**37**	**41**	**45**	**50**	**54**	**59**	**63**	**67**	**72**	**76**
14	—	2	7	11	16	21	26	31	36	41	46	51	56	61	66	71	77	82	87	92
	—	**1**	**5**	**9**	**13**	**17**	**22**	**26**	**31**	**36**	**40**	**45**	**50**	**55**	**59**	**64**	**67**	**74**	**78**	**83**
15	—	3	7	12	18	23	28	33	39	44	50	55	61	66	72	77	83	88	94	100
	—	**1**	**5**	**10**	**14**	**19**	**24**	**29**	**34**	**39**	**44**	**49**	**54**	**59**	**64**	**70**	**75**	**80**	**85**	**90**
16	—	3	8	14	19	25	30	36	42	48	54	60	65	71	77	83	89	95	101	107
	—	**1**	**6**	**11**	**15**	**21**	**26**	**31**	**37**	**42**	**47**	**53**	**59**	**64**	**70**	**75**	**81**	**86**	**92**	**98**
17	—	3	9	15	20	26	33	39	45	51	57	64	70	77	83	89	96	102	109	115
	—	**2**	**6**	**11**	**17**	**22**	**28**	**34**	**39**	**45**	**51**	**57**	**63**	**67**	**75**	**81**	**87**	**93**	**99**	**105**
18	—	4	9	16	22	28	35	41	48	55	61	68	75	82	88	95	102	109	116	123
	—	**2**	**7**	**12**	**18**	**24**	**30**	**36**	**42**	**48**	**55**	**61**	**67**	**74**	**80**	**86**	**93**	**99**	**106**	**112**
19	0	4	10	17	23	30	37	44	51	58	65	72	80	87	94	101	109	116	123	130
		2	**7**	**13**	**19**	**25**	**32**	**38**	**45**	**52**	**58**	**65**	**72**	**78**	**85**	**92**	**99**	**106**	**113**	**119**
20	0	4	11	18	25	32	39	47	54	62	69	77	84	92	100	107	115	123	130	138
		2	**8**	**13**	**20**	**27**	**34**	**41**	**48**	**55**	**62**	**69**	**76**	**83**	**90**	**98**	**105**	**112**	**119**	**127**

Source: This tables is from *Elementary Statistics*, 2nd Edition, by Roger E. Kirk. Copyright © 1984, 1978 by Roger E. Kirk. Adapted by permission of the author.

TABLE H

continued

For a two-tailed test at the 2% level (roman type, $\alpha = 0.02$) and at the 1% level (boldface type, $\alpha = 0.01$). For a one-tailed test, halve the probabilities.

Dashes in the body of the table mean that no decision is possible at the given α.

N_2	1	2	3	4	5	6	7	8	9	10	11	12	13	14	15	16	17	18	19	20
1	—	—	—	—	—	—	—	—	—	—	—	—	—	—	—	—	—	—	—	—
2	—	—	—	—	—	—	—	—	—	—	—	—	0	0	0	0	0	0	1	1
													—	—	—	—	—	—	0	0
3	—	—	—	—	—	—	0	0	1	1	1	2	2	2	3	3	4	4	4	5
							—	—	0	0	0	1	1	1	2	2	2	2	3	3
4	—	—	—	—	0	1	1	2	3	3	4	5	5	6	7	7	8	9	9	10
					—	0	0	1	1	2	2	3	3	4	5	5	6	6	7	8
5	—	—	—	0	1	2	3	4	5	6	7	8	9	10	11	12	13	14	15	16
				—	0	1	1	2	3	4	5	6	7	7	8	9	10	11	12	13
6	—	—	—	1	2	3	4	6	7	8	9	11	12	13	15	16	18	19	20	22
				0	1	2	3	4	5	6	7	9	10	11	12	13	15	16	17	18
7	—	—	0	1	3	4	6	7	9	11	12	14	16	17	19	21	23	24	26	28
			—	0	1	3	4	6	7	9	10	12	13	15	16	18	19	21	22	24
8	—	—	0	2	4	6	7	9	11	13	15	17	20	22	24	26	28	30	32	34
			—	1	2	4	6	7	9	11	13	15	17	18	20	22	24	26	28	30
9	—	—	1	3	5	7	9	11	14	16	18	21	23	26	28	31	33	36	38	40
			0	1	3	5	7	9	11	13	16	18	20	22	24	27	29	31	33	36
10	—	—	1	3	6	8	11	13	16	19	22	24	27	30	33	36	38	41	44	47
			0	2	4	6	9	11	13	16	18	21	24	26	29	31	34	37	39	42
11	—	—	1	4	7	9	12	15	18	22	25	28	31	34	37	41	44	47	50	53
			0	2	5	7	10	13	16	18	21	24	27	30	33	36	39	42	45	48
12	—	—	2	5	8	11	14	17	21	24	28	31	35	38	42	46	49	53	56	60
			1	3	6	9	12	15	18	21	24	27	31	34	37	41	44	47	51	54
13	—	0	2	5	9	12	16	20	23	27	31	35	39	43	47	51	55	59	63	67
	—	—	1	3	7	10	13	17	20	24	27	31	34	38	42	45	49	53	56	60
14	—	0	2	6	10	13	17	22	26	30	34	38	43	47	51	56	60	65	69	73
	—	—	1	4	7	11	15	18	22	26	30	34	38	42	46	50	54	58	63	67
15	—	0	3	7	11	15	19	24	28	33	37	42	47	51	56	61	66	70	75	80
	—	—	2	5	8	12	16	20	24	29	33	37	42	46	51	55	60	64	69	73
16	—	0	3	7	12	16	21	26	31	36	41	46	51	56	61	66	71	76	82	87
	—	—	2	5	9	13	18	22	27	31	36	41	45	50	55	60	65	70	74	79
17	—	0	4	8	13	18	23	28	33	38	44	49	55	60	66	71	77	82	88	93
	—	—	2	6	10	15	19	24	29	34	39	44	49	54	60	65	70	75	81	86
18	—	0	4	9	14	19	24	30	36	41	47	53	59	65	70	76	82	88	94	100
	—	—	2	6	11	16	21	26	31	37	42	47	53	58	64	70	75	81	87	92
19	—	1	4	9	15	20	26	32	38	44	50	56	63	69	75	82	88	94	101	107
	—	0	3	7	12	17	22	28	33	39	45	51	56	63	69	74	81	87	93	99
20	—	1	5	10	16	22	28	34	40	47	53	60	67	73	80	87	93	100	107	114
	—	0	3	8	13	18	24	30	36	42	48	54	60	67	73	79	86	92	99	105

TABLE I

Critical values of T

N	.05	.02	.01
6	0	—	—
7	2	0	—
8	4	2	0
9	6	3	2
10	8	5	3
11	11	7	5
12	14	10	7
13	17	13	10
14	21	16	13
15	25	20	16
16	30	24	20
17	35	28	23
18	40	33	28
19	46	38	32
20	52	43	38
21	59	49	43
22	66	56	49
23	73	62	55
24	81	69	61
25	89	77	68

Source: This table is from Table 1 of Wilcoxon, F., *Some Rapid Approximate Statistical Procedures,* American Cyanamid Company, 1949, p. 13, and is reproduced with permission of American Home Products.

5

Answers to Odd-Numbered Exercises

CHAPTER 1

1. Statistics was defined as (1) the summary numbers that result from the analysis of data and (2) a set of procedures and tools used to organize and interpret facts, events, and observations that can be expressed numerically. Studying statistics will make you a better everyday consumer of statistics, help you read and understand the literature in the behavioral sciences, and give you the tools to calculate and interpret data in your own research.

CHAPTER 2

1a. The independent variable is the variable manipulated by the experimenter; the dependent variable is the measurement of behavior.

b. A population is a complete collection of objects or individuals; a sample is a population subset.

c. A parameter is a measurable characteristic of a population; a statistic is a measurable characteristic of a sample.

d. In sampling with replacement, each subject chosen is returned to the population before the next selection. Subjects are not returned in sampling without replacement.

e. Descriptive statistics is used to illustrate data or some feature of data; inferential statistics allows conclusions to be made about populations based on sample results.

3. From school rolls, you could obtain a list of all fifth-graders. This list would be your population. You could write the names on slips of paper and draw a sample from a container, either with or without replacement. Students in the sample would be contacted, and their body mass computed. From the individual values, you could compute the average (a statistic, because it is a

sample characteristic) and use this to estimate the population average (a parameter).

5. The independent variable is the type of reading instruction; the dependent variable is student reading performance.

CHAPTER 3

1. Frequency distribution:

X	f	X	f	X	f
50	2	35	1	20	2
48	1	34	1	18	2
47	1	33	2	16	2
45	1	29	2	15	1
44	1	28	1	14	2
40	2	27	1	13	2
38	2	25	2	12	1
37	1	23	1	11	1

Grouped frequency distribution with $i = 5$:

Class Intervals

Apparent Limits	Real Limits	f	Cum f	%age	Cum %age
50–54	49.5–54.5	2	35	5.71	100.00
45–49	44.5–49.5	3	33	8.57	94.29
40–44	39.5–44.5	3	30	8.57	85.71
35–39	34.5–39.5	4	27	11.43	77.14
30–34	29.5–34.5	3	23	8.57	65.71
25–29	24.5–29.5	6	20	17.14	57.14
20–24	19.5–24.5	3	14	8.57	40.00
15–19	14.5–19.5	5	11	14.29	31.43
10–14	9.5–14.5	6	6	17.14	17.14

3. Grouped frequency distribution with $i = 7$:

c_i	f	c_i	f
154–160	1	119–125	2
147–153	2	112–118	0
140–146	3	105–111	3
133–139	2	98–104	3
126–132	2	91–97	2

5. Grouped frequency distribution with $i = 5$:

Class Intervals

Apparent Limits	Real Limits	f	Cum f	%age	Cum %age
70–74	69.5–74.5	1	30	3.33	100.00
65–69	64.5–69.5	0	29	0.00	96.67
60–64	59.5–64.5	1	29	3.33	96.67
55–59	54.5–59.5	2	28	6.67	93.33
50–54	59.5–54.5	2	26	6.67	86.67
45–49	44.5–49.5	4	24	13.33	80.00
40–44	39.5–44.5	6	20	20.00	66.67
35–39	34.5–39.5	6	14	20.00	46.67
30–34	29.5–34.5	5	8	16.67	26.67
25–29	24.5–29.5	3	3	10.00	10.00

7. Grouped frequency distribution with $i = 5$:

Class Intervals

Apparent Limits	Real Limits	f	Cum %age
110–114	109.5–114.5	1	100.00
105–109	104.5–109.5	0	96.67
100–104	99.5–104.5	1	96.67
95–99	94.5–99.5	2	93.33
90–94	89.5–94.5	1	86.67
85–89	84.5–89.5	2	83.33
80 84	79.5–84.5	5	76.67
75–79	74.5–79.5	7	60.00
70 74	69.5–74.5	5	36.67
65–69	64.5–69.5	6	20.00

9a. A continuous variable is one whose measurement can take an infinite number of values; there are no gaps in its measurement, or the gaps are apparent rather than real.

  b. Range is the difference between the highest and lowest scores in a distribution.

  c. A discrete variable is one whose measurement results in a finite number of values.

CHAPTER 4

1.

X	f
12	1
11	2
10	5
9	4
8	3
7	2
6	1

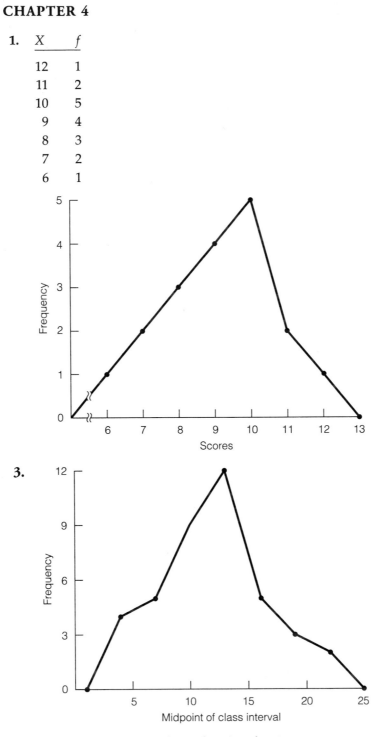

Frequency polygon of number of sentences
unscrambled in 10 minutes

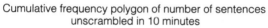

Cumulative frequency polygon of number of sentences
unscrambled in 10 minutes

Cumulative percentage polygon of number of sentences
unscrambled in 10 minutes

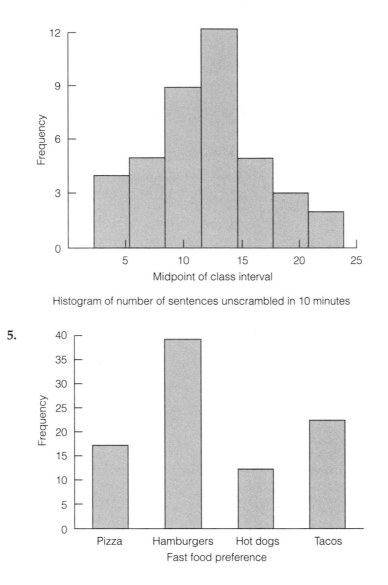

Histogram of number of sentences unscrambled in 10 minutes

5.

Fast food preference

7a. A positively skewed curve is a distribution that has much smaller frequencies for large X values than it does for small X values; the resulting frequency polygon has a tail to the right.

b. A symmetrical curve results in a distribution whose left half would fold to precisely cover its right half.

d. A negatively skewed curve is a distribution that has smaller frequencies for small X values than it does for large X values; the resulting frequency polygon has a tail to the left.

9. (1) The Y axis should be approximately three-fourths as long as the X axis; this is called the three-quarters rule. (2) Values on the Y axis should begin with 0 and should reflect reasonable deviations in the data.

11.

Stems	Leaves
1	5 1 2 8 6 3 3 6 8 4 4
2	7 8 3 9 9 5 0 5 0
3	7 4 3 8 5 3 8
4	4 8 7 5 0 0
5	0 0

CHAPTER 5

Note: Beginning with Chapter 5, some of the answers you get when you work the exercises may differ slightly from the answers given here. In solving the problems, we used the memory function on a pocket calculator. If you do not use the memory function of your calculator, more frequent rounding decisions will be made, and the final answer you get will reflect these rounding decisions. Slight differences in answers can be overlooked.

1. $\bar{X} = 16.95$, $Md = 19$, $Mo = 19$; the median is the most appropriate measure, and the distribution is negatively skewed.

3a. $Md = 11$, $\bar{X} = 17$.

  b. $Md = 121.5$, $\bar{X} = 108.22$

  c. $Md = -0.5$, $\bar{X} = -4.9$

5a. negatively

  b. positively

7. $\bar{X} = 4.28$, $Mo = 3$, $Md = 3.5$ (interpolation), $Md = 3.5$ (counting)

9. $\bar{X} = 420.3$, $Md = 419.5$, $Mo = 425.5$

11. $\bar{X} = 11.95$, $Md = 13$ (counting), $Md = 11.67$ (interpolation), $Mo = 13$

CHAPTER 6

1. $s = 2.0$, $s^2 = 4.0$

3. $s = 3.16$

5. $R = 8$, $\bar{X} = 6$, $s = 1.96$, $s^2 = 3.85$

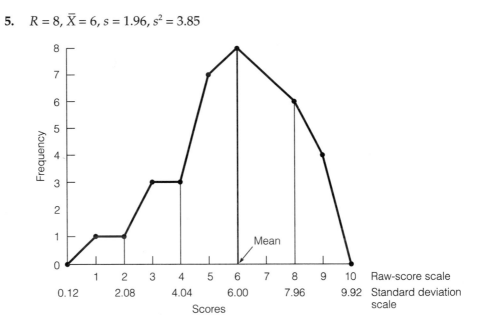

7. $s^2 = 17.74$, $s = 4.21$

9. $R = 10$, $s^2 = 7.01$, $s = 2.65$

11a. population variance
  b. population standard deviation
  c. population mean
  d. sample variance
  e. sample standard deviation
  f. range of a set of scores

13. $z = -0.53$, $z = 1.8$; IQ = 117.6, IQ = 92.5

15. $SS = 9089.6$, $s^2 = 908.96$, $s = 30.15$

CHAPTER 7

1. The normal curve is a unimodal, symmetrical curve whose tails never reach the X axis. The standard normal curve has a mean equal to 0, and its standard deviation is 1.

3a. 22.66%
  b. 72.57%ile rank
  c. 44.01%
  d. 6.2, rounded to 6
  e. 11.34; 8.32

5a. 13.57%ile rank
  b. 14
  c. 1.6 or less, 6.86 or more
  d. 4; 3
  e. 5.21

7a. 30.85%ile rank
  b. 7
  c. 62.47%
  d. 6.38 or less, 13.62 or more

CHAPTER 8

1a. $r = .82$
  b. $\ddot{Y} = 1.13 + 0.73X$
  c. $b = 0.73$
  d. $a = 1.13$
  e. $\hat{Y} = 5.51$

3a. $r = .64$
  b. $b = 0.67$
  c. $a = 0.512$
  d. $\hat{Y} = 3.86$

5. From highest to lowest, the ranking is: $-.98, +.95, +.85, +.57, -.37, +.08; +1.22$ is impossible.

7. $r = .86$

9. $r = .18$

11.

Subject	Stimulus A	X^2	Stimulus B	Y^2	XY
1	65.3	4,264.09	71.8	5,155.24	4,688.54
2	75.7	5,730.49	73.5	5,402.25	5,563.95
3	85.6	7,327.36	99.3	9,860.49	8,500.08
4	73.7	5,431.69	81.7	6,674.89	6,021.29
5	69.5	4,830.25	75.7	5,730.49	5,261.15
6	68.2	4,651.24	73.5	5,402.25	5,012.70
7	70.1	4,914.01	79.8	6,368.04	5,593.98
8	72.5	5,256.25	70.3	4,942.09	5,096.75
9	71.0	5,041.00	85.3	7,276.09	6,056.30
10	83.5	6,972.25	107.1	11,470.41	8,942.85
	735.1	54,418.63	818.0	68,282.24	60,737.59

$$CP = \Sigma XY - \frac{(\Sigma X)(\Sigma Y)}{N} = 60{,}737.59 - \frac{(735.1)(818)}{10} = 60{,}737.59 - 60{,}131.18$$

$$= 606.41$$

$$SS_X = \Sigma X^2 - \frac{(\Sigma X)^2}{N} = 54{,}418.63 - \frac{(735.1)^2}{10} = 54{,}418.63 - 54{,}037.201$$

$$= 381.429$$

$$SS_Y = \Sigma Y^2 - \frac{(\Sigma Y)^2}{N} = 68{,}282.24 - \frac{(818)^2}{10} = 68{,}282.24 - 66{,}912.4$$

$$= 1{,}369.84$$

$$r = \frac{CP}{\sqrt{(SS_X)(SS_Y)}} = \frac{606.41}{\sqrt{(381.429)(1{,}369.84)}} = \frac{606.41}{\sqrt{522{,}496.7}} = \frac{606.41}{722.839} = .84$$

CHAPTER 9

1. Without replacement, the probability is

$$\left(\tfrac{1}{52}\right)\left(\tfrac{1}{51}\right)\left(\tfrac{1}{50}\right)\left(\tfrac{1}{49}\right)\left(\tfrac{1}{48}\right) = .000000003120$$

3. $p = \left(\tfrac{1}{2}\right)\left(\tfrac{1}{6}\right)\left(\tfrac{1}{13}\right) = .0064$

5. $p = \left(\tfrac{4}{52}\right)\left(\tfrac{3}{51}\right)\left(\tfrac{2}{50}\right)\left(\tfrac{1}{49}\right) = .0000036$

7. 57.94 or less, 94.06 or more; $p = .011$

9. 1.19%; 0.82%; 0

CHAPTER 10

1a. 99% CI: 88.81 to 111.19

  b. 95% CI: 96.11 to 103.89

3. 95% CI: 21.13 to 25.67, 99% CI: 20.33 to 26.47

5. $t(136) = 4.41$, $p < .01$. There is a significant difference between the running time of these rats and the population mean.

7a. Power is defined as the probability of rejecting a false H_0 and is equal to $1 - \beta$.

  b. Rejecting a true H_0 is called an α error.

  c. A β error is failing to reject a false null hypothesis.

    d. A directional hypothesis is an alternative hypothesis that states the direction of the difference between a population parameter and the value assumed by H_0.

  9. $t(9) = 3.84$, $p < .01$. Lack of sleep increases the average brainstem auditory response latency.

CHAPTER 11

  1. $t(18) = 2.26$, $p < .05$. Sleep deprivation resulted in slower cognitive performance.

  3. $t(24) = 0.29$, $p < .05$. The speeches did not differ signficantly in distractibility. The numerators of the t test are the same in Exercises 2 and 3. However, the denominator in Exercise 3 is much larger. This illustrates the gain in power and precision when a design is used in which the dependent t is appropriate.

  5. $t(9) = 3.97$, $p < .01$. Order of presentation is important. The pattern discrimination is easier because the animals have experience with the task after learning the brightness discrimination task.

  7. $t = -1.90$, $p < .05$, $t_{.05} = -1.7459$, $t_{.01} = -2.5835$; directional. Viewing the film significantly increased aggression.

  9. The assumptions are homogeneity of variance and sampling from normal populations. Both assumptions can be violated without affecting conclusions drawn from the test.

11. $t(5) = 8.01$, $p < .01$. Brain response to sound was increased by alcohol.

13. $t(28) = -4.77$, $p < .01$. Students responded more quickly to an "emergency" if they were alone than if they were in a group.

CHAPTER 12

  1. $F(2, 21) = 6.29$, $p < .05$. The three hypnotic susceptibility groups differed significantly in their dream recall.

  3.

Group A	Group B	Group C
$N = 8$	$N = 8$	$N = 8$
$\Sigma X = 260$	$\Sigma X = 78$	$\Sigma X = 36$
$\Sigma X^2 = 8,492$	$\Sigma X^2 = 788$	$\Sigma X^2 = 196$

$$N = N_A + N_B + N_C = 8 + 8 + 8 = 24$$

$$\Sigma X = \Sigma X_A + \Sigma X_B + \Sigma X_C = 260 + 78 + 36 = 374$$

$$\Sigma X^2 = \Sigma X_A^2 + \Sigma X_B^2 + \Sigma X_C^2 = 8,492 + 788 + 196 = 9,476$$

$$SS_{tot} = \Sigma X^2 - \frac{(\Sigma X)^2}{N} = 9,476 - \frac{(374)^2}{24} = 9,476 - 5,828.167 = 3,647.833$$

$$SS_w = \left[\left(\Sigma X_g^2 \right) - \frac{(\Sigma X_g)^2}{N} \right] = \left[8,492 - \frac{(260)^2}{8} \right] + \left[788 - \frac{(78)^2}{8} \right] + \left[196 - \frac{(36)^2}{8} \right]$$

$$= 42 + 27.5 + 34 = 103.5$$

$$SS_b = SS_{tot} - SS_w = 3,647.833 - 103.5 = 3,544.333$$

ANOVA Summary Table

Source	SS	df	MS	F
Between groups	3,544.333	2	1,772.166	359.47
Within groups	105.50	21	4.930	
Total	3,647.833	23		

5. $F(3, 12) = 20.48$, $p < .01$. The number of errors committed differed significantly across the four time periods.

7.

Diet 1	X_1^2	Diet 2	X_2^2	Diet 3	X_3^2	Diet 4	X_4^2
13	169	10	100	7	49	14	196
20	400	20	400	17	289	19	361
31	961	34	1,156	11	121	27	729
18	324	27	729	23	529	31	961
11	121	7	49	14	196	15	225
11	121	27	729	13	169	21	441
11	121	10	100	26	676	14	196
12	144	12	144	23	529	141	3,109
12	144	32	1,024	4	16		
12	144	11	121	138	2,574		
140	2,649	190	4,552				
$N = 10$		$N = 10$		$N = 9$		$N = 7$	

$$\Sigma X = \Sigma X_1 + \Sigma X_2 + \Sigma X_3 + \Sigma X_4 = 140 + 190 + 138 + 141 = 609$$

$$N = N_1 + N_2 + N_3 + N_4 = 10 + 10 + 9 + 7 = 36$$

$$\Sigma X^2 = \Sigma X_1^2 + \Sigma X_2^2 + \Sigma X_3^2 + \Sigma X_4^2 = 2,649 + 4,552 + 2,574 + 3,109 = 12,884$$

$$SS_{tot} = \Sigma X^2 - \frac{(\Sigma X)^2}{N} = 12,884 - \frac{(609)^2}{36} = 12,884 - 10,302.25 = 2,581.75$$

$$SS_w = \sum_g \left[(\Sigma X_g^2) - \frac{(\Sigma X_g)^2}{N_g} \right] = \left[2,649 - \frac{(140)^2}{10} \right] + \left[4,552 - \frac{(190)^2}{10} \right]$$

$$+ \left[2,574 - \frac{(138)^2}{10} \right] + \left[3,109 - \frac{(141)^2}{7} \right]$$

$$= 689 + 942 + 458 + 268.857 = 2,357.857$$

$$SS_b = SS_{tot} - SS_w = 2,581.75 - 2,357.857 = 223.893$$

ANOVA Summary Table

Source	SS	df	MS	F
Between groups	223.893	3	74.631	1.01
Within groups	2,357.857	32	73.683	
Total	2,581.75	35		

9. $F(3, 24) = 3.85$, $p < .05$. Therapy significantly affected the frequency of recall of intrusive thoughts. Compared to the within-subjects ANOVA in Exercise 4, the F value is lower. Note that SS and MS for groups is the same in both summary tables, but SS_w here is larger than SS_{error} in Exercise 4.

CHAPTER 13

1. **HSD Tests on Mean Differences**

			Groups		
			3	2	1
		Means	19.63	13.88	9.38
Group	3	19.63	—	5.75	10.25**
Group	2	13.88		—	4.50
Group	1	9.38			—

$HSD_{.05} = 7.33$
$HSD_{.01} = 9.50$

*$p < .05$
**$p < .01$

Summary of LSD Comparisons

		Groups		
		3 **High HS**	**2** **Medium HS**	**1** **Low HS**
Group	**3**	—	1.99	3.54**
Group	**2**		—	1.55
Group	**1**			—

$t_{.05} = 2.0796$
$t_{.01} = 2.8314$

*$p < .05$
**$p < .01$

3. **HSD Tests on Mean Differences**

				Groups			
			1	**2**	**3**	**4**	**5**
		Means	5.17	3.50	3.33	1.83	0.33
Group	**1**	5.17	—	1.67	1.84	3.34**	4.84**
Group	**2**	3.50		—	0.17	1.67	3.17**
Group	**3**	3.33			—	1.50	3.00**
Group	**4**	1.83				—	1.50
Group	**5**	.33					—

$HSD_{.05} = 2.15$
$HSD_{.01} = 2.66$

*$p < .05$
**$p < .01$

Summary of LSD Comparisons

		Groups				
		1	**2**	**3**	**4**	**5**
Group	**1**	—	2.32*	2.56*	4.64**	6.72*
Group	**2**		—	0.24	2.32*	4.40**
Group	**3**			—	2.08*	4.17**
Group	**4**				—	2.08*
Group	**5**					—

$t_{.05} = 2.0595$
$t_{.01} = 2.7874$

*$p < .05$
**$p < .01$

5. **HSD Tests on Mean Differences**

			Groups			
			1	2	3	4
		Means	29.17	11.67	7.50	3.17
Group	1	29.17	—	17.50**	21.67**	26.00**
Group	2	11.67		—	4.17	8.50
Group	3	7.50			—	4.33
Group	4	3.17				—

$HSD_{.05} = 11.30$
$HSD_{.01} = 14.32$

*$p < .05$
**$p < .01$

Summary of LSD Comparisons

		Groups			
		1	2	3	4
Group	1	—	4.36**	5.40**	6.48**
Group	2		—	1.04	2.12*
Group	3			—	1.08
Group	4				—

$t_{.05} = 2.0860$
$t_{.01} = 2.8453$

*$p < .05$
**$p < .01$

7. $F = 110.54, p < 0.01.$

HSD Tests on Mean Differences

			Groups			
			A	B	C	D
		Means	9.50	8.00	5.00	1.25
Group	A	9.50	—	1.50*	4.50**	8.25**
Group	B	8.00		—	3.00**	6.75**
Group	C	8.00			—	3.75**
Group	D	1.25				—

$HSD_{.05} = 1.45$
$HSD_{.01} = 1.90$

*$p < .05$
**$p < .01$

Summary of LSD Comparisons

| | Groups | | | |
	A	B	C	D
Group A	—	3.06**	9.18**	16.84**
Group B		—	6.12**	13.78**
Group C			—	7.65**
Group D				—

$t_{05} = 2.1788$
$t_{.01} = 3.0545$

*$p < .05$
**$p < .01$

CHAPTER 14

1a. all nonsignificant
b. significant A main effect; B main effect and interaction nonsignificant
c. significant A and B main effects; no interaction
d. A and B main effects nonsignificant; significant interaction
e. A main effect nonsignificant; B main effect significant; significant interaction

3. The main advantage is the ability to test for an interaction of factors. A significant interaction is a mixed blessing because it makes the interpretation of results more complicated.

5. A significant interaction is usually revealed by crossing or converging lines on a graph.

CHAPTER 15

1. $\chi^2(2, N = 270) = 26.68, p < .01$. Liberals were more likely than conservatives to vote for the levy.

3.

	Gave Aid	Did not Give Aid
Well-dressed	20	6
Shabbily dressed	10	20

$\chi^2(1, N = 56) = 10.64, p < .01$. Help was less likely to be given to the shabbily dressed person.

5. $\chi^2(2, N = 90) = 18.78, p < .01$. First borns and later borns differ significantly on need for affiliation.

7. $\chi^2(1, N = 50) = 6.52, p < .05$. A higher percentage of the rural people exhibit abnormal behavior.

9. $\chi^2(3, N = 134) = 32.13, p < .01$. Religious affiliation was related to voting practices.

11. $\chi^2(1, N = 3{,}195) = 364.35, p < .01$. The drug was effective in preventing relapse.

CHAPTER 16

1. $U = 1, p = .02$. Isolate-reared monkeys exhibited more self-directed behavior.

3. The parametric test is normally more powerful; that is, it is more likely to result in rejection of the null hypothesis.

5. OC vs. SEP, $U' = 1.5, p < 0.01$
   OC vs. OB, $U' = 31.5, p > 0.10$
   OC vs. VMH, $U' = 1.5, p < 0.01$
   SEP vs. OB, $U' = 4, p < 0.01$
   SEP vs. VMH, $U' = 20.5, p > 0.10$
   OB vs. VMH, $U' = 5, p < 0.01$
   SEP and VMH rats are more reactive than OCs and OBs.

7. $T = 31, p = .05$. There is no reason to believe that an attitude change resulted from watching the film.

9. $H = 3.13, p = .05$. These occupations did not differ in rated sociability.

MATH–ALGEBRA REVIEW

1. 0.06

3. 0.03

5. 25

7. 121

9. 8.50

11. −3.4

13. 21

15. 2

Index

Descriptive Statistics Formulas

Formula 5-1—Median for a frequency distribution

$$Md = \text{LRL} + i\left(\frac{N/2 - \text{Cum}\,f}{f}\right)$$

Formulas 5-2 and 5-3—Sample mean

$$\overline{X} = \frac{\sum X}{N} \quad \text{or} \quad \frac{\sum fX}{N}$$

Formula 6-1—Range of a distribution

$$R = \text{HS} - \text{LS}$$

Formula 6-3—Average deviation for a frequency distribution

$$AD = \frac{\sum f\,|X - \overline{X}|}{N}$$

Formula 6-8 and 6-9—Sample variance

$$s^2 = \frac{\sum X^2 - \dfrac{(\sum X)^2}{N}}{N} \quad \text{or} \quad \frac{\sum fX^2 - \dfrac{(\sum fX)^2}{N}}{N}$$

Formula 6-11—Sum of squares

$$SS = \sum X^2 - \frac{(\sum X^2)}{N} \left[\sum fX^2 - \frac{(\sum fX^2)}{N} \text{ for a frequency distribution}\right]$$

Formula 6-12—Sample variance

$$s^2 = \frac{SS}{N}$$

Formula 6-17 and 6-18—Sample standard deviation

$$s = \sqrt{\frac{\sum X^2 - \dfrac{(\sum X^2)}{N}}{N}} \quad \text{or} \quad \sqrt{\frac{\sum fX^2 - \dfrac{(\sum fX)^2}{N}}{N}} \quad \text{or} \quad \sqrt{\frac{SS}{N}}$$

Formula 6-20—z-score from a raw score

$$z = \frac{X - \overline{X}}{s}$$

Formula 6-22—Raw score from a z score

$$X = zs + \overline{X}$$

Formulas 8-1 and 8-4—Pearson r

$$r = \frac{\sum z_X z_Y}{N} \quad \text{or} \quad \frac{CP}{\sqrt{(SS_X)(SS_Y)}}$$

Formula 8-3—Cross products

$$CP = \sum XY - \frac{\sum X \sum Y}{N}$$

Formula 8-5—Equation for predicting Y from X

$$\hat{Y} = \left(\frac{rs_r}{s_X}\right)X - \left(\frac{rs_r}{s_X}\right)(\overline{X}) + \overline{Y}$$

Formula 8-6—Regression coefficient

$$b = \frac{CP}{SS_X}$$

Formula 8-7—Y intercept of the regression line

$$a = \overline{Y} - b\overline{X}$$

Formula 8-9—Coefficient of determination

$$r^2 = \frac{\text{explained variation}}{\text{total variation}}$$

Formula 8-10—Spearman rank order correlation coefficient

$$r_s = 1 - \frac{6\sum d^2}{N(N^2 - 1)}$$